WHO'S WHO

IN SOUTH AFRICAN POLITICS

NUMBER 5

SHELAGH GASTROW

Ravan Press   Johannesburg

Published by Ravan Press (Pty) Ltd
PO Box 145, Randburg 2125, South Africa

© Shelagh Gastrow, 1995

All rights reserved. No part of this publication may be reproduced, stored in a retrieval system, or transmitted in any form or by any means, electronic, mechanical, photocopying, recording, or otherwise, without the prior permission of the copyright owner.

First published 1995

ISBN 0 86975 458 0

Cover design: Centre Court Studio/Ingrid Obery

DTP: Rob Irvine

Printed and bound by Galvin & Sales, Cape Town
(0831)

Contents

Entries in *Who's Who in South African Politics 1, 2, 3, 4, 5*   ix
Preface xix
Office bearers and portfolio holders xxi

Asmal, Abdul Kader 1
Bengu, Sibusiso Mandlenkosi Emmanuel 5
Botha, Thozamile 8
Botha, Roelof Frederik 'Pik' 12
Buthelezi, Mangosuthu Gatsha 17
Carolus, Cheryl 27
Cobbett, William John 30
Coetsee, Hendrick Jacobus 32
De Klerk, Frederik Willem 36
De Lange, Johannes Hendrik 'Johnny' 43
De Villiers, Dawid Jacobus 47
Dipico, Emsley Manne 50
Duarte, Yasmin 'Jessie' 52
Erwin, Alexander 55
Fanaroff, Bernard Lewis 58
Felgate, Walter Sidney 61
Fismer, Christiaan Loedolff 64
Fivaz, John George 66
Fraser-Moleketi, Geraldine 68
Gasa, Faith Xolile 72
Gerwel, Gert Johannes 'Jakes' 75
Ginwala, Frene Noshir 77
Gomomo, John 80
Gordhan, Pravin Jamnadas 81
Hanekom, Derek Andre 87
Hartzenberg, Ferdinand 90
Holomisa, Harrington Bantubonke 95
Holomisa, Sango Patekile 98
Jiyane, Ziba Bonginkosi 101
Jordan, Pallo Zweledinga 105

Kasrils, Ronald 108
Khoza, Themba 112
Kriel, Hermanus Jacobus 115
Lekota, Mosiuoa Patrick 'Terror' 117
Leon, Anthony James 120
Liebenberg, Christo Ferro 123
Mabandla, Brigitte Sylvia 125
Maduna, Penuell Mpapa 126
Maharaj, Satyandranath Ragunanan 'Mac' 130
Makwetu, Clarence Mlami 133
Mandela, Nelson Rolihlahla 137
Mandela, Nomzamo Zaniewe Winnifred 'Winnie' 147
Manganyi, Noel Chabani 155
Mangena, Mosibudi 157
Manuel, Trevor Andrew 160
Marcus, Gill 164
Matthews, Vincent Joseph 166
Mbeki, Thabo Mvuyelwa 169
Mboweni, Tito Titus 172
Mdlalose, Frank Themba 176
Meiring, Georg 180
Meshoe, Kenneth Raselabe 181
Meyer, Anthon Tobias 183
Meyer, Roelof Petrus 185
Mhlaba, Raymond 187
Modise, Johannes 190
Mokaba, Peter Ramoshoane 193
Molefe, Popo Simon 197
Moosa, Mohammed Valli 201
Msane, Angela Thoko 205
Mtetwa, Celani Jeffrey 208
Mthembu-Nkondo, Sankie Dolly 210
Mtintso, Thenjiwe 212
Mufamadi, Sydney Pholisani 215
Mulder, Pieter Willem Adriaan 218
Myakayaka-Manzini, Yvette Lillian 'Mavivi' 220
Mzimela, Sipo Elijah 222

Naidoo, Jayaseelan 'Jay' 225
Naidoo, Jayendra 228
Ngubane, Baldwin Sipho 231
Nhlanhla, Joseph Mbuku 234
Nqakula, Charles 236
Nzimande, Emmanuel Bonginkosi 'Blade' 238
Nzo, Alfred Baphethuxolo 241
Omar, Abdulah Mohamed 244
Pahad, Aziz Goolam Hoosein 246
Phosa, Nakedi Mathews 249
Pityana, Sipho Mila 252
Radebe, Jeffrey Thamasanqa 255
Ramaphosa, Matamela Cyril 257
Ramatlhodi, Ngoako 260
Schoeman, Renier Stephanus 262
Sexwale, Mosima Gabriel Tokyo 264
Shilowa, Sam 267
Sigcau, Stella Margaret Nomzamo 269
Sigxashe, Sizakele Whitmore 271
Sisulu, Zwelakhe 273
Skweyiya, Zola Sidney Themba 275
Steyn, Pierre Derksen 278
Stofile, Makhinketi Arnold 280
Terre Blanche, Eugene Ney 282
Tshwete, Steve Vukile 287
Tutu, Desmond Mpilo 290
Van Niekerk, Andre Isak 294
Van Schalkwyk, Marthinus Christoffel Johannes 296
Viljoen, Constand Laubscher 298
Wessels, Leon 302
Williams, Abraham 304
Zulu, Sifiso Thokosani 306
Zuma, Jacob 309
Zuma, Nkosazana 312
Zwelithini, Goodwill 315

Entries in *Who's Who in South African Politics 1, 2, 3, 4, 5*

Surname	First Names	1	2	3	4	5
Alexander	Benny	✗	✗	✓	✓	✗
Alexander	Neville Edward	✓	✓	✓	✓	✗
Alexander	Rachel Esther	✗	✓	✗	✗	✗
Andrew	Kenneth Michael	✗	✓	✗	✗	✗
Arenstein	Rowley Israel	✗	✓	✓	✗	✗
Asmal	Abdul Kader	✗	✗	✗	✗	✓
Baard	Frances	✓	✗	✗	✗	✗
Badenhorst	Petrus Johannes	✓	✗	✗	✗	✗
Barayi	Elijah	✗	✓	✓	✗	✗
Barnard	Lukas Daniel	✗	✓	✓	✓	✗
Bengu	Sibusiso Mandlenkosi Emmanuel	✗	✗	✗	✗	✓
Beyers	Andries	✗	✗	✗	✓	✗
Boesak	Allan	✓	✓	✓	✓	✗
Bonhomme	Virgile Joseph	✓	✗	✗	✗	✗
Boraine	Alexander Lionel	✓	✗	✓	✓	✗
Boraine	Andrew Michael	✗	✓	✗	✗	✗
Boshoff	Carel Willem Hendrik	✓	✓	✓	✓	✗
Botha	Jan Christoffel Greyling	✗	✓	✗	✗	✗
Botha	Pieter Willem	✓	✓	✗	✗	✗
Botha	Roelof Frederik 'Pik'	✓	✓	✓	✓	✓
Botha	Thozamile	✗	✗	✗	✗	✓
Breytenbach	Wynand Nicolas	✗	✗	✓	✓	✗
Burton	Maria MacDiarmid	✗	✓	✗	✗	✗
Buthelezi	Mangosuthu Gatsha	✓	✓	✓	✓	✓
Cachalia	Azhar	✗	✗	✓	✗	✗
Camay	Piroshaw	✓	✓	✗	✗	✗
Carolus	Cheryl	✗	✗	✓	✓	✓
Chikane	Frank	✗	✓	✓	✗	✗
Cindi	Zithulele	✗	✓	✗	✗	✗
Clase	Petrus Johannes	✗	✓	✓	✗	✗
Cobbett	William John	✗	✗	✗	✗	✓
Coetsee	Hendrick Jacobus	✓	✓	✓	✓	✓

Surname	First Names	1	2	3	4	5
Coetzer	Pieter Willem	✗	✗	✓	✓	✗
Conco	Simon Zwelinjani	✗	✓	✗	✗	✗
Cooper	Sathasivan	✓	✗	✗	✗	✗
Coovadia	Hoosen	✓	✗	✗	✗	✗
Cronin	Jeremy Patrick	✗	✗	✗	✓	✗
Curry	David Michael George	✗	✗	✓	✗	✗
De Beer	Samuel Johannes	✗	✓	✓	✓	✗
De Beer	Zacharias Johannes	✗	✗	✓	✓	✗
De Klerk	Frederik Willem	✓	✓	✓	✓	✓
De Lange	Jan Pieter	✓	✓	✗	✗	✗
De Lange	Johannes Hendrik 'Johnny'	✗	✗	✗	✗	✓
De Lille	Patricia	✗	✗	✗	✓	✗
Delport	Jacobus Tertius	✗	✗	✗	✓	✗
Desai	Barney	✗	✗	✗	✓	✗
De Villiers	Dawid Jacobus	✓	✓	✓	✓	✓
De Villiers	Willem Johannes	✗	✗	✓	✗	✗
Dhlomo	Oscar Dumisani	✓	✓	✓	✓	✗
Dlamini	Christopher Ndodebandla	✗	✓	✓	✓	✗
Dlamini	Langalethu Griffiths	✓	✗	✗	✗	✗
Dipico	Emsley Manne	✗	✗	✗	✗	✓
Duarte	Jasmin 'Jessie'	✗	✗	✗	✗	✓
Dudley	Richard Owen	✗	✓	✗	✗	✗
Duncan	Sheena	✓	✗	✗	✗	✗
Du Plessis	Barend Jacobus	✓	✓	✓	✗	✗
Du Plessis	George Kenrick	✓	✗	✗	✗	✗
Du Plessis	Pieter Theunis	✓	✓	✗	✗	✗
Durr	Kent	✗	✗	✓	✗	✗
Ebrahim	Ebrahim Ismail	✗	✗	✓	✓	✗
Eglin	Colin Wells	✓	✓	✗	✓	✗
Erwin	Alexander	✗	✗	✓	✗	✓
Fanaroff	Bernard Lewis	✗	✗	✗	✗	✓
Fazzie	Henry Mutile	✗	✓	✓	✗	✗
Felgate	Walter Sydney	✗	✗	✗	✓	✓

Surname	First Names	1	2	3	4	5
Fismer	Christiaan Loedolff	✗	✗	✗	✓	✓
Fivaz	John George	✗	✗	✗	✗	✓
Foster	Joseph Alexander	✓	✗	✗	✗	✗
Fraser-Moleketi	Geraldine	✗	✗	✗	✗	✓
Gasa	Faith Xolile	✗	✗	✗	✗	✓
Gastrow	Peter Hans Paul	✗	✓	✗	✗	✗
Geldenhuys	Johannes Jocobus	✗	✓	✓	✗	✗
Gerwel	Gert Johannes 'Jakes'	✗	✗	✗	✗	✓
Ginwala	Frene Noshir	✗	✗	✗	✗	✓
Gomomo	John	✗	✗	✗	✓	✓
Gordhan	Pravin Jamnadas	✗	✗	✗	✗	✓
Gqozo	Oupa Josh	✗	✗	✓	✓	✗
Grobler	Johannes Petrus	✓	✗	✗	✗	✗
Gumede	Archibald Jacob	✓	✓	✓	✗	✗
Gumede	Simon Hulumeni	✓	✓	✗	✗	✗
Gwala	Harry Themba	✗	✗	✗	✓	✗
Hadebi	Daniel Ntjammu	✗	✓	✗	✗	✗
Hanekom	Derek Andre	✗	✗	✗	✗	✓
Hani	Martin Thembisile 'Chris'	✗	✓	✓	✓	✗
Hartzenberg	Ferdinand	✓	✓	✓	✓	✓
Hayward	Sarel Antoine Strydom	✓	✗	✗	✗	✗
Hendrickse	Helenard Joe 'Alan'	✓	✓	✓	✓	✗
Heunis	Jan Christiaan	✓	✓	✗	✗	✗
Holomisa	Sango Patekile	✗	✗	✗	✗	✓
Holomisa	Harrington Bantubonke	✗	✗	✓	✓	✓
Howa	Hassan	✓	✗	✗	✗	✗
Issel	John James	✓	✗	✗	✗	✗
Jack	Mkuseli	✗	✓	✓	✗	✗
Jassat	Essop	✓	✗	✗	✗	✗
Jiyane	Ziba Bonginkosi	✗	✗	✗	✗	✓
Jones	Peter Cyril	✓	✗	✗	✗	✗
Jordan	Pallo Zweledinga	✗	✗	✓	✓	✓
Joseph	Helen Beatrice May	✓	✗	✗	✗	✗

Surname	First Names	1	2	3	4	5
Kasrils	Ronald	✗	✗	✗	✓	✓
Kathrada	Ahmed	✗	✗	✓	✗	✗
Keys	Derek Lyle	✗	✗	✗	✓	✗
Kgositsile	Baleka Mmakota	✗	✗	✗	✓	✗
Khanyile	Vusumuzi Philip	✗	✓	✗	✗	✗
Khoza	Themba	✗	✗	✗	✓	✓
Koornhof	Nicolaas Jacobus	✗	✗	✗	✓	✗
Koornhof	Pieter Herhardus	✓	✗	✗	✗	✗
Kotzé	Gert Jeremias	✓	✗	✗	✗	✗
Kriel	Hermanus Jacobus	✗	✗	✓	✓	✓
Le Grange	Louis	✓	✗	✗	✗	✗
Lekota	Musiuoa Patrick 'Terror'	✓	✓	✓	✓	✓
Leon	Anthony James	✗	✗	✗	✗	✓
Le Roux	Francois Jacobus	✗	✗	✓	✗	✗
Liebenberg	Andreas Jacobus	✗	✗	✓	✓	✗
Liebenberg	Christo Ferro	✗	✗	✗	✗	✓
Louw	Eli van der Merwe	✓	✓	✓	✗	✗
Louw	Eugene	✗	✗	✓	✓	✗
Mabandla	Brigitte Sylvia	✗	✗	✗	✗	✓
Mabasa	Lybon Tiyani	✓	✓	✗	✗	✗
Mabhida	Moses	✓	✗	✗	✗	✗
Mabuza	Nganani Enos John	✓	✓	✓	✗	✗
Macozoma	Sakumzi Justice	✗	✗	✗	✓	✗
Madide	Dennis Bhekokwake	✓	✓	✓	✗	✗
Maduna	Penuell Mpapa	✗	✗	✗	✗	✓
Mafolo	Titus Magashe	✗	✗	✓	✗	✗
Maharaj	Satyandranath 'Mac'	✗	✓	✓	✓	✓
Mahomed	Yunus Ismail	✗	✗	✓	✗	✗
Makwetu	Clarence Mlami	✗	✗	✓	✓	✓
Malan	Magnus André de Merindol	✓	✓	✓	✓	✗
Malan	Wynand Charl	✓	✓	✓	✗	✗
Malindi	Zollie Zolile	✗	✓	✗	✗	✗
Mandela	Nelson Rolihlahla	✓	✓	✓	✓	✓

Surname	First Names	1	2	3	4	5
Mandela	Nomzamo Zaniewe Winnifred	✓	✓	✓	✓	✓
Manganyi	Noel Chabani	✗	✗	✗	✗	✓
Mangena	Mosibudi	✗	✗	✓	✓	✓
Mangope	Lucas Manyane	✓	✓	✓	✓	✗
Manuel	Trevor Andrew	✓	✓	✓	✓	✓
Maphumulo	Mhlabunzima	✗	✗	✓	✗	✗
Marais	Georg	✗	✓	✓	✓	✗
Marais	Jacobus Albertus	✓	✓	✗	✓	✗
Marais	Pieter Gabriel	✗	✗	✓	✗	✗
Marais	Pieter Jacobus	✓	✗	✗	✗	✗
Marcus	Gill	✗	✗	✗	✗	✓
Marks	Joseph Johannes	✓	✗	✗	✗	✗
Masekela	Barbara Mosima Joyce	✗	✗	✗	✓	✗
Matanzima	George Mzimvube	✗	✓	✗	✗	✗
Matanzima	Kaiser Daliwonga	✓	✗	✗	✗	✗
Matthews	Vincent Joseph	✗	✗	✗	✗	✓
Mayekiso	Moses Jongizizwe	✗	✓	✓	✓	✗
Mbeki	Govan Archibald Mvuyelwa	✓	✓	✓	✗	✗
Mbeki	Thabo Mvuyelwa	✗	✓	✓	✓	✓
Mboweni	Tito Titus	✗	✗	✗	✗	✓
Mchunu	Abby	✗	✓	✗	✗	✗
Mdlalose	Frank Themba	✓	✓	✓	✓	✓
Mdlalose*	James Themba	✗	✗	✓	✓	✓
Meiring	George	✗	✗	✗	✗	✓
Mentz	Marthinus Johannes	✗	✗	✓	✓	✗
Meshoe	Kenneth Raselabe	✗	✗	✗	✗	✓
Meyer	Anthony Tobias	✗	✗	✗	✗	✓
Meyer	Roelof Petrus	✗	✓	✓	✓	✓
Mhlaba	Raymond	✗	✗	✓	✗	✓
Mkhatshwa	Smangaliso Patrick	✓	✓	✓	✗	✗
Mkwayi	Wilton Zamisile	✗	✗	✓	✗	✗
Mlambo	Johnson Phillip	✗	✓	✓	✓	✗

*previously entered as James Mndaweni

Surname	First Names	1	2	3	4	5
Mlangeni	Andrew Mokete	✗	✗	✓	✗	✗
Modise	Johannes	✓	✓	✓	✓	✓
Mohammed	Ismail Jacobus	✗	✓	✗	✗	✗
Mokaba	Peter Ramoshoane	✗	✗	✓	✓	✓
Mokoape	Maitshue Nchaupe Aubrey	✗	✗	✓	✓	✗
Mokoena	Aubrey	✓	✗	✗	✗	✗
Molala	Nkosi	✗	✓	✗	✗	✗
Molefe	Popo Simon	✓	✓	✓	✓	✓
Molobi	Eric	✗	✗	✓	✗	✗
Mompati	Ruth	✗	✗	✓	✗	✗
Moodley	Strinivasa	✓	✗	✓	✓	✗
Moosa	Mohammed Valli	✗	✗	✓	✓	✓
Mopeli	Tsiame Kenneth	✗	✗	✗	✓	✗
Morobe	Murphy	✗	✓	✓	✗	✗
Mosala	Ithumeleng Jeremiah	✗	✗	✓	✗	✗
Moseneke	Dikgang Ernest	✗	✗	✗	✓	✗
Mothopeng	Zephania Lekoane	✓	✓	✓	✗	✗
Motlana	Nthato Harrison	✓	✓	✗	✗	✗
Motsoaledi	Elias	✗	✗	✓	✗	✗
Mpetha	Oscar	✓	✗	✗	✗	✗
Msane	Angela Thoko	✗	✗	✗	✗	✓
Mtetwa	Celani Jeffrey	✗	✓	✗	✗	✓
Mthembu-Nkondo	Sankie Dolly	✗	✗	✗	✗	✓
Mti	Linda	✗	✗	✗	✓	✗
Mtintso	Thenjiwe	✗	✗	✗	✗	✓
Mufamadi	Sydney Pholisani	✗	✓	✓	✓	✓
Mulder	Cornelius Petrus	✓	✓	✗	✗	✗
Mulder	Pieter Willem Adriaan	✗	✗	✗	✓	✓
Munnik	Lourens Albertus Petrus	✓	✗	✗	✗	✗
Mxenge	Victoria Nonyamezelo	✓	✗	✗	✗	✗
Myakayaka-Manzini	Yvette Lillian 'Mavivi'	✗	✗	✗	✗	✓
Myeni	Musawenkosi Bethuel	✗	✗	✗	✓	✗
Myeza	Muntu	✗	✓	✓	✗	✗

Surname	First Names	1	2	3	4	5
Mzimela	Sipo Elijah	✗	✗	✗	✗	✓
Naidoo	Jayaseelan 'Jay'	✗	✓	✓	✓	✓
Naidoo	Jayendra	✗	✗	✗	✓	✓
Nair	Billy	✗	✓	✓	✗	✗
Nathan	Laurie	✗	✓	✗	✗	✗
Naudé	Christiaan Beyers	✓	✓	✗	✗	✗
Ncube	Sister Bernard	✗	✗	✓	✗	✗
Ndlovu	Curnick Muzuvukile	✗	✓	✓	✗	✗
Nefolovhodwe	Pandelani	✗	✓	✗	✓	✗
Nel	Daniel Jacobus Louis	✓	✗	✗	✗	✗
Netshitenze	Joel Khathutshelo	✗	✗	✗	✓	✗
Ngcuka	Bulelani Thandabantu	✗	✗	✓	✗	✗
Ngcukana	Cunningham Thozamile	✗	✗	✓	✓	✗
Ngoyi	Edgar Dumine	✗	✓	✓	✗	✗
Ngubane	Baldwin Sipho	✗	✗	✗	✗	✓
Nhlanhla	Joseph Mbuku	✗	✗	✗	✓	✓
Nkadimeng	Donald Kglake	✗	✗	✗	✓	✗
Nkadimeng	John Kgoana	✓	✓	✓	✗	✗
Nkobi	Thomas Titus	✓	✓	✓	✓	✗
Nkondo	Curtis	✓	✗	✗	✗	✗
Nothnagel	Albertus Erik	✓	✓	✗	✗	✗
Nqakula	Charles	✗	✗	✗	✓	✓
Ntloko	Phambili ka	✗	✓	✗	✗	✗
Ntsanwisi	Hudson William Edison	✗	✗	✗	✓	✗
Ntsebeza	Dumisa Buhle	✗	✗	✓	✗	✗
Nyanda	Siphiwe	✗	✗	✗	✓	✗
Nyembe	Dorothy	✓	✗	✗	✗	✗
Nzimande	Emmanuel Bonginkosi 'Blade'	✗	✗	✗	✗	✓
Nzo	Alfred Baphethuxolo	✓	✓	✓	✗	✓
Omar	Abdulah Mohamed	✗	✗	✓	✗	✓
Pahad	Aziz Goolam Hoosein	✗	✗	✗	✗	✓
Paulus	Petrus Jacobus	✓	✗	✗	✗	✗
Phatudi	Cedric Nameni	✓	✓	✗	✗	✗

Surname	First Names	1	2	3	4	5
Phosa	Nakedi Mathews	✗	✗	✗	✗	✓
Pienaar	Cehill Hercules	✗	✗	✗	✓	✗
Pienaar	David Schalk	✗	✗	✗	✓	✗
Pienaar	Louis Alexander	✗	✗	✗	✓	✗
Pityana	Sipho Mila	✗	✗	✗	✗	✓
Pokela	Nyati John	✓	✗	✗	✗	✗
Poovlingam	Pat Thungaval	✓	✓	✗	✗	✗
Rabie	Jacobus Albert	✓	✓	✗	✓	✗
Rachidi	Kenneth Hlako	✓	✗	✗	✗	✗
Radebe	Jeffrey Thamsanqa	✗	✗	✗	✓	✓
Rajbansi	Amichand	✓	✓	✓	✗	✗
Ramaphosa	Matamela Cyril	✓	✓	✓	✓	✓
Ramatlhodi	Ngoako	✗	✗	✗	✗	✓
Ramgobin	Mawalal	✓	✗	✗	✗	✗
Ramodike	Mogoboya Noko Nelson	✗	✗	✓	✗	✗
Raw	Wyatt Vause	✓	✗	✗	✗	✗
Reddy	Jayaaran Narinsamy	✓	✓	✓	✓	✗
Roux	Johannes Petrus	✗	✗	✓	✗	✗
Saloojee	Ebrahim	✓	✗	✗	✗	✗
Saloojee	Rashid Ahmed Mahmood	✓	✓	✗	✗	✗
Scheepers	Johannes Hendrikus	✗	✗	✗	✓	✗
Schlebusch	Alwyn Louis	✗	✓	✗	✗	✗
Schoeman	Hendrik Stephanus	✓	✗	✗	✗	✗
Schoeman	Renier Stephanus	✗	✗	✓	✓	✓
Schutte	Daniel Pieter Antonie	✗	✗	✓	✓	✗
Schwartz	Harry Heinz	✓	✗	✗	✗	✗
Sebe	Lennox Leslie Wongama	✓	✓	✗	✗	✗
Sewpershad	Chanderden George	✓	✓	✗	✗	✗
Sexwale	Mosima Gabriel Tokyo	✗	✗	✗	✓	✓
Shilowa	Sam	✗	✗	✗	✓	✓
Shope	Gertrude	✗	✓	✓	✓	✗
Sigcau	Stella Margaret Nomzamo	✗	✗	✗	✗	✓
Sigxashe	Sizakele Whitmore	✗	✗	✗	✗	✓

Contents

Surname	First Names	1	2	3	4	5
Sisulu	Nonsikelelo Albertina	✓	✓	✓	✓	✗
Sisulu	Walter Max Ulyate	✓	✓	✓	✓	✗
Sisulu	Zwelake	✗	✓	✓	✗	✓
Sizane	Stone Phumelele	✗	✓	✓	✗	✗
Skweyiya	Zola Sidney Themba	✗	✗	✗	✗	✓
Slabbert	Frederik van Zyl	✓	✓	✓	✓	✗
Slovo	Joe	✓	✓	✓	✓	✗
Sonn	Franklin Abraham	✗	✗	✓	✗	✗
Steyn	Daniel Wynand	✓	✗	✗	✗	✗
Steyn	Pierre Derksen	✗	✗	✗	✗	✓
Stofberg	Louis Frans	✗	✓	✗	✗	✗
Stofile	Makhinketi Arnold	✗	✗	✗	✗	✓
Suzman	Helen	✓	✓	✗	✗	✗
Tambo	Oliver Reginald	✓	✓	✓	✓	✗
Terre Blanche	Eugene Ney	✓	✓	✓	✓	✓
Tinto	Christmas Fihla	✗	✓	✓	✗	✗
Tloome	Daniel	✗	✗	✓	✗	✗
Treurnicht	Andries Petrus	✓	✓	✓	✓	✗
Tsele	Molefe Samuel	✗	✓	✗	✗	✗
Tshwete	Steve Vukile	✗	✗	✗	✓	✓
Tutu	Desmond Mpilo	✓	✓	✓	✗	✓
Van der Horst	Frank	✓	✓	✗	✗	✗
Van der Merwe	Christoffel	✓	✓	✓	✓	✗
Van der Merwe	Cornelius Visser	✓	✗	✗	✗	✗
Van der Merwe	Jacobus Hercules	✗	✗	✓	✓	✗
Van der Merwe	Stephanus Sebastian	✗	✗	✓	✗	✗
Van der Westhuizen	Pieter	✗	✓	✗	✗	✗
Van Niekerk	André Isak	✗	✗	✗	✓	✓
Van Niekerk	Willem Abraham	✗	✓	✗	✗	✗
Van Schalkwyk	Marthinus Christoffel Johannes	✗	✗	✗	✗	✓
Venter	Elizabeth Hendrina	✗	✗	✓	✓	✗
Viljoen	Constand Laubscher	✗	✗	✗	✗	✓
Viljoen	Gerrit van Niekerk	✓	✓	✓	✓	✗

Surname	First Names	1	2	3	4	5
Vlok	Adriaan Johannes	✗	✓	✓	✓	✗
Vos	Suzanne Christina	✗	✗	✗	✓	✗
Wauchope	George Mpapa	✗	✓	✗	✗	✗
Wentzel	Jacob Johannes Greyling	✓	✗	✗	✗	✗
Wessels	Leon	✗	✗	✓	✗	✓
Wiley	John Walter Edington	✓	✗	✗	✗	✗
Wilkens	Benjamin Hugh	✓	✗	✗	✗	✗
Williams	Abraham	✗	✗	✗	✗	✓
Worrall	Denis John	✗	✗	✓	✗	✗
Xundu	Mcebisi Osman	✓	✓	✗	✗	✗
Zitha	Mangisi Cephus	✗	✗	✗	✓	✗
Zondi	Keith Musakawukhethi	✗	✗	✓	✗	✗
Zulu	Sifiso Thokosani	✗	✗	✗	✗	✓
Zuma	Jacob	✗	✗	✓	✓	✓
Zuma	Nkosazana	✗	✗	✗	✗	✓
Zwelethini	Goodwill	✗	✗	✗	✓	✓

Preface

The last few years in South Africa's political process have been dramatic indeed, and this is reflected in the remarkable changes in formal leadership patterns.

In selecting the political leaders to be included in this, the fifth *Who's Who in South African Politics*, two important new trends emerged.

Firstly, there has been a major shift in the leadership echelons from the sphere of civil society to that of political society. Up until 1994, civil society leadership played a key political role, especially in the anti-apartheid movement, peace structures, women's organisations, voter education, new policy formulation, etc. However, many of the key individuals from this sector have moved into party politics. As a result, the leadership in the institutions of civil society has weakened, with relatively unknown figures taking over positions in structures which themselves may have only a limited lifespan and viability. Other activists in civil society have moved into the new state bureaucracy: some of the new directors-general of departments included in this *Who's Who*, for example, were trained in institutions of civil society such as non-governmental organisations, and will play a key role in policy-making over the next few years.

Secondly, despite their increased numbers in parliament, women are still a conspicious minority in this book although, compared to previous years, there is a marked increase in the numbers of entries for women. However, the number of entries for women in this *Who's Who* does not necessarily reflect the substantial impact women are making on parliamentary select committees, nor the fact that more and more women are occupying senior leadership positions in those civil society structures which are often the seed-bed for formal political leadership.

Various individuals and organisations were very helpful to me during the research period for this book. I would like to thank the Institute for Democracy in South Africa (Idasa) for providing me with working conditions enabling me to proceed with my ongoing research; the *Daily News* in Durban, which gave me unhindered use of their library; and staff of the South African Communication Services (SACS) who have supplied me with regular updates on government appointments. I am also grateful to the *Daily News, The Star, The New Nation* and SACS for the use of their photographs.

Whilst I was editing *People in Politics* for Idasa, various individuals undertook research for that journal, and some of the information in this *Who's Who* is based on their interviews. I would therefore like to thank Elsabe Wessels, Trudie du Toit, Shelley Gielink and Sarah Blecher-Collins for their contributions made in this way.

Many thanks, once again, to my publishers, Ravan Press. Its staff have been a pleasure to work with and have always been flexible enough to permit additions and alterations at the very last moment to enable this book to be as up-to-date as possible.

Last, but not least, thanks to the members of my family, whose patience, humour and input have been of great support and who must be wondering how many editions still face them in the future!

Shelagh Gastrow
Cape Town
July 1995.

Office bearers and portfolio holders

Cabinet of the Republic of South Africa

Ministers

President . . . . Mr Nelson Mandela (ANC)
First Executive Deputy President . . . Mr Thabo Mbeki (ANC)
Second Executive Deputy President . Mr FW de Klerk (NP)
Agriculture . . . . Dr Kraai van Niekerk (NP)
Arts, Culture, Science and
    Technology . . . . Dr Ben Ngubane (IFP)
Correctional Services . . . . Mr Sipo Mzimela (IFP)
Defence . . . . Mr Joe Modise (ANC)
Education . . . . Mr Sibusiso Bengu (ANC)
Environment Affairs . . . . Dr Dawie de Villiers (NP)
Finance . . . . Mr Chris Liebenberg
Foreign Affairs . . . . Mr Alfred Nzo (ANC)
General Affairs . . . . Mr Chris Fismer (NP)
Health . . . . Dr Nkosazana Zuma (ANC)
Home Affairs . . . . Chief Mangosuthu Buthelezi
                                  (IFP)
Housing . . . . Ms Sankie Nkondo (ANC)
Justice . . . . Mr Dullah Omar (ANC)
Labour . . . . Mr Tito Mboweni (ANC)
Land Affairs . . . . Mr Derek Hanekom (ANC)
Mineral and Energy Affairs . . . . . . Mr Pik Botha (NP)
Minister without Portfolio . . . . Mr Jay Naidoo (ANC)
Posts, Telecommunications and
    Broadcasting . . . . Mr Pallo Jordan (ANC)
Provincial Affairs and
    Constitutional Development . . . . Mr Roelf Meyer (NP)
Public Enterprises . . . . Ms Stella Sigcau (ANC)
Public Service and Administration . . Dr Zola Skweyiya (ANC)
Public Works . . . . Mr Jeff Radebe (ANC)
Safety and Security . . . . Mr Sydney Mufamadi (ANC)
Sport and Recreation . . . . Mr Steve Tshwete (ANC)
Trade, Industry and Tourism . . . . . . Mr Trevor Manuel (ANC)
Transport . . . . Mr Mac Maharaj (ANC)
Water Affairs and Forestry . . . . Prof Kadar Asmal (ANC)
Welfare and Population Development Mr Abe Williams (NP)

Deputy Ministers

Agriculture . . . . Ms Thoko Msane (ANC)

Arts, Culture, Science and
  Technology .... Ms Brigitte Mabandla (ANC)
Defence .... Mr Ronnie Kasrils (ANC)
Education .... Mr Renier Schoeman (NP)
Environment Affairs .... Mr Bantu Holomisa (ANC)
Finance .... Mr Alec Erwin (ANC)
Foreign Affairs .... Mr Aziz Pahad (ANC)
Home Affairs .... Mr Penuell Maduna (ANC)
Intelligence .... Mr Joe Nhlanhla (ANC)
Justice .... Mr Gert Myburgh (NP)
Land Affairs .... Mr Tobie Meyer (NP)
Provincial Affairs .... Mr Valli Moosa (ANC)
Safety and Security .... Mr Joe Matthews (IFP)
Welfare .... Ms Geraldine Fraser-Moleketi
                               (ANC)

Ministerial Advisers
Agriculture .... No advisers
Arts, Culture, Science and
  Technology .... No advisers
Correctional Services .... No advisers
Defence .... Mr Fana Hlongwane
Education .... Ms Sheila Sisulu,
                               Mr Trevor Abrahams
Environmental Affairs and Tourism . No advisers
Finance .... Mr Charles Stride
Foreign Affairs .... No advisers
Health .... No advisers
Home Affairs .... Dr Mario Oriani-Ambrosini
Housing .... No advisers
Justice .... Mr Enver Daniels,
                               Mr Vusi Pikoli
Labour .... Mr David Lewis,
                               Mr Papi Moloto
Land Affairs .... Mr Bahle Sibisi,
                               Ms Joanne Yawitch
Mineral and Energy Affairs .... No advisers
Posts, Telecommunications and
  Broadcasting .... Mr Willie Currie (Broadcasting)
Provincial Affairs and Constitutional
  Development .... No advisers
Public Enterprises .... Vacant
Public Service and Administration .. Mr John Ernstzen,
                               Mr Sandile Nogxine
Public Works .... Mr Sipho Shezi,
                               Mr Sivi Gounden

Reconstruction and Development .. Mr Raymond Mabope,
Mr Howard Gabriel
Safety and Security .... Mr Peter Gastrow
Sport and Recreation .... No advisers
Trade and Industry .... Dr Alistair Ruiters
Transport .... Dr CF Scheepers
Water Affairs and Forestry .... Mr A Heard
Mr I Abrams
Welfare and Population Development No advisers

Directors General

Office of the President .... Prof GJ Gerwel
Agriculture .... Dr FJ van der Merwe
Arts, Culture, Science and
   Technology .... Mr JJM Lotter (Acting)
Constitutional Development ...... Dr LD Barnard
Correctional Services .... Gen HJ Bruyn (Commissioner)
Education .... Dr NC Manganyi
Environmental Affairs and Tourism . Dr CM Cameron
Finance .... Dr E Calitz
Foreign Affairs .... Mr LH Evans (Acting)
Health .... Dr Olive Shisana
Home Affairs .... Mr PJ Colyn
Housing .... Mr WJ Cobbett
Justice .... Adv JJ Noeth
Labour .... Mr SM Pityana
Land Affairs .... Mr GC de Villiers
Mineral and Energy Affairs .... Dr PJ Hugo
National Intelligence Agency ..... Dr SW Sigxashe
Public Service Commission .... Dr LCA Stoop (Acting)
Public Works .... Mr TPC van Robbroeck (Acting)
South African National Defence
   Force .... Gen GL Meiring
(Chief of the SANDF)
Mr P Steyn
(Secretary for Defence)
South African Police Service ...... Maj Gen George Fivaz
(National Commissioner)
Sport and Recreation .... Mr M Tyamzashe
State Expenditure .... Mr GJ Smit
Trade and Industry .... Mr KM Gordhan
Water Affairs and Forestry .... Mr M Erasmus
Welfare .... Dr JH Schoeman (Acting)

Parliamentary Portfolio Committees (chairpersons)

Joint Committees

Joint Standing Committee on Defence Mr TS Yengeni
Joint Standing Committee on Finance
  (National Assembly and Senate) . Ms G Marcus
Joint Standing Committee on Public
  Accounts . . . . Mr KM Andrew

National Assembly

Agriculture, Water Affairs and
  Forestry . . . . Ms JY Love
Arts, Culture and Language, Science
  and Technology . . . . Dr MW Serote
Constitutional Affairs . . . . Mr PJ Gordhan
Correctional Services . . . . Mr CG Niehaus
Defence . . . . Mr PJ Groenewald
Education . . . . Dr BE Nzimande
Environmental Affairs and Tourism . Mr PR Mokaba
Finance . . . . Ms G Marcus
Foreign Affairs . . . . Adv RS Suttner
Health . . . . Dr ME Tshabalala
Home Affairs . . . . Mr D Lockey
Housing . . . . Mr MT Mafolo
Justice . . . . Adv JH de Lange
Labour . . . . Mr GG Oliphant
Land Affairs . . . . Adv SP Holomisa
Mineral and Energy Affairs . . . . Mr MJ Golding
Public Enterprises . . . . Mr MD Msomi
Public Service and Administration . . Ms PG Mlambo-Ngcuka
Public Works . . . . Mr MM Chikane
Reconstruction and Development
  Programme . . . . Mr MV Sisulu
Safety and Security . . . . Mr LM Mti
Sport and Recreation . . . . Ms LM Xingwana
Trade and Industry . . . . Mrs BEE Sethema
Transport . . . . Mrs P de Lille
Welfare . . . . Mr E Saloojee

Ad Hoc Select Committee, National Assembly

Statements by Minister for Safety
  and Security . . . . Mr CL Fismer

Senate

Constitutional and Provincial Affairs,
 Public Service and Administration   Sen M Bhabha
Education, Sport and Recreation, Arts,
 Culture, Science and Technology . Sen TGG Mashamba
Environmental Affairs and Tourism,
 Water Affairs and Forestry . . . . . . Sen SP Grove
Finance and Public Accounts . . . . . . Sen CE Lausberg
Health, Welfare and Population
 Development and Home Affairs . Sen Dr SC Cwele
Housing and Public Works . . . . Sen JL Kgoali
Justice . . . . Sen MW Moosa
Mineral and Energy Affairs,
 Transport, Posts, Telecommunica-
 tions and Broadcasting . . . . Sen SJ Mongwaketse
Reconstruction and Development
 Programme and Labour . . . . Sen SM Rasmeni

Provincial Executive Councils

Northern Transvaal

Premier . . . . Mr Ngoako Ramatlhodi (ANC)
Agriculture and Forestry . . . . Prof Tiny Burgers (ANC)
Economic Affairs, Commerce and
 Industry . . . . Mr Thaba Mafumadi (ANC)
Education and Culture . . . . Dr Aaron Motsoaledi (ANC)
Environment and Water . . . . Ms Maris Stella Sexwale-
        Mabitje (ANC)
Finance and Expenditure . . . . Mr Edgar Mushwana (ANC)
Health and Welfare . . . . Dr Joe Phaahla (ANC)
Land, Housing and Local
 Government . . . . Mr J Dombo (ANC)
Police and Protection Services . . . . . Mr Seth Nthai (ANC)
Public Transport . . . . Mr Johan Kriek (FF)
Public Works . . . . Mr Dikeledi Magadzi (ANC)

KwaZulu-Natal

Premier . . . . Dr Frank Mdlalose (IFP)
Agriculture . . . . Mr George Bartlett (NP)
Auxiliary Services and Traditional
 Affairs . . . . Inkosi Nyanga J Ngubane (IFP)
Education and Culture . . . . Dr Vincent Zulu (IFP)
Finance and Economic Affairs . . . . . Dr Senzele Mhlungu (IFP)
Health . . . . Dr Zweli Mkhize (ANC)

Housing and Local Government ... Mr Peter Miller (IFP)
Nature Conservation and Tourism .. Prince Gideon Zulu (IFP)
Police Services .... Rev Celani Mtetwa (IFP)
Roads, Transportation and Traffic
   Controls .... Mr S'bu Ndebele (ANC)
Social Welfare .... Mr Jacob Zuma (ANC)

Eastern Cape
Premier .... Mr Raymond Mhlaba (ANC)
Administration and Development
   Planning .... Mr Ezra Sigwela (ANC)
Agriculture and Environmental
   Planning .... Dr Tertius Delport (NP)
Economic Affairs .... Mr Smuts Ngonyama (ANC)
Education and Culture .... Mr Ziziwe Balindela (ANC)
Finance, Provincial Expenditure ... Mr Shepherd Mayatula (ANC)
Health and Welfare .... Dr Trudy Thomas (ANC)
Local Government, Housing and
   Traditional Authorities .... Mr Maxwell Mamase (ANC)
Police Services .... Mr Raymond Mhlaba (ANC)
                    (Acting)
Public Works .... Mr Tobile Mahlahlo (ANC)
Transport .... Mr Mandisa Marasha (ANC)

Free State
Premier .... Mr Patrick Lekota (ANC)
Agriculture and Environmental
   Affairs .... Mr Cas Human (ANC)
Education and Culture .... Mr Saki Belot (ANC)
Finance and Expenditure .... Mr Tate Makgoe (ANC)
Health and Welfare .... Mr Senorita Ntlabathi (ANC)
Housing .... Mr Vax Mayekiso (ANC)
Local Government Management ... Mr Ouma Motsumi (ANC)
Police Services .... Mr Papi Kgnare (ANC)
Public Transport .... Mr Louis van der Walt (NP)
Public Works and Roads .... Mr Gregory Nthatisi (ANC)

Gauteng
Premier .... Mr Tokyo Sexwale (ANC)
Agriculture and Conservation ..... Mr John Mavuso (NP)
Economic Affairs .... Mr Jabu Moleketi (ANC)
Education .... Ms Mary Metcalfe (ANC)
Health .... Mr Amos Masondo (ANC)
Local Government and Housing ... Mr Dan Mofokeng (ANC)

Public Safety and Security .... Ms Jessie Duarte (ANC)
Public Transport and Roads .... Mr Olaus van Zyl (NP)
Social Welfare .... Mr Sakkie Blanche (NP)
Sport, Recreation, Arts and Culture . Mr Peter Skosana (ANC)
Urban/Rural Development and
   Environment .... Mr Sicelo Shiceko (ANC)

Eastern Transvaal
Premier .... Mr Matthews Phosa (ANC)
Agriculture .... Dr Lucas Nel (NP)
Economic Affairs .... Mr Jabulani Mabena (ANC)
Education .... Mr David Mabuza (ANC)
Environmental Affairs .... Mr David Mkhwanazi (ANC)
Finance .... Mr Jacques Modipane (ANC)
Health and Welfare .... Mr Candith Mashego (ANC)
Housing .... Mr Craig Padayachee (ANC)
Law and Order .... Mr Steve Jabulane Mabona
                                       (ANC)
Local and Regional Government ... Mr January Che Masilela (ANC)
Minister without Portfolio .... Mr Joseph Mbazima (ANC)
Minister without Portfolio .... Mr Steve Mbuyisa (ANC)
Roads and Transport .... Mr Lackson Nthimane
                                      Mathebula (ANC)

Northern Cape
Premier .... Mr Emsley Manne Dipico
                                      (ANC)
Agriculture .... Mr Jacobus Marais (NP)
Economic Affairs, Trade and
   Industry .... Mr Goolam Akharwaray (ANC)
Education and Culture .... Mr Tina Joemat (ANC)
Finance .... Mr Jan Brazelle (NP)
Health and Welfare .... Dr Modise Matlaopane (ANC)
Local Government, Housing and
   Land Reform .... Mr Ouneas Dikgetsi (ANC)
Police Services, Safety and Security . Ms Eunice Komane (ANC)
Public Works .... Ms Peggy Hollander (NP)
Transport .... Mr Charl van Wyk (NP)
Unspecified .... Prof Jozef Henning (FF)

North West
Premier .... Mr Popo Molefe (ANC)
Agriculture .... Rev Johannes Tselapedi (ANC)
Economic Affairs .... Mr Amie Venter (NP)

Education	Mr Mamokoena Gaoretelelwe (ANC)
Finance	Mr Martin Kuscus (ANC)
Health	Dr Paul Sefularo (ANC)
Housing	Mr Darkie Afrika (ANC)
Justice	Mr Satish Roopa (ANC)
Public Media	Mr Riani de Wet (ANC)
Public Works	Mr Zacharia Tolo (ANC)
Transport	Mr Frans Vilakazi (ANC)

Western Cape

Premier	Mr Hernus Kriel (NP)
Agricultural Planning and Toursim	Mr Lampie Fick (NP)
Economic Affairs and RDP	Rev Chris Nissen (ANC)
Education, Arts and Culture	Ms Martha Olckers (NP)
Finance, Nature and Environment Conservation	Mr Kobus Meiring (NP)
Health and Welfare	Mr Ebrahim Rasool (ANC)
Housing and Leader of the House	Mr Gerald Morkel (NP)
Local Government	Mr Peter Marais (NP)
Police Services	Mr Patrick McKenzie (NP)
Sport and Recreation	Mr Lerumo Kalako (ANC)
Transport and Public Works	Mr Leonard Ramatlakane (ANC)

African National Congress

National Executive Committee

President	Mr Nelson Mandela
Deputy President	Mr Thabo Mbeki
Chairperson	Mr Jacob Zuma
Secretary General	Mr Cyril Ramaphosa
Deputy Secretary General	Ms Cheryl Carolus
Treasurer General	Rev Arnold Stofile

General Members

Prof Kader Asmal	Mr Peter Mokaba
Prof Sibusiso Bhengu	Ms Ruth Mompati
Mr Thozamile Botha	Mr Mohamed Valli Moosa
Mr Jeremy Cronin	Mr Linda Mti
Mr Ebrahim Ismail Ebrahim	Ms Thenjiwe Mtintso
Mr Alec Erwin	Mr Sydney Mufamadi
Ms Frene Ginwala	Mr S'bu Ndebele
Mr John Gomomo	Mr Joel Netshitenzhe

Mr Derek Hanekom
Ms Limpho Hani
Gen Bantu Holomisa
Mr Lulu Johnson
Dr Pallo Jordan
Mr Ahmed Kathrada
Ms Baleka Kgositsile
Mr Patrick 'Terror' Lekota
Mr Saki Macozoma
Mr Penuell Manduna
Mr 'Mac' Maharaj
Ms Winnie Mandela
Mr Trevor Manuel
Ms Mavivi Manzini
Ms Gill Marcus
Mr Moses Mayekiso
Mr Tito Mboweni
Mr Raymond Mhlaba
Mr Wilton Mkwayi
Mr Joe Modise
Ms Thandi Modise

Mr Smuts Ngonyama
Mr Joe Nhlanhla
Mr Carl Niehaus
Ms Sankie Nkondo
Mr Charles Nqakula
Mr Blade Nzimande
Mr Alfred Nzo
Mr Dullah Omar
Mr Essop Pahad
Mr Aziz Pahad
Mr Jeff Radebe
Mr Sam Shilowa
Ms Stella Sigcau
Mr Max Sisulu
Mr Zola Skweyiya
Adv Raymond Suttner
Ms Adelaide Tambo
Mr Steve Tshwete
Mr Tony Yengeni
Dr Nkosazana Zuma

Ex officio members

All provincial chairpersons and secretaries, and the Youth and
Women's Leagues' presidents and secretaries.

Women's League
Ms Winnie Mandela
Ms Noxiviwe Maphisa

KwaZulu-Natal
Mr Jacob Zuma
Mr Senzo Mchunu

Gauteng
Mr Tokyo Sexwale
Mr Paul Mashatile

Youth League
Mr Lulu Johnson
Mr Mpho Lekgoro

Free State
Mr Pat Matosa
Mr Kaiser Sebothelo

Northern Transvaal
Mr Ngaoko Ramathlodi
Mr Collins Chabane

Northern Cape
Mr Manne Dipico
Mr William Steenkamp

North West
Mr Popo Molefe
Mr Ndleleni Duma

Eastern Cape
Mr Dumisani Mafu
Mr Bongani Gxilishe

Eastern Transvaal
Mr Mathews Phosa
Mr Solly Zwane

Western Cape
Rev Chris Nissen
Mr James Ngculu

Azanian People's Organisation

President .... Mr Mosibudi Mangena
Deputy President .... Mr Pandelani Nefolovhodwe
Assistant National Organiser ...... Mr Fundile Mafongosi
Assistant Secretary General .... Mr Don Nkadimeng
Cape Vice-President .... Mr Danile Landingwe
Deputy Political Commissar ...... Mr Mzukisi Madlavu
Natal Vice-President .... Mr Patrick Mkhize.
National Organiser .... Mr Strike Thokoane
National Treasurer .... Mr Godfrey Africa
Political Commissar .... Mr Nkutsoeu Motsau
Publicity Secretary .... Mr Vuyisa Qunta
Secretary General .... Mr Mpotseng Kgokong
Transvaal Vice-President .... Ms Joyce Kalaote

Congress of South African Trade Unions

President .... Mr John Gomomo
First Vice-President .... Mr George Nkadimeng
Second Vice-President .... Ms Connie September
General Secretary .... Mr Sam Shilowa
Assistant General Secretary .... Mr Zwelinzima Vavi
Treasurer .... Mr Ronald Mofokeng

Democratic Party

Leader .... Mr Anthony James Leon
Deputy Leader .... Mr William Fettie Mnisi
Deputy Leader .... Mr Chris April
Chairperson of the Federal Council . Mr Dave Gant
Chairperson of Finance Committee . Mr Douglas Gibson
Deputy Chairperson of the Federal
   Council .... Mr Roger Hulley
Executive Director .... Mr James Selfe
National Chairperson .... Ms Dene Smuts

Freedom Front

National Executive Committee
Dr Pieter WA Mulder (Chairperson)
General Constand L Viljoen (Leader)
Dr Corne P Mulder
Mr Joseph Chiole
Dr Willie J Botha
Mr Pieter J Groenewald
General PH (Tienie) Groenewald
Mr Leon Louw
Mr Abrie Oosthuizen

Leader Council
General Constand Viljoen
Dr Pieter WA Mulder
Dr WJ Botha
Mr WA Botha
Mr J Chiole
Professor CWH Boshoff
Mr Carl Werth
Mrs Eleanor Lombard
Advocate Moolman Mentz
Dr CP Mulder
Mr Leon Louw
Mr AB Oosthuizen
Mr Pieter Groenewald
General Tienie Groenewald

Inkatha Freedom Party

Leadership Portfolios
President .... Chief Mangosuthu Buthelezi
Chief Executive Officer .... Mr Joe Matthews
National Chairperson .... Dr Frank Mdlalose
National Spokesperson .... Dr Ziba Jiyane
Women's Brigade Chairperson .... Ms Faith Gasa
Youth Brigade Chairperson .... Mr Musa Zondi

Portfolio Chairpersons
Communications .... Dr Z Jiyane
Community Development .... Mr MV Ngema
Education and African Affairs ..... Mr LPHM Mtshali
Environment .... Mr MM Mackenzie
External Relations .... Chief MG Buthelezi
   (Co-chairperson) .... Dr BS Ngubane)
Financial Affairs .... Mr J Mhlungu
Internal Relations .... Dr FT Mdlalose
Media Liaison .... Ms S Vos
Party Organisation and Development Mr WS Felgate
Public Relations .... Ms I Mars
Research and Documentation ..... Prof SJ Maphalala
Security .... Rev CJ Mtetwa

Sport .... Dr BS Ngubane
Training .... Dr RDB Madide

National Party of South Africa

National Leader .... Mr FW de Klerk
Eastern Cape Leader .... Dr Tertius Delport
Eastern Transvaal Leader .... Mr Chris Fismer
Free State Leader .... Mr Inus Aucamp
Gauteng Leader .... Mr Pik Botha
KwaZulu-Natal Leader .... Mr Danie Schutte
Northern Cape Leader .... Dr Kraai van Niekerk
Northern Transvaal Leader ...... Mr Andre Fourie
Northwest Leader .... Mr Amie Venter
Western Cape Leader .... Dr Dawie de Villiers

Federal Council
Executive Director .... Mr Fanus Schoeman
Director Information .... Mr Marthinus van Schalkwyk
Director, Management Services .... Mr Kobus du Plessis
Director, Organisation and
   Development .... Mr PW Saaiman
Director, Research and Information . Mr Melt Hamman
Director, Special Projects .... Mr Coetzee Bester

Pan-Africanist Congress

National Executive Council
President .... Mr Clarence Mlamli Makwetu
Deputy President .... Dr Motsoko Pheko
Civil Local Affairs .... Mr Bathembu Lugulwana
Culture, Sports and Recreation .... Mr Siphiwe Sithole
Economic Affairs .... Mr Mosesjane Malatsi
Education and Human Resources .. Dr Mandla Tshabalala
Environmental Affairs .... Dr Solly Skosana
Finance Secretary .... Mr Siphiwe Cele
Foreign Affairs .... Mr Mogole Mphahlele
Health .... Dr Selva Saman
Legal and Constitutional .... Mr Mandisa Tsitsi
Labour .... Mr Khoisan X
Land and Natural Resources ...... Dr Ben Marengwa
National Organiser .... Mr Bamba Ndwandwe

Political Affairs .... Mr Johnson Mlambo
Projects and Development .... Ms Cynthia Bekwa
Publicity and Information .... Mr ZB Moete
Religious Affairs .... Mr Joe Mkhwanazi
Relief and Aid .... Mr Kwedie Mkhaliphi
Secretary General .... Mr Maxwell Nemadzivhanani
Transport .... Ms Patricia de Lille
Without Portfolio .... Mr Gora Ebrahim
Without Portfolio .... Mr Mfanasekhaya Gqobose

South African Communist Party

Central Committee Executive
Chairperson .... Mr Raymond Mhlaba
Deputy Chairperson .... Mr Blade Nzimande
General Secretary .... Mr Charles Nqakula
Deputy General Secretary .... Mr Jeremy Cronin
Treasurer .... Ms Kay Moonsamy

Other Members
Mr Brian Bunting
Mr Yunis Carrim
Mr Manne Dipico
Mr Chris Dlamini
Ms Geraldine Fraser-Moleketi
Mr Enoch Godongwana
Mr John Gomomo
Mr Pravin Gordhan
Mr Ronnie Kasrils
Mr Gwede Mantashe
Mr Ben Dikobe Martins
Mr George Mashamba
Mr Kgalema Mothlanthe

Ms Thenjiwe Mthinso
Mr Sydney Mufamadi
Mr Billy Nair
Mr John Nkadimeng
Mr Godfrey Oliphant
Dr Essop Pahad
Mr Jeff Radebe
Ms Jenny Schreiner
Mr Sam Shilowa
Mr Garth Strachan
Adv Raymond Suttner
Mr Tony Yengeni

Members of the Constitutional Court

Adv Arthur Chaskalson, Chairperson
Mr Justice Thole Madala
Mr Justice Ismail Mohammed
Mr Justice Richard Goldstone
Mr Justice Laurie Ackermann
Mr Justice John Didcott

Mr Pius Langa
Mr Justice Johann Kriegler
Professor Yvonne Mokgoro
Professor Catherine O'Regan
Professor Albie Sachs

ABDUL KADER ASMAL

*Minister of Water Affairs
and Forestry, 1994.*

Kader Asmal, nicknamed 'The Bee' for his prodigious energy, was born on 8 October 1934 in Stanger, Natal, one of the seven children of Rassool and Ahmed Asmal, a shopkeeper. He was particularly close to his father who encouraged reading, debate and independent thinking in his children.

Asmal started his schooling in Stanger and subsequently attended the Oriental Primary School in Pietermaritzburg, returning to Stanger where he matriculated in 1952. At school his leadership and debating abilities were recognised and he became a prefect and house captain and won the province-wide Islamic Debating trophy. During his school years several factors influenced his later life and political thinking. From the age of ten, his love of books and newspapers (particularly the *New Statesman*) turned him into a lifelong Anglophile with the ambition to study at the London School of Economics. After seeing films of Nazi concentration camp victims at the age of 12 he decided to become a lawyer in order to root out practices which could lead to such atrocities.

Meeting Albert Luthuli, who was restricted to the Lower Tugela area, was the start of his lifelong commitment to human rights and the ideals of the African National Congress (ANC). He sold newspapers for the organisation and later arranged the first public meeting for Dr Luthuli in Stanger. Asmal's love of cricket led to his first political act as a schoolboy when he opposed the segregation of cricket clubs. In his matric year he led a stay-at-home as part of the 1952 Defiance Campaign of the Congress movement. Daily encounters and experiences in the small racially-segregated rural community in which he lived helped to form his strong aversion to inequality and injustice.

After matriculating, Asmal qualified as a teacher at the Springfield Training College in 1954. He then taught in the sugar cane company town of Darnall and in Stanger while studying for his BA degree in History, English and Politics through the University of South Africa.

Asmal realised his childhood ambition when he enrolled as a law student at the London School of Economics in 1959. Within a few months after his arrival in London, he started the Boycott Movement with a group of fellow South Africans (he shared a house with ex-South Africans, among them 'Mac' Maharaj), members of the Labour government and student groups.

Asmal was a founder member of the British Anti-Apartheid Movement which later became unique in the world for the solidarity shown by ordinary middle-class people for a specific cause. The movement scored its first victory in 1963 when it succeeded in stopping the sale of arms to South Africa by the British government. During this time Asmal also met and married his wife, Louise, who later ran the Irish Anti-Apartheid Movement from their home in Ireland.

Despite his time-consuming political involvement, Asmal won an academic award as a law student and lectured in law at the London Polytechnic.

In 1963 Asmal was offered a post as junior lecturer in law at Trinity College, Dublin University, and moved to Ireland. There he founded the Irish Anti-Apartheid Movement (he was chairman from 1974) and acted as vice-president for the International Defence and Aid Fund which, over the years, made millions of pounds available for the relief and defence of apartheid victims.

Asmal obtained his LLM from the London School of Economics (1964), qualified as a barrister at Lincoln's Inn, London (1964) and as barrister at law at King's Inn, Dublin (1975). In 1966 he obtained his MA degree from the University of Dublin.

Asmal's campaigns against inequality also made him aware of gender issues and he became a supporter of the Irish feminist movement. In 1966 he was the only Irish lawyer willing and able to discuss the legal aspects of contraception at a conference in Dublin. Visits to the USSR alerted him to the fact that equal employment opportunities for women are alone insufficient to guarantee gender equality in societies where social values remain patriarchal.

As founder and chairman of the Irish Council for Civil Liberties (1976), Asmal became involved in various campaigns for human rights. The Council became a public watchdog and pace-setter for changing attitudes (for example, promoting freedom of speech and trade unionism and opposing abuse of police power and the repression of information concerning sexual abuse).

Asmal's prominence as a campaigner for civil liberties led to international recognition. In 1979 he became a member of the International Commission of Inquiry into the Crimes of the Apartheid Regime and in 1982 was appointed rapporteur of the International Commission of Inquiry into Violations of International Law by Israel. In 1983 he chaired an international lawyers' inquiry into the lethal use of firearms in Northern Ireland. In the same year he was awarded the Prix Unesco for Human Rights.

Despite his involvement in campaigns, Asmal's stature as a lawyer and academic grew. In 1974 he became president of the Irish Federation of University Teachers and the following year he lectured at Christ's College, Cambridge, as visiting academic. During 1980 he was appointed dean of the Faculty of Arts at Trinity College, Dublin. Late in the 1980s he was given the inaugural Nelson Mandela Chair at Rutgers, the State University of New Jersey, and lectured as a visiting academic at the University of Warwick.

In 1979 Asmal was elected vice-president of the Haldane Society of Socialist Lawyers and became vice-president of the African Association of International Law in 1986. He also acted as legal advisor to Sanroc from 1980-90. In addition, his interest in labour and consumer issues resulted in his appointment to the Irish National Consumer Advisory Council in 1973.

Since 1963 Asmal has written numerous chapters in books as well as articles and reports for the United Nations and Commission of the European Communities on various aspects of law, workers' and human rights and apartheid. He was invited to deliver special lectures in Amsterdam, New York and Ottowa and his DN Pritt Memorial Lecture at the London School of Economics in 1989 was published as 'If Law is the Enemy ...' He delivered many papers at conferences in Europe, Africa, India and, after 1990, in South Africa.

Although Asmal considers himself to have been an ANC member for 35 years, he officially joined the movement in 1965 when Oliver Tambo moved to London. He believes that the contribution he made through the Anti-Apartheid and Boycott Movements played an important role in creating the climate that led to the unbanning of the ANC on 2 February 1990. Despite all his achievements he considers his work for the ANC as the most important part of his life. As a result, he declined full-time appointment as secretary of the National Council for Civil Liberties because accepting it would have meant that he could not continue with his work against apartheid.

In 1986 Asmal became a member of the ANC's Constitutional Committee which had the task of preparing the organisation's proposals for a new constitution for South Africa.

He returned to South Africa in September 1990 and at the ANC

Congress in July 1991 was elected to serve on its National Executive Committee. In addition to the Constitutional Committee, Asmal served on the organisation's Elections Committee and the Commission on Gender Discrimination and assisted with the establishment of new ANC branches.

Asmal moved to Cape Town where he was appointed professor of Human Rights at the University of the Western Cape. In this capacity he actively promoted the concept of affirmative action which he preferred to call 'positive action'. He defined this as deliberate actions aimed at making amends for past inequalities by providing education for all, adult education, extended education in rural areas, training and re-training of the work force and the provision of basic rights such as housing, water, electricity and schools. In the employment sphere he believes that the civil service should be more representative of the country's demography and that skills such as languages are as important as qualifications.

Asmal has served as a member of the Board of Sponsors of Nicro, as a trustee of the Street Law Project and a member of the National Association of Democratic Lawyers and the Friends of the South African National Gallery. In February 1993 Asmal was elected chairman of the council of the University of the North.

In the April 1994 general election, Asmal stood as number 22 on the ANC's national list for the National Assembly and he became a member of Parliament. In May 1994 he was appointed Minister of Water Affairs and Forestry.

Asmal is married to Louise, an executive assistant, and has two sons who live in Ireland.

SOURCES

1. *People in Politics*, First Quarter 1993, Institute for Democracy in South Africa (Idasa), Durban, 1993.
2. *Sunday Tribune*, 10 March 1991.

SIBUSISO MANDLENKOSI EMMANUEL BENGU

Minister of Education,
Arts and Culture,
May 1994.

Born on 8 May 1934 in Kranskop, Natal, Sibusiso Bengu was the second of the seven children of Augusta and the Reverend Jackonia Bengu, a Lutheran pastor.

Bengu attended Entomeni Primary School at Eshowe and the Umpumulo Teachers' Training College from 1950-51 where he received his Teachers' Certificate 4. He then taught for three years at the Entomeni Primary School before returning to teach at the teachers training college. He matriculated through private studies in 1957.

Bengu was a member of the African National Congress (ANC) while teaching in Eshowe and Umpumulo. At the time, the organisation was banned and his strongest connection with the movement was through his uncle-by-marriage, Chief Albert Luthuli, then ANC president.

Before enrolling at the University of Zululand, Bengu and others consulted Luthuli to establish his views on their attending a tribal university established by the apartheid authorities. Luthuli encouraged them to attend with the view to proving their academic abilities. Bengu was part of the first intake at the university in 1960 and became president of the Students' Representative Council. At the end of 1963 he completed his BA degree, majoring in English and History, and in 1964 achieved his Honours degree by correspondence through the University of South Africa.

Bengu was then employed by the radio station 'Voice of the Gospel' which was based in Addis Ababa, Ethiopia, with production studios in Roodepoort. There Bengu produced programmes in English, Afrikaans and the Nguni and Sotho languages. They were transmitted to Addis

Ababa and then beamed back to South Africa. During this time, relations between Ethiopia and South Africa were antagonistic and Bengu was harassed by the local authorities.

Bengu returned to Eshowe in 1966 to teach and at the same time lectured at the teachers' training college until 1969 when he was appointed founding principal of the Dlangezwa High School. This school was attached to the University of Zululand and functioned as a practical school for the training of teachers studying through the university.

In 1971 Bengu left South Africa to begin studying for his doctorate at the University of Geneva, Switzerland, at the Graduate Institute of International Studies. He completed his doctorate in Political Science with a thesis on African cultural identity and international relations. To this end, Bengu visited Nigeria and Ghana. He remained in Geneva until the end of 1974 and then resumed his position as principal of the Dlangezwa High School.

While studying in Europe Bengu met a number of South African political exiles. This encouraged him to return to the country to become active in political mobilisation. In this capacity he carried letters and messages to Chief Buthelezi requesting him to re-establish Inkatha, previously formed as a cultural organisation for Zulus. The intention in 1975 was to create a cultural organisation – 'culture' being defined very broadly to include politics. Inkatha yeNkululeko yeSizwe (National Cultural Liberation Movement) was formed on 21 March 1975 at a meeting in Mhlabatini, with Chief Buthelezi as president, and Bengu as secretary-general. Bengu drafted the preamble to the Inkatha constitution.

In 1977 Bengu was appointed professor and dean at the University of Zululand. During this time he continued to serve as secretary-general of Inkatha and participated in the establishment of Inkatha branches. He was also involved in attempts to promote Inkatha to other homelands in South Africa in order to gain the support of non-Zulus.

At this time Bengu was not permitted to teach history or political science (his areas of specialisation) because his ideas were considered too radical by the authorities. His position was further complicated when students communicated their political views to him and, in some cases, their plans to leave the country to join the liberation movement. The university administration expected him to report these students, and he found himself isolated and came into conflict with the police on several occasions.

His position within Inkatha became untenable when he and Buthelezi clashed on the issue of mass democratic action against apartheid, with his views being misinterpreted to imply the need for violent action. As he was unable to find support for his position, he lost faith in both Buthelezi and Inkatha and decided to leave the country.

Bengu resigned from his university position in July 1978 to go into exile. He left the country in August to work in Geneva as executive secretary for research and social action with the Lutheran World Federation. His special assignment there was the analysis of the root causes of socio-economic injustice especially as these affected development. He was responsible for stimulating and co-ordinating research in Asia, Africa and Latin America and promoting education regarding development for the countries of Europe and North America.

The Lutheran World Federation supported the Southern African liberation movements with financial and material aid. From time to time Bengu visited the camps of these movements and had close contact with Oliver Tambo, then president of the ANC. Following the unbanning of the ANC in February 1990 he was asked to serve as a delegate of its Geneva branch at the ANC's first conference in Johannesburg in 1990. However, he was unable to attend.

On 1 July 1991 Bengu was appointed vice-chancellor and rector of the University of Fort Hare. As rector he did not actively participate in ANC structures, but retained his membership. However, in January 1994 he accepted nomination to the national election list of the ANC (as candidate number 74) for the April 1994 elections.

Following the elections, Bengu was appointed Minister of Education, Arts and Culture in the first post-apartheid cabinet.

Bengu is married to Ethel Funuka (born Msizi) and they have five children.

SOURCE

1. Interviewed 20 April 1994, Durban.

THOZAMILE BOTHA

Member of Parliament,
African National Congress,
1994-95.
Chairperson, Commission on
Provincial Government, 1994.
Director-General,
Eastern Cape Province.

Thozamile Botha was born in 'White Location', Port Elizabeth, on 15 June 1948, the eldest of the six children of Miriam Skhenjana, a domestic worker, and James Thembile Botha, a teacher.

As a baby he was cared for by his maternal grandmother who lived on a farm near the small Eastern Cape town of Alexandria. At the age of six, Botha had an accident which left him with a permanent limp. He fell from a tree and injured his back but received no medical treatment. A year later his mother took him back to Port Elizabeth where he was admitted to hospital for spine dislocation. It was in Walton Hospital that he started school and passed Sub A. A year later he was sent back to Alexandria. Despite his disability, he insisted on attending school which involved walking a distance of 20 km twice daily. Botha found it difficult to make progress at school because he, like the rest of the young boys on the farm, was periodically obliged to work in the chicory plantation. For this reason he was unable to write examinations on two occasions.

In 1963, at the age of 14, Botha realised that his disability would exclude him from strenuous labour. Because he wanted to further his education, he left his grandmother's house and went in search of his mother who had remarried and moved to the Port Elizabeth township of KwaZakhele. However, he was not registered as living in Port Elizabeth and, in terms of influx control legislation of the time, was prohibited from being in an urban area. He was therefore unable to obtain a permit to register for school. By dodging the police, lying to school authorities about his permit and working part-time to pay for his clothes and books, Botha managed to pass Standard 6 in 1968.

In 1969 Botha was granted permanent residence in Port Elizabeth, but financial difficulties forced him to leave school. Determined to go back to school, Botha spent a year working as a machine operator at a paper mill company and later as a 'tea boy' at a timber company.

In 1970 Botha returned to KwaZakhele and thereafter completed four further years of secondary education. In March 1974, the year he was due to matriculate, his widowed mother fell ill and financial difficulties again forced Botha to leave school and seek employment.

With the assistance of a former headmaster, Botha managed to register and study part-time. He matriculated while working for Murray and Roberts as a time keeper.

Botha obtained a scholarship and in 1975 registered at Fort Hare University for a BSc degree. Poor health forced him to abandon his studies but he returned the following year and enrolled for a BA Law degree.

The political events of 1976 affected his studies. Within two months of the Soweto student uprising in June the university had closed down and students were sent home.

Returning to KwaZakhele, Botha was recruited to teach mathematics at the local high school. Noticing that science teaching was hampered by lack of equipment, Botha and a number of colleagues formed an Association for Science and Technology (Afsat), bringing together teachers and people in the field of science with the aim of setting up a community laboratory for Port Elizabeth townships. Botha was elected vice-president of the project.

In 1977, as tension continued to mount between principals and students in the Port Elizabeth township schools, ex-Fort Hare students, including Botha, intervened. Afsat became increasingly involved in community matters and launched a support group for the students arrested in the student resistance. Following an Afsat fundraising rally, Botha and others were arrested and tortured in police custody. He was detained for 14 days and charged with incitement to public violence. This charge was later converted to one of sabotage. Botha was tried and acquitted.

On his release from jail, he continued teaching in KwaZakhele. In 1979 he took up employment with Ford as a time-and-work-study technician and moved to Zwide.

Zwide had been established to accommodate the residents of Ford village where many elderly people lived in houses built in 1948 out of packing cases supplied by the Ford Motor Company. Ford village was destroyed by the authorities in 1979 and some of its inhabitants were moved to Zwide while others were moved to hostels. Homes in Zwide were in such poor condition that Zwide residents opposed rent increases, the metering of water and re-siting of electrical sub-stations. It was in this context that the Zwide Residents' Association (ZRA), led by Botha, was formed in September 1979.

As most residents of Port Elizabeth townships were experiencing similar problems, pressure developed for the creation of a unifying organisation and a larger civic grouping, and the Port Elizabeth Civic Organisation (Pebco) was established. Botha served as convenor of a Committee of Ten which drafted Pebco's constitution.

On 30 October 1979, a meeting in New Brighton attended by some 8 000 people adopted the Pebco constitution and an executive was elected with Botha as president. The aims and objectives of Pebco included demands for equal civic rights for all the people of Port Elizabeth; opposition to all discriminatory legislation enacted by the government and local authorities; participation in decision-making on all matters affecting South African citizens; and resistance to any attempt to deprive blacks of their South African citizenship.

Pebco refused to negotiate on national issues unless the government accepted black participation in administration. Negotiations would only be approved if an all-race national convention was called where political prisoners, exiled leaders and participants in the armed struggle could be involved. Pebco also adopted the principle of non-collaboration with organisations participating in government institutions.

Botha's involvement with Pebco caused concern among his white colleagues at Ford. He was given an ultimatum to choose between his work and politics. He chose the latter and the following day 700 Ford workers downed tools, demanding Botha's reinstatement. Management agreed to Botha's reinstatement, thereby ending the three-day strike.

However, the action sparked further labour demands. Ford was issued with an ultimatum to meet certain demands, which it failed to do. This was followed by a walkout supported by other workers in the motor industry. Those who participated were dismissed. Their union, claiming that the action was political, refused to become involved and Ford refused to communicate with the dismissed workers who had by then organised themselves as the Ford Workers' Committee, chaired by Botha.

To force recognition of dissatisfaction among workers, a boycott aganst white businesses and Ford products was launched. National support was sought for the boycott as well as backing from the African National Congress (ANC). The strike, which led to the intervention of the US ambassador, ended in February 1980 with the reinstatement of all dismissed workers.

Following these events, Botha and Pebco's entire executive were detained. Botha was interrogated in an attempt to ascertain his link with the ANC. News of their detention led to protest action in the townships which was broken up by riot police using tear gas.

After his release from detention on 27 February 1980, Botha was issued with a three-year banning order which, *inter alia*, prohibited him from entering any factory. He was therefore unable to take up Ford's offer of re-employment. Receiving assistance from Ford workers, he set up a vegetable vending business in the township.

His underground activities were, however, noted by the security police. Anticipating another clampdown, Botha fled to Lesotho, leaving South Africa on 1 May 1980. Botha conntiued to work for the ANC in Lesotho. In 1981, he enrolled at Lesotho University for an LLB degree. In the aftermath of the December 1982 cross-border raid which devastated the ANC community in Lesotho, Botha was advised to leave.

From 1983-86 Botha lived in Lusaka where he was elected to the national executive committee of the exiled trade union movement, the South African Congress of Trade Unions (Sactu), and worked as an administrative secretary for Sactu. He also acted as convenor of a local government commission.

In 1986 Botha enrolled for a diploma in Public Administration and Management at Glasgow College of Technology in Scotland, followed by a masters degree in Political Science and Public Administration at Strathclyde University in Scotland. In 1989 he registered for a PhD at Essex University and became regional chairperson of the United Kingdom's ANC region.

Following the unbanning of the ANC in February 1990, Botha returned briefly to South Africa in May 1991 to head the Local Government Planning and Policy Research Project at the University of the Western Cape.

In July 1991, at its congress in Durban, Botha was elected to the national executive committee of the ANC. He was appointed head of the ANC's Department of Local and Regional Government and Housing. He served on the organisation's negotiations commission, played a central role in the local government negotiating forum and was a founder member of the national housing forum. He serves as an executive member of the South African National Civic Organisation (Sanco).

Botha stood as candidate number 11 on the ANC's national list for the national assembly in the April 1994 general election and became a member of parliament.

In June he was appointed chairman of the Commission on Provincial Government dealing with issues concerning the finalisation of the number and boundaries of the provinces; constitutional dispensations of the provinces; final delimitation of the powers and functions of national and provincial governments; fiscal arrangements between national and provincial governments; and powers and functions of local governments. On his appointment to this post, Botha resigned from parliament.

On 1 February 1995, he took up the post of director-general of the

Eastern Cape. In this capacity he oversees a bureaucracy of 150 000 employees, created through the merging of the Ciskei, Transkei and Eastern Cape regional civil services.

At the ANC's Bloemfontein congress held in December 1994, Botha was re-elected to the organisation's national executive committee.

Botha and his wife, Fezeka (born Makimana), live in Rustadal in Cape Town. They have two children.

SOURCES

1. *People in Politics*, Third Quarter 1993, Institute for Democracy in South Africa (Idasa), Durban, 1993.
2. *Negotiation News*, 21 July 1994.
3. *Weekly Mail & Guardian*, 17 March 1995.

ROELOF FREDERIK 'PIK' BOTHA

Member of Parliament,
National Party, Westdene,
1977-94.
Member of Parliament,
National Party, 1994.
Minister of Foreign Affairs,
1977-94.
Minister of Mineral and
Energy Affairs, 1994

The son of a school principal, Pik Botha was born on 27 April 1932 in Rustenburg, Transvaal. He attended the Hoër Volkskool, Potchefstroom, and was a good all-round pupil, becoming chairman of the debating society, head of the Voortrekkers, a member of the rugby team and an officer in the school cadets.

He completed his BA and LLB at the University of Pretoria and in

February 1953 joined the South African Department of Foreign Affairs. In June 1956 he was transferred to the South African Mission in Stockholm, Sweden, as third secretary, and in January 1960 he moved to the South African Embassy in Cologne, West Germany. Following his transfer back to Pretoria in January 1963, he became a member of the South African legal team in the case concerning South African administration of South West Africa (*Ethiopia and Liberia vs South Africa*) at the International Court of Justice, The Hague, from 1963-66. He represented the South African Government in the case from 1965-66.

Botha was appointed legal adviser to the Department of Foreign Affairs in February 1966, and between 1966 and 1974 attended seven sessions of the United Nations (UN) General Assembly as a member of the South African delegation. During this time he was promoted to the post of under-secretary and head of the South West Africa and UN Section of the Department of Foreign Affairs. However, a month after presenting his credentials as ambassador to the UN, South Africa was suspended and Botha returned home.

In 1970 Botha's life turned from that of career diplomat to politics and on 22 April he won the the Wonderboom seat for the National Party, and held it again in 1974.

Botha again served as a member of the South African legal team on the South West Africa question which came before the International Court of Justice in 1970-71.

As an MP, Botha served on a number of special committees, including the Committee of Public Accounts from 1970-74.

In 1975 Botha was appointed South African ambassador extraordinary and plenipotentiary to the USA, combining this post with that of permanent representative at the UN. During this time he was much in the public eye and, with his distinctive, assertive style of diplomacy, became a popular figure among white South Africans.

In April 1977 he was appointed Minister of Foreign Affairs and in the same year became MP for Westdene, the constituency he represented until the April 1994 election.

As Minister of Foreign Affairs, Botha recognised the connection between domestic policy and foreign affairs and openly indicated his *verligte* viewpoint. In March 1980 the portfolio of Information was added to his Foreign Affairs Ministry.

In 1978 Botha stood for the premiership in a move to block Dr Connie Mulder from succeeding BJ Vorster as prime minister. Although his candidature had no chance of succeeding, it drew votes away from Mulder, thus enabling PW Botha to become prime minister. The year 1984 was a high point in Botha's career with numerous spectacular foreign affairs coups including the signing of the Nkomati Accord with Mozambique and a tour to European countries arranged for PW Botha in May and June. In addition, a meeting between the administrator-general of South West Africa, representatives from the internal parties, the South African authorities and South West African People's Organisation leader, Sam Nujoma, was set up in Zambia. Coupled with this was on-going contact with the Angolan government to prepare the way for a cessation of hostilities and the independence of South West Africa/Namibia.

However, in September 1984 South Africa's relations with Great Britain deteriorated when Botha announced that the South African government would renege on an undertaking to produce four South Africans charged with customs and excise offences in the United Kingdom for illegally exporting military hardware to South Africa. Botha claimed this was a response to Britain's tardiness in resolving the Durban British consulate sit-in by six United Democratic Front leaders who had sought consular protection to avoid detention by the South African authorities.

In June 1985, South Africa's diplomatic relations deteriorated further with the recall of the United States ambassador to Washington following an alleged South African intelligence-gathering operation in Cabinda, Angola.

In July 1985 Botha had to deal with the De Jonge affair. Klaas de Jonge, suspected of assisting the African National Congress, allegedly led police to the Dutch Embassy on the pretext of exposing an arms cache. He then sought sanctuary at the embassy which he partially entered before being recaptured by the police. De Jonge was later returned to the Dutch Embassy where he remained for two years before his repatriation to Holland in 1988.

In February 1986, Pik Botha told reporters that South Africa could be ruled by a black president in the future, provided agreement was reached on protecting minority rights. At the end of the no-confidence debate in parliament, State President Botha publicly repudiated the statement made by his Foreign Minister and reaffirmed apartheid policy outlined by other senior National Party MPs during the week's debate. The state president stated that no member of the cabinet had the right to compromise the government in such a way. Pik Botha was forced to acknowledge, by means of a letter to the state president, that entertaining the idea of a black president did not conform with government policy. Botha later admitted that at the time he considered resigning from the NP and launching a rival party.

Botha played a key role in the negotiation process which led to the withdrawal of Cuban and South African troops from Angola and which culminated in Namibian independence. Negotiations held in Brazzaville, Congo, in May 1988 were followed by talks between South Africa, Cuba and Angola in Cairo in June. At a meeting of representatives of the three governments in New York in July, agreement was reached on a set of principles to establish peace in Angola. On 22 December, Botha attended the formal signing of the New York peace accord between Cuba, South Africa and Angola at the United Nations headquarters. This agreement cleared the way for the implementation of UN Resolution 435 and Namibian independence.

In January 1990 Botha visited Budapest for talks with Hungarian Foreign Minister, Gyulu Horn. The visit was seen as a breakthrough for the South African government in normalising relations with Eastern bloc countries.

After the unbanning of the ANC and the release from prison of Nelson Mandela in February 1990, Botha formed part of the South African government delegation at subsequent talks with the ANC at Groote Schuur in Cape Town.

Following the talks he accompanied President de Klerk on an official trip to Europe where they visited nine countries and held talks with heads of state and senior government officials. In 1990 and 1991 he travelled to many other countries including Cote d'Ivoire (to attend the consecration by Pope John Paul II of the Basilique Notre Dame de la Paix), Czechoslovakia, Yugoslavia, Zambia, Kenya, Israel, Ukraine, Lithuania, Russia, Latvia, Taiwan, New Zealand and Australia. In 1992 he travelled to Senegal and in 1993 visited Tunisia, Pakistan, India, Egypt, Oman, Jordan and Qatar.

In July 1991 it was revealed that the Department of Foreign Affairs had channelled R250 000 to Inkatha. In a television interview Botha admitted he had authorised the transfer of state money from the Foreign Affairs special account to Inkatha as part of a world-wide anti-sanctions campaign.

In December 1991 Botha was appointed to serve as the South African government's representative on the Convention for a Democratic South Africa (Codesa) working group dealing with the future of the TBVC states.

In January 1992 Botha travelled to Angola to sign an agreement which would lead to an exchange of diplomatic missions between South Africa and Angola. However, following the Angolan election and allegations of collusion between South Africa and Unita, which refused to accept the election result and went back to the bush, diplomatic contact was broken and Botha was declared *persona non grata* in Luanda.

Following deadlock in the negotiation process after Codesa 2 in May 1992, and the start of the ANC's mass action campaign in the wake of the Boipatong massacre, the Organisation of African Unity raised the issue of violence in South Africa at the United Nations security council. Botha represented the government at this debate, where he alleged that the ANC/communist alliance was attempting to infiltrate arms into the country. Following the resignation of Finance Minister Barend du Plessis in April 1992, Botha was elected leader of the National Party in the Transvaal. He was also appointed to the board of governors of the Development Bank of Southern Africa.

In October 1993 Botha made a controversial statement apologising for the raid on an Azanian People's Liberation Army house in Umtata, Transkei, as well as for the government's handling of the petrol price increase. The statement conflicted with the views of his cabinet colleagues responsible for these matters.

Following the 1994 general election, Botha was appointed Minister of Mineral and Energy Affairs in the government of national unity. The appointment was criticised by the National Union of Mineworkers.

He is married to Helena Susanna (born Bosman) and they have two sons and two daughters.

SOURCES

1. *Curriculum vitae* supplied by Department of Information.
2. South African Institute of Race Relations, *Race Relations Survey 1983*, Johannesburg, 1984.
3. *Fair Lady*, 18 April 1984.
4. *Sunday Tribune*, 13 May 1984.
5. *Argus*, 25 September 1984.
6. *Argus*, 18 June 1985.
7. *Cape Times*, 12 July 1985.
8. *Argus*, 8 February 1986.
9. *Natal Mercury*, 14 November 1990.
10. *Natal Witness*, 25 July 1991.
11. *Natal Mercury*, 24 January 1992.
12. *Daily News*, 15 November 1992.
13. *Daily News*, 1 November 1993.
14. *A-Z of South African Politics,* Mail & Guardian/Penguin Books, Johannesburg 1995.

MANGOSUTHU GATSHA BUTHELEZI

Leader, Inkatha
Freedom Party, 1990.
Member of Parliament,
Inkatha Freedom Party,
1994.
Minister of Home Affairs,
1994.

Mangosuthu Buthelezi was born on 27 August 1928 in Mahlabatini, Zululand, heir to the chieftainship of the Buthelezi tribe. His mother, Princess Constance Magogo Zulu, was the grand-daughter of King Cetshwayo and daughter of King Dinizulu. His father, Chief Mathole, was the grandson of Chief Mnyamana Buthelezi, prime minister to King Cetshwayo.

Buthelezi grew up in a traditional household at Dlamahlahla, spending his early years as a herdboy. He attended Impumalanga Primary School from 1934-43 and in 1944 enrolled at Adams College, Amanzimtoti, where he matriculated. In 1948 he was admitted to Fort Hare University at Alice, Cape, to major in History and Bantu Administration. He came under the influence of Prof ZK Matthews of the African National Congress (ANC) and joined its Youth League, meeting Robert Sobukwe, then Youth League president at the university, and Robert Mugabe, now president of Zimbabwe.

In 1950, as a result of student boycotts and protests against the visit of Governor-General G Brand van Zyl to the university, Buthelezi was one of a number of students who were expelled. He completed his BA by attending lectures at the University of Natal where he was permitted to write his Fort Hare examinations.

In 1951 Buthelezi was offered employment as a clerk in the Department of Bantu Administration. He resigned a year later and was then employed by a firm of Durban attorneys. In 1953 he returned to Mahlabatini to take up the position of chief of the Buthelezi tribe. Despite the fact that his position was hereditary, the government only recognised his chieftainship in September 1957, regarding him as an acting chief up to that date.

In 1970 the KwaZulu Territorial Authority was established with Buthelezi as its chief executive officer. In 1972 he became chief executive councillor of the KwaZulu Legislative Assembly and in 1976 chief minister of KwaZulu, a position he held until April 1994.

In 1975 Buthelezi founded Inkatha yeNkululeko yeSizwe, a black liberation movement. Its predecessor, Inkatha ka Zulu, founded for Zulus by his uncle, King Solomon ka Zulu in 1928, collapsed in the early 1930s. However, Buthelezi, as president of Inkatha (which was renamed Inkatha yeNkululeko yeSizwe – Freedom of the Nation), changed the nature of the 1975 organisation, portraying it as a liberation movement pursuing a policy of non-violence. In 1984 it claimed a membership of close to one million people. Inkatha's philosophy included liberation at all levels, particularly in respect of political, economic and cultural aspects. Apart from the process of peaceful evolution, it took the view that liberation would also come through education for equal citizenship, equitable land distribution and the encouragement of foreign investment to provide employment for a growing population.

In 1976, during the Soweto disturbances, Buthelezi visited the area primarily to defuse a violent confrontation between Mzimhlophe residents and hostel dwellers. In October of that year, he held a meeting with leaders representing various black community groupings, including trade unionists, members of the Black Consciousness Movement, 'homeland' leaders and businessmen in an attempt to launch a Black Unity Front. Buthelezi also called for a national convention to work out South Africa's constitutional future. However the Black Unity Front failed when some of those present at its inaugural meeting withdrew.

In 1978 Buthelezi was instrumental in the formation of the South African Black Alliance (SABA) which initially consisted of the coloured Labour Party of South Africa, the Indian Reform Party and Inkatha. It was later joined by Enos Mabuza's Inyandza National Movement of KaNgwane. However, the alliance suffered a major split in February 1983 when the Labour Party was suspended and subsequently resigned as a result of its decision to participate in the South African government's tricameral constitutional dispensation. In 1986 a further rift appeared when Buthelezi criticised Enos Mabuza, chief minister of KaNgwane, for holding discussions with the ANC in Lusaka.

In May 1980 the Buthelezi Commission, under the chairmanship of Prof GDL Schreiner of the University of Natal, was established on the initiative of Inkatha's central committee. It released its report in March 1982 and its recommendations were supported by Inkatha as a basis for a future negotiated political settlement. In December 1982 Buthelezi stated that the KwaZulu government had accepted the commission's report as a basis for negotiation with the South African government.

Buthelezi had repeatedly stated that although Inkatha stood for one-man-one-vote in a unitary state, it was prepared to seek alternatives to find a peaceful solution. The commission had proposed a consociational government as the most acceptable political option, with a legislative assembly elected by universal adult suffrage from a number of community-of-interest areas, not necessarily based on ethnicity. It incorporated the principle of proportional representation, a bill of rights, a delimitation of powers and functions by the central government, a minority veto and control of the legislature through the courts.

In 1982 Buthelezi was instrumental in preventing the South African authorities from excising a part of KwaZulu (Ingwavuma) for incorporation into Swaziland. In June of that year Minister of Co-operation and Development Piet Koornhof informed the KwaZulu government that the area was to be ceded to Swaziland. The decision was contested in the Natal Supreme Court and the excision of Ingwavuma declared illegal on the grounds that there had been insufficient consultation with the KwaZulu cabinet as required by the Black States Constitution Act of 1971. This decision was confirmed by the Appellate Division. Following another unsuccessful attempt by the South African government to excise the area in terms of the Black Administration Act of 1927, officials of the Department of Co-operation and Development were ordered to leave Ingwavuma and the South African government was banned from interfering in the area.

In 1983 Buthelezi launched a major campaign against the government's new constitutional proposals, organising mass rallies and public meetings. In the same year, he opposed the black local authorities elections on the grounds that he would not be drawn into participation while the community councils were being used as stage props for what he viewed as the political farce of the tricameral parliament. He also opposed participation because, in his opinion, the government was using the councils and the 'homelands' as alternatives to the inclusion of Africans in parliament.

During 1983 Buthelezi visited the USA and Europe, and called for increased investment in South Africa if this could be linked to pressure for change, claiming that the free enterprise system was vital to the development of Southern Africa.

In 1985 Buthelezi participated in the Convention Alliance, a grouping of political, church and business organisations which called for a national convention in South Africa, but which subsequently collapsed.

In the same year a joint strategic committee of the KwaZulu cabinet and the Natal provincial executive was set up to deal with many policy and planning matters which affected both regions. As a consequence various political and business organisations called for a KwaNatal constitutional Indaba to discuss the possible formation of a single Natal/KwaZulu legislative authority. The Indaba, which brought together 37 organisations, began its deliberations in April 1986 and in July published its agreed bill of rights. In November it finally agreed to a recommended constitution for the region.

At the opening of parliament in January 1986, State President PW Botha announced the formation of a national council which would be a forum under his chairmanship for negotiation with South African black leaders. Buthelezi indicated that he would not serve on the council until certain prerequisites were met, including the release of ANC leader Nelson Mandela from jail.

From 1985, following the assassination of Victoria Mxenge, a human rights lawyer working within the United Democratic Front (UDF), violence in Natal townships between supporters of Inkatha and the UDF began to escalate. Buthelezi called for unity talks with ANC President Oliver Tambo, but the ANC responded by saying that Buthelezi's statements and actions did not accord with a desire for black unity. In addition, ANC and other leaders viewed his support for the formation of the United Workers Union of South Africa (Uwusa) as a rival to the Congress of South African Trade Unions (Cosatu) as divisive.

The conflict continued into 1987 and attempts to make peace during the year broke down. Buthelezi denied that Inkatha was the perpetrator of the violence and claimed that the ANC mission in exile was waging an armed struggle and that the UDF and Cosatu were working together to make the country ungovernable. It was his view that the ANC had declared war on Inkatha and had repeatedly called for the murder of anyone it stigmatised as a collaborator.

In March 1987 Buthelezi met with Law and Order Minister Adriaan Vlok, and called on the South African government to hand over control of its police stations in KwaZulu to the KwaZulu administration. As a result police stations in certain areas, including KwaMashu, Umlazi and Umbumbulu, were taken over by the KwaZulu police.

In January 1988 Inkatha and the UDF issued a joint and unconditional call on their members to end the violence. Shortly thereafter, Buthelezi indicated that he wanted to hold talks with the national rather than the local leadership of the UDF. He appealed to UDF President Archie Gumede to secure black unity and maintained that he saw peace talks as a first attempt towards consolidating black power in opposition to apartheid.

An agreement was finally reached in September 1988 in the Pietermaritzburg area, but unrest continued. Peace talks in the Durban area broke down in 1989.

Buthelezi consistently opposed sanctions against South Africa as a means to end apartheid. He maintained that large-scale sanctions would condemn South Africa to Third World poverty. He encouraged foreign investment in the country, repeatedly indicating his support for the free enterprise system.

Following the unbanning of the ANC, the Pan-Africanist Congress and the South African Communist Party on 2 February 1990, and the release of Nelson Mandela from jail on 11 February, Buthelezi indicated that he was now ready to negotiate with the South African government in a process leading to a new constitution for South Africa.

Violence between supporters of the ANC and Inkatha continued to gain momentum, not only in Natal, but also in the Transvaal. On 29 January 1991 Buthelezi and Nelson Mandela met in Durban to negotiate a peace agreement between the two organisations. Despite reaching agreement, the violence continued.

In July 1991 Buthelezi was involved in a controversy arising out of revelations that certain Inkatha rallies held in 1990 had been funded by the South African government. He denied any knowledge of the funding and repaid the amount involved. He rejected suggestions that he had received covert funding from South African intelligence services since the founding of Inkatha.

In the same month Inkatha was converted into a political party named the Inkatha Freedom Party (IFP). Buthelezi was unopposed in the election for leader at the IFP's first conference.

In September 1991 Buthelezi participated in the signing of the National Peace Accord together with Nelson Mandela and State President FW de Klerk. The following month he rejected the formation of a Patriotic Front, and reiterated his view that the IFP was a fulcrum at the centre of South African politics and that a settlement was impossible without its participation.

In 1991 Buthelezi's lawyers threatened legal action against libraries which held copies of the book *Gatsha Buthelezi: Chief with a Double Agenda* by Mzala. Although certain libraries initially withdrew this book, it was subsequently reinstated despite Buthelezi's claim that it contained material defamatory of him.

Although the IFP and the KwaZulu government sent representatives to the Convention for a Democratic South Africa (Codesa) in December 1991, Buthelezi himself did not attend, protesting that Zulu King Goodwill Zwelithini had not been permitted full delegate status at the convention. In February 1992 he threatened to remove the IFP from Codesa unless a full working delegation from the Zulu king was accepted and the ANC's military wing, Umkhonto we Sizwe, disbanded.

During 1992, it was alleged that IFP supporters, especially those living in Reef hostels, were promoting violence in collaboration with elements of the security forces. This view was supported in a June 1992 report of the International Commission of Jurists. Buthelezi responded that he had never been a proponent of violence, and that it was the ANC's policy of ungovernability which was at the core of the violence.

At the IFP's annual conference, held at Ulundi in July 1992, Buthelezi gave notice that the party would withdraw from the negotiation process if Umkhonto we Sizwe was not disbanded by mid-September. He accused ANC President Nelson Mandela of lying to the United Nations Security Council of July, when he claimed that the IFP was a surrogate of the government 'in its business of killing to oppose democratic forces'. As a result of this, Buthelezi indicated that he would not attend the next scheduled meeting of the National Peace Accord. During this speech, Buthelezi also attacked Mandela and the ANC, accusing them of lacking a commitment to peace.

Following the breakdown of negotiations and the subsequent rolling mass action campaign of the ANC, the government and the ANC began bi-lateral talks which led to a Record of Understanding between Mandela and De Klerk agreed on 26 September 1992. At a Shaka Day rally in KwaMashu on 27 September Buthelezi rejected the Record of Understanding and stated that he was appalled at the inference that South Africa's future could be decided by the South African government and the ANC. He then announced the IFP's withdrawal from the negotiation process.

Buthelezi and others subsequently formed the Concerned South African Group (Cosag), which consisted of the KwaZulu government, the IFP, the Transvaal Hostel Dwellers' Association, the National Forum, the Ciskei government, the Bophuthatswana government, the Conservative Party, the Afrikaner Volksunie, the Afrikaner Vryheidsbeweging and the Indian Reform Party. It opposed the concepts of a transitional government and transitional constitution as well as a constituent assembly and sought to resume multi-party negotiations towards a new constitution.

Buthelezi continued to refuse to resume talks during 1993 while the negotation process continued at the World Trade Centre. He indicated that the IFP could not accept the setting of an election date before there was agreement on the form of state, the final constitution and the process in terms of which it would be written.

Buthelezi, a proponent of federalism, indicated in October 1993 that he did not envisage KwaZulu as a unitary state, but only as a federal state in a federal republic. He also raised the the future of the Zulu nation.

Secret talks between the IFP, the government and the ANC took place in an attempt to bring the IFP back into the negotiation process, but these failed. In December 1993 Buthelezi stated that it was impossible for the IFP to take part in the 1994 general election.

In February 1994 the ANC announced substantial concessions to the IFP and its partners in the Freedom Alliance (a group including Cosag members and repesentatives of the Afrikaner Volksfront), but Buthelezi criticised the proposals as 'cheap politicking'.

In March a meeting between Nelson Mandela and Buthelezi was held in Durban and an accord was reached with Buthelezi's provisional agreement to register for the April elections and an ANC guarantee of international mediation to deal with outstanding problems. However, registration did not guarantee participation by the IFP.

Attempts at finding mediators delayed the process and in March Buthelezi, as Minister of Police in KwaZulu, faced claims in a report to the Transitional Executive Council (TEC) that IFP officials and senior South African police had colluded in the supply of arms to his supporters in Natal and that KwaZulu police atrocities in the region had been covered up.

At the end of March, KwaZulu civil servants in Ulundi staged a march protesting against suggestions that the administration be taken over by the South African authorities and supporting Buthelezi's demands for self-determination of the Zulu people and the institution of the monarchy.

Towards the end of March Buthelezi and State President de Klerk met in Durban in an effort to deal with the massive upsurge of violence in the province, IFP participation in the elections and matters pertaining to the king. Buthelezi opposed the sending of troops to Natal as he felt people would view this as an invasion. It was agreed that solutions needed to be found on the issues of the Zulu king and the Zulu nation's right to self-determination. A state of emergency was declared in Natal on 31 March.

On 8 April Buthelezi attended a leaders' summit at Skukuza in the Kruger National Park which was attended by De Klerk, Mandela and the Zulu king, Goodwill Zwelithini. He proposed a postponement of the coming election and amendments to the constitution to protect the Zulu monarchy and the IFP's KwaZulu/Natal constitution. He also called for the immediate lifting of the state of emergency in the province. However, the talks once again failed.

An attempt at international mediation took place in the second week of April, with the mediation team including Henry Kissinger of the USA, Lord Carrington of the United Kingdom and Professor Washington Okumu from Kenya. Okumu had met Buthelezi many years earlier at a prayer breakfast in the USA and they had developed a firm friendship. Okumu, at the request of various South African religious groups, had become active in behind-the-scenes attempts at mediation. When terms of reference could not be agreed to, Kissinger and various other mediators left South Africa, but Okumu remained and met with Buthelezi. Arising out of this mediation, Buthelezi accepted participation in the April election in return for constitutional recognition of the Zulu king.

The IFP, ANC and government agreed that the IFP would participate in the April elections; that the parties would do everything in their power to ensure a free and fair election; that they would recognise and protect the institution, status and role of the constitutional position of the king of the Zulus and the kingdom of KwaZulu; that outstanding issues in respect of the king and the 1993 constitution would be addressed through international mediation; that the South African government would place the necessary facilities at the disposal of the Independent Election Commission to facilitate the full participation of the IFP in the election; and that proper provision would be made for registration of the IFP, the IFP candidate list and marking by voters of ballot papers.

In the April 1994 elections the IFP won ten per cent of the national vote and in May Buthelezi was appointed Minister of Home Affairs in the government of national unity.

Following the elections, Buthelezi's relationship with the Zulu king began to deteriorate and it was alleged that the king was attempting to oust him from his position as 'traditional prime minister'. This came to a head in September 1994 when the king invited President Mandela to attend a Shaka Day rally in Stanger. Buthelezi claimed that the king had breached protocol by not consulting him on this matter. A meeting between the three men took place, after which Mandela announced that he would not attend the rally. Following this meeting the king's palace was damaged by young IFP supporters. The next day the king cancelled all Shaka Day rallies and announced a day of prayer instead. However, the IFP and the KwaZulu-Natal government insisted that the rallies take place as they had been planned months in advance and could not be cancelled by the king without consultation.

In the meantime the king built around him an interim royal committee consisting of people known not to support Buthelezi. One of these, Prince Sifiso Zulu, was given the brief of communicating to KwaZulu-Natal Premier, Dr Frank Mdlalose, the royal family's displeasure regarding the attack on the king's palace. On Sunday 24 September Zulu appeared on national television, and stated that Buthelezi had never been the king's 'traditional prime minister'. Buthelezi was present at the South African Broadcasting Corporation headquarters in Durban at the time, and he and his body guards burst into the studio and began to admonish Zulu. A gun was drawn, although there was some confusion as to whether the gun belonged to Zulu or to one of the body guards. Zulu fled the studios and Buthelezi then took the microphone and participated in the programme.

The incident led to a major political uproar and Buthelezi was criticised by all political parties except the IFP and the Conservative Party. On 29 September, at a cabinet meeting in Pretoria, he offered to resign his position. However, his unconditional apology to President

Mandela and the cabinet was accepted after the cabinet passed a motion of severe censure for his conduct which was viewed as inimical to good government and the protection of fundamental human rights.

In December the relationship between Buthelezi and Mandela again deteriorated after Mandela discovered that a meeting to be held between himself and KwaZulu-Natal *amakhosi* (chiefs) was to be headed by top IFP officials. Mandela allegedly accused Buthelezi of undermining the government of national unity and attempts at reconciliation.

The relationship between the king and Buthelezi continued to simmer and in January 1995 Buthelezi was unanimously elected chairman of the executive committee of KwaZulu-Natal's House of Traditional Leaders. The House had been established in 1994 but had been rejected by King Goodwill on the grounds that there had been no consultation with him as to its functions and that it undermined his status as king.

On 21 February 1995 Buthelezi led a walkout of all 48 IFP members of parliament on the grounds that the ANC and the National Party had reneged on promises of international mediation for all outstanding issues regarding the constitution, including the status of the Zulu king and the borders of KwaZulu-Natal. He indicated that they would continue to boycott parliament until they received a fresh mandate from IFP supporters at a special conference to be held on 5 March. However, IFP members of the cabinet, including Buthelezi, continued to function within their portfolios and Buthelezi announced a crackdown on the wave of illegal immigrants flooding into South Africa by the introduction of forgery-proof passports and amendments to the Aliens Control Act.

IFP members subsequently returned to parliament, but the party suspended its participation in the constitutional assembly. The ANC claimed that the terms of reference for mediation had not been clarified, but the IFP maintained that issues agreed for mediation were clear, and included the extent of provincial powers; fiscal and financial autonomy for provinces; preservation of provincial autonomy during future constitutional development; autonomy of constitution-making at provincial level; the role of the constitutional court in national and provincial constitutions; procedures for future constitutional amendments that could affect provincial autonomy; the process of empowering the new provincial governments and the transfer of functions and assets to them; citizenship and residential requirements for voting rights; and the restoration of the kingdom of Zululand.

When it appeared that the ANC was not prepared to follow the route of international mediation, Buthelezi called upon his supporters to 'rise and resist'. This was followed by an attack by President Mandela, who accused Buthelezi of fomenting violence and an uprising against central government. Mandela also threatened to cut off central government funds to the KwaZulu/Natal province if initiatives in that area continued to undermine the constitution.

Following a war of words, Buthelezi and Mandela met in an attempt to settle their differences. Despite their meeting's conciliatory tone, the issue associated with international mediation remained unresolved

While visiting Liberia as the guest of President Tolbert in 1975, Buthelezi was awarded the Knight Commander of the Star of Africa for outstanding leadership. In 1976 he was awarded an honorary Doctorate of Law from the University of Zululand and in 1983 he received the George Meaney Human Rights Award from the American Federation of Labour and Congress of Industrial Organisation, USA. Buthelezi has met many political leaders abroad, including US Presidents Richard Nixon, Jimmy Carter, Ronald Reagan and George Bush; British Prime Ministers Margaret Thatcher and John Major, French Prime Minister (now President) Jacques Chirac, Italian Prime Minister Giulio Andreotti; and West German Chancellor Helmut Kohl.

Buthelezi married Irene Audrey Thandekile Mzila, a nurse from Johannesburg, in 1952, and the couple have three sons and four daughters.

SOURCES

1. South African Institute of Race Relations, *Race Relations Survey, 1982*, Johannesburg, 1983/1984.
2. Ben Temkin, *Gatsha Buthelezi: Zulu Statesman*, Purnell, Cape Town, 1976.
3. Tom Lodge, *Black Politics in South Africa since 1945*, Ravan Press, Johannesburg, 1983.
4. Dee Shirley Dean, *Black South Africans: A Who's Who: 57 Profiles of Natal's Leading Blacks*, Oxford University Press, Cape Town, 1978.
5. *SA Foundation News*, November 1985, p3.
6. South African Institute of Race Relations, *Race Relations Surveys 1986, 1987/88 and 1988/89*, Johannesburg, 1987, 1988 and 1989.
7. *Daily News*, 20 July 1991.
8. *Natal Witness*, 1 August 1991.
9. *Natal Mercury*, 17 October 1991.
10. *Daily News*, 29 December 1991.
11. *Natal Witness*, 15 February 1992.
12. *Natal Mercury*, 28 September 1992.
13. *Natal Witness*, 28 September 1992.
14. *Negotiation News*, 17 December 1992.
15. SAPA in English 1236 GMT 6 September 1993, Johannesburg.
16. *Business Day*, 4 October 1993.
17. *Financial Mail*, 22 October 1993.
18. *New York Times*, 21 December 1993.
19. *Natal Mercury*, 18 February 1994.

20. *Sunday Tribune*, 6 March 1994.
21. *Sunday Times*, 20 March 1994.
22. *Sunday Tribune*, 27 March 1994.
23. *Sunday Times*, 27 March 1994.
24. *Saturday News*, 9 April 1994.
25. *Daily News*, 20 April 1994.
26. *Sunday Times*, 24 April 1994.
27. *Natal Witness*, 29 September 1994.
28. *Cape Times*, 23 December 1994.
29. *Cape Times*, 10 January 1995.
30. *Cape Times*, 22 February 1995.
31. *Weekend Argus*, 25 February 1995.
32. *Weekend Argus*, 29 April 1995.
33. *Cape Times*, 4 May 1995.

CHERYL CAROLUS

Deputy Secretary-General,
African National Congress,
1994.

Born on 27 May 1958 in Silvertown on the Cape Flats, Cheryl Carolus came from a working class background. Her father was a printer's assistant and her mother a nurses' aide. She became politicised as a high school student in the 1970s when she joined the South African Black Students' Association. Chosen as head prefect of her school, Carolus organised a petition to replace the prefect system with a democratically-elected Students' Representative Council. Following her matriculation she enrolled at the University of the Western Cape, registering for a BA degree and a teachers diploma. She became active in the Black

Consciousness South African Students' Organisation (Saso) and was detained for five months in 1976.

Carolus subsequently taught English and History at schools on the Cape Flats and during this period became involved in the 1981 school boycotts and participated in grassroots organisations.

Carolus returned to the University of the Western Cape in 1981 where she served on the Students' Representative Council. Between 1982 and 1983 she worked for the Churches Urban Planning Commmission.

In 1983 Carolus helped in the formation of the Western Cape region of the United Democratic Front (UDF), and following its launch in August served as its general secretary. Between 1983 and 1987 she served on the UDF national executive.

Carolus was a founder member of the United Women's Organisation (later the United Women's Congress) in the Western Cape and from 1987 served as general secretary of the Federation of South African Women (Fedsaw), both of which were affiliated to the UDF.

In January 1986 Carolus, at the invitation of the international centre for the Swedish labour movement, travelled to Sweden as part of a UDF delegation which included Murphy Morobe, Rev Arnold Stofile and Raymond Suttner. There the group met officials of Sweden's ruling Socialist Democratic Party, key labour figures and the Minister of Foreign Affairs and Development Aid. They also met ANC executive committee members Alfred Nzo, Thomas Nkobi and Thabo Mbeki.

When she returned to South Africa in January 1986 Carolus was detained under emergency regulations and held at John Vorster Square, Johannesburg, for three weeks. On her release she was served with a restriction order confining her to the Cape magisterial area of Wynberg. She was also prohibited from participating in UDF activities, associating herself with any publication, entering educational institutions and attending meetings where government policies were attacked or discussed.

During the 1989 general election Carolus became the Western Cape spokesperson for the defiance campaign organised by the Mass Democratic Movement.

Carolus was a member of a joint delegation of the UDF, the Congress of South African Trade Unions and the National Education Crisis Committee which attended the 1989 Organisation of African Unity meeting in Harare. This was the first time South Africans from inside the country had formally attended an OAU meeting. The delegation lent its support to a document, tabled by the ANC, setting out agreed preconditions for negotiations in South Africa.

Carolus was again detained on 5 November 1989 in terms of emergency regulations and held at Ravensmead police station, Cape Town, until her release on 16 November.

Following the unbanning of the ANC and the release of Nelson Mandela in February 1990, Carolus formed part of the ANC team which met South African government representatives at Groote Schuur in Cape Town in May.

When the South African Communist Party was relaunched as a legal party on 29 July 1990, Carolus was named as a member of its interim leadership group.

At the ANC's July 1991 conference held in Durban, Carolus was elected to its national executive committee. She also served on the movement's working committee, occupying a full-time position based in Johannesburg and held the portfolios of health, human resources development, education and arts and culture. In order to take up this position she resigned from her job as a staff development officer at the Education, Resource and Information Project at the University of the Western Cape.

Carolus declined nomination as an ANC representative to parliament, and accepted appointment as head of the ANC's Reconstruction and Development department. At the organisation's December 1994 conference, she was elected to the post of deputy secretary-general. Carolus is married to Graeme Bloch.

SOURCES

1. *Sowetan*, 24 January 1986.
2. *Argus*, 24 January 1986.
3. *Star*, 13 February 1986.
4. *Leadership*, Volume 8, October 1989.
5. *Cape Times*, 15 November 1989.
6. *Vrye Weekblad*, 17 November 1989.
7. *Weekly Mail*, 30 July 1990.
8. *Sunday Tribune*, 15 April 1990.
9. *Tribute*, August 1990.
10. *A-Z of South African Politics*, *Weekly Mail & Guardian*/Penguin Books, Johannesburg, 1994.
11. *Sunday Times*, 8 January 1995.

WILLIAM JOHN COBBETT

Director-General,
Ministry of Housing,
1994.

Born in Johannesburg on 27 December 1957, William Cobbett was the third of the seven children of Angela Margaret and David John Cobbett, a merchant banker and stockbroker.

From 1963 Cobbett attended Parktown Convent Primary School before spending six years at St David's Marist Brothers. He then attended Parktown Boys' High School for two years, matriculating in December 1976 from Woodmead School.

At the time, military service was compulsory for all school leavers. To avoid this call-up, Cobbett left South Africa for the United Kingdom in April 1977.

Cobbett's political views were largely shaped by his mother's connections with the Black Sash and the Christian Institute, both anti-apartheid organisations. In the early 1970s he came into contact with journalists as well as some of the major figures representing the opposition in the country. Cosmos Desmond, a priest active in anti-apartheid politics, banned and house arrested at the time, had a particular influence on the young Cobbett. In addition, when Cobbett's mother was arrested and jailed for being in Soweto without a permit, this left a deep impression on him. Cobbett was also aware of political developments such as the Durban strikes of 1973, the coup in Portugal and its impact on the region in 1974 and the student riots of 1976.

In London Cobbett worked as a shop assistant, eventually becoming a buyer until the store closed in 1983. While working at the store, Cobbett met Mary, a fellow employee, and they married in 1983. In 1981, Cobbett started studying for a degree in modern European history and

English literature and completed his BA Honours in 198₃ at the Middlesex Polytechnic in London.

Cobbett's renewed interest in South Africa led him to register for a higher degree, originally in labour studies, but later for a PhD based on a study of a specific area in South Africa, namely Botshabelo in the Orange Free State.

Cobbett returned to South Africa in 1984 and tutored in the Department of Sociology at the University of the Witwatersrand from 1985-86 while preparing his field workers. However, following the second state of emergency in 1986 his field workers were either detained or had left South Africa and he was unable to continue with his research.

Cobbett again left South Africa in August 1986 and rejoined his wife in Coventry, United Kingdom. He spent two years at the University of Warwick doing research. He joined the editorial board of the *Review of African Political Economy* and in 1988, in collaboration with Robin Cohen, wrote the book *Popular Struggles in South Africa*. During this time he also became active in the Anti-apartheid Movement.

Cobbett returned to South Africa in August 1988 and became the co-ordinator of Planact, a non-governmental organisation providing advice on developmental issues to community organisations. He remained with Planact for four years and during this time provided back-up to the Soweto People's Delegation regarding the Soweto negotiations on rent and service boycotts. Cobbett became increasingly involved in local-level negotiations. By acting as advisor to community organisations and non-statutory bodies he gained substantial expertise in the fields of electricity, housing and development.

Following the unbanning of the African National Congress (ANC) in February 1990 Cobbett joined the organisation. However, he had had a certain amount of contact with the ANC during the 1980s concerning local government issues, mainly in Harare and Lusaka.

In 1992 Cobbett was asked by the ANC to serve as its representative on the National Housing Forum and he later served on the Electricity Forum. He also became involved in hostel negotiations on the Record of Understanding reached in September 1992 and the constitutional negotiations where he assisted with in drfating the section dealing with local government.

In December 1993 Cobbett was appointed ANC representative on the Transitional Executive Council and co-chaired the sub-council on local and regional government and traditional authorities. On 16 May 1994, following the general election, he was appointed special adviser to Minister of Housing, Joe Slovo, and became director-general of the department on 4 August 1994.

Cobbett is married to Mary Louise (born Clilverd) and they have three children.

SOURCE

Interviewed 9 November 1994, Cape Town.

HENDRICK JACOBUS COETSEE

Member of Parliament,
National Party,
Bloemfontein West, 1994.
Chairman, National Party of the
Orange Free State, 1979-85.
Deputy Minister of Defence and
National Security, 1978-80.
Minister of Justice, 1980-94.
Leader, National Party of the
Orange Free State, 1985.
President of the Senate, 1994.

'Kobie' Coetsee was born in Ladybrand, Orange Free State, on 19 April 1931, the only child of Josephine (born Van Zyl) and Jan Johannes Coetsee, a printer. He attended local schools, matriculating at Ladybrand School in 1948 where he had been a prefect and Dux scholar.

Coetsee then attended the University of the Orange Free State, completing his BA and LLB in 1954, with Latin as a major. During this time he served on the students' council for extra-mural studies and was chairman of the youth branch of the National Party (NP). He subsequently lectured Law part-time while qualifying as an attorney, eventually practising at the Side Bar for 17 years. In 1972 he was admitted to the Bar as an advocate in Bloemfontein.

Between 1962-68 Coetsee, who had not been balloted to do military service, volunteered to join the President Steyn Regiment where he served in the armoured car section.

Coetsee came from a politicised home where his parents were active in local NP politics. However, it was his grandfather, who had been NP chairman in Ladybrand at the time CR Swart had been the town's MP, who taught Coetsee his politics. With two grandfathers who had fought in the Anglo-Boer War, Afrikaner liberty was a key sentiment in Coetsee's environment.

In 1968 Coetsee was elected MP for the Bloemfontein West constituency. He served on the head committee of the NP in the Orange Free State and was its chairman from 1979-85. Coetsee took over the leadership of the party in the Orange Free State on 22 June 1985 at a time when debate was raging over the repeal of the measures preventing Asians from entering and living in the Orange Free State. The repeal was eventually effected as a result of the request by an overwhelming majority of delegates at the September 1985 NP congress in the Orange Free State.

As an MP, Coetsee served on various parliamentary committees and commissions, including the Schlebusch Commission of Inquiry into Certain Organisations (1974-76), the Commission for Co-operation and Development (1976-78) and the Select Committee on the Constitution (1983). He was elected chairman of the Defence Group of the NP caucus in 1978 and, in this position, took the Civil Defence Act through parliament.

Upon his appointment as Deputy Minister of Defence and National Security on 12 October 1978, Coetsee restructured the National Intelligence Service following the Information Scandal. In addition, he tailored national service requirements to protect people from suffering monetary loss while doing their service, and to prevent unnecessary travelling.

As the department fell within the responsibility of then-Prime Minister PW Botha, Coetsee, as Deputy Minister, was, to a large extent, entrusted with the administration of the two departments.

Coetsee was appointed Minister of Justice on 7 October 1980. In this capacity, he instituted changes in the legal system, including the introduction of the small claims courts, a new concept of administering and dispensing justice at a local level. In addition, he piloted the Matrimonial Property Act through parliament in 1984, a measure which had major repercussions on the status of married women and introduced the accrual system of property sharing between spouses. Coetsee was instrumental in making community service a viable alternative sentence to imprisonment and did away with the racially-specific commissioners' courts.

Until 1992 Coetsee's portfolio also covered prisons and, in this capacity, he developed a new managerial style of running the prisons which provided for maximum delegation balanced by a system of report-back and monitoring.

Coetsee made increasing use of the Law Commission to promote legal reform. In April 1986 he requested the commission to investigate a larger role for the courts in protecting group and individual rights. The commission was later asked to draw up a report on group and human rights.

In 1987 the case of the Sharpeville Six became prominent when six people were sentenced to death for their part in the murder of the deputy mayor and town councillor of Lekoa on 3 September 1984. The six were granted various stays of execution: their fourth reprieve, granted on 12 July 1988 by Coetsee, deferred their execution indefinitely. Coetsee said he made this move to enable lawyers for the condemned to exhaust all legal avenues open to them to protect their clients from the death penalty. The death sentence passed was eventually converted to life imprisonment.

In August 1987 State President Botha stated that he had asked Coetsee to investigate the possible release of Govan Mbeki, Rivonia trialist, who had received a life sentence. Mbeki was released later in the year and in 1989 Coetsee was again involved in procedures to release others serving life sentences for political offences, most of the other Rivonia trialists. He held discussions with Nelson Mandela prior to their eventual release in October 1989.

Following the unbanning of the ANC and the release of Nelson Mandela in February 1990, Coetsee formed part of the South African government delegation which held talks with the ANC in May at Groote Schuur, Cape Town. Prior to the talks, Coetsee piloted the Indemnity Act through parliament, granting temporary immunity to those who might serve in negotiation delegations. This Act also contained a provision for conditional and unconditional permanent indemnity.

In July 1991 Coetsee amended the Internal Security Act by repealing sections dealing with, inter alia, the prohibition of publications promoting the aims of communism or banned organisations; restrictions on the registration of newspapers; restrictions on the movements of people on a consolidated list; and the maintaining of the consolidated list of names of people belonging to unlawful organisations. In addition, amendments were made to Section 29 of the Act by providing for a definite period of initial detention without trial (not more than ten days) after which periods of detention would be determined by a judge. (Previously this section permitted indefinite detention without trial.) Section 50(A) which allowed for 180 days' detention was also repealed.

Coetsee became a key figure in the South African government's negotiation team and attended the meetings of the Convention for a Democratic South Africa (Codesa) in December 1991 and May 1992. He served on Codesa working group 1 which dealt with the creation of a climate for free political participation and the role of the international community.

From 20 January 1992 to 31 March 1993, Coetsee's portfolio was extended to include the National Intelligence Service. From 1 April 1993 until the April 1994 general elections Coetsee served as Minister of Justice and of Defence. Following the first democratic elections in April 1994, Coetsee was elected president of the senate.

On 6 October 1956 Coetsee married Helena Elizabeth Malan and they have three daughters and two sons.

SOURCES

1. *Curriculum vitae* submitted by the Department of Information 1984.
2. *Nuntius*, 1983.
3. Interviewed 2 June 1986, Cape Town.
4. *Weekly Mail*, 13 October 1989.
5. South African Institute of Race Relations, *Race Relations Survey, 1987/88*, Johannesburg 1988.
6. *New Nation*, 17 April 1990.
7. South African Institute of Race Relations, *Race Relations Survey, 1991/92*, Johannesburg 1992.
8. *Profile '94*, South African Communication Services, Pretoria, 1994

FREDERIK WILLEM DE KLERK

Member of Parliament,
National Party,
Vereeniging, 1972-94.
State President, 1989-94.
Member of Parliament,
National Party, 1994.
Deputy State President,
1994.

FW de Klerk was born on 18 March 1936 in Johannesburg, one of the two sons of Jan and Corrie (born Coetzer) de Klerk. He came from a political family: his great-grandfather was a senator, his grandfather stood twice for parliament (both times unsuccessfully) and his aunt was married to Prime Minister JG Strydom.

De Klerk's father, Jan de Klerk, served as secretary of the Herenigde Nasionale Party in 1947, and then became Transvaal general secretary of the National Party in the Transvaal from 1948-54. He was elected a member of the provincial council in 1949 and simultaneously became member of the executive committee responsible for education. He was appointed to the senate in January 1955 and held the cabinet portfolio of Minister of Labour and Public Works. He subsequently held other portfolios, and on 12 August 1968 was elected president of the senate, a post he held until his retirement in January 1976.

When De Klerk was born, his father was a school principal. The family lived in Johannesburg, subsequently moving to Germiston. De Klerk matriculated at the Hoërskool Monument in Krugersdorp.

He received an early training in politics through membership of the *Jeugbond*, the youth section of the National Party.

De Klerk studied further at the Potchefstroom University for Christian Higher Education and graduated BA LLB *(cum laude)* in 1958. He won the Abe Bailey Travel Scholarship in the same year and travelled to the United Kingdom.

While at university he played a leading role in student affairs and was an executive member of the Afrikaanse Studentebond, vice-chairman of the Students' Representative Council and editor of the campus newspaper.

It was at university that he met his wife-to-be, Marike Willemse, whom he married on 11 April 1969 in Pretoria. She is the daughter of the late Professor WA Willemse and Susan Steyn (formerly Willemse, born Heyns).

De Klerk served his legal articles in Klerksdorp and Pretoria and thereafter practised as an attorney in Vereeniging from 1961-72. During this time he continued to play an active role in the National Party at constituency level and became chairman of the local divisional council.

During this period he became chairman of the Law Society (Vaal Triangle) and served on the Council of the Vaal Triangle College for Advanced Technical Education. In addition, he became chairman of the *Federasie van Junior Rapportryers*.

In 1972 De Klerk was appointed to the Chair of Administrative Law at Potchefstroom University, effective from January 1973. However, in 1972 the sitting member of parliament for Vereeniging, Blaar Coetzee, was appointed South African ambassador to Rome and De Klerk was elected to succeed him as MP for the constituency in November of that year.

In the 1974 general election De Klerk was returned to parliament unopposed and in 1975 he became information officer of the Transvaal National Party. On 3 April 1978 he was appointed to the cabinet as Minister of Posts and Telecomunications. Subsequently he held the portfolios of Social Welfare and Pensions, Sport and Recreation, Mining and Environmental Planning and Energy and Internal Affairs. For a period he also held the Civil Service portfolio under delegation by the prime minister. Following the 1982 split in the National Party and the resignation of Andries Treurnicht, De Klerk became Transvaal leader of the NP on 6 March of that year.

In September 1984 he was appointed Minister of Home Affairs and National Education. With the introduction of the tricameral parliament he was appointed chairman of the Ministers' Council in the House of Assembly and Minister of the Budget on 1 July 1985. These posts were held concurrently with the general affairs portfolio of National Education.

On 1 December 1986 De Klerk became leader of the House of Assembly and in the 1987 general election again won his Vereeniging seat. As Minister of Education, he reponded to student protest on university campuses by announcing that the state would cut university subsidies unless the universities themselves maintained order and policed their students.

In the subsequent confrontation between the universities and the state, a court ruled that the conditions attached to university subsidies were out of order, and De Klerk was forced to withdraw them.

On 18 January 1989 State President PW Botha suffered a stroke; on 2 February he resigned as leader of the National Party, but retained the position of state president. De Klerk was elected NP leader at a caucus meeting, his nearest rival being Barend du Plessis who lost by nine votes.

Tension built up between Botha and De Klerk and a public rift over whether the Minister of Foreign Affairs had advised Botha of De Klerk's trip to meet the president of Zambia occurred. This eventually led to a caucus meeting on 14 August, in the middle of the general election campaign, at which PW Botha was asked to resign. That night Botha appeared on television and, in a bitter statement, announced his resignation. De Klerk became acting state president the next day.

Following the 6 September general election which left the NP with a slashed majority in the House of Assembly, De Klerk was elected state president. His actions showed marked differences from those of his predecessor, and he permitted the holding of peaceful, mass marches by extra-parliamentary groupings. In October 1989 he released eight long-term political prisoners, including Walter Sisulu, former secretary general of the African National Congress (ANC) and senior figure in its armed wing, Umkhonto we Sizwe. De Klerk soon declared his intention to initiate negotiations with all groupings in South Africa at a 'great Indaba'.

At the opening of parliament on 2 February 1990, De Klerk announced the unbanning of the ANC, the Pan-Africanist Congress, the South African Communist Party and a range of other banned or restricted organisations. Later that month, Nelson Mandela was released from prison.

Talks between an ANC delegation headed by Mandela and a government delegation led by De Klerk were held at Groote Schuur in Cape Town in May 1990. Later that month, De Klerk travelled abroad, visiting nine European countries including France, West Germany, Switzerland, Great Britain, Spain and Italy, where he held official talks with heads of state. He has subsequently travelled abroad frequently, including visits to Japan and Russia.

During the 1991 session of parliament most apartheid statutes were rescinded including the Population Registration Act whereby South Africans were classified by race at birth. Public facilities were desegregated and the Land Acts of 1913 and 1936 as well as the Group Areas Act were repealed thereby allowing black South Africans to buy land anywhere in the country. The security branch of the South African police was incorporated into the detective branch. Some of the most oppressive elements of the Internal Security Act were repealed, and the Universities Amendment Act returned the right to universities to admit whom they chose, regardless of race.

In May 1991 the ANC issued an ultimatum to De Klerk, demanding that unless he dealt with violence in the country, they would withdraw from negotiations. In an attempt to respond to the ANC's demands certain measures to stem the violence were taken including a ban on the carrying of dangerous weapons in public. However, De Klerk refused to comply with the ANC's demand the he fire the Ministers of Law and Order and Defence. The ANC declined to attend a peace summit initiated by De Klerk later in May.

In July 1991 De Klerk had to face a storm over his security forces' clandestine funding of Inkatha rallies. While he appeared to weather this storm, distancing himself from the issue, he was forced to demote his Ministers of Law and Order and Defence to minor cabinet posts.

After further talks between the ANC and De Klerk's government on the transitional process, the 'Pretoria Minute' made provision for the granting of indemnity to exiles and those involved in underground activity.

In September 1991 De Klerk joined the leaders of a range of other political organisations in signing a peace accord aimed at defusing the widespread political violence wracking the country. De Klerk served on the national peace committee, one of the structures established by the Peace Accord.

De Klerk led his government's delegation to the first meeting of the Convention for a Democratic South Africa (Codesa) where 17 of the 19 delegations present endorsed a declaration of intent. At the plenary session, De Klerk indicated that the ANC's failure to abandon the armed struggle was a major obstacle to negotiating progress. Mandela responded with a scathing attack on De Klerk and the manner in which he had behaved.

In his opening speech at the 1992 parliamentary session, De Klerk attempted to woo the right wing into the negotiation process by indicating that the concept of self-determination should be brought to the negotiating table.

In February 1992 De Klerk and Mandela were jointly awarded Unesco's Houphouet-Boigny Peace Prize at a ceremony in Paris.

In March 1992 De Klerk called a snap whites-only referendum in an attempt to gain a mandate for constitutional reform. Following a campaign which placed considerable emphasis on his own leadership, he achieved a landslide victory.

The second plenary session of Codesa began in May 1992, but broke down when there was deadlock on the issue of constitution-making. De Klerk and Mandela made public efforts to retrieve the initiative, but this failed and the ANC prepared for a rolling mass action campaign which began on 16 June (Soweto Day). The campaign aimed to force the government to agree to certain demands, including a transitional government and one-person one-vote elections for a constituent assembly. De Klerk subsequently criticised the campaign, arguing that it would result in violence, inflammatory rhetoric and false accusations against political leaders.

On 17 June 1992, KwaMadala hostel dwellers rampaged through Boipatong, killing 39 people. De Klerk subsequently attempted to visit the area, but was forced to withdraw when faced with threatening demonstrators. The ANC's position hardened as a result of the Boipatong massacre, and it rejected De Klerk's overtures for urgent talks. The ANC argued that the collapse of the negotiation process was the result of the violence which involved security forces and their surrogates.

After the mass action campaign, which included a march on Pretoria's Union Buildings, De Klerk reaffirmed his commitment to a process of negotiation.

In September 1992, following bi-lateral negotiations, a Record of Understanding between the National Party and the ANC was signed by De Klerk and Mandela. This made provision for an elected constitution-making body to draft and adopt a new constitution. It was further agreed that this body would act as an interim government of national unity in terms of an interim constitution which would provide for regional government during the interim period as well as for a bill of rights. The two delegations also agreed that in cases where the release of political prisoners could contribute to reconciliation, this would be done. As a result of these talks, the ANC agreed to return to multi-lateral constitutional negotiations. Talks subsequently began at the World Trade Centre in 1993.

On 26 November 1993 De Klerk signed a proclamation establishing the Transitional Executive Council which held its first meeting on 8 December. The body was established to level the playing fields in the run-up to the April 1994 elections.

From January to April 1994 De Klerk spent a great deal of his time electioneering across the country, the NP campaign strongly emphasising his personal image. Highly popular in the Western Cape, De Klerk was, however, unable to campaign in areas such as Kimberley and Bloemfontein as ANC supporters blocked access roads and broke up meetings.

The election took place on 26-28 April 1994 and on 3 May De Klerk conceded defeat to the ANC, the NP drawing the second largest number of votes. In his concession speech De Klerk pointed out that his vision had been realised in that South Africa now had a new dynamic constitution; there was assurance that no single group of South Africans could dominate any other; there was an end to discrimination and inequality before the law; minority rights had been secured and individual rights and other rights were guaranteed by a charter of fundamental rights and by a strong and effective constitutional court.

On 10 May 1994 De Klerk was sworn in as second deputy president. At the inauguration Mandela referred to him as 'one of the greatest sons of Africa'. In a subsequent debate on the president's opening speech in parliament, De Klerk stated that Mandela could rely on the NP's co-operation to secure reconciliation, peace, justice and a better life for all South Africans.

During 1994 it became clear that the National Party was having difficulty in defining its role in the context of a government of national unity, with the party's profile of critical ally creating confusion as to its function. Questions also arose in the media as to De Klerk's role as he seemed to be taking a back seat to Mandela and First Deputy President, Thabo Mbeki. These matters were raised at the NP congresses and within its caucus.

In January 1995 a crisis within the government of national unity was sparked when the relationship between De Klerk and President Mandela nearly collapsed over a row concerning a secret attempt by two former cabinet ministers and 3 500 police to obtain indemnity shortly before the April 1994 elections. Mandela believed that De Klerk had known of the attempt to by-pass the agreement that indemnities for security force personnel would only be granted by the new democratic government. Mandela accused De Klerk of speaking in a manner in which 'white men used to speak to blacks' and questioned his commitment to the government's reconstruction and development programme. He stated that should De Klerk resign from the government of national unity, this would 'not cause even a ripple'.

De Klerk and his ministers then faced the decision as to whether to resign from the government of national unity or to suspend their operations until Mandela apologised. Following meetings between NP ministers, Mandela and other ANC ministers at which Mandela indicated that they could make a 'fresh start', De Klerk stated at the NP conference that he would meet with Mandela on condition that the attack on his integrity be addressed. In addition he wanted the issue of indemnities to be resolved and a new set of conventions for the working of government outlined. Following the meeting a diplomatically-worded statement was released which addressed De Klerk's demands without compromising the dignity of either side. The two leaders accepted each other's integrity and good faith and jointly stated that the two parties had agreed to develop conventions in a government of national unity concerning the rights of all parties.

As deputy president, De Klerk has travelled abroad extensively to give feedback to political and business leaders. He delivered his Nobel Laureate peace lecture in Britain, after he and Mandela were jointly awarded the 1993 Nobel Peace Prize.

The De Klerks have two sons, Jan and Willem, and a daughter, Susan.

SOURCES

1. *Curriculum vitae* submitted by Department ofInformation.
2. *Fair Lady*, 30 June 1982.
3. Questionnaire returned by The Hon FW de Klerk.
4. *Daily News*, 5 June 1985.
5. *Weekly Mail*, 21 September 1988.
6. *The Star*, 21 September 1989.
7. *Daily News*, 23 September 1989.
8. *Daily News*, 18 June 1991.
9. *Daily News*, 21 June 1991.
10. *Natal Mercury*, 4 February 1992.
11. *Sunday Tribune*, 1 March 1992.
12. *Natal Witness*, 25 June 1992.
13. *Natal Mercury*, 6 August 1992.
14. South African Institute of Race Relations, *Race Relations Surveys 1992/93 and 1993/94*, Johannesburg, 1993 and 1994.
15. *Sunday Tribune*, 13 February 1994.
16. *Natal Mercury*, 24 February 1994.
17. *Daily News*, 3 May 1994.
18. *Natal Witness*, 26 May 1994.
19. *The Argus*, 19 January 1995.
20. *Sunday Times*, 22 January 1995.
21. *Cape Times*, 17 February 1995.

JOHANNES HENDRIK (JOHNNY) DE LANGE

Member of Parliament,
African National Congress,
1994.

Born on 8 January 1958, Johnny de Lange was one of the four children of Johanna Wilhelmina and Jan Simon de Lange, an electrician. His early years were spent in Eshowe, Natal, where he attended the local primary school, but he later went to live with his mother and step-father in Durban where he matriculated from the Hoërskool Port Natal in 1975.

Apart from the prejudices prevalent in white working class families, De Lange's parents were largely apolitical. He, however, had an inquiring mind and from a young age questioned authority as personified by the school and the Dutch Reformed Church. He also found the antagonism of the predominantly English-speaking group towards the Afrikaners in Durban unpleasant and confusing, especially as he spoke both languages at home.

Being a keen rugby player, De Lange chose to further his studies at the University of Stellenbosch. His choice was also influenced by the excellent reputation of the university's Law faculty. However, he was not happy there. Coming from a poor background, he felt alienated from his fellow students and stifled by the authoritarian attitudes of staff members. Even rugby at university level was a disappointment to him.

The 1976 uprising and the ensuing riots made De Lange feel uncomfortable. He knew that something was wrong in the country, but did not have a sufficiently clear understanding of politics on which to base his concerns. The student upheaval was also largely ignored on the Stellenbosch campus.

After obtaining his BA Law degree at the end of 1978, De Lange's financial position compelled him to enter the army instead of completing his LLB. In mid-1979 De Lange began his national service in the infantry, completing an officer's course as lieutenant. During his training as an officer, his platoon was deployed in Angola for three months. Although the platoon was at no time involved in combat, De Lange was sickened by the burning of villages and crops in an attempt to create a no-man's-land where the South West Africa People's Organisation (Swapo) could not obtain food.

One incident left an indelible impression on De Lange: an old man and his family were returning to Namibia from Angola with hundreds of cattle. Despite the old man's begging and pleading, the captain in charge ordered that all the cattle be shot. The reason given was the prevention of the spread of cattle disease to Namibia.

De Lange was sent to the Angolan/Namibian border for the last year of his training and was stationed in Kaokoland, in charge of a platoon of local Ovahimbas. He was shocked by the way the local Ovahimba population was lured by high salaries to join the army in the fight against Swapo. This not only caused resentment among South African troops, but also disrupted the social structure of the Ovahimba society. Some areas of Kaokoland became depopulated when young people opted to join the army, leaving the remaining inhabitants without the resources to fend for themselves at the end of the war.

De Lange completed his national service in 1981. He once again obtained a state bursary and, using the money he had saved in the army, managed to continue his LLB studies, this time at the University of Cape Town.

Here his unhappiness and unease with society were crystallised. Via open political discussions and the activities of the National Union of South African Students (Nusas), he was exposed to a view of society which opened his eyes. He further broadened his understanding by reading as much as possible about history, society and apartheid. He considers this period in his life as an intense learning experience.

However, De Lange did not have sufficient confidence to join Nusas structures. This was partly because he felt that he was still grappling with concepts with which the student leaders had grown up, and partly because of feeling self-conscious of his working class background and his sense that others were suspicious of his Afrikaner and army background.

After completing his LLB degree in 1983, De Lange was obliged in terms of his bursary to work for the government, but he was adamant that he would not implement apartheid laws by working as a public prosecutor. In the six-month periods before and after his national service, he chose the least controversial option by agreeing to work in the Master's Office. A year later, he left the civil service.

While completing his pupilage with an advocate at the Bar, he gained valuable experience in civil law, which served as a background to his intended civil and humanitarian practice. De Lange was admitted as an advocate in January 1985.

His own practice focused on cases involving public violence and other prosecutions generated by resistance to apartheid, in particular the state of emergency. This included the year-long terrorism trial of Ashley Forbes and fourteen others; the trial of Tony Yengeni, Jenny Schreiner and others; and proceedings which resulted in the first Western Cape case of a detainee being released by court order.

In 1983, after the formation of the United Democratic Front (UDF), De Lange was invited to a meeting of the Democratic Lawyers Organisation (DLO), a UDF affiliate. At the meeting De Lange met Dullah Omar – now Minister of Justice – a prominent advocate and political activist, who was to become his mentor. Through the DLO De Lange became involved with the formation of the National Association of Democratic Lawyers (Nadel) in 1987 and he served on its Western Cape Executive Committee. His work brought him into contact with rural communities and his organisational involvement in Nadel gave him first-hand, practical experience of the theories about which he had been reading.

The Children's Conference in Harare at the end of 1987 made a profound impression on him. It was there that he learned of the evidence of torture of children in South Africa. He also met senior officials of the African National Congress (ANC), including Oliver Tambo and Thabo Mbeki. This contributed to his personal growth and commitment to the ideals of the ANC. This relationship with the ANC deepened when he attended the November 1987 ANC Consultative Conference in Arusha, Tanzania, under a veil of secrecy.

During 1988 De Lange was elected assistant general secretary of Nadel and in this way became closely involved with organisations and individuals opposed to apartheid, falling under the umbrella of the Mass Democratic Movement (MDM). Thereafter he was re-elected to the Nadel national executive committee several times, until his work with the ANC became too demanding after 1992.

Towards the end of 1987 De Lange also became involved on an executive level with the Cape Democrats, a UDF affiliate concentrated in the white areas. In December 1988 he was elected treasurer of the UDF Western Cape Region (the last person to hold this position) until the organisation was disbanded after the unbanning of the ANC.

Through Nadel and the UDF, De Lange became involved with the Western Cape Defiance Campaign. He was arrested once when he tried to intervene when police fired tear gas at a crowd gathered at Groote Schuur Hospital in honour of Oscar Mpetha. During a march which became known as the 'Purple Rain March' he was severely assaulted by police. Both cases were settled out of court in his favour.

After the ANC was unbanned in 1990, De Lange was elected and later re-elected to its Western Cape regional executive committee. As head of the regional negotiations desk, he became part of the ANC negotiating team at the World Trade Centre, which he describes as a highlight of his political career.

De Lange closed his legal practice in April 1993 to become the first director of the Legal Education Research Training Project of Nadel. After his election to the top position on the ANC's regional candidates' list for the national assembly, he resigned in March 1994 to devote himself to the ANC's Western Cape election campaign. In the April 1994 general election he was elected a member of the National Assembly.

In parliament De Lange chairs the Select Committee on Justice. In this respect he has played a key role in changing the ethos and role of the parliamentary committee system, establishing a more open and inclusive process of consultation both within parliament and with the public in general. De Lange also serves on the Parliamentary Rules Committee and was primarily responsible for drafting new rules on law-making that gave the select committees real power for the first time. He is also a member of its sub-committee dealing with proposed amendments to the rules as well as the Select Committee on Constitutional Affairs. In addition, De Lange chairs the ANC's parliamentary study group on justice and the ANC Caucus Rules Committee.

De Lange is also active in the Constituent Assembly and serves on its Rules Committee, its Judiciary and Legal Systems Theme Committee and its Constitutional Committee.

De Lange married Pamela Claire Haddad in 1990. They live in Cape Town.

SOURCES

1. *People in Politics, Second Quarter 1994*, Institute for Democracy in South Africa (Idasa), Durban, 1994.
2. *Negotiation News*, 15 October 1994.
3. *Weekly Mail & Guardian*, 26 August 1994.

DAWID JACOBUS DE VILLIERS

*Member of Parliament,
National Party, Piketberg,
1982-94.
Member of Parliament,
National Party, 1994.
Minister of Economic
Co-ordination and Public
Enterprises, 1991-94.
Minister of Public Enterprises,
1992-94.
Minister of Environment Affairs,
1994.*

Born in Burgersdorp on 10 July 1940, Dawie de Villiers was one of the three children of Elsa and Coenie de Villiers, a railway clerk who later became a National Party (NP) organiser and member of parliament for Vasco from 1953-61.

The family moved to Caledon where De Villiers began school, but after his first year they moved again to Bellville where he completed his junior and senior schooling, matriculating from Bellville High School in 1959.

De Villiers attended the University of Stellenbosch where he completed his BA (Hons) in Philosophy (1963) and his B Theology (1966). During this time he served on the house committee of the Dagbreek Residence and was chairman of the Students' Representative Council in 1962-63. He was involved in heated debates at the university and was regarded as being out of line with traditional NP politics. When a notice was sent out warning students against extreme leftists who posed as Afrikaner nationalists, De Villiers' name was among those cited. An article subsequently appeared in *Die Burger* newspaper mentioning him as the son of an MP who held views contrary to the NP establishment. De Villiers was active in the university debating and philosophy societies. He excelled at rugby and involved himself at all levels of the sport, including administration. He also served on the NP committee at the university. De Villiers also captained the Springbok Rugby team in the 1960s.

From 1963-64, De Villiers held a temporary lectureship in Philosophy at the University of the Western Cape. He was awarded the Abe Bailey scholarship in 1963 and the Markotter scholarship in 1964.

On completion of his theology degree, De Villiers became minister at the Dutch Reformed Church at Wellington from 1967-69. His duties were largely associated with youth work and he ministered to students at the Wellington Teachers' Training College and at the Huguenot College. He then took up a lecturing post in Philosophy at the Rand Afrikaans University (RAU) and completed his MA in philosophy in 1972.

Although De Villiers had grown up in a political household, he had not harboured political ambitions as he had seen the negative effects of public life. In 1972 he had received a scholarship to continue his studies in Europe. En route back to South Africa, he received a telephone call at Heathrow Airport, London, asking him to consider standing for the NP in a Johannesburg West by-election.

On his return, De Villiers sought advice from his father who supported his wish to further his studies. However, it was Gerrit Viljoen, then rector at RAU, who encouraged him to take a political role. As a result, De Villiers became MP for Johannesburg West and subsequently kept his seat during the 1974 and 1977 general elections. During this period he served as president of the RAU convocation and as chairman of the NP's Foreign Affairs committee in parliament. In 1979 he was awarded his DPhil from the University of Stellenbosch.

In April 1979 De Villiers was appointed South African ambassador to London, a post he held until October 1980. He arrived in the United Kingdom prior to the British Conservative Party victory and met many of its prominent leaders before they became ministers. The change in government offered the South African ambassador a new situation resulting in improved relations between the two countries. During his term of office the Lancaster House discussions on Zimbabwe took place and, although not party to the talks, De Villiers was involved in consultations and informal discussions with many of the participants.

In October 1980 De Villiers returned to South Africa to take up the post of Minister of Industries, Commerce and Tourism (now designated Minister of Trade and Industry). In the April 1981 general election he stood as the NP candidate in the Gardens constituency, Cape Town, but lost the seat to Ken Andrew of the Progressive Federal Party. He subsequently became MP for Piketberg, Cape.

As Minister of Trade and Industry, De Villiers announced government plans to permit hotels and restaurants to open their premises to all races. In 1986 this was extended by changes to the Liquor Act resulting in the desegregation of South Africa's bars. In the field of tourism the South African Tourist Board was established to include the Department of Tourism, the South African Tourist Corporation and the Hotel Board. This was seen as an example of co-operation between the public and private sectors. Other aspects covered by De Villiers' department included the establishment of a strategy for the electronics industry – still in its infancy in South Africa – and the removal of numerous control measures, restrictions and other obstacles in the way of a freer market. In September 1983 De Villiers announced an investigation into monopolies by the competition board, the recommendations of which were adopted and gazetted in May 1986, including a ban on price collusion. In May 1984 he initiated new incentives for small businesses in decentralised areas with the policy of promoting small business continuing to receive high priority.

Following the September 1989 general election, De Villiers became Minister of Mineral and Energy Affairs and Public Enterprises. This portfolio included matters pertaining to the privatisation of many state functions, including the post office. He also became leader of the House of Assembly. In April 1991, he was appointed Minister of Economic Co-ordination and Public Enterprises. Later that year, responsibility for posts and telecommunications was removed from his portfolio.

In July 1989 De Villiers was elected leader of the NP in the Cape. This led to contact with members of the house of representatives who wished to join the NP in 1991 and 1992.

In September 1990 De Villiers travelled for economic discussions in Angola, and in February 1991 visited Gabon and Cameroon to hold talks on joint economic matters.

In May 1990 De Villiers served on the government team at talks held with an African National Congress delegation at Groote Schuur, Cape Town.

In December 1991 De Villiers was appointed the National Party representative on the Convention for a Democratic South Africa (Codesa) working group dealing with transitional arrangements. He remained on the party's negotiating team and again served as one of its delegates at the multi-party negotiating process which followed Codesa. From December 1993-April 1994 he served as NP member on the Transitional Executive Council, prior to the first democratic elections in April.

During the early 1990s De Villiers held the following cabinet portfolios: Mineral and Energy Affairs and Public Enterprises (September 1989-April 1991); Economic Co-ordination and Public Enterprises (8 April 1991); Public Enterprises (January 1992).

In the April 1994 general election De Villiers stood as an NP candidate and was returned as a member of parliament. In May he was appointed Minister of Environment Affairs in the government of national unity.

De Villiers married Suzaan Mangold in 1964 and they have three daughters and a son.

SOURCES

1. *Curriculum vitae* supplied by the office of the Minister of Trade and Industry.
2. *Rand Daily Mail*, 9 January 1981.
3. *Argus*, 1 May 1981.
4. *Cape Times*, 17 March 1983.
5. *Cape Times*, 9 September 1983.
6. *Cape Times*, 19 May 1984.
7. Interviewed 17 April 1986, Cape Town.
8. *Natal Mercury*, 31 July 1991.
9. *Daily News*, 22 February 1991.
10. *Profile 94*, South African Communication Services, Pretoria, 1994.

EMSLEY MANNE DIPICO

Premier, Northern Cape
Province, 1994.

Manne Dipico was born in Kimberley's Greempoint township on 21 April 1959, the eldest of the four children of a domestic worker at a hospital.

He attended Mankurwane Lower Primary School (1967-70) and Boitshoko Higher Primary School (1971-74) before going on to Tidimalo Secondary School in 1975. From 1978-79 he attended St Boniface High School where he matriculated.

Dipico was employed as a fitter's assistant by De Beers Consolidated Mines in March 1980 but was dismissed in July after a general strike which lasted for two weeks. He subsequently worked for Barlows Northern Cape Caterpillars as a cleaner.

In 1981 Dipico enrolled for a BA degree at Fort Hare University where he became active in the Azanian Students' Organisation (Azaso) and underground structures of the African National Congress (ANC) which he joined in 1982. Dipico remained at Fort Hare until 1984 when he was appointed local Azaso treasurer and the organisation's standing representative on the Border region of the United Democratic Front (UDF).

He was detained in 1984 for involvement in anti-Ciskei homeland activities and as a result was refused readmission to Fort Hare. He returned to Kimberley and became active in youth structures. He also served as an executive member of the UDF in the Northern Cape from 1985-86 and of the Detainees' Support Committee, as well as becoming active in the National Union of Mineworkers (NUM) as an organiser. In June 1986 Dipico was detained in terms of state of emergency regulations until October of that year.

In August 1987 Dipico was arrested and charged with terrorism and furthering the aims and objects of the ANC. He received a five-year sentence and was imprisoned at the Johannesburg Prison and Pollsmoor Prison, Cape Town. He was released in 1990 before completion of his sentence. Dipico then served as national education co-ordinator of NUM.

In March 1991 he was elected regional secretary of the ANC's Northern Cape region, becoming regional chair in 1992. He also served as the region's elections co-ordinator.

Dipico led the ANC's Northern Cape provincial list in the April 1994 democratic elections and became premier after a close ANC victory over the National Party. The Northern Cape is the country's largest province but has the smallest population – 726 000. Its economy is based on mining – mainly diamonds, limestone, iron ore and manganese.

At the ninth national congress of the South African Communist Party (SACP), held in April 1995, Dipico was elected to the central committee of the party.

A keen football administrator who enjoys table tennis and jogging, Dipico is single and has one child. He lives in Kimberley.

SOURCES

1. *Curriculum vitae* supplied by the Premier's Office, Northern Cape.
2. *RSA Review,* June 1994.
3. *Sunday Tribune,* 8 May 1994.

YASMIN 'JESSIE' DUARTE

*Member of Gauteng
Executive Council, Safety
and Security, 1994.*

Born in Johannesburg on 19 September 1953, Jessie Duarte was the fifth of the nine children of Julie, a seamstress, and Ebrahim Dangor, a shoe salesman, van driver and receiving clerk.

Duarte grew up in Newclare and began school in 1958 at the Johannesburg Indian Girls' School. She then attended the Coronation-ville High School where she matriculated in 1971. While at high school Duarte (then aged about 15) and a fellow pupil organised a stayaway on 31 May, Republic Day, and were suspended. At about this time she and her brothers formed a residents' association in Newclare to oppose the expropriation of land in the area. However, they were unable to organise the community to protest and the association was disbanded.

As a 16-year-old standard eight pupil, Duarte joined the Labour Party youth movement and was elected provincial treasurer at the Transvaal youth congress. However, she had difficulty with the leadership when the youth suggested that the party be transformed from a coloured to a non-racial party. This was not possible in terms of the apartheid laws of the time. During this time she met with representatives of the Progressive Party youth and the Transvaal Indian Congress youth and although they felt they should be able to work together, this proved to be difficult and their attempts were unsuccessful.

Duarte's early political influence was her paternal grandmother who spoke of politics and the history of South Africa, including the Anglo-Boer War and the position of blacks in the country. A strict traditional Muslim, Duarte's grandmother was critical of existing government and the class structures.

Duarte's mother, a garment worker, made her aware of women's struggles on the factory floor and developed her understanding of women's issues. Duarte was also influenced by their family friend, Don Mattera, who taught her the right to self-respect and the need to create her own black identity. Her brother, Ahmed, encouraged her to be clear and precise about her goals in life. Later, during the 1980s, Duarte worked closely with Albertina Sisulu, whom she admires greatly.

In 1972 Duarte travelled to Pittsburg, USA, as an American Field Service (AFS) scholar, and on her return to South Africa was employed as a bookkeeper/accountant with Techno Machinery, where she worked for the next seven years.

In 1977 Duarte became involved in organising AFS scholarships and came into contact with teachers and students from Soweto. This rekindled her interest in politics.

From 1980-81 she worked for Syfrets and then Amaprop, a property service company. She then served as the national programmes co-ordinator for the American Field Service before becoming an accountant with Ravan Press in 1983.

While working, Duarte enrolled with the University of South Africa for a BCom degree by correspondence. She still hopes to continue her studies and would like to study for an MBA.

In 1982 Duarte was elected general secretary of the Federation of Transvaal Women (Fedtraw), a position she held until 1989. In 1983 Fedtraw became an affiliate of the United Democratic Front (UDF), an umbrella organisation consisting of hundreds of civil society organisations opposing the new tricameral parliamentary system and apartheid laws.

Some of Fedtraw's campaigns included an anti-Depoprovera campaign and the campaign to unban the African National Congress (ANC). Fedtraw's main interest was the upliftment of women and it ran 17 pre-school projects in various areas. From 1984-90 Duarte served as the women's representative on the Regional Executive Council of the UDF.

In 1985 Duarte met exiled ANC leader, Ray Alexander, in Lusaka, Zambia, and was recruited into the ANC underground. She reported to Alexander on issues regarding the women's movement and Alexander provided input on the formation of a women's coalition. They tried to revive the Federation of South African Women which had been active in the 1950s, but this was unsuccessful.

Duarte was issued with a restriction order on 9 March 1985 which was renewed in 1986 and 1987. She was restricted from participating in any organisations and from leaving the magisterial district of Johannesburg. She was not permitted to attend gatherings where more than 12 people would be present. On 17 March 1988 Duarte was detained at the

Johannesburg Women's Prison in terms of the state of emergency regulations and held until 5 December 1988.

In 1987 she was appointed director of the African Scholarship Trust organised by Beyers Naude. When the ANC was unbanned in February 1990, Duarte was asked to serve on its Transvaal interim regional leadership group which was charged with the establishment of internal ANC structures. She subsequently served as a member of the ANC's Regional Executive Council from 1992 to the present. From 1992-93 she also served on the executive committee of the ANC Women's League.

Besides working in ANC structures, from 1990 to April 1994, Duarte served as Nelson Mandela's personal assistant until he assumed the presidency.

In the April 1994 elections, Duarte stood on the ANC list for the PWV region (now Gauteng) and was elected to the provincial legislature. She was appointed member of the executive council with the portfolio of Safety and Security. She views her priorities as transforming the police from a force to a service; improving training and management skills within the police service in order to promote efficiency; and changing the face of police management through affirmative action programmes so that the service fully represents the people of the country.

Duarte is married to John Duarte and they have two children.

SOURCE

1. Interviewed 6 December 1994, Johannesburg.

ALEXANDER ERWIN

*Deputy Minister of Finance,
1994.*

Born in Cape Town on 17 January 1948, Alec Erwin is the son of Rosamund and Dennis Erwin, a concert violinist who began farming and undertook various business enterprises after World War II.

Erwin grew up in Southern Africa, including Cape Town, Johannesburg, Lusaka, Harare and Mutare, attending various schools and matriculating at Durban High School in 1965.

He then worked briefly on the railways before travelling abroad for some months. In 1967 he enrolled at the University of Natal, Durban, and completed his B Econ (Hons) in 1970. During this time he served as chairman of the Commerce Students' Council and in his Honours year assisted the Wages Commission, a project which linked students, academics and workers in the organisation of trade unions.

Erwin accepted a post lecturing in economics at Natal University. In mid-1974 he travelled to the United Kingdom for a year to undertake his own research and study at the Centre for Southern African Studies, York University, where he also lectured.

On his return he again lectured at the University of Natal until April 1978 when he began work for the Trade Union Advisory and Co-ordinating Council, established in 1974 as a co-ordinating body for trade unions in Natal and the Transvaal.

Erwin was also involved in the activities of the Institute for Industrial Education together with with noted Natal academics Rick Turner and Eddie Webster, and union organiser Halton Cheadle. The institute ran a correspondence course on a range of worker and industrial relations-related issues as well as training courses for workers and shop stewards.

Through the institute and the Wages Commission, he had some involvement with the 1973 Durban strikes. Erwin's involvement in the union movement stemmed from his interest in economics, his belief that the economic dispensation in South Africa was unjust and his knowledge that unions constituted an effective means of change.

In 1977 discussions began regarding the formation of the Federation of South African Trade Unions (Fosatu) which was launched in 1979. Erwin served as its general secretary from 1979-81 when he resigned to return to grassroots work in the unions, this time as branch secretary in the Pinetown area for the National Union of Textile Workers (now South African Clothing and Textile Workers' Union).

When talks concerning the formation of a larger federation began in 1981 Erwin served on the Fosatu delegation. The Congress of South African Trade Unions (Cosatu) was launched in December 1985 and from February 1986 Erwin served as education officer with the task of developing training programmes within Cosatu and its affiliates. He was also involved in liaising with organisations researching and investigating the nature and structure of the economy.

At the end of 1987 Erwin became national education secretary of the National Union of Metalworkers of South Africa (Numsa), based in Durban.

In debates on economic and financial sanctions against South Africa, Erwin maintained that disinvestment would be beneficial to the country as an effective means of bringing about change. He argued that the South African economy was heavily dependent on foreign loans, foreign trade and new investments which depended on an atmosphere of confidence in the country. Disinvestment would affect all these areas and weaken apartheid government. He believed that workers were prepared to make sacrifices, and it would be up to them to intervene if they felt that disinvestment was counter-productive.

From November 1987 Erwin represented Cosatu in various capacities in talks relating to the violence in Natal. Talks began in Pietermaritzburg but little was achieved until September 1988 when an agreement between Inkatha and Cosatu was reached regarding the establishment of a complaints adjudication board, although the latter eventually fell away. Erwin also served on the joint Cosatu/United Democratic Front committee dealing with violence.

From 1986 onwards, Cosatu initiated a major economic research programme, and Erwin became responsible for co-ordinating this work within the federation. He participated in the economic trends project, a group involving academics and intellectuals concerned with economic policy, serving as the group's link with Cosatu. As a result of these projects, Cosatu's views on economic policy developed a more precise formulation.

Erwin subsequently became involved with the African National Congress's Macro-Economic Research Group and also played a leading role on behalf of organised labour in the National Economic Forum where attempts were made to find common ground between the state, labour and business on South Africa's economic future. He also provided input for the ANC's reconstruction and development programme and edited its final policy document.

In the first democratic elections in April 1994, Erwin stood as a candidate for the ANC and became a member of parliament. In May he was appointed Deputy Minister of Finance in the government of national unity. Following his appointment he repeatedly emphasised the government's determination to maintain financial discipline despite pressures for state spending to improve the lot of the masses.

At the ANC's Bloemfontein congress held in December 1994, Erwin was elected a member of the organisation's national executive committee.

He is married to Annie Pretorius and has two children from a previous marriage.

SOURCES

1. Interviewed 15 March 1990, Durban.
2. *Daily News*, 29 August 1985.
3. *Sunday Times*, 22 May 1994.
4. *Sunday Tribune*, 29 May 1994.
5. *Profile 94*, South African Communication Services, Pretoria, 1994.

BERNARD LEWIS FANAROFF

*Deputy Director General
and Head, Management Team,
Reconstruction and Development
Programme, Office of the
State President, 1994.*

Bernie Fanaroff was born on 11 September 1947 in Sydenham, Johannesburg, the eldest of the two children of Isaac and Fanny Fanaroff who had immigrated to South Africa from Latvia. Both his parents were teachers who, during the 1930s and 1940s, involved themselves in the trade union movement and participated in the establishment of night schools on the Reef. Their progressive political commitment shaped Fanaroff's political consciousness.

Fanaroff attended Fairmount Primary School and Northview High School in Glenhazel where he matriculated in 1964. The following year he enrolled at the University of the Witwatersrand where he graduated with a BSc in Physics and Mathematics. In 1970 he completed his Honours degree in Theoretical Physics and in 1974 was awarded his PhD in Radio Astronomy by Cambridge University.

Long before he had completed his studies, Fanaroff had decided that he wanted to involve himself in the development of the trade union movement in South Africa. He returned to the country and obtained a lecturing post at the University of the Witwatersrand in the Physics Department. On a part-time basis he joined the Industrial Aid Society, established by a small group of dedicated university-based and other activists to act as a worker advisory body for the formation of trade unions on the Reef.

Fanaroff involved himself in worker education in a climate where the fledgling trade union movement was facing severe repressive measures, including large-scale bannings of trade union organisers. Although trade unions for black workers were not outlawed, organising activities in the factories were severely hampered by the business sector's refusal to recognise organised labour.

Fanaroff joined the Metal and Allied Workers Union (Mawu) on a full-time basis in 1977 in direct response to the banning of a co-organiser.

The repressive conditions improved following the introduction of the Wiehahn labour reforms in 1979. An amended Labour Relations Act enabled trade unions with black members to register and participate in the official bargaining machinery. This led to a rapid increase in trade union membership and a major wave of strikes involving, in particular, Mawu members.

The mid-1980s saw a uniting of trade union, civic and church groups in political resistance which resulted in Mawu assuming a strong political position. The detention of Mawu general secretary, Moses Mayekiso, resulted in Fanaroff serving as acting general secretary for two years.

In 1987, when Mawu was absorbed into the newly formed National Union of Metalworkers of South Africa (Numsa), Fanaroff became its first national secretary for the engineering sector. As head of Numsa's collective bargaining department, Fanaroff played a key role in the organisation as its front person for wage negotiations during the 1980s. The union, which was the result of a merger of five unions, is the largest in the manufacturing industry and a key affiliate of the Congress of South African Trade Unions (Cosatu).

In 1990 he was elected Numsa's National Secretary for Organising which involved working to strengthen Numsa's structures on the ground.

Fanaroff also served as a member of Cosatu's Political Task Force set up in 1991 to liaise with its alliance partners (the African National Congress and South African Communist Party) and prepare position papers on key political issues. He was convenor and chairperson of the VAT Co-ordinating Committee (VCC) established following the introduction of VAT in 1991. Under VCC pressure VAT was reduced from 12 to 10 per cent. The VCC subsequently broadened its focus to investigate food prices and campaign for a poverty relief programme.

Fanaroff was the Numsa delegate on the interim management committee of the National Electrification Forum. In November 1993 he was involved in the establishment of the Telecommunications Forum which supported Cosatu's view that the state should negotiate the granting of licences for the manufacture and marketing of cellular telephones. He was also active in talks with Armscor, South Africa's major arms manufacturer, in an attempt to encourage transparency.

In the early 1990s Fanaroff played an important role in the development of socio-economic strategies for Numsa and Cosatu. He participated in discussions within Cosatu which conceptualised a 'social contract' between the unions and the African National Congress (ANC), having studied a similar relationship between Australia's labour movement and its Labour Party. This concept was expanded into a more concrete economic and development programme which was eventually adopted by the tripartite alliance of Cosatu, the ANC and SACP as its election manifesto – the Reconstruction and Development Programme (RDP).

In July 1994 Fanaroff was appointed head of the management team dealing with the implementation of the RDP under Jay Naidoo, Minister without Portfolio responsible for the RDP.

Fanaroff's partner of 17 years is Wendy Vogel, a psychiatrist.

SOURCES

1. *People in Politics, First Quarter 1993*, Institute for Democracy in South Africa (Idasa), Durban, 1993.
2. *Sunday Times*, 24 July 1994.
3. Anton Harber and Barbara Ludman (eds), *A-Z of South African Politics*, Penguin, Johannesburg, 1994.

WALTER SIDNEY FELGATE

Member, Central Committee,
Inkatha Freedom Party, 1991.
Member of Parliament,
Inkatha Freedom Party, 1994.

Born in Pretoria in 1930, Walter Felgate was the second of the three children of Antoinette and Sidney Albert Felgate. Felgate attended Pretoria Boys' High School where he matriculated in 1949. When he completed school he worked on the SA Railways as a ticket clerk, and later at Lever Brothers where he introduced computerised stock control.

Felgate studied at the University of Natal, Durban, and completed a degree in social anthropology in 1958. This was followed by an Honours degree in 1959. Thereafter, he was employed by the Institute for Social Research at the university and undertook research in Tongaland (north-eastern Zululand). When the government withdrew his permit for the area, he was seconded to Lisbon University through the University of Lourenco Marques and worked in the rural areas of southern Mozambique for a year.

During the 1950s, when Felgate was a lay preacher in the Methodist Church, he began to question the morality of apartheid when confronted with segregation in the church. He left a white congregation to worship with an Indian mission in Lorne Street, Durban. He wished to become actively involved in combating racism, and held discussions with Albert Luthuli about involvement in the African National Congress. However, membership of the ANC at the time was open to Africans only, and he was asked to involve himself in the whites-only Congress of Democrats (COD). Felgate could not reconcile himself with the strong Marxist tendencies in the COD and therefore joined the Liberal Party, serving as its Southern Natal regional secretary until its dissolution.

On his return from Mozambique, Felgate lectured at Rhodes

University for three years in the Department of Social Anthropology and then undertook labour motivational research with the Chamber of Mines in Johannesburg for the following three years. Thereafter he was appointed African affairs adviser to Rio Tinto Zinc's Phalaborwa Mining Company. Since 1972 he has worked as a business consultant specialising in social and political research related to the establishment of new business ventures.

While in Phalaborwa, Felgate established an external monitoring panel to assess Rio Tinto's labour policies, and he invited, among others, Beyers Naude and Mangosuthu Buthelezi to serve on this committee. As a result of his contact with Naude, Felgate joined the Christian Institute and in the mid-1970s became involved in liaison between the Black People's Convention and the African National Congress in an effort to promote political reconciliation. In his Christian Institute capacity, he often functioned as a contact between Steve Biko, Oliver Tambo and Mangosuthu Buthelezi.

Felgate held a number of meetings with the then-ANC president, Oliver Tambo, during the 1970s. In 1974 Felgate played a role in advising Buthelezi about the establishment of Inkatha and its constitution. By the late 1970s tensions between Inkatha and the ANC had developed, partly, in Felgate's view, because of Inkatha's rapid growth. In 1977 Felgate helped to plan a summit meeting between the two organisations for 1978, but this failed when both Tambo and Buthelezi declined to attend it.

Felgate was active in the establishment of a Christian Institute office in Leyden, Holland, at the beginning of 1977, prior the Institute's banning in October of that year. After the break between the ANC and Inkatha in 1979, Felgate parted with Naude and his colleagues from the now-banned Christian Institute. He maintains that he was expected to take an anti-Buthelezi and anti-Inkatha position, but that he believed that Buthelezi, rather than the ANC, was the injured party in ANC-Inkatha relations, and he decided to continue working with him.

From 1980 onwards Felgate became closely involved with the work of Inkatha. He undertook research and provided a documentation service, initially on a part-time, but later full-time, basis. When membership of the Inkatha Freedom Party was opened to all races in 1990, Felgate was the first white to join. He was appointed to its central committee and served on its executive committee with the portfolio of organisational development, structures and leadership development. He also continued to undertake research for the party.

Felgate has represented Inkatha on various committees relating to the Natal violence and was active in the process leading up to the signing of the National Peace Accord. He served as an IFP representative on the National Peace Committee and on its sub-committees dealing with socio-economic issues and a code of conduct for the South African Defence Force. Felgate served as an IFP representative at the Convention for a Democratic South Africa (Codesa) and attended its plenary sessions in December 1991 and May 1992. He was also a member of the Codesa working group dealing with interim transitional mechanisms. He served as the IFP's chief negotiator at the World Trade Centre in 1993 until the party walked out over the issue of 'sufficient consensus' in decision-making concerning the election date of 27 April 1994.

In September 1993, following the dismissal with costs of the KwaZulu government's Supreme Court application to have certain negotiated decisions taken by 'sufficient consensus' set aside, Felgate allegedly threatened that the IFP would launch a mass action campaign to ensure that the scheduled April 1994 elections would not take place. He indicated that if the elections went ahead without the IFP, there would be civil war. He also stated that the IFP would not abide by decisions of the Transitional Executive Council as it was viewed as a 'weapon of the ANC to carry on its political vendetta of annihilating KwaZulu and Inkatha.' Following his statements there were indications of internal discontent over Felgate's role in the IFP and his close relationship with Buthelezi. He was openly criticised by other IFP office-bearers for his threats.

In March 1993 Democratic Party MP, Kobus Jordaan, implied in a question in parliament that Felgate could have been a spy or informer for one of the state's intelligence agencies. Felgate strongly denied these allegations.

Following the agreement by the IFP in April 1994 to contest the elections at the end of the month, Felgate stood as an IFP candidate for the national assembly and became a member of parliament.

In April 1994 Felgate married his personal assistant, Rose Butler. He has two daughters from his first marriage. He lives in Richards Bay.

SOURCES

1. Interviewed 6 August 1991, Durban.
2. *Daily News*, 11 March 1993.
3. *Natal Mercury*, 8 April 1993.
4. *Natal Mercury*, 10 September 1993.
5. *Daily News*, 11 September 1993.
6. *Natal Witness*, 15 September 1993.
7. *Natal Mercury*, 12 April 1994.

CHRISTIAAN LOEDOLFF FISMER

. *Member of Parliament,*
National Party, Rissik,
1987-94.
Member of Parliament,
National Party, 1994.
Deputy Minister of
Justice, 1994.
Minister of General
Affairs, 1995.

Born in Pretoria on 30 September 1956, Chris Fismer was the youngest of the four children of Elizabeth Catharina (born Loedolff) and Eric William Fismer, a general practitioner. He attended the Laërskool Pretoria Oos and the Afrikaanse Hoër Seunskool, Pretoria, matriculating in 1974.

Fismer then enrolled at the University of Pretoria where he completed a BCom degree in 1978, a BLC in 1981 and an LLB in 1983. While at univeristy Fismer became active in student politics and served as chairman of the Rag Committee in 1977. He became chairman of the Students' Representative Council in 1978; deputy president of the Afrikaanse Studentebond (ASB) in 1979 and its president in 1980.

At that time changes were starting to take place at Afrikaans universities and the growing divergence between the political views of students were later to be found in the differences between the Conservative Party and the National Party. Contacts with other student groupings began, and Fismer attended a National Union of South African Students (Nusas) conference as an observer while observers from Inkatha were invited to attend ASB conferences. By the time Fismer left university, increased tension had developed in Afrikaans student circles between those supporting a new approach to politics and those who supported Verwoerdian policies.

As Fismer had received a bursary from the Department of Justice to study law, he was employed as a public prosecutor at the Pretoria magistrate's court after qualifying. From 1982-83 he underwent his national service in the army at Voortrekkerhoogte where he qualified as an officer.

On his discharge from the army, Fismer returned to the Department of Justice for a further six months. He then served legal articles from 1984-85 in Pretoria and qualified as an attorney. In 1986 he joined the Pretoria Bar and practised as an advocate until his election to parliament as the member for Rissik in the 1987 general election.

Fismer joined the National Party (NP) while in his first year at university. He had developed an interest in politics through his family (his uncle was a cabinet minister) and during his high school days when he was active in debating societies. In the mid-1980s, while doing legal articles, Fismer was asked to become involved in the creation of a new youth action within the NP. He became active in setting up the new organisation, writing its constitution. In 1984-85 Fismer served as chairman of the NP's Youth Action in the Transvaal.

As an MP Fismer served on the parliamentary finance standing committee and the public accounts standing committee. He participated in an investigation into parliamentary privilege in 1988. In 1991 he was appointed to serve on the standing committee dealing with land reforms. In 1989 Fismer was elected senior Transvaal whip of the NP.

In December 1991 Fismer was appointed National Party representative to the Convention for a Democratic South Africa (Codesa) working group dealing with time frames and implementation of decisions.

In 1993 he was appointed FW de Klerk's parliamentary and political assistant with the responsibility of communicating the views of the president to the general public. In 1994 this post held the rank of Deputy Minister.

Fismer stood as a candidate for the National Party's Eastern Transvaal list for the national assembly in the April 1994 general elections and was returned to parliament. In May he was appointed Deputy Minister of Justice in the government of national unity. In the same month he was elected leader of the NP in the Eastern Transvaal.

Fismer also chairs the legal commission of the NP in the Transvaal and is therefore a member of the executive committee of the Transvaal NP.

In 1994 the Minister of Finance in the government of national unity – an NP member – resigned. His replacement was not affiliated to any particular party. As a result, an additional NP cabinet post had to be created and in January 1995 Fismer was appointed Minister of General Affairs.

Fismer is married to Linda (born Mills) and they have twin daughters.

SOURCES

1. Interviewed 8 April 1991, Cape Town.
2. *Curriculum vitae* supplied by Ministry of Justice, July 1994.

JOHN GEORGE FIVAZ

National Commissioner,
South African Police Services,
1995.

Born on 23 December 1945 in Reitz, Orange Free State, George Fivaz was one of the six children of Joey and Gert Fivaz, a farmer. He grew up in Bultfontein, a small town in the Free State, where he attended Bultfontein High School, matriculating in 1963.

Fivaz had always been interested in serving his community in some way and the police force seemed an interesting option to him. He therefore joined the South African Police (SAP) immediately after leaving school in 1964 and underwent his initial training at the Pretoria Police College.

Fivaz then served as a station police officer at Bayswater, one of the substations in Bloemfontein, where he became involved in grassroots police work such as patrolling, investigating minor crimes and attending to complaints. In 1967 he was transferred to the detective branch and promoted to the rank of sergeant.

In 1969 Fivaz became a warrant officer and was transferred to the Harrington Street detective branch in Cape Town. He was promoted to the rank of lieutenant in 1970 and was appointed branch commander of the housebreaking unit. He later also commanded the units dealing with motor theft and common theft. For a short period he also served as branch commander of the fraud unit in Cape Town.

At the end of 1972 Fivaz was transferred back to Bloemfontein to take up the post of branch commander of the South African Narcotics Bureau in the Orange Free State. In 1973 he registered as a part-time student at the University of the Orange Free State for a BAdmin degree which he completed in 1976. During this period he served as district detective officer and in 1974 became a captain. At the end of 1976 Fivaz settled in Pretoria where he became a member of the National Inspectorate of the SAP. He also qualified as an organisation and work-study officer during 1977.

Fivaz developed a particular interest in studying various policing styles such as community and community-supported policing. Original policing styles in South Africa were based on the British system founded by Robert Peel. In the 1970s South Africa had a highly centralised policing style of management with the top echelons enjoying a great deal of power, but with very little empowerment lower down the line of command. Fivaz investigated the decentralisation of authority and powers in policing structures and became involved in the restructuring of the SAP on various occasions. In this capacity he visited Europe, South America, the USA and Canada in order to study structures and policing styles.

During 1989-90 he was engaged in the process of revamping and improving police structures when, for the first time, authority was decentralised lower down on the hierarchy and delegated to regional commissioners. The intention was to make the police force more flexible in terms of its managerial process. This laid a sound foundation for the creation of the new structures prescribed by the new South African constitution which will be based on the principle of increased authority at the lower echelons of the line of command. The process of command has been further streamlined by removing blockages in communication channels and shortening these channels.

In the early 1980s Fivaz was promoted to major and subsequently to lieutenant-colonel. He was appointed colonel in 1987, brigadier in 1989 and major-general in 1992.

In October 1992 Fivaz was appointed head of Efficiency Services and in 1994, following the first democratic elections, was appointed to serve as a member of the interim advisory team of the new Minister of Safety and Security with the responsibility of advising the Minister on issues concerning the rationalisation, transformation and amalgamation of the 11 separate police forces established in terms of apartheid policy.

On 29 January 1995 his appointment as national commissioner of the South African Police Services (SAPS) was announced by President Nelson Mandela. In February of that year Fivaz had to deal with a policing crisis in the former Transkei area of the Eastern Cape when some two thousand heavily armed Transkei police rebels blockaded the town of Umtata because of a pay dispute. Police and defence force troops were sent in to break up the revolt. Fivaz stated that undisciplined actions by civil servants, especially police officials, could no longer be tolerated and would be dealt with appropriately. He also stated that it was time to act decisively against undisciplined elements within police ranks as failing to do so would mean that South Africans would be at the mercy of increasing crime and violence.

Fivaz and his wife, Anna-Beth, whom he married in 1969, have four sons.

SOURCES

1. *Curriculum vitae* provided by General JG Fivaz, January 1995.
2. Telephonic interview, 27 January 1995.
3. *Sunday Times*, 26 February 1995.

GERALDINE FRASER-MOLEKETI

Member, Central Committee,
South African Communist
Party, 1992.
Member of Parliament,
African National Congress,
1994.
Deputy Minister of Welfare,
1995.

Geraldine Joslyn Fraser was born in Cape Town on 24 August 1960, the eldest of the six children of Cynthia, a factory worker, and Arthur Fraser, a teacher working at specialised schools in the Cape Peninsula.

Fraser spent her formative years with her maternal grandmother who lived in the small Klipfontein community adjacent to Cape Town's sprawling squatter camp, Crossroads. Her outlook on life was shaped by the beliefs of her grandmother who was an active trade unionist.

Politics further impacted on her family life. Fraser was eight years old when her mother's sister, whose husband was active in the Non-European Unity Movement, left the country to assume a life in exile. By the time she reached Standard 8 Fraser had developed a keen political awareness. She attended Livingstone High School in Landsdowne which had a history of providing its pupils with alternative perspectives on South African history and socio-political issues. Years of apartheid on Cape Town buses, where half the bus was reserved for whites, had also sharpened her political perspective and Fraser recalls battles with white school children on municipal buses travelling to and from school.

Fraser was also influenced by events in and around Cape Town, such as the bulldozing of shacks in Crossroads in the early 1970s, the 1976 school protests and the Fatti's and Monis strike and consumer boycott. Racial tensions between the coloured community and Africans residing in the growing squatter settlements were also emerging. Fraser stepped forward in an attempt to resolve these tensions. Being from Xhosa and English lineage, Fraser lived and felt at home in both Xhosa and coloured communites and she felt that this background put her in a prime position to mediate. She joined the Bellville Association for Community Action, the forerunner to the Bellville Civic Association.

When Fraser was in Standard 8, she unsuccessfully contested the chairperson's position for the school's Students' Representative Council (SRC). She was, however, later elected to the executive of the SRC and also served as a prefect and on the executives of the Debating and History Societies.

On matriculating from Livingstone High School in 1977, Fraser enrolled at the University of the Western Cape in 1978 for a Lower Secondary Teacher's Diploma. In the June holidays of 1980, Fraser and a number of friends travelled to Zimbabwe and during this four-week visit they met Zanla and Zipra combatants who had fought in the liberation struggle for the recently independent Zimbabwe. The political euphoria engendered by these meetings and events in Zimbabwe made a profound impression on her. On her return to South Africa she decided to leave the country for military training.

In August 1980 Fraser and a friend travelled to Zimbabwe where Fraser had previously had links with members of the African National Congress (ANC). She arrived in Zimbabwe on her 20th birthday and a month later met with the ANC's first chief representative in Zimbabwe, Joe Gqabi, who was in the process of setting up an office in Harare. Fraser's goal of undergoing military training was delayed when she became involved in assisting with the establishment of the office.

Nearly a year later, on 30 July 1981, as Fraser was about to leave for military training, Gqabi was assassinated. Fraser and a colleague had spent the evening with her mother who had made a special trip to Harare to say farewell to her daughter. On their return to the office late that night they found the body of Gqabi who had been ambushed in his car.

On the day of her 21st birthday, Fraser was arrested and detained by the Zimbabwe police in connection with Gqabi's murder. It was her view that elements in the Zimbabwe special branch were attempting to frame her for Gqabi's death and she suspected collusion between South African security operatives and former Rhodesian security personnel who had retained their positions after Zimbabwean independence.

Fraser was kept in solitary confinement and interrogated for 17 days in an attempt to extract information from her about the ANC and its operations. Following the arrival of an ANC deputation from Lusaka, she was released.

After a short spell in Lusaka, Fraser moved to Angola where she completed a three-month military training course. In February 1982 she left for a specialised commander's training course in the Soviet Union with the aim of being infiltrated back into South Africa. However, Fraser's pregnancy thwarted her goal of active military service. She had met her husband, Jabu Moleketi, during training in Angola and both had been sent to the Soviet Union.

Days after Fraser and Moleketi were married in Lusaka in April 1983, Moleketi left for active operations in Lesotho while Fraser later returned to Zimbabwe. With Zimbabwean authorities refusing to accept the presence of Umkhonto we Sizwe (MK) cadres, Fraser applied to study. She enrolled for part-time study for a diploma in journalism at the Christian College of Southern Africa.

While in Zimbabwe Fraser was invited to join the South African Communist Party (SACP) and served in its regional underground structures. In 1985 she was seconded by the ANC to the Lutheran World Federation office in Harare. She continued to represent the ANC and was the ANC delegate at the United Nations Decade of Women conference held that year. Her husband, who was seconded to the ANC office, joined her in Harare in 1985.

In January 1990 Fraser attended the historic Malibongwe women's conference in Amsterdam. On the day of her return to Harare, the South African government lifted its ban on the ANC and other political organisations.

Three months later, Fraser was asked by the SACP to return to South Africa to assist in the establishment of the SACP office. As she was not indemnified, Fraser returned at her own risk. As an *ex-officio* member of the internal leadership core, Fraser worked tirelessly in setting up the party headquarters and the public launch of the SACP at the First National Bank stadium in Johannesburg on 29 July 1990. At the eighth congress of the SACP in December 1991 Fraser was elected to the party's central committee and subsequently to the Politburo. She was one of only two women in the Politburo and one of four on the central committee. She was re-elected to the SACP's central committee at its ninth congress, held in April 1995.

Fraser continued to work as a full-time official at the SACP headquarters and served as personal assistant to SACP secretary general, Chris Hani, (and later Charles Ngqakula) as well as national head of administration.

One of a handful of women who held senior positions at the Convention for a Democratic South Africa (Codesa), Fraser acted as adviser on the management committee to then-SACP chair, Joe Slovo. She caused a stir by arriving at management committee meetings with her baby and breastfeeding when necessary. Fraser is severely critical of the lack of consideration for women with children shown by political parties and business organisations. She identifies the lack of social infrastructures catering to women's needs as a major obstacle to women wanting to assume leadership positions.

During the April 1994 elections Fraser stood as an ANC candidate for the national assembly and became a member of parliament. Following the cabinet reshuffle after the death of Joe Slovo, Minister of Housing, in January 1995, Fraser was appointed Deputy Minister of Welfare.

Fraser and Jabu Moleketi, ANC member of the Gauteng Executive Council with the portfolio of Economic Affairs, have three children.

SOURCE

1. *People in Politics*, First Quarter 1993, Institute for Democracy in South Africa, Durban, 1993.

FAITH XOLILE GASA

Member of Parliament,
Inkatha Freedom Party,
1994.

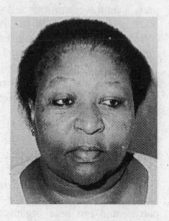

Faith Xolile Gasa (born Tshabangu) was born on 30 June 1945 in Bloemfontein. She was brought up by adoptive parents who were teachers by profession – Peter Timothy Tshabangu (a Presbytarian Church of Africa minister and moderator of the Synod) and Vidah Gladys Tshabangu.

She grew up in the parish house in Bloemfontein's Batho location, also known as '4 and 6' (because the plots had cost four shillings and sixpence). Gasa attended the local Mangaunga Primary School until her father was called to Cape Town to reconcile different factions in the church and she was enrolled at Langa Primary School. She matriculated in Bloemfontein at Batho High School in 1963.

As a youngster, Gasa interacted with many of the Afrikaans children on the farms she visited with her father, but noticed that as they became teenagers, they distanced themselves from her. Yet she acquired a passion for the Afrikaans language and today speaks Afrikaans as well as English, Xhosa, Zulu, South Sotho, North Sotho, Tswana, Swazi and Rolong.

As a young teenager, Gasa accompanied her father to African National Congress (ANC) meetings on the surrounding farms where he went to conscientise people. It was during these journeys that her political beliefs and personal values were formed.

Following matriculation Gasa enrolled at what was then the National Hospital in Bloemfontein (now the Pelonomi Hospital) where she attained her General Nursing Diploma in 1967. Gasa was then awarded a bursary to attend the University of Zululand where she studied from 1968-72, graduating with a BA degree in History and Afrikaans. In 1971 she was elected to the Students' Representative Council (SRC).

While at university in 1970, Gasa met her future husband, Enock Doctor Gasa. Enock Gasa was SRC president during that year and was responsible for changing the affiliation of the University of Zululand from the liberal National Union of South African Students (Nusas) to the Black Consciousness grouping, the South African Students' Organisation (Saso).

Gasa became involved with the Black Consciousness movement and worked with people such as Strini Moodley, Barney Pityana, Steve Biko and Harry Ngwenkhulu. These activists would visit the university to raise awareness among students through meetings and workshops.

Gasa and Fikile Mazibuko (now president of the South African Black Social Workers' Association) were among the few women involved in the political conscientisation taking place at the university. They organised sit-ins and other forms of activism around issues affecting students such as living conditions at the university and racial harassment by white lecturers. Although these were localised issues, they took their cue from the broader political movements that were growing in the country.

In 1973 Gasa and her husband moved to Vryheid, Northern Natal. She taught at Ikhethelo High School where her husband held the post of principal. She became a member of the Natal African Teachers' Union of which she is life president. She also became involved in community work, particularly among the disadvantaged, and started two creches in the area – Bambanani and Zamokwake pre-schools in Mondlo, the township of Vryheid.

Gasa worked with the Young Women's Christian Association and set up workshops for women in areas such as deportment and assertiveness.

During this period Enock Gasa became active in the newly-formed Inkatha movement. He founded the branch in Vryheid and was elected chairperson. Faith Gasa also became a member and greatly admired Chief Mangosuthu Buthelezi. She felt he was mobilising and uniting people after the political vacuum of the 1960s and early 1970s. Gasa worked to encourage teachers to join the movement and received a mandate from Buthelezi to conduct workshops aimed at raising women's levels of awareness.

In 1977 Gasa returned to the University of Zululand where her husband took up a permanent post. She taught at Dlangezwa High School but, because of political disturbances, the school was forced to close before the end of the year. She then taught at Amangwangwe High School until 1980 and at Mdlamfe High School in 1981. In 1982 she became founder principal of Hlakaniphani Junior Secondary School under the KwaZulu Department of Education and Culture (DEC), and the following year founded Khula Junior Secondary School.

In 1991 a call from the National Education Crisis Committee to bring children back to school precipitated a clash with the KwaZulu DEC which could not provide the necessary infrastructure by way of sufficient classrooms, books and other resources. Gasa formed the Mehlwesizwe Education Committee and pleaded with the DEC to open a temporary school for children who were unable to gain admission to other schools. She was granted permission to do so and became the founder principal of yet another school, the Nhlamvana Junior Secondary School in Esikaweni near Empangeni.

In 1991 Gasa became press secretary for the Inkatha Freedom Party (IFP) and was asked to serve as an *ex-officio* member of all its committees, including the central committee. She also became chairperson of the Inkatha Women's Brigade.

At the Convention for a Democratic South Africa (Codesa) I and II she represented the IFP as a full delegate. Later, at the Multi-Party Negotiating Forum in 1993, Gaza and Mavivi Manzini of the ANC were elected co-chairpersons of an *ad hoc* committee that led to compulsory participation by women at the multi-party talks. Gasa and Frene Ginwala of the ANC were appointed to the steering committee of the Women's National Coalition, whose mission was to deliver a women's charter for inclusion in the new constitution.

Gasa, then an inspector of schools, also held the following positions: women's consultant for the African Teachers' Association of South Africa and Southern African regional consultant for women's affairs; member of the World Confederation of the Teaching Profession; life president of the Natal African Teachers' Union and co-convenor in training trainers on curriculum development for the post-apartheid era; national council member of Women for South Africa; council member of the Mother's Union Church of the Province of South Africa, Diocese of Zululand; member of the Third Order of St Francis of Assisi; convenor, Teenage Pregnancy and Child Abuse Concerned Committee (Northern Natal Region); council member for Dice (Do I Care Enough?) and secretary of the Mehlwesizwe Education Trust.

In the April 1994 elections, Gasa was candidate number four on the IFP's regional list to the national assembly and became a member of parliament. In this capacity she serves on the parliamentary portfolio committees on education and home affairs.

She has travelled in Southern Africa, the United States of America, Canada, Germany and Togo. Faith Gasa has five children.

SOURCE

1. *People in Politics*, First Quarter 1994, Insitute for Democracy in South Africa (Idasa), Durban, 1994.

GERT JOHANNES 'JAKES' GERWEL

Director-General,
Office of the State President.

Born on 18 January 1947 on Kommadagga farm in the Somerset East district of the Eastern Cape, Jakes Gerwel was one of the ten children of Sara (born Beckett) and John Richard Gerwel, a farm worker.

Gerwel attended the local farm school, later moving to Dower College in Uitenhage. He matriculated at Paterson High School in Port Elizabeth.

In 1963 Gerwel registered at the University of the Western Cape for a BA degree and graduated in 1967 *cum laude*. He completed his BA (Hons) in 1968. From April 1969 to September 1970 Gerwel lectured at Hewat Teachers' Training College in Cape Town before taking up a Belgian government scholarship to the Free University of Brussels where he completed a licentiate in Germanic Philosphy in 1971. In 1979 he completed his doctorate in Literature and Philosophy (*magna cum laude*) at the same university with a thesis on literature and apartheid. In 1986 he was awarded a doctorate in humanities (*honorus causa*) by Clarke College, Atlanta, Georgia.

On his return from Belgium in 1971, Gerwel taught for six months at Grassy Park High School in Cape Town, following which he began lecturing in Afrikaans and Dutch literature at the University of the Western Cape. In July 1976 he was promoted to senior lecturer and in January 1980 became professor. Two years later he became dean of the faculty of Arts and in January 1987 was appointed vice-chancellor of the university.

Gerwel became involved in the Black Consciousness movement in the late 1960s and early 1970s, serving as educational advisor to the South African Students' Organisation (Saso) in the early 1970s. There were objections by the university authorities to his political involvement and he served three probations before his appointment to permanent staff.

During the 1980 education boycotts, police detained Gerwel for a few days at the end of May.

When his appointment as vice-chancellor was announced in 1986, Gerwel indicated that the South African left needed an intellectual home and that the University of the Western Cape could become that base. He later designated the university as a vehicle for change in South Africa. A month after the announcement of his appointment, Gerwel led a march of several thousand students towards the Bellville police station to demand the release of those detained under emergency regulations. Later that year he travelled to Lusaka to hold discussions with the then-banned African National Congress.

During 1988, frequent class boycotts took place at the university and Gerwel warned against the negative effects of this but conceded that they constituted a valuable lesson. However, he reiterated the fact that frequent interruptions to studies were not conducive to achieving the goals of a liberal education. In 1989 classes were suspended during the general election campaign.

In September 1989 Gerwel was briefly arrested together with Archbishop Tutu and Franklin Sonn during a march in the city centre.

Gerwel has served on various boards and community organisations, including the Mowbray Inter-race Group (Merge); the board of the Council for Black Education and Research; the board of directors of the Mauerberger Foundation; the board of trustees of the Kagiso Trust; the board of trustees of the Ukunilungisela Trust; the board of trustees of the South Publications Trust; and the board of trustees of the Institute for a Democratic Alternative for South Africa. He also serves as chairman of the board of the Careers Research and Information Centre (CRIC) and of the Equal Opportunity Foundation.

In September 1991 Gerwel was elected a member of the Western Cape regional committee of the ANC and, following the April 1994 general elections, was asked to take over the post of director-general in the office of State President Nelson Mandela.

Gerwel is married to Phoebe (born Abrahams) and they have two children.

SOURCES

1. *People in Politics*, Fourth Quarter 1991, Institute for Democracy in South Africa (Idasa), Durban, 1991.
2. *Directory of Contacts*, South African Communication Services, February 1995.

FRENE NOSHIR GINWALA

Speaker, House of Assembly, 1994.
Member of Parliament, African National Congress, 1994.

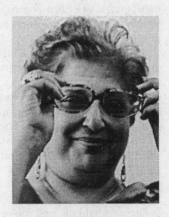

Born on 25 April 1932, the daughter of Banoo (born Bodhadwala) and Nassarwangee Sohrabji Ginwala, Frene Ginwala travelled abroad to study law at the University of London where she completed her LLB. She returned to South Africa to complete her legal training at a time when it was becoming clear that the South African government would outlaw the African National Congress (ANC).

The leadership of the organisation had started to make arrangements for an ANC office to be established outside the country and on 22 March 1960, immediately after the Sharpeville massacre, Ginwala was asked by the ANC to leave South Africa for Mozambique where her parents resided, and to assist in smuggling the ANC deputy president, Oliver Tambo, out of the country. While in Maputo (then Lourenco Marques) she heard that the ANC acting president, Oliver Tambo, had left South Africa and was in Botswana.

Ginwala then travelled to Salisbury, Southern Rhodesia, where she made arrangements for Tambo, Congress activists, Ronald Segal, Yusuf Dadoo, and herself to travel to Tanzania to establish an ANC office in exile. Because of the state of emergency in South Africa at the time Ginwala could not return.

Ginwala subsequently arranged for other ANC leaders including Nelson Mandela, Andrew Mlangeni, Raymond Mhlaba and Wilton Mkwayi, to travel out of South Africa clandestinely, and return in the same way.

In Tanzania Ginwala established a monthly journal, *Spearhead*, and worked as a journalist until she was deported and declared a prohibited immigrant. At the time she had injured her leg in an accident and was hospitalised in the United Kingdom. When she was permitted to return to Tanzania, Ginwala did not return immediately as her injuries required bone grafts. She then began producing radio programmes and writing scripts for a non-profit organisation which produced cultural programmes for Africans.

While in the United Kingdom Ginwala gave lectures to trainee diplomats at Oxford University and was eventually admitted to study at the university. She began her studies in the late 1960s but they were interrupted in 1969 when President Nyerere of Tanzania asked her to become managing editor of the national English-language newspaper, *The Standard*, which was to be nationalised. Although government-owned, the newspaper was given a charter to enable it to be independent. With the support of Oliver Tambo, Ginwala accepted the position. She also worked as a frelance journalist in East Africa for British newspapers, including *The Guardian*, *The Observer* and *The Economist* as well as for the British Broadcasting Corporation.

Ginwala held the position of managing editor of the monthly political journal, *Spearhead*, until 1972 when she was dismissed for publishing an article attacking General Mamare who had executed members of the Communist Party in the Sudan. She had been unaware that he was due to pay a state visit to Tanzania. Ginwala returned to Oxford and completed her DPhil. She then obtained legal chambers with the aim of establishing her own legal practice.

In 1974, after the coup in Portugal, Ginwala returned to Mozambique to see her parents. As a result of political changes in the region, it was decided that she should work full-time for the ANC and she was asked to assist in establishing its Department of Information and Publicity. She never returned to pursue her legal career.

Ginwala worked in Tanzania, Zambia, Mozambique and the United Kingdom as an ANC official and as a journalist and broadcaster in East Africa and Europe. She also lectured at universities and institutions in a number of countries and participated at various United Nations, Unesco and other international conferences on South Africa, covering conflict research, women's issues, development and technology transfer. She was one of 14 international experts invited to advise the director-general on Unesco's programme on Peace and Conflict Research (1987-88).

Prior to her return from exile in 1991, Ginwala was head of the Political Research Unit in the office of President Tambo where she conducted research focusing on the transfer of military and nuclear technology. She also served as ANC spokesperson in the United Kingdom on sanctions, the nuclear programme and the arms and oil embargo relating to South Africa.

After she returned to South Africa in 1991 Ginwala formed part of the task force to establish the ANC Women's League in South Africa. She helped to set up the Women's National Coalition which was made up of organisations from across the political spectrum with the aim of drawing up a women's charter, and was elected its national convenor. She has also held the following positions: member of the ANC's PWV regional executive committee; member of the secretariat in the ANC president's office; member of the ANC's negotiating team at the Convention for a Democratic South Africa (Codesa); and member of the technical committee on the Independent Electoral Commission set up by the Multi-party Negotiating Forum in 1993.

Ginwala stood as an ANC candidate for the national assembly in the April 1994 general elections and became a member of parliament. She was then elected speaker of the national assembly. In this capacity, she has been instrumental in many of the changes in parliament which have opened up the committee process to the public and the press; eased the dress codes; and relaxed restrictions regarding entrance to the public gallery.

In addition, Ginwala has served as head of the ANC's research department and as its representative on the Science and Technology Initiative. At present she is deputy head of the ANC Commission on the Emancipation of Women; member of the board of Land and Agriculture Policy Centre; member of the board of the Group for Environmental Monitoring; trustee of the Govan Mbeki Fellowship (University of Fort Hare) Multi-media Trust; and trustee of the Democratic Media Trust.

Ginwala has been widely published on anti-apartheid and women's issues.

At the ANC's December 1994 congress held in Bloemfontein, Ginwala was elected to the party's national executive committee. In February 1995 she was elected to the organisation's national working committee.

SOURCES

1. *Profile 94*, Directorate Research, South African Communication Services.
2. Hilda Bernstein, *The Rift*, Jonathan Cape, London, 1994.
3. *The Women's Directory, 1994-95*, Political addendum, *Femina* magazine in association with Old Mutual, 1995.
4. *Femina*, December 1994.
5. *Curriculum vitae* supplied by the office of Frene Ginwala, May 1955.

JOHN GOMOMO

President, Congress of
South African Trade Unions,
1991.
Member, Central Committee,
South African Communist
Party, 1991.

Born on 25 October 1945 on a farm in the Eastern Cape, John Gomomo was one of seven children. He left school in Standard Six, because of family poverty, and subsequently completed his matriculation through correspondence courses.

Gomomo first worked as a machine operator in a textile factory, then joined Volkswagen in Uitenhage, where he became a spot-welder, later moving to brazing and arc-welding

He became a member of the United Automobile Workers (UAW) at Volkswagen in 1977, which subsequently merged with a set of other unions to form the National Automobile and Allied Workers Union (Naawu), affiliated to the Federation of South African Trade Unions.

In the early 1980s Gomomo became a full-time shop steward at Volkswagen. He and other union members played a role in building civic structures in Uitenhage as well, but avoided leadership roles because of tensions between community-based organisations and the trade unions. Gomomo was elected vice-president of Naawu which, in 1987, merged with other unions to form the National Union of Metalworkers of South Africa. In 1989, he was elected second vice-president of the Congress of South African Trade Unions (Cosatu).

Following the unbanning of the African National Congress (ANC) and the South African Communist Party (SACP) in February 1990, Gomomo was appointed to the ANC's Eastern Cape internal leadership core and the SACP's internal leadership group. He was elected to the SACP's central committee at its December 1991 congress, and re-elected at the party's ninth national congress, held in April 1995.

Gomomo replaced Elijah Barayi as president of Cosatu at the federation's fourth national congress, held in 1991.

At the December 1994 ANC conference held in Bloemfontein, Gomomo was elected to the organisation's national executive committee.

Gomomo lives in KwaNobuhle, Uitenhage. He is a widower and has eight children.

SOURCES

1. *South African Labour Bulletin*, 15(3), September 1990.
2. *The Shop Steward*, 1(1), June 1992.

PRAVIN JAMNADAS GORDHAN

Member of Parliament,
African National Congress,
1994.

Born on 12 April 1949 in Durban, Pravin Gordhan was the third of the four children of Rumbha and Jamnadas Gordhan, a jeweller and later a businessman. Gordhan grew up in Durban, attending the Surat Hindu State Aided School and Sastri College where he matriculated in 1967. He graduated with a BPharm from the University of Durban-Westville in 1973.

Gordhan completed his pharmacy internship at King Edward VIII Hospital in 1974, and continued to work there after qualifying until 1981 when he was dismissed by the Natal Provincial Administration while in detention for his political activities.

After his release from jail in May 1982 Gordhan was issued with banning orders which were effective until June 1983. He was restricted to the Durban central area and worked as a locum pharmacist. In 1984 he worked as a full-time volunteer for the Natal Indian Congress (NIC) in its anti-tricameral parliament campaign. At the beginning of 1985 Gordhan opened his own pharmacy, but in mid-1986 he was forced to go underground.

During his high school years, Gordhan became aware of human rights issues. When he later attended the University of Durban-Westville he found the climate on campus to be very repressive and this sparked off conflicts between students and the administration. For example, monitors were appointed to check the length of students' hair and in 1970 students walked out of the Chemistry II class because the professor insisted on their wearing ties.

In 1971 there was a movement to establish a Students' Representative Council (SRC) on the campus and Gordhan served on the committee established to draft its constitution. He was subsequently elected to the first elected SRC on the basis of that constitution.

In April 1972 the university rector presented the SRC with his own constitution and Gordhan chaired the first mass meeting on the new campus where it was agreed to suspend the SRC, all clubs and societies and to refuse to participate in any extra-curricular activities on campus until a democratic SRC was established. This decision held for five years.

In the 1971-72 period Gordhan became aware of, and became associated with, members of the Natal Indian Congress (NIC), including George Sewpershad. In 1974 Gordhan was elected to the executive committee of the NIC. At this time the organisation was the only legal representative of the Congress Alliance in the country. Charles Diggs, a US congressman, became involved with the NIC human rights committee and helped to expose the working conditions of labourers on the Natal sugar plantations.

As a political activist Gordhan was exposed to Marxist philosophy and he and some of his graduate colleagues began to look for opportunities to relate to the masses and become involved in mass activity. One such watershed event took place in March 1976 when the banks of the Umgeni River burst and the river flooded, affecting families living in the area. Gordhan and others offered medical and legal assistance and later helped to establish a residents' association. When those affected moved to Phoenix he assisted with the formation of a community-based organisation in the area.

Gordhan had to maintain the sensitive and delicate balance between his political identity and his involvement on the ground. He continued to help establish grassroots organisations in other areas such as Chatsworth. This work had to be done in a clandestine way to avoid security police becoming aware of these activities. At this time, the organisations began to engage the Durban City Council on various issues. In 1978 the city council tried to force autonomy on the Phoenix area in an attempt to create a separate Indian town and Gordhan was active in an 18-month long campaign to resist the move. The idea was eventually dropped by the city council and the Natal Provincial Administration. The campaign combined mass action, door-to-door canvassing, coalitions with various organisations, cultural activities with political connotations and mobilisation.

As a result of similar work taking place in different areas, including the coloured community, the NIC convened a meeting of civics on 20 March 1980 where the Durban Housing Action Committee (DHAC) was launched and Gordhan was elected secretary.

Gordhan then became involved in a campaign to promote DHAC which co-incided with the city council increasing rentals by 15% throughout the areas under its jurisdiction. Mass meetings attended by residents were held in October 1980 which led to a six-week rent boycott and negotiations with the Durban City Council. At that time the NIC also helped to bring a group of people together to launch the Release Mandela Committee in Durban and Gordhan served on this body.

In 1981 Gordhan became active in the campaign against the elections to the South African Indian Council (SAIC) and attended a conference of organisations held on 10 October where the Freedom Charter was affirmed and where opposition to the elections was declared.

Following the murder of human rights lawyer, Griffiths Mxenge, Gordhan was involved in preparations for his funeral and the drafting of a pamphlet. The next day, on 27 November 1981, he and others were detained and held in solitary confinement in terms of section 6 of the Terrorism Act.

During the 1970s Gordhan began associating with people who had been released from Robben Island, such as Judson Kuzwayo, Jacob Zuma and Mac Maharaj. In the late 1970s he became involved in underground activities and became associated with the African National Congress (ANC) and later the South African Communist Party (SACP).

In late 1982 and early 1983 discussions began regarding the creation of what eventually became the United Democratic Front (UDF). NIC representatives had attended an anti-SAIC conference in the Transvaal early in 1983 and had opened debate on this development. Although Gordhan was banned, he took part in these discussions. In August 1983 Gordhan attended the launch of the UDF in Cape Town and the NIC became an affiliated organisation.

During the period of his banning, Gordhan maintained his involvement in civic issues. Following his unbanning, Gordhan became involved in more assertive campaigns such as the placard demonstration outside the Durban City Hall in November when State President PW Botha addressed a gathering. Gordhan was arrested, but was released on bail.

Gordhan helped to build up NIC structures and by March 1984 regional councils and area committees were established, based on the clandestine work of the previous six to seven years.

The anti-tricameral election campaign organised by the UDF was highly sophisticated. Gordhan maintains that 100 000 Indian homes were visited in Natal and on election day, activists were very visible ensuring that voters were not forced to go to the polls. The week before the election, leaders of the NIC (including Gordhan) were arrested and held at the Pietermaritzburg prison. Following the elections, they were released on bail and taken by their colleagues into hiding. Some of the UDF and NIC leaders took refuge at the British Consulate in Durban and Gordhan helped to co-ordinate the campaign surrounding their plight.

Gordhan and a number of others were detained in Durban in September 1985 in terms of Section 29 of the Internal Security Act and held for one month. The detentions were linked with the outbreak of violence in the Durban area, particularly in Inanda, when many members of the Indian community lost their homes and possessions.

During 1985-86 Gordhan liaised with civic organisations in other parts of the country and worked with the UDF towards arranging a national civic conference which was eventually held under semi-underground conditions in Cape Town in May 1986.

A few days before 16 June 1986, it became clear to political activists that there would be mass detentions in terms of the state of emergency and Gordhan went underground, remaining in hiding until his arrest on 12 July 1990 when he was named as a key figure in the ANC underground network, Operation Vula. Gordhan was secretary of Operation Vula's Durban political committee and from 1988 had been a member of the operation's political military leadership.

Gordhan spent three and a half months in detention in Bethlehem, Orange Free State, under section 29 of the Internal Security Act and appeared in court on 28 October on charges of terrorism and illegal possession of arms, ammunition and explosives. It was alleged that he and others had conspired to create a national underground network to recruit, train, arm and lead a 'people's army' to seize power from the government by means of an armed insurrection. He was held for two weeks at the Westville Prison and released on bail of R40 000. He was granted indemnity on 25 March 1991.

Gordhan served on the Interim Leadership Group of the SACP and chaired its Durban Western Areas branch. He was also a member of the executive committee of the Western Areas branch of the African National Congress (ANC) and vice-chairman of the Southern Natal Civic Association. He played a key role in the campaign for a democratic Durban.

From 1986 Gordhan served on the People's Education Commission of the National Education Co-ordinating Committee and was involved in the establishment of the Education Policy Unit at the University of Natal, Durban. He chaired the ANC's national education committee and sat on the policy frameworks committee of the National Education Policy Investigation initiated by the ANC.

Gordhan served as a NIC delegate at the Patriotic Front Conference held in Durban in October 1991.

The preparatory meeting for the Convention for a Democratic South Africa (Codesa) was held on 29-30 November 1991 in Johannesburg and Gordhan attended as a joint NIC/Transvaal Indian Congress (TIC) representative. That meeting established a steering committee which was charged with the responsibility of organising Codesa 1 and Gordhan was appointed NIC/TIC delegate to the steering committee, together with two advisers.

After Codesa 1, the steering committee became the management committee which had at that stage one delegate and one adviser from each participating organisation. The first meeting of the management committee took place on 13 January 1992 and a daily eight-person management committee was appointed, including Gordhan.

At the first daily management committee meeting on 20 January Gordhan was mandated to replace Zach de Beer as chairman, subject to review on 10 February. On that date it was agreed that Gordhan continue to chair the committee until Codesa 2 (which took place at the end of May). In this capacity he became spokesperson for Codesa. Gordhan also served on Codesa Working Group 3 which dealt with issues concerning an interim government and transitional arrangements. This working group was unable to reach consensus on various issues and the Codesa initiative eventually broke down.

In March 1993 new multi-party negotiation initiatives took place and Gordhan served on the planning committee of the multi-party negotiation process. He was appointed to the panel of chairpersons of the new forum and developed a good reputation as a chair. In this position on 2 July 1993 he ruled that the negotiation forum had adopted by sufficient consensus 27 April 1994 as the date for an election for a transitional parliament which would also be a constitution-making body. He made the ruling despite the fact that seven of the 26 participating organisations opposed its adoption. This led to a walk-out by the Inkatha Freedom Party and in September the KwaZulu administration challenged his ruling in court. However, the case was dismissed with costs and subsequently both the KwaZulu administration and the IFP refused to return to talks.

From December 1993 to May 1994 Gordhan served as one of the four co-chairpersons of the Transitional Executive Council established to level the playing fields in preparation for the elections. During this time Gordhan also worked as a research consultant at the Centre for Community and Labour Studies.

In the general election of April 1994 Gordhan stood as an ANC candidate for the national assembly and became a member of parliament. In parliament he serves as chairperson of the select committee on provincial affairs and constitutional development and as a member of the select committees on housing and the public service. He is also a member of the constitutional committee of the Constituent Assembly.

At the ninth national congress of the South African Communist Party, Gordhan was elected as a member of the party's central committee.

Gordhan is married to Vanitha (born Raju), and they have one child. He has another child from a previous marriage. They live in Durban.

SOURCES

1. Interviewed 1992, Durban.
2. Anton Harber and Barbara Ludman (eds), *A-Z of South African Politics*, *Weekly Mail & Guardian*/Penguin Books, Johannesburg, 1994.
3. South African Institute of Race Relations, *Race Relations Survey 1993/94*, Johannesburg, 1994.
4. Telephonic discussion with P Gordhan, 1 March 1995.

DEREK ANDRE HANEKOM

Minister of Land Affairs, 1994.
Member of Parliament,
African National Congress,
1994.

Born in Cape Town on 13 January 1953, Derek Hanekom was the youngest of the three children of Sheila Mary (born Delany) and Alfonso Hanekom, a clerk at Cape Town's Groote Schuur Hospital.

Hanekom grew up in Cape Town, attending the Deutsche Schule and Jan van Riebeeck High School. He matriculated in 1970 and the following year underwent national service with the 3rd South African Infantry Battalion at Potchefstroom. During this time he spent two months at Katima Mulilo in the Caprivi Strip, South West Africa.

On completion of his army service Hanekom worked part-time until entering the University of Stellenbosch to study for a law degree in 1972. However, he left the university after six months.

To give himself time to assess his future, he left for the UK where he was employed first as a labourer in Hastings and then a petrol pump attendant in Battle. He then travelled to the United States at the invitation of his uncle who had a business in the coal mining district of Pennsylvania. There he worked on a coal delivery truck in the winter, and in summer at a coal factory.

In 1973 Hanekom returned to England and was employed as a labourer to pick apples and hops. He then travelled to Austria, working in Salzburg as a casual labourer on the mountains preparing for the skiing season. In December 1973 he visited Israel and worked on the docks in Eilat after which he worked on a kibbutz for a few months. He then travelled to Greece and worked as a deckhand on a private boat for six months.

Hanekom returned to South Africa at the end of 1974. His exposure to farm work in England and in Israel had kindled his interest in farming, but until the end of 1977 he held odd jobs.

Hanekom had came from a politically conscious family. His father stopped supporting the National Party after the introduction of the Group Areas Act, and although his parents' views were generally conservative, they took an anti-apartheid stance.

Hanekom's experiences of racism in the army and his need to defend South Africa during his travels abroad exposed him to views highlighting the absurdity of the apartheid system in South Africa. He had also worked in factories where there was a strong union influence and he was exposed to the issue of workers' rights. When he returned to South Africa he felt alienated and was fired from his first two jobs. In the second case, he was working for the Swedish company, ASEA, and was warned by his foreman not to fraternise with black workers after hours. Management took the side of the foreman and Hanekom lost his job.

Throughout this period Hanekom's brother was actively involved in politics, initially as a full-time organiser for the Progressive Party in Stellenbosch and subsequently as a Young Christian Students activist. The events of 1976 and the Soweto revolt increased Hanekom's resistance to the system. The following year his friend, Tom Waspe, a Christian activist, was arrested and at the end of the year Christian activists organised a demonstration outside John Vorster Square in Johannesburg where they sang Christmas carols and lit candles. Hanekom was arrested and detained at John Vorster Square where he was assaulted the following morning. He was charged in terms of the Riotous Assemblies Act, pleaded guilty and was warned.

He had in the meantime met his future wife, Patricia Elizabeth Murray, who had played a key role in organising the event, and they both joined the African National Congress (ANC) which was banned at the time.

In 1978 they moved to the Western Cape and rented a farm in Kuilsrivier for a year. During this year, Hanekom was arrested in Cape Town and again charged under the Riotous Assemblies Act for participating in a protest against the eviction of squatters at Crossroads. He was acquitted.

At the end of 1978 he and Murray moved to a farm in the Magaliesberg, Transvaal, and built up a dairy herd of Jersey cows and a poultry enterprise. After five years the farm became a viable operation. The decision to move to the Magaliesberg was made partly on the grounds that it was strategically positioned between Johannesburg and Botswana, where they had political contacts.

They made their first trip to Botswana in 1980 where they established a communications system and explored the role they could play in the liberation struggle. Many people from left-wing student and Christian circles visited them on the farm and Hanekom and Murray undertook political work with them, identifying possible recruits and focusing their attention on the issue of conscription. Hanekom and Murray married in 1981.

In 1983 a military conscript, Roland Hunter, visited the Hanekoms. He held a position in the office of the chief of staff intelligence in the special operation aimed at destabilising the Mozambican Frelimo government. Hunter was driver and general assistant to a Colonel van Niekerk who served as paymaster to the Renamo training camps. Over a period of several months Hunter passed on substantial information and the Hanekoms arranged for him to meet with representatives of the liberation movement in Botswana. The nature of the information being supplied to the liberation movement was very sensitive and it later appeared that it was being used by Frelimo. In particular, it was clear to the operation that Frelimo knew the whereabouts of the Renamo training camp which was subsequently moved. Hunter passed on information about the site of the new camp and was arrested soon after.

The Hanekoms were arrested at the end of 1983 and charged with high treason. The security branch refused to release documents which had been seized from their farm to their defence lawyers as the documents revealed South African support for Renamo and the existence of other destablising operations in Lesotho, Angola and Zimbabwe.

The Hanekoms spent four and a half months in detention, mostly in Pretoria, and then four and a half months on trial, which was held *in camera*. Following negotiations between their defence lawyers and the state, the high treason charges were dropped and by agreement they pleaded guilty to alternative charges of possession of banned literature. Hunter was charged in terms of the Defence Act which carried a maximum sentence of five years. Hanekom was sentenced to two years imprisonment, his wife to three years and two months and Hunter to five years. When Hanekom's wife (a Zimbabwean citizen) was released from prison in November 1987 she was deported to Zimbabwe and they spent the next three years there.

While in Zimbabwe Hanekom worked for the Popular History Trust in Harare and his wife attended the university to study veterinary science.

Following the unbanning of the ANC in February 1990, Hanekom returned to South Africa to work on the organisation's land and agriculture desk. His wife returned several months later as she had been implicated in certain clandestine operations and needed to obtain indemnity before re-entering South Africa.

Hanekom spent the following four years working on the ANC's land and agriculture policies. He stood for election to the ANC's national list and, following the ANC majority in the April 1994 elections, was appointed Minister of Land Affairs in the government of national unity.

Hanekom views his priorities as follows: dealing with the issue of land restitution either through the return of land or by monetary compensation; the opening up of opportunities to those who do not qualify through the court process, but who were denied access to land; provision of secure tenure to those already on the land, especially those living in conditions of insecure tenure; ensuring that those who are already on the land or beneficiaries of the programme obtain adequate support so that they are able to make a living on the land and use it productively in the context of the government's reconstruction and development programme.

SOURCE

1. Interviewed 24 June 1994, Cape Town.

FERDINAND HARTZENBERG

Member of Parliament,
Conservative Party,
Lichtenburg, 1987-94.
Leader, Conservative
Party, 1993.

Born on 8 January 1936 on his father's farm, Klein Uitschot, in the Sannieshof district, Western Transvaal, Ferdie Hartzenberg is the son of the late Maria Aletta (born Coetzee) and Ferdinand Hartzenberg.

He attended primary school in Sannieshof, and then went to the Hoër Volkskool, Potchefstroom, where he matriculated in 1953. He registered at the University of Pretoria and completed his BSc (Agriculture) in 1957 and his MSc (Agriculture) in 1959. While at university,

Hartzenberg won the Geyer Floating Trophy for the best agriculture student of that year. During 1960-61 he was employed by the Department of Agricultural Technical Services as a researcher, returning to full-time study for a further year before beginning to manage the family farm. He completed his DSc in 1972 with a thesis on factors which influence the early growth of cattle.

While at university, Hartzenberg played an active role on the Students' Representative Council and the Afrikaanse Studentebond as well as other university committees. He also worked for the National Party (NP) during election campaigns. From 1959-60 he served as secretary of the NP divisional council for Rissik. When he returned to farm on Klein Uitschot, he participated in NP activity at branch level and served on the divisional council for Lichtenburg.

In 1964 Hartzenberg was nominated as a candidate for the Transvaal Provincial Council, and won the seat the following year. In 1970 he became MP for Lichtenburg.

In parliament, Hartzenberg's special interests concerned Agriculture and Co-operation and Development, and he also served on the NP caucus study groups dealing with Water Affairs and Economic Affairs. In 1974 he was appointed chairman of the Commission for Co-operation and Development which dealt with proposals for consolidating the 'homelands'.

In 1976 he was appointed Deputy Minister of Development, and in 1979 was promoted to the position of Minister of Education and Training, a post he held until his resignation in March 1982. At the time he took over the portfolio, black schools were affected by countrywide boycotts. Hartzenberg indicated that he was not prepared to repair damage to school property when finance could be used to improve facilities at schools not involved in the protests. As a result, several schools were closed, particularly in the Bloemfontein and Port Elizabeth areas.

Hartzenberg's parents were involved in the NP at a local level, but his political views were also influenced by Jan Pienaar, who had been divisional council chairman for Rissik, as well as Piet Koornhof and Gerrit Viljoen. However, it was Hendrik Verwoerd, whose meetings and publications provided Hartzenberg with the greatest inspiration.

Hartzenberg's break with the NP was the result of a fundamental difference in outlook regarding the concept of power-sharing with other racial groups. He believed that power-sharing in any form was not viable and had never worked successfully in any society. He maintained that the basic objective in South African politics was to reduce conflict by granting each nation control over its own destiny through the division of land and political power.

Hartzenberg argues that, until 1982, NP policy created institutions for each nation in South Africa to rule itself. But he believes that in that year the policy changed, allowing for the inclusion of others in central government. Following the split in the NP in February 1982, a mass meeting was held at the Skilpad Hall in Pretoria on 20 March at which a decision was taken to form a new party. The Conservative Party (CP) manifesto was submitted for approval in August 1982 at the party's first congress where Hartzenberg was elected vice-chairman of the Transvaal CP. He held his parliamentary seat during the 1987 and 1989 elections.

Hartzenberg is widely viewed as a hardliner within the CP. He is alleged to have been a key mover in the CP's initial decision to boycott the March 1992 whites-only referendum called by FW de Klerk – a decision subsequently overturned by the party's caucus. During August 1992, a dispute developed within CP ranks between the old guard (including Hartzenberg) and the 'new right' led by Andries Beyers, over whether the right wing should enter the national negotiation process in an attempt to secure a *volkstaat* for the Afrikaner people. On 13 August, members of the 'new right' resigned from the party after their discussions with the CP's executive committee broke down.

Having marginalised the CP from the mainstream of political activity in the country, the party and some conservative black groups in South Africa formed the Freedom Alliance (originally known as the Concerned South Africans Group). The Freedom Alliance was linked with the Inkatha Freedom Party (IFP) and some homeland governments.

Following the death of Andries Treurnicht in 1993, Hartzenberg was elected CP leader in May. That month the Afrikaner Volksfront (AVF) was formed as an umbrella structure for 21 right-wing organisations with the aim of uniting and mobilising Afrikaners towards self-determination. In July 1993 Hartzenberg announced the withdrawal of the CP from multi-party negotiations.

At the official opening of the CP's Transvaal congress in September Hartzenberg indicated that the establishment of a multi-party Transitional Executive Council (TEC) would be regarded as a declaration of war and that Afrikaners would not subject themselves to the TEC or any interim administration approved by the multi-party constitutional negotiations. A dispute within the AVF arose in October 1993 when Hartzenberg forced AVF leader, Constand Viljoen, to suspend negotiations with the National Party and the African National Congress.

Tension continued between Hartzenberg and other hardliners on the one hand and Viljoen and more pragmatic supporters on the other. In November 1993 the AVF revealed a revised *volkstaat* plan which provided for limited autonomy for Afrikaners within South Africa, but with restrictions on black voting rights within the area. However, low-key negotiations between the Viljoen group and the ANC were resumed.

A deal was almost reached in December, but was turned down by the Hartzenberg faction. In January Hartzenberg attacked Viljoen for his continued attempts at negotiations, and on Hartzenberg's insistence, the talks were terminated.

In an attempt to make the elections as inclusive as possible, the ANC and the NP made wide-ranging concessions to the Freedom Alliance, but the Hartzenberg group rejected the proposals as inadequate.

However, faced with an imminent election, Viljoen registered a new conservative party, the Freedom Front (FF), 20 minutes short of the deadline for registration on 4 March 1994. In an attempt to maintain unity, Hartzenberg thanked Viljoen for his foresight but stated that the AVF would not legitimise the new interim constitution by participating in the elections.

In the same month Hartzenberg outlined the constitution and map for the proposed *Boerevolksrepubliek* announced by the CP. The area included most of the Transvaal, the Orange Free State and Northern Natal, excluding the 'homelands' and state-owned land such as the Kruger National Park. The constitution stated that citizenship would be granted to all 'Boere-Afrikaners' living within the boundaries of the republic on the date of independence. It allowed for the creation of cantons to accommodate concentrations of non-citizens within the boundaries of the republic, such cantons being connected to other states in Southern Africa.

In January 1994 a *Volks Verteenwoordigende Raad* (People's Representative Council) was formed as a first step towards the unilateral creation of an Afrikaner *volkstaat*. The council was to administer the election for the first house of assembly for the new republic and Hartzenberg was appointed to serve as council president. This body was seen as an alternative to the multi-party Transitional Executive Council (TEC) and as the embryonic parliament of the *volkstaat*. In his inaugural speech as president, Hartzenberg indicated that although he would prefer to achieve independence through non-violent means, if Afrikaners were not granted freedom, they would 'take it'.

In the second week of March, Lucas Mangope, then president of the government of Bophuthatswana and a partner in the Freedom Alliance, called for assistance from Viljoen in an effort to maintain control over his mutinying soldiers and striking bureaucracy. Viljoen sent in a force of about 4 000 men who were forced to leave by South African Defence Force troops. Humiliated by this experience, Viljoen resigned from the leadership of the AVF and handed in his list of candidates to ensure that the Freedom Front would play a role in the elections.

In the meantime a split took place within the CP over election participation. Hartzenberg adopted a boycott position and, as a result, nine of the CP caucus, including Pieter and Corne Mulder, Willem Botha and Joseph Chiole, announced that they would fight the election under the banner of the Freedom Front. They were then expelled from the CP. About 150 key grassroots members of the CP also indicated that they would join General Viljoen and this disrupted plans by the CP and the Afrikaner Volksfront to use their control over many rural towns to prevent change and disrupt the elections.

Viljoen continued to try to bring the CP into the electoral process, but Hartzenberg refused to participate unless the NP and the ANC constitutionally guaranteed the establishment of the *volkstaat* if the right-wing won more than 800 000 votes. This was rejected by both the NP and the ANC.

The FF won nine seats in the House of Assembly and it was estimated that of the 86% of white Afrikaners who voted, approximately 20% of that vote went to the FF. Hartzenberg responded to the results by stating that because of irregularities, the election should be declared null and void and that the party's boycott position had been correct. He would therefore view the new ANC-led government as the illegal product of an invalid election.

Hartzenberg is married to Judy (born De Wet) and they have two sons, Ferdinand and Benjamin de Wet. They live on the family farm where they grow maize and breed cattle and sheep.

SOURCES

1. Interviewed 22 May 1984, Cape Town.
2. *Sunday Times*, 1 March 1992.
3. *Sunday Times*, 16 August 1992.
4. *Natal Mercury*, 27 July 1993.
5. SAPA, Johannesburg, 1952 GMT 3 September 1993.
6. *Sunday Times*, 30 January 1994.
7. *Daily News*, 21 February 1994.
8. *Sunday Times*, 20 March 1994.
9. *Weekend Argus*, 2/3 April 1994.
10. Andrew Reynolds (ed), *Election '94*, David Philip, Cape Town and Johannesburg, 1994.

HARRINGTON BANTUBONKE HOLOMISA

*Commander of the Transkei
Defence Force, April 1987-94.
Chairman, Transkei Military
Council, December 1987-94.
Transkei Minister of Defence
and Minister of Audit,
January, 1988-94.
Member of Parliament,
African National Congress, 1994.
Deputy Minister of
Environment Affairs, 1994.*

Born on 25 July 1955 at Mqanduli, Transkei, Bantu Holomisa was the son of the late Chief Bazindlovu Holomisa of the AmaHegebe tribe and his second wife, Constance. His father served in the Second World War and had been a member of the Transkei Legislative Assembly.

Holomisa attended primary school at Mqanduli and junior and senior secondary school at Jongilizwe College, Tsolo, a school for the sons of chiefs and headmen. He matriculated in 1975, and was rugby captain and vice-head prefect.

In 1976 Holomisa worked for the Department of Posts and Telecommunications in Umtata for six months before joining the Transkei Defence Force. In the army he undertook a parachute course, a combat team commander's course and a candidate officer's course (he was commissioned in 1978). In addition, he was one of the first blacks to undertake the South African staff and management course at the Army College in Pretoria.

Holomisa's military career has included the following positions: lieutenant, platoon commander (1978-9); captain, training wing (1979-81); major, second-in-command of a battalion (1981); lieutenant-colonel, battalion commander (1981-83); colonel, operations and training (1984-85); brigadier, chief of staff (1985-87); and major general, commander of the Transkei Defence Force (April 1987 – April 1994).

Holomisa was also active in sports and in 1978 he managed the national gymkhana squad which competed in Zimbabwe. In 1980-81 he was manager of the Transkei national rugby squad. He also served as national secretary of the Transkei Rugby Board in 1982-84 and as president of the Combined Forces Sport from 1981-83. From 1984-87 he was manager of the Tembu Royals Football Club, Umtata.

On 21 January 1987 Holomisa was detained by Transkei security police under section 47 of the Transkei Public Safety Act, but was never questioned by them. He was, however, interrogated by an advisor to General Ron Reid-Daley, former Selous Scout and adviser to the head of the Transkei Defence Force, Zodwa Mtirara. During his detention Holomisa contracted pneumonia but received inadequate medical care. Because prison authorities differed with police about his treatment, he was transferred to military cells.

On 1 April 1987 Holomisa was advised that he would be released. Later that day he was instructed to appear in court and face charges and was told bail would be set. Holomisa refused to appear in court without lawyers appointed by himself. He then had meetings with security police chief, General Kawe, and military officers. Holomisa was released later that night, apparently as a result of a confrontation between Transkei's George Matanzima and army officers who had demanded to know why Holomisa was under arrest.

Following Holomisa's release, General Reid-Daley and other ex-Selous Scouts were detained briefly and then ordered to leave Transkei. The Transkei Defence Force chief, Mtirara, was dismissed and Holomisa took over as head of the defence force. On 23 September 1987 six cabinet ministers and two deputies were ordered to resign, and Prime Minister George Matanzima fled Transkei.

Stella Sigcau was then elected Prime Minister, but less than three months later it emerged that she had accepted R50 000 in return for her support for a gambling rights application in the homeland.

In January 1988 Holomisa announced that a military council would run the country together with the ministers' council, at least until the auditor-general had completed his investigations into corruption by government ministers and officials. The military council was chaired by Holomisa who was also responsible for the Department of Defence and the Department of Audit.

In 1989, at a reburial service for Chief Sabata Dalindyebo, Holomisa indicated that he would hold a referendum to see whether Transkeians wished to rejoin South Africa. In November 1989 he attended a rally for the released ANC leaders in Umtata where he shared the platform with them and National Union of Mineworkers' general secretary, Cyril Ramaphosa.

From 1989-90 Holomisa embarked on a process aimed at normalising political life in Transkei. He unbanned 33 political organisations, including the ANC and the PAC, and released political prisoners. However, Transkei remained under military rule until democratic elections were held in 1994. In November 1990 an unsuccessful coup led

by a former member of the military council, lieutenant-colonel Craig
Duli attempted to remove Holomisa from power.

In December 1991 and May 1992 Holomisa participated in the
Convention for a Democratic South Africa (Codesa) representing the
Transkei Government. At these deliberations, he formed part of the
'patriotic front' grouping which included the ANC, Natal and Transvaal
Indian Congresses, the Labour Party, the South African Communist
Party, the Venda administration and the governing parties of Lebowa,
KwaNdebele and Kangwane. During 1991 Holomisa visited India and
France together with representatives of the ANC.

In May 1992, Holomisa claimed that he was in possession of
documents which proved state complicity in violence and
destabilisation, but did not reveal their contents to the South African
authorities.

Early in 1993 a committee of the Goldstone Commission investigating
the location of the Azanian People's Liberation Movement (Apla) bases
and activities was told that Transkei was a base for attacks on South
Africa. Holomisa refused to allow his administration to give evidence to
the committee and stated that it would hold its own judicial inquiry.

In March 1993 Holomisa supplied the press with a signal from
Military Intelligence which indicated authorisation of the murder of
UDF activist, Matthew Goniwe in 1985. As a result the inquest into the
murder was reopened.

In the April 1994 general election, Holomisa stood as an ANC candidate and became a member of parliament. Following the ANC victory at
the polls he was appointed Deputy Minister of Environment Affairs.

At the December 1994 ANC congress, Holomisa drew the most votes
in elections to its national executive committee. In February he
challenged President Nelson Mandela's allegation that Transkei
government officials had stolen millions of rands. It was his view that
Mandela's allegations could not be regarded as the last word on the
matter. Holomisa's comments followed a warning by Mandela that he
would take a tough position against lack of discipline within the cabinet.
This followed a clash with Winnie Mandela, an ally of Holomisa, over
her criticism of the government of national unity.

Holomisa is married to Tunyelwa and they have two daughters and a
son.

SOURCES

1. Interviewed 15 November 1989, Umtata.
2. *Curriculum vitae* supplied by Major General Bantu Holomisa.
3. *Daily News*, 31 December 1987.
4. *Natal Witness*, 1 January 1988.

5. *Daily News*, 6 January 1988.
6. *Natal Witness*, 12 January 1988.
7. *Weekly Mail*, 27 May 1988.
8. *Weekly Mail*, 1 December 1989.
9. *Sunday Times*, 17 May 1992.
10. *Natal Mercury*, 7 August 1992.
11. *The Republic of Transkei*, 31 August 1989.
12. South African Institute of Race Relations, *Race Relations Survey 1993/94*,
    Johannesburg, 1994.
13. *Cape Times*, 17 February 1995.

SANGO PATEKILE HOLOMISA

Member of Parliament,
African National Congress,
1994.
President, Congress of
Traditional Leaders of
South Africa, 1990.

Born on 26 August 1959 at Mqanduli, Transkei, Patekile Holomisa was
the eldest of the five children of the late Chief Jongisizwe Holomisa and
Chieftainess Nodumile Holomisa of the Hegebe tribe of the Thembu
nation.

Holomisa grew up under the guardianship of his uncle, Chief Douglas
Ndamase, one of the senior chiefs in western Pondoland. As heir to the
chieftainship it was traditional practice that Holomisa be removed from
his immediate family because of potential rivalries and also to allow him
to grow up in surroundings where he would not be accorded any special
privileges. His uncle was involved in Transkei homeland politics as a
member of the opposition Democratic Party, which was established to
oppose independence for the Transkei.

While growing up Holomisa learnt of the tremendous influence traditional leaders had over their communities, with people consulting them on issues ranging from their children's education to employment problems. In addition, members of the community voluntarily tilled the land of the traditional leader and in exchange, at times when food was in short supply, destitute families were fed and maize was sold at a drastically reduced price.

Holomisa also learned that the bantustan system was not popular among the people and political organisations were opposed to traditional leaders participating in the system. However, traditional leaders who refused to co-operate with the authorities were deposed, suspended or jailed and some fled. As a result, others decided to collaborate to protect the system of traditional leadership and to look after their communities. Holomisa also noticed that the people had pride in their traditional institutions with which they closely identified.

He attended the Mampondomiseni School at Ngqeleni during his primary school years, and subsequently St John's College, Umtata, and Ndamase High School at Ngqeleni, matriculating in 1980. From 1981-83 he studied for his BA degree at the University of Transkei and from 1984-85 attended the University of Natal, Durban, where he completed his LLB.

While attending the University of Transkei, Holomisa joined the Azanian Students' Organisation (Azaso) which was subsequently renamed the South Africa Students' Congress (Sasco). He did not associate himself with political organisations affiliated with Black Consciousness, although he did acquaint himself with their politics. At university he began to take part in debates on issues which affected the community such as detention of activists, and at the University of Natal he became actively involved in Azaso and the Black Students' Society, serving as vice-president of the latter in 1984-85. During this time he campaigned against the establishment of the tricameral parliament and distributed pamphlets in the coloured and Indian communities, becoming involved in the activities of the United Democratic Front (UDF), a mass-based organisation consisting of hundreds of anti-apartheid affiliates.

It was Holomisa's view that black students at the University of Natal were treated as second-class members of the university community. Unlike white students, black students, including Holomisa, were accommodated at the Alan Taylor residence in Wentworth. They demanded the right to accommodation in on-campus residences and after a demonstration this was agreed to by the university authorities.

Holomisa's education was financed by his community and merit bursaries made available by the university. As a result, he felt obligated to take on his responsibility as traditional head of his community. However, towards the end of his education he realised that a return to his traditional role would automatically mean involvement in homeland politics (his regent was an *ex officio* member of the Transkei parliament). He therefore decided to consult with the exiled and then banned African National Congress (ANC). He made his first contact with the organisation in Lesotho in 1985 and subsequently met with representatives on an annual basis in Botswana, Lesotho, Zambia and Zimbabwe. It was the ANC's view that he should not only take up his position but also go to parliament as a member of the Transkei National Independence party of Chief Matanzima so that the organisation would have someone inside these structures.

After completing his studies, Holomisa asked his community to allow him to undertake his legal articles which he completed with HKV Siwisa in East London from 1986-87. However, he later opted to become an advocate and in 1988 served his pupilage for the Bar in Umtata and Durban. He was admitted as an advocate of the Supreme Court of South Africa in 1989 and practised at the Umtata Bar until 1994. In 1987 Holomisa became a founder member of the National Association of Democratic Lawyers (Nadel).

After qualifying as an advocate, Holomisa expected his community to insist that he take up his leadership role but, as he was as yet unmarried, this was postponed. As a result he was able to establish a legal practice and also became involved in political activities.

In 1989 Holomisa was elected vice-president of the Congress of Traditional Leaders of South Africa (Contralesa), an organisation initially established in KwaNdebele to fight the imposition of independence on the homeland and which subsequently grew to include all regions of South Africa.

As vice-president, Holomisa assisted in drafting the organisation's constitution and principles and this involved travelling to most parts of the country and consulting with political and traditional leaders. Most of the homeland rulers were prepared to co-operate with the exception of Bophuthatswana and KwaZulu which opposed the establishment of Contralesa.

Holomisa was elected president of Contralesa at its national conference in 1990, a position he still holds. Following the unbanning of the ANC in February 1990 he was appointed to the movement's interim regional committee in the Transkei – a position he subsequently relinquished as he wanted to dedicate more time to Contralesa.

In 1991 Holomisa attended the initial meeting of the Convention for a Democratic South Africa (Codesa) as part of the Transkei government delegation.

In the democratic elections of April 1994 Holomisa stood as candidate number 64 on the ANC's national list and became a member of parliament. He chairs the parliamentary portfolio committee on land affairs and also serves on the justice committee. He was appointed to the constitutional committee of the Constituent Assembly and is also deputy-chairman of Arts and Culture in South Africa.

As president of Contralesa, Holomisa has promoted the concept of full participation of traditional leaders in the law-making process in South Africa. He proposes that the House of Traditional Leaders which, at present, acts only in an advisory capacity regarding laws pertaining to customs and tradition, should operate like the senate or be incorporated into it. This proposal is based on his belief that traditional leaders are involved in day-to-day meetings (*imbizos*) of the people and are in touch with the grassroots.

Holomisa is unmarried and lives in Mqanduli, Transkei.

SOURCES

1. Interviewed 11 August 1994, Cape Town
2. *Curriculum vitae* of SP Holomisa, August 1994.

ZIBA BONGINKOSI JIYANE

National Politics Director,
Inkatha Freedom Party, 1993-94.
Secretary General, Inkatha
Freedom Party, 1994.
Member of Parliament,
Inkatha Freedom Party, 1994.

Ziba Jiyane was born on 22 September 1958 in Empangeni, Natal, the son of Agnes Phoqiwe and Hambayedwa Jiyane, and has two brothers and two sisters. His father was a chief councillor to the tribal court Reserve 5 KwaKhoza, Nseleni. His mother was a housewife and leading member of civic organisations, active on school and church committees.

While he was growing up, his mother often related stories of proceedings at the courts. These included complaints by the community about poll taxes, dog taxes, concerns about education and possible removals. He often heard about the 'government' which he, as a young boy, thought was one person, and when asked what he would like to be when he grew up, he would declare that he would like to be a government.

His family was deeply religous, belonging to the Dutch Reformed Church of which he is still a member. He attended Bejane Lower Primary School and Lubane Higher Primary and went on to Amagwe High School where he matriculated in 1977. He was the only pupil in his class to gain university exemption and received Best Student awards in Leadership, Oratory and Physical Science from 1973 to 1977.

His first became politically aware in 1974 when, as a Standard 7 pupil, he spent many hours commuting to and from school by bus. His daily journey took him through Empangeni where he saw election banners for the whites-only general elections. He frequently questioned his English teacher (a privately-appointed man from the University of Zululand who had been influenced by the Black Consciousness movement on that campus at the time) as to why blacks could not vote. His teacher opened his eyes to many of the issues of the day and this, together with his avid reading of newspapers, developed his political thinking.

Jiyane was chairman of the debating society and also chaired the newly-formed Inkatha Youth Brigade in 1975. In addition, he was a member of the Student Christian Movement.

In 1973 Jiyane's father fell seriously ill and under normal circumstances he would have been obliged to find employment to support the family. However, the principal of his school offered him a bursary which allowed him to complete his education. In 1978 he enrolled at the University of Zululand for a B Proc degree but only completed one semester before going underground and travelling to Botswana. During his short stay at the university he held the position of national secretary of the Inkatha Youth Brigade and was at the forefront of student political activism on campus.

The Soweto student uprising had a profound effect on Jiyane and he recalls Inkatha leader Mangosuthu Buthelezi travelling to Johannesburg to visit victims and to donate R1 000 which the youth brigade had collected. After reading Martin Luther King's book, *Strength to Love*, he attempted to influence the Inkatha Youth Brigade to become more active in civil disobedience although he always advocated non-violent resistance to apartheid, particularly after events in Soweto. He tried to convince the Youth Brigade to adopt this strategy at their national conference in 1978 and was at the forefront of the protest against Minister Connie Mulder opening the KwaZulu Legislative Assembly buildings in Ulundi. Senior leaders of Inkatha were opposed to this type of behavior and Dr Bhengu, then secretary general of Inkatha was accused of having influenced the youth brigade and expelled from the party.

Jiyane's parents were then visited by the security branch and told that he was regarded as a radical. Fearing arrest, he went underground in July 1978 and with the help of the Black Consciousness movement in Umlazi, he travelled to Botswana where he gained political asylum until December 1978.

He moved to Tanzania in January 1979 where he joined the Pan-Africanist Congress (PAC) and lived in Dar es Salaam until 1984. During this period he served as director of Publicity and Information of the PAC and head of Radio Freedom. He was leader of the youth division of the PAC and represented the PAC at international conferences in many countries including Kenya, Zambia, Ethiopia, Nigeria, Yugoslavia, Cyprus, Germany, France and England.

In 1984 Jiyane was awarded a scholarship to study at the University of California, Los Angeles, by the African-American Institute. There he completed a BA degree in Political Science and Public Administration. This was also the year when he went home for the first time since his exile only to hear the sad news that his father had passed away the previous year.

During this time Jiyane was very active in the United States Anti-Apartheid Movement and the disinvestment campaign. He travelled extensively in the United States as an exiled South African enlightening people about apartheid.

He completed his degree at UCLA in three years, instead of the allotted four, graduating *Magna Cum Laude* and *Phi Beta Kappa* which is the highest academic honour at American colleges. He was also made a member of the Golden Key National Honor Society. He was then awarded the Yale Graduate School Tuition Award to study from 1987 to 1991. His living expenses were paid through a United Nations Award from 1987 to 1989. At Yale he completed a Masters degree in Political Science in 1988. He was then admitted to a prestigious dual degree programme in Law and Political Science – Juris Doctor – specialising in Constitutional Law and International Law which he completed in 1992. He also received the Harry Oppenheimer Memorial Trust Doctoral Merit Award in the same year. During 1990 Jiyane was a summer associate at the Covington and Burling law firm in Washington DC.

During his years in the United States of America, Jiyane remained a member of the PAC but sympathised with the Inkatha Freedom Party (IFP) and corresponded with Buthelezi regarding the escalating violence. Although he had become a Marxist, Jiyane began to be disillusioned by the incoherence of some of its theories. Having personally witnessed the hardships and sadness of people in Eastern Europe before the collapse of communism, he perceived a huge disparity between communist theory and practice. He began to believe that Marxist theories were not flawless and that a system of free enterprise was preferable.

In January 1992 Jiyane returned to South Africa on a grant from the United Nations. He became a senior lecturer in Political Science and Public Administration at the University of Zululand and was a lecturer and consultant in the political leadership programme of the Institute for Multi-party Democracy.

In May 1993 he formally rejoined the IFP, of which he had been a founder member, and was appointed to its central committee and central committee executive in July 1993. He was appointed IFP spokesperson in the same month. He became legal and political adviser to the KwaZulu government and IFP delegations to the Multi-Party Negotiations Forum and served as communications director of the IFP Elections Committee in 1993. In November 1993 Jiyane was appointed national political director of the IFP. This involved press liaison, managing the party's national structures and conducting branch and regional elections.

In the April 1994 general election, Jiyane stood as number nine candidate on the IFP's election list to the national assembly and became a member of parliament.

At the IFP's annual conference in Ulundi on 17 July 1994, Jiyane was elected IFP secretary general. This position had been vacant since the resignation of Oscar Dhlomo in 1990 and was re-established to deal with wide-ranging changes to the party's constitution. The party's central committee was to be replaced by a national council and a 13-person national executive committee consisting of IFP members elected through branch, constituency, regional and provincial structures.

In 1993 Jiyane married Zodwa Dlamini who is studying Pedagogics at the University of Zululand and they have one son, Nkululeko (Freedom). He continues to maintain a keen interst in soccer, being a supporter of Kaiser Chiefs. He also enjoys reading on the subjects of politics, social issues, law, religion and philosophy; public speaking; listening to gospel music and African rhythms; and playing chess.

SOURCES

1. *People in Politics*, 1st Quarter 1994, Institute for Democracy in South Africa (Idasa), Durban, 1994.
2. *Daily News*, 18 July 1994.

PALLO ZWELEDINGA JORDAN

Member of Parliament,
African National Congress,
1994.
Minister of Posts,
Telecommunications and
Broadcasting, 1994.

Pallo Jordan was born in B Location, Kroonstad, Orange Free State, on 22 May 1942, the son of Priscilla Phyllis (born Ntantala), a teacher who subsequently became a researcher and lecturer, and Dr Archibald Campbell Jordan, a lecturer in Bantu Languages at Fort Hare University College.

Jordan spent his early years in Kroonstad and Alice before his father was appointed senior lecturer in African Languages at the University of Cape Town. The family moved to Cape Town and Jordan attended St Marks Primary School and Athlone High School.

Jordan came from a highly politicised family, with both parents prominent members of the Non-European Unity Movement. At age seven he began selling *Torch*, a newspaper produced by the All-African Convention. Jordan's political views matured in the mid-1950s following the Suez crisis and Ghana's independence, and he was strongly influenced by the Modern Youth Society, a Congress-inclined youth organisation of that time.

Jordan enrolled at the University of Cape Town and during this time was active in the Modern World Society, and began a serious study of Marxist classics. Jordan joined the African National Congress (ANC) in 1960.

In the early 1960s his father received a Carnegie fellowship but was refused a passport to travel abroad. He therefore left the country via Botswana. Jordan left South Africa in September 1962 and completed a degree at the University of Wisconsin, Madison, and a post-graduate degree at the London School of Economics.

While in the US, Jordan came under the influence of those espousing ideas of the non-communist Marxist currents associated with the 'New Left'. He also became active in the anti-Vietnam war campaigns.

Jordan began to work full-time for the ANC in 1975 in London as a member of the research unit of the Department of Information and Publicity (DIP). From 1977-79 he headed Radio Freedom, based in Luanda, Angola. In 1980 he moved to Lusaka to head the DIP's research unit.

In the early 1980s, the ANC's security department detained Jordan in Lusaka for six weeks.

In 1984 Jordan served on the conference preparatory committee for the ANC's 1985 Kabwe Conference, where he was elected to the organisation's national executive committee.

That year he became deputy director of the DIP as well as administrative secretary of the NEC's secretariat. From 1985-89 Jordan served as convener of the ANC's strategy and tactics committee and also served on the sub-committee on negotiations and constitutional guidelines. When Johnny Makathini died in 1989, Thabo Mbeki replaced him as head of the ANC's Department of Foreign Affairs. In turn, Jordan took over Mbeki's post as director of the Department of Information and Publicity.

Following the unbanning of the ANC in February 1990, Jordan returned to South Africa. At the ANC's national conference held in Durban in July 1991 Jordan was re-elected to the organisation's national executive committee. He also serves on the ANC's national working committee.

In December 1991 Jordan represented the ANC on the Convention for a Democratic South Africa (Codesa) working committee dealing with time-frames and implementation of decisions.

Jordan, a prolific writer, has been published in various journals. He has also written a number of articles for the ANC publication, *Sechaba*. While attending a conference on South Africa in December 1989 in Paris he addressed a sitting of the French National Assembly on behalf of the ANC.

In July 1990, Jordan caused a stir when he published an article harshly criticising SACP leader Joe Slovo's reassessment of socialism. Jordan argued that Slovo had misunderstood the historical context of the Russian revolution, and attacked previous practices of the South African Communist Party.

In 1992 Jordan was appointed to serve on the ANC's civil service commission and its elections commission. In November 1992 he criticised the ANC's paper entitled 'Strategic Perspective' on its strategy for negotiations. The ideas in the paper were originally conceived by Joe Slovo and subsequently refined by top ANC negotiators, including Mac

Maharaj and Thabo Mbeki. The strategy included a general amnesty for the future and the protection of existing public service job contracts, as well as a 'sunset clause' that would provide for compulsory power-sharing for a fixed number of years in the period immediately following the adoption of the constitution. In response Jordan produced a document of his own in which he described the authors of 'Strategic Perspective' as confused and ignorant of the history of the 20th century. He argued that long-held ANC goals aimed not only at the creation of a democratic state, but also the dismemberment of the racist state.

In the April 1994 general election, Jordan stood as the ANC's number five candidate for the national assembly and became a member of parliament. In May he was appointed Minister of Posts, Telecommunications and Broadcasting.

At the December 1994 ANC conference Jordan was re-elected to the organisation's national executive committee.

Jordan is separated from his wife and has one daughter, Nandipha Esther.

SOURCES

1. *Curricula vitae* submitted by Pallo Jordan, May 1990 and July 1994.
2. *Weekly Mail*, 23 August 1991.
3. *Sunday Times*, 8 November 1992.
4. *Profile 94*, South African Communication Services, Pretoria, 1994.

RONALD KASRILS

Member of Parliament,
African National Congress, 1994.
Deputy Minister of Defence,
1994.

Born on 15 November 1938 in Yeoville, Johannesburg, Ronnie Kasrils was the son of Rene (born Cohen) and Isidore Kasrils, a Lithuanian immigrant who came to South Africa as an infant in 1900. Kasrils' father was a commercial traveller and strong union supporter, who was a member of the National Union of Commercial Travellers.

Kasrils grew up during the war years and although he was very young, this left a deep impact on him. He learnt about anti-semitism and compared this to racism in South Africa. Kasrils attended Yeoville Boys' Primary School and King Edward VII High School, matriculating in 1956.

After he left school, Kasrils developed extensive social contacts with blacks and felt that he had been able to avoid the constraints of the colour bar. However, he was extremely shocked by the Sharpeville shootings which convinced him to become politically involved, and in 1961 he joined the South African Communist Party (SACP), at that stage an unlawful organisation in South Africa.

From 1957-58 Kasrils was an articled clerk with a law firm, studying part-time, but left to work as a film script writer. In 1960 he moved to an advertising agency in Durban to work in its film and television division and remained there until his arrest in 1962 when he was charged with contravening the Pondoland emergency regulations.

Kasrils, who was by then secretary of the Congress of Democrats (COD) in Natal, was tried together with the organisation's chairman and treasurer. The preparatory examination was held at Flagstaff in the Transkei, and the trial continued in Kokstad where they were acquitted of the charges. He was fired from his advertising job after the trial. In July 1961 Kasrils joined Umkhonto we Sizwe (MK). In 1962 he received a five-year banning order prohibiting him from public speaking. The Congress of Democrats was itself banned in April 1962.

Kasrils became a member of the regional command of MK under the leadership of Curnick Ndlovu and Billy Nair. He participated in a number of operations, including a raid on a road construction site for dynamite. He was active in sabotaging electric pylons around Durban which resulted in the cutting off of light and electricity in the city.

In 1963 Kasrils enrolled at the University of Natal, Durban, to study towards a BA degree. However, the 90-day detention clause was about to become law, and Kasrils knew that the security police wanted to arrest him together with Billy Nair and Curnick Ndlovu. He managed to evade arrest by using a trap door in his bedroom and hiding under the floorboards when police raided his home.

During his brief period at the university Kasrils joined the cross-country club and was due to run in the South African cross-country championship when he was forced to go underground in June 1963. He remained in hiding until October when the movement's leadership asked him to leave the country to undergo military training.

Kasrils's wife Eleanor (born Logan) had been arrested in August 1963, but managed to escape from police custody, and they left South Africa together in October 1963.

From the years 1963-90 Kasrils worked for the African National Congress (ANC). He underwent military training in 1964 in the USSR and at the end of 1965 was sent to London to work for the movement there. During this time Kasrils worked with Yusuf Dadoo, Joe Slovo and Jack Hodgson and they formed a special committee (1966-76) to develop underground activities in South Africa from the United Kingdom. During this time he trained various people including Raymond Suttner, Jeremy Cronin, Ahmed Timol, Alex Moumbaris, Tim Jenkins and Dave and Sue Rabkin, with the aim of establishing underground propaganda units in South Africa.

In 1977 Kasrils was transferred to Angola where he lived in the ANC camps for three years. He served as political instructor to the Soweto generation who left South Africa following the 1976 uprising, and became the MK regional commissar in Angola.

In 1980 Kasrils was transferred to Maputo to help develop the underground and in 1983 became head of military intelligence and a member of the political-military council of the ANC in Lusaka in 1985.

In 1987 Kasrils was co-opted onto the national executive committee of the ANC with the portfolio of military intelligence.

At the beginning of 1990, prior to the unbanning of the ANC and the SACP, Kasrils returned to South Africa to participate in Operation

Vulindlela (Vula). He was underground in Durban when the Groote Schuur talks between the government and the ANC took place, after which indemnity was given to the whole national executive committee. At that time Kasrils was at a consultative conference of the internal SACP underground discussing how the party should re-emerge. Shortly after, in June, the ANC leadership instructed Kasrils and Mac Maharaj, another NEC member, to leave South Africa secretly so that they could return publicly and legally.

On 18 June Kasrils publicly entered South Africa and was given a position in the organising department of the ANC, working in its headquarters in Johannesburg.

In July some of his colleagues on the Vula project were arrested in Durban, and police learned about his previously-illegal presence in the country. While Maharaj was arrested, Kasrils continued to operate underground. Police described him as 'armed and dangerous' and offered a reward for his capture. His indemnity was withdrawn but reinstated in June 1991. He emerged to participate in the July 1991 conference of the ANC held in Durban and he was elected to the national executive committee of the ANC with the seventh highest number of votes.

Kasrils then worked in the organising department of the ANC with the portfolio of campaigns. Following the breakdown of the Convention for a Democratic South Africa (Codesa) negotiations in May 1992, the ANC/SACP/Cosatu alliance launched a mass action campaign to pressure the government into accepting a transitional government and constituent assembly, and to take firm steps to end political violence. Kasrils was appointed national organiser of this campaign which included rallies on Soweto Day (16 June), a stayaway (29 June) in the Transvaal to commemorate the Boipatong massacre, a two-day national stayaway on 3-4 August, and marches and demonstrations in all major cities.

The mass action campaign also involved a march on Bisho, capital of Ciskei, on 7 September 1992. Restrictions were placed on the march to prevent participants from reaching the headquarters of Oupa Gqozo, Ciskei's military ruler, and they were diverted to Independence Stadium. Kasrils attempted to lead a group of people to the central business district of Bisho through a gap in the stadium fence. Without warning, members of the Ciskei Security Force opened fire on the group and 29 were killed, and hundreds injured. Kasrils was harshly criticised for his role in the march, but the ANC did not take action against him.

Since 1979 Kasrils has been a member of the central committee of the SACP and since 29 July 1990 has served on its interim leadership group. In December 1991, at the party congress, he was re-elected to the central committee and also serves on the party's politburo (the executive of the central committee).

At the SACP's ninth congress held in April 1995, Kasrils was again re-elected to the party's central committee.

Kasrils is a prolific writer, publishing regularly in the *African Communist* under the pseudonym of Alexander Sibeko. He has also published poetry under the name of ANC Khumalo. Publications under his own name include *Dear Bertrand Russell* and *Bertrand Russell's America*. In 1993 his autobiography *Armed and Dangerous* was published.

Prior to the first democratic general election in April 1994, Kasrils worked in the ANC's electoral commission and was a member of MK's team negotiating with the South African Defence Force on issues dealing with integration and the future of the force. From December 1993-April 1994 Kasrils served on the defence sub-council of the transitional executive council established to level the playing fields in the run-up to the election.

In the general election Kasrils stood as candidate number eight on the ANC list for the national assembly and became a member of parliament. In June he was appointed Deputy Minister of Defence.

Kasrils is married to Eleanor (born Logan) and has two sons and a stepdaughter.

SOURCES

1. Interviewed 17 November 1991, Durban.
2. *Daily News*, 9 September 1992.
3. *Weekly Mail*, 11 September 1992.
4. *Natal Mercury*, 1 October 1992.
5. Anton Harber and Barbara Ludman (eds), *A-Z of South African Politics*, *Weekly Mail & Guardian*/Penguin Books, Johannesburg, 1994.

THEMBA KHOZA

Member of Parliament,
Inkatha Freedom Party,
1994.

Thembinkosi Samson Khoza was born on 17 May 1959 in Eshowe, Zululand. He was one of three children born to Alfred Mkhohlweni Khoza, a Zulu headman, and his third of six wives, Phillipina Khonzaphi Khoza.

Khoza started his education at the Samungu Primary School in Eshowe and in 1980 matriculated from the Ndluyesilo High School. In 1981-82 he enrolled at the Isithebe Training Centre where he acquired a Technical Teaching Certificate in industrial skills.

Khoza moved to Johannesburg in search of employment in 1983. He joined Excludex furniture manufacturers in the same year and worked as a sales person in the company until 1985. During this period he became involved in the Metal and Allied Workers' Union (Mawu). By 1986 Khoza had joined SA Perm as a clerk, later to be promoted to the position of promotion officer, where he was responsible for public as well as in-house promotions. In 1989 Khoza was asked to join labour consultants, Brentwood Associates, as a training officer, specialising in communication skills. After a year he left to become a full-time organiser for Inkatha.

In January 1990 Khoza opened the first organisational office of Inkatha in Johannesburg. At the same time he established an employment agency under the auspices of the Inkatha Youth Project. He encouraged businessmen to employ IFP youth members, describing the venture as a self-upliftment project with Inkatha supplying a labour force while at the same time promoting the training of unskilled workers.

Acording to Khoza, lack of communication between Inkatha branches was the biggest obstacle he faced as the first full-time grassroots organiser for Inkatha on the Witwatersrand. Having established a 'nerve centre', Khoza claims that Inkatha grew rapidly in the Transvaal. In July 1990 Inkatha transformed itself into the Inkatha Freedom Party.

Khoza traces his political awareness to his childhood, which was filled with stories about the victorious battle of Isandlwana, where Zulu forces defeated the British. His great-grandfather was killed in this battle. Khoza's mother is a descendent of the Zulu royal family, while one of his father's ancestors, Mfusi Khoza, was prominent in the fight against the reduction of the Zulu kingdom during King Cetshwayo's period of exile. Although politically minded, Khoza was not exposed to national politics until he attended an Inkatha meeting in 1975 when he joined the organisation's youth brigade.

In the mid-1970s Khoza was attracted to the Black Consciousness movement and Africanism. However, the formation of the United Democratic Front (UDF) in August 1983 entrenched Khoza's commitment to Inkatha. Khoza maintains that he initially welcomed the UDF, but later regarded it as a divisive factor in the black community.

He again started attending Inkatha meetings and was elected onto the executive of its Meadowlands branch in 1985. Later the same year, he was elected regional youth leader for the area covering Johannesburg, Krugersdorp, Roodepoort and Soweto. Khoza identified his main task as reorganising Inkatha and mobilising youth structures.

He maintains that the youth became the uniting force in Inkatha and by 1989 the organisation was well established in the Transvaal. In the same year he was nominated Transvaal youth leader, a position which allowed him to expand his organisational influence. In 1991 Khoza was voted onto the central committee of the IFP.

In September 1990, during township violence in the Vaal, Khoza was accused of supplying weapons to Sebokeng hostel inmates. He stood trial after police found arms, including AK47 rifles, in the boot of his car. In January 1992 he was acquitted on charges of illegal possession of firearms, ammunition and explosives. In May 1992 Khoza was arrested after attempting to avoid a police roadblock in Meadowlands. He was charged with reckless driving and defeating the ends of justice.

After the signing of the National Peace Accord in 1991, Khoza became active in negotiations on violence in the National Peace Committee and represented the IFP on the Local Dispute Resolution Committee in Soweto. As an IFP central committee member, Khoza also served on the party's negotiation secretariat, an advisory body to the IFP negotiating team and the transition committee which focused on building the IFP into a political party.

In 1994 Khoza and another IFP member, Victor Ndlovu, were named in a Goldstone Commission report as members of a gunrunning network involved in destabilisation of the Reef. The report alleged that they formed links in the movement of arms from Namibia and Mozambique to hostel dwellers. It was further alleged that the arms were provided by a network controlled by Colonel Eugene de Kock, a former head of the Vlakplaas military base, and other senior police officials, including Lieutenant-General Basie Smit, Major-General Krappies Engelbrecht and former Kwazulu police commissioner, General Jac Buchner. It was reported that Khoza and Ndlovu were paid under false names as informers. Khoza denied these allegations.

In the general election of April 1994, Khoza stood as an IFP PWV regional candidate for the national assembly and became a member of parliament.

Khoza is a devout Christian and an active member of the Rhema Church. He is unmarried and lives in Soweto.

SOURCES

1. *People in Politics*, First Quarter 1992, Institute for Democracy in South Africa (Idasa), Durban, 1992.
2. *Weekly Mail*, 30 January 1992.
3. *Sunday Times*, 20 March 1994.
4. *Weekly Mail*, 25 March 1994.

HERMANUS JACOBUS KRIEL

Minister of Law and Order,
1991-94.
1994-95.
Premier, Western Cape Province,
1994.

Born in Kakamas, Cape, on 14 November 1941, Hernus Kriel was the only child of Rachel Catarina (born Jacobs) and Cornelius Johannes Kriel, a minister.

The family left Kakamas when Kriel was seven years old and moved to Wellington where he attended primary and senior school, matriculating from Huguenot High School in 1959. Kriel studied at the University of Stellenbosch from 1960-64 where he completed his BA and LLB degrees. After graduating, Kriel worked as a state prosecutor in Bellville for six months. He then travelled through Europe for six months, during which time he attended the South West Africa case at the International Court of Justice, The Hague, Netherlands.

On his return, Kriel completed his legal articles with a Goodwood firm of attorneys from 1966-67, and in 1968 opened his own practice in Parow. He remained in the profession for ten years before becoming involved in ocean diamond mining between 1978 and 1980. When he sold his business interests he joined the Cape Town Bar as an advocate. He left the Bar in 1981 after his election to the executive committee of the Cape Provincial Council.

While a student at the University of Stellenbosch, Kriel was a staunch supporter of the National Party (NP). He became more involved in party structures when he opened his legal practice, serving as chairman of the Parow branch of the NP.

In 1974 he was elected to the Cape Divisional Council, becoming chairman of finance in 1975. In 1977 he became chairman of the divisional council, but resigned in November of that year following his election to the provincial council. He was re-elected to the divisional council in 1981, becoming an executive committee member. In 1984 Kriel won the parliamentary by-election in Parow after Pen Kotze, who had held the seat, had resigned to take up his appointment as deputy chairman of the President's Council.

Kriel's father, a missionary in the coloured community, had conveyed his opposition to the strict petty apartheid of the Verwoerd era to his son. Kriel, who believes that John Vorster was the father of political reform in South Africa, supported Vorster's application of the theory of separate development. Other influences on Kriel's political ideals were Professor Nic Olivier, who taught Kriel at Stellenbosch, and Pen Kotze, with whom Kriel worked closely in the Parow NP.

As an MP, Kriel was a member of the following study groups of the NP caucus: law and order; constitutional affairs (vice-chairman); trade and industry; environmental affairs; and local government and housing (vice-chairman). In addition, he was chairman of the Cape provincial joint committee, and a member of the constitutional affairs standing committee and the constitutional development and planning standing committee. During 1988 he served as a member of the commission on the Promotion of Orderly Internal Politics Bill. Following the September 1989 general election, Kriel was appointed Minister of Planning and Provincial Affairs. In this portfolio he dealt with the scrapping of the Separate Amenities Act during the 1990 session of parliament.

Following the July 1991 controversy surrounding government funding of Inkatha rallies, Kriel was appointed Minister of Law and Order, replacing Adriaan Vlok. In this capacity he represented the South African government on the Convention for a Democratic South Africa (Codesa) working committee dealing with the creation of a climate for free political participation and the role of the international community.

In 1993, while multi-party negotiations were in progress, a police raid took place on Pan-Africanist Congress activists and several leaders were arrested, including the organisation's key negotiator, Benny Alexander. Kriel was summoned by the multi-party negotiating council to account for police actions. He responded by pointing out that the PAC was talking peace at the World Trade Centre while propagating and waging a racist terrorist campaign against civilians and security forces.

In the general election of April 1994, Kriel led the NP list for the Western Cape regional legislature and was elected premier of the region. He pledged himself to reconciliation with political opponents and co-operation with the central government.

Kriel, who is divorced, has two daughters and a son.

SOURCES

1. *Sunday Star*, 19 November 1989.
2. Interviewed 16 June 1988, Cape Town.
3. *Daily News*, 28 May 1993.
4. *Natal Witness*, 4 May 1994.
3. Author's research undertaken for the Institute for Democracy in South Africa (Idasa), 1994.

MOSIUOA PATRICK 'TERROR' LEKOTA

Premier, Free State Province, 1994.

'Terror' Lekota, the first of the seven children of Mamasiuoa, a domestic worker, and Meshack Lekota, a truck driver, was born on 13 August 1948 in Kroonstad, Orange Free State, where he grew up. As a young child he walked 14 miles a day to and from the farm school which he and the other children attended. He then attended a Catholic school and completed Standard Eight in Matatiele, Transkei. In 1968 he enrolled at St Francis College, Mariannhill (near Pinetown, Natal) where he matriculated in 1969.

While at school Lekota began to be aware of sport segregation, and his political awareness grew when former students of St Francis College came to help tutor matriculation pupils. One of the tutors was Steve Biko, leader of the Black Consciousness South African Students' Organisation (Saso), who had a major influence on Lekota's political views.

In 1970 he worked part-time as a teacher at St Francis College before enrolling at Turfloop (University of the North) to study law. However, he left the university for financial reasons and took a position as a court interpreter. At this time he also played for a semi-professional soccer team, Clermont Home Defenders, in Durban.

In 1972 Lekota returned to the University of the North to study for a social science degree. In that year he was elected to the Students' Representative Council (SRC).

Following the expulsion of Saso organiser, Abram Ongepotse Tiro, from the university, the SRC called a boycott. University authorities responded by closing the university, sending students home, and expelling members of the SRC.

Because he was prohibited from returning to university, Lekota took a job as a teller at the South African Permanent Building Society in Pinetown, in 1973. He resigned from the job at the end of the year to fill the post left vacant after Tiro had gone into exile following police harassment. Lekota remained permanent organiser for Saso until his arrest in September 1974.

Following the holding of pro-Frelimo rallies in September 1974, Lekota and eight other Black Consciousness leaders were charged under the Terrorism Act. After a 17-month trial, he was found guilty of conspiring to commit acts capable of endangering the maintenance of law and order and was sentenced to six years imprisonment, which he served on Robben Island. He was released in December 1982. Between 1974 and 1982, Lekota broadened his political perspective to embrace non-racialism and a commitment to the African National Congress's Freedom Charter.

In 1983 Lekota joined the Release Mandela Campaign and was elected national publicity secretary for the recently-formed United Democratic Front (UDF). He played a prominent role in the campaign for a 'No' vote in the 1983 whites-only referendum on a new constitution for a tricameral constitution and the boycott of the 1984 elections to the Houses of Delegates and Representatives. He was detained briefly in October 1983. In August 1984, just prior to the tricameral elections, police detained Lekota. Lekota was again detained in April 1985, and in June he and 21 others were charged with treason. During the course of the trial, held in Pretoria and Delmas, Eastern Transvaal, Lekota was denied bail several times on grounds that he posed a threat to state security. He and his co-accused were alleged to have conspired with each other, the African National Congress (ANC) and the South African Communist Party, to promote national unrest in order to overthrow the government by revolutionary means.

In November 1988 Lekota and four of the other accused were convicted of treason. Lekota was sentenced to a 12-year jail sentence.

However, those convicted were granted leave to appeal, and on 15 December 1989 the Appeal Court quashed all the convictions. In April 1990, following the February unbanning of the ANC, Lekota was appointed its convener for the Southern Natal region. Shortly after that, he was asked to chair the ANC's convening committee in Southern Natal. As a result of these appointments, he also served on the ANC's interim leadership committee. During this time Lekota helped to establish over 60 ANC branches in the area. In addition, he was centrally involved in attempts to establish a peace initiative in Natal.

In December 1990, the ANC asked Lekota to move to the northern Orange Free State to help build the organisation in that province. In May 1991 he was transferred to the ANC's Department of Information and Publicity, based in Johannesburg.

At the July 1991 ANC conference held in Durban, Lekota was elected to the organisation's national executive committee and also served on its national working committee. In August 1991 he was appointed chief of intelligence for the ANC, and deputy in its Department of Security and Intelligence. In the same month, he published a book of his prison letters, written to his daughter while he was in jail.

In September 1992 Lekota was appointed deputy head of the ANC's elections department and played a key role in its national campaign up to the first democratic elections of April 1994. In those elections Lekota stood as ANC leader in the Free State and became that region's premier.

In November 1994 Lekota lost the vote for chairperson of the ANC's Free State region at its provincial congress. He was beaten by Pat Matosa in a tense election and some ANC members indicated that the result was a reflection of members' attitudes to Lekota's reconciliatory attitude towards whites. Others indicated that they believed the governmental and political posts should be separated. He remains a member of the ANC's provincial executive committee.

At the ANC conference held in Bloemfontein in December 1994, Lekota was re-elected to the organisation's national executive committee.

Lekota (nicknamed 'Terror' as a result of his soccer-playing skills) is married to Cynthia and they have four children.

SOURCES

1. South African Institute of Race Relations, *Race Relations Survey, 1983*, Johannesburg, 1984.
2. *Rand Daily Mail*, 31 October 1983.
3. *Daily News*, 25 August 1984.

4. *Weekly Mail*, 2 May 1986.
5. *Frontline*, June 1987.
6. *Natal Mercury*, 16 December 1989.
7. *Learn and Teach*, March 1992.
8. Discussion with Terror Lekota, 13 March 1992, Durban.
9. *Natal Witness*, 28 November 1994.

ANTHONY JAMES LEON

Member of Parliament,
Democratic Party, 1994.
Leader, Democratic Party,
1994.

Born on 15 December 1956 in Durban, Tony Leon is the youngest of the two sons of Sheila Jean Schulz (born Herman) and Ramon Nigel Leon, a retired Supreme Court judge. His parents were both politically active, his father serving as the first Natal chairman of the Progressive Party and his mother an activist in organisations such as the Black Sash and the South African Institute of Race Relations.

Leon became fascinated by electoral politics from a young age and assisted his parents in political campaigns from the age of 12. He was also an active member of the Young Progressives.

He attended Kearsney College in Botha's Hill, Natal. Considered a rebel, he did not distinguish himself academically at school, matriculating in 1974.

Leon then enrolled at the University of the Witwatersrand for a BA degree majoring in Political Science. He not only distinguished himself academically, but also took an active part in student politics. He served four terms on the Students' Representative Council (SRC), including one as vice-president, and during this time became involved in intense debate around the ideological differences between liberals, and left and right wingers.

Leon had initially avoided law studies, because of his father's prominence in the profession and because his brother had excelled as a law student, winning a scholarship to Cambridge. While contemplating doing his honours degree in Political Science, Leon decided that he needed to qualify for a profession and registered as a LLB student. He completed his degree in 1982 having won the jurisprudence prize for conflict of laws and the Moot Court contests twice in succession.

Leon then worked for three years as an articled clerk and professional assistant for the Johannesburg law firm with which he is still associated. In 1986 Professor Louise Tager, dean of the Law faculty at the University of the Witwatersrand, encouraged him to apply for a lectureship in constitutional and human rights law.

Shortly after joining the faculty, he was persuaded to stand in the municipal by-election in the Bellevue constituency. The Progressive Federal Party (PFP) campaigned under very difficult circumstances. It was shortly after the party's leader had resigned and Leon's opponent, Sam Bloomberg, received considerable publicity for his work among potential suicide cases. Leon won the seat by 39 votes.

During 1988 he was elected leader of the PFP caucus in the city council and in the city-wide elections of that year he won the seat for Houghton. After the PFP's resounding defeat in the 1987 general election, when the Conservative Party became the official opposition, PFP members were demoralised. Leon, however, put together a strong team for the municipal elections and managed to regain voter support.

In 1989, shortly after the formation of the Democratic Party, an amalgamation of the PFP, the National Democratic Movement and the Independent Party, Leon was faced with a difficult decision when Helen Suzman retired as member of parliament for Houghton. Activists from the constituency asked him to stand for nomination as candidate, despite another candidate being favoured by the senior party hierarchy. The major changes taking place in South African politics and a belief that the 1989 election would be the last of its kind, persuaded Leon to risk a successful and comfortable career in local politics and law and to stand for nomination. He won the nomination contest and went on to win the seat with a 6 000 majority.

During the negotiations preceding the first democratic elections, Leon argued strongly for free market guarantees in the Charter of Fundamental Human Rights and took the technical committee to task for emphasising equality, rather than freedom. He also led and won the fight against the proposal that the cabinet appoint constitutional court judges.

In the 1994 democratic election, Leon was placed second on the DP's

list of candidates for the national assembly and was returned to
parliament. The DP was unable to extend its traditional support and
achieved only seven seats in the Assembly. The DP leader, Zac de Beer,
immediately announced his resignation and Leon was elected acting
leader of the party.

At the DP's national congress later in the year, Leon was elected party
leader.

Because of logistical problems concerning the DP's small
representation in parliament, Leon believes that members of parliament
will have to use their ingenuity to continue to play a role. With only six
per cent of parliamentarians outside the government of national unity,
this will be vital to ensure that parliamentary democracy and public
accountability are upheld. Major problems are the lack of speaking time
and resources to cover the work of 27 ministerial departments.

Leon hopes to expand the DP's liberal democratic base and believes
that a party or political movement which promotes the individual will
have an increasingly important role to play in future politics.

Leon is unmarried and lives in Johannesburg.

SOURCE

People in Politics, 3rd Quarter 1994, Institute for Democracy in South Africa
(Idasa), Durban, 1994.

CHRISTO FERRO LIEBENBERG

Minister of Finance,
October, 1994.

Born on 2 October 1934 in Touwsriver, Cape, Chris Liebenberg is the son of Christiaan Rudolf Liebenberg and Helene Henrietta Liebenberg (born Griessel). He matriculated at Worcester Boys' High School in 1951.

He joined Nedbank in Cape Town (Barrack Street branch) on 12 January 1952 and in the late 1950s worked for Nedbank in London and the Nederlandsche Oorzee Bank in Amsterdam, Rotterdam and Hamburg before returning in 1967 as sub-manager at Cape Town's St George's Street branch. In 1971 he served as a trainee with the Banker's Trust in New York and subsequently became manager of the Strand Street, Cape Town branch.

After spending some time in New York with Morgan Guaranty, he returned to South Africa in 1981 as general manager Advances/ Corporate Banking. In 1986 he was promoted to senior general manager of this division and in 1988 became its managing director when the bank merged with the Perm. In 1990 he became chief executive officer of Nedcor, retiring in February 1994. He was also chairman of Syfrets and served as director of various other companies. Liebenberg has undertaken training at Cranfield School of Management (UK), Insead (France) and Harvard. He has completed his CAIB (SA); his AMP (Harvard) and AMP (Insead); and PMD (Cranfield).

In 1990 he expressed the view that South Africa no longer required the financial rand and that it should be done away with as he felt the negative effects of the two-tier currency outweighed the positive. He believed that although the finrand attracted foreign investment, he was concerned that local investors had difficulty competing with foreigners for local investments. At his last Nedcor annual general meeting in 1993, Liebenberg put forward his view that business needed to be involved in the changes in South Africa and that the country's financial services markets had to comply with international standards to maintain confidence in the country's banking system.

Liebenberg played a role in assisting the African National Congress (ANC) in its investigation of various aspects of economic policy, especially the position of the banking industry.

Following the shock resignation of the Minister of Finance, Derek Keys, it was announced on 6 July 1994 that Liebenberg would take over as Minister when Keys left in October. President Nelson Mandela announced that Liebenberg would not be involved in party politics and that another cabinet post would be created to accommodate the National Party.

Liebenberg has also held the following positions: chairman, Credit Guarantee Insurance Corporation; director, Nedcor; director, Mutual and Federal Insurance Company; director, Oceana Fishing Group; member, Policy Board for Financial Services and Regulation; member, council University of Stellenbosch School of Business; chairman, Salvation Army National Advisory Board.

He is married to Elly and they have two sons.

SOURCES

1. *Financial Mail*, 6 April 1990.
2. *Natal Witness*, 6 July 1994.
3. *Natal Mercury*, 6 July 1994.
4. *Natal Mercury*, 7 July 1994.
5. *Profile 94*, South African Communication Services, Pretoria, 1994.

BRIGITTE SYLVIA MABANDLA

Member of Parliament,
African National Congress, 1994.
Deputy Minister of Arts,
Culture, Science and Technology,
1995.

Brigitte Mabandla obtained her LLB degree from the University of Zambia in 1979, having been excluded from the University of the North because of her political activities in the Black Consciousness South African Students' Organisation (Saso). In 1974, following the independence of Mozambique, she was involved in the organisation of pro-Frelimo rallies and was subsequently detained and banned.

Mabandla spent a number of years teaching law in Botswana and during this time was involved in the underground structures of the African National Congress (ANC).

In 1986 she became a member of the ANC's Legal and Constitutional Affairs department, based in Lusaka. She was also active in the ANC's Women's Section.

Mabandla returned to South Africa after the unbanning of the ANC in February 1990 and served on its Legal and Constitutional Committee. As a result, she became involved in the negotiations process. Her work also focused on research and policy development regarding constitutional recognition of social and economic rights, particularly those dealing with gender and children.

In pursuit of these interests, she became a founder member of the National Committee for the Rights of the Child and of the National Women's Coalition and worked with national and international agencies in these fields.

In the April 1994 elections she stood as an ANC canditate and became a member of parliament. In this capacity, she became a member of the management committee of the Constitutional Assembly; the parliamentary Rules Committee; the committee on Constitutional Affairs (including provincial affairs and local government) and the Justice Committee. She also served on the select committee on Abortion and Sterilisation. Mabandla also headed the Gender Project of the Community Law Centre of the University of the Western Cape.

At the December 1994 conference of the ANC in Bloemfontein, she was elected to the organisation's national executive committee.

Following the dismissal of Winnie Mandela as Deputy Minister of Arts, Culture, Science and Technology at the end of March 1995, Mabandla was appointed to that post.

SOURCES

1. *The Argus*, 28 March 1995.
2. *The Women's Directory*, Political Addendum 1994-95, *Femina* in association with Old Mutual, 1995.
3. SABC radio interview with Pippa Green, 28 March 1995.

PENUELL MPAPA MADUNA

Member of Parliament,
African National Congress, 1994.
Deputy Minister of Home
Affairs, 1994.

Penuell Maduna was born in Johannesburg on 29 December 1952, the younger of two brothers. His father died when he was very young and his uncle, who acted as patriarch of an extended family of cousins living in his house, filled the role of a father-figure. His mother, Priscilla, was a domestic worker in Langlaagte.

Although poor, the household was filled with life and activity. Maduna's grandmother was a card-carrying member of the African National Congress (ANC) until her death, and she cherished the signatures of Chief Albert Luthuli and Oliver Tambo to such an extent that she refused to relinquish her membership card when the organisation was banned. Her close friend was a banned member of the ANC and the young Maduna became aware of political issues by listening to their conversations. The poverty of township life compared with affluent white society, the pass laws, arrests and Bantu education were daily facts of life which further sensitised him politically, and the family often discussed these issues.

Being a bright scholar, Maduna was given the opportunity to attend the Eshowe Government Bantu School in Natal, after attending local primary schools. Education was highly regarded by his family and a love of reading was encouraged in all the children. Although it involved sacrifices, the family rallied round to help him take advantage of the opportunities offered by scholarships. He matriculated in 1972.

A bursary enabled Maduna to continue his studies at the University of Zululand. Following the class boycotts arising from the arrest of Black Consciousness student leader, Abraham Tiro, the leaders of the South African Students' Organisation (Saso) were expelled or detained. During his first year as a law student, Maduna was elected chairperson of the interim committee which had the task of reviving the Saso branch structures, and he chaired the committee until 1974.

During 1975-76 Maduna was elected to the Students' Representative Council (SRC) at a time when students and scholars all over the country revolted against the confines of Bantu education and the compulsory use of Afrikaans as a teaching medium in some subjects.

After a student meeting on 18 June 1976 to protest against the shooting of Soweto students on 16 June, certain buildings in the university were set on fire. Maduna was arrested and detained from 25 June 1976 until July 1977. He was charged under the Terrorism Act of 1967, but acquitted. Following his release, Maduna briefly participated in underground ANC activities, but was again arrested with others at the end of November. He was again charged and acquitted, and released in July 1979.

Maduna tried to continue his studies by registering with the University of South Africa (Unisa), but found it difficult to study while operating underground for the ANC. At the beginning of 1980, the ANC realised that Manduna's re-arrest was likely and an operative was sent to remove him from the country. His future wife, Nompumelelo Cheryl, whom he married in Swaziland, left the country with him.

Maduna re-registered with Unisa and continued his law studies during 1981-82 from Swaziland, where he was based. In order to justify his presence in the country, he also worked with a firm of attorneys who were sympathetic to the ANC. His wife was employed by the Swaziland government.

Maduna was, however, arrested with other ANC members during 1983 and held in Mawelawela Prison until deported from Swaziland. King Sobhuza II had protected the ANC members in the country, but after his death the government acted on pressure from South African authorities, and expelled ANC and Pan-Africanist Congress exiles.

Maduna subsequently worked for the ANC in Mozambique and Tanzania, where he was regional administrative secretary in the office of the ANC treasurer-general. During 1985 a friend, Judson Kuzwayo, requested that Maduna come to Zimbabwe to work there in the ANC office. While working in Harare, he completed his LLB degree at the University of Zimbabwe.

Maduna also worked as staff member in the ANC headquarters in Lusaka, Zambia, for six years. He represented the ANC at numerous international meetings and conferences and at the end of 1985 participated in the establishment of the ANC's Department of Legal and Constitutional Affairs. The focus of the legal department's work was to prepare for a future accessible legal system and to provide a legal perspective for the development of the constitution. The legal department also kept a watch on political trials in South Africa, liaised with lawyers working in the country and kept in touch with the International Defence and Aid Fund, an anti-apartheid organisation which raised funds for the defence of activists charged with political offences in South Africa.

As a founder member of the ANC's constitutional committee, Maduna played an active role in the formulation and adoption of the ANC's Constitutional Guidelines which laid the foundation for the organisation's current human rights orientation. During 1987 he attended Columbia University Law School in New York as a visiting scholar of constitutional law.

The ANC, aware that negotiations with the South African government might be a possibility in the future, began working on its constitutional guidelines towards the end of 1985.

From the mid-1980s, Maduna was a member of various ANC teams which met with white South Africans, meetings which further opened avenues for the formal negotiation process. He participated in the July 1987 Dakar meeting organised by Idasa, at which predominantly Afrikaans-speaking South Africans met with a group of ANC representatives, as well as the 1989 Oxfordshire meeting with members of the South African judiciary.

Maduna played an active role in the formulation, promotion and adoption of the ANC's Harare Declaration in 1989, in which the ANC spelled out its pre-conditions for negotiation with the South African government.

After the February 1990 unbanning of the ANC, the South African Communist Party and other proscribed organisations, and the release of Nelson Mandela, Maduna was part of a two-person delegation sent to South Africa in March 1990 to launch the process of talks that led to eventual negotiations. He was subsequently part of the ANC team which met with South African government representatives at Groote Schuur and Pretoria in May and August respectively to start the negotiation process. In February 1991 he was a member of the ANC team that participated in the DF Malan Airport talks where the ANC reaffirmed its commitment to its unilateral decision to suspend the armed struggle.

Maduna's return to South Africa was marred when shots were fired at him in Soweto and he was struck on the head by a panga in August 1990. A month later he was again attacked and his car stolen.

Maduna was an active role player in the formal negotiation process which led to the establishment of a democratic government. As such he played a vital part in the entire process that established the Convention for a Democratic South Africa (Codesa) in 1991-92.

After the Boipatong massacre in 1992 in which scores of residents were killed by attackers from nearby hostels, multi-party negotiations broke down. Maduna was a member of the team led by Cyril Ramaphosa of the ANC and Roelf Meyer of the South African government that revived the negotiation process. On 26 September 1992 Maduna was an ANC representative at the Mandela-De Klerk summit at which a Record of Understanding was adopted and the negotiations put back on track.

During the negotiation process at the World Trade Centre in 1993, Maduna played an active role in the development of the chapter on fundamental human rights which forms an important part of the interim constitution. This led to his co-authorship with Azhar Cachalia of the book *Fundamental Rights in the New Constitution* published in 1994.

Following the deaths of Chris Hani and President Oliver Tambo in 1993, Maduna was co-opted to fill one of the vacancies left on the ANC's national executive committee.

While part of the ANC's negotiating team at Codesa in 1992, Maduna completed his masters degree through the University of the Witwatersrand. He is currently undertaking a Higher Diploma in Tax Law at the university where he is a member of the Board of the Faculty of Law.

Maduna was elected to the national executive committee of the ANC at the organisation's Durban conference in July 1991. He was re-elected at the December 1994 conference.

Following the April 1994 general election in which Maduna stood as

an ANC candidate, he was appointed Deputy Minister of Home Affairs.
Maduna and his wife, Nompumelelo Cheryl, have two daughters and
a son. They live in Johannesburg.

SOURCES

1. Interviewed by Trudie du Toit, Cape Town, 1994.
2. *Profile 94*, South African Communication Services, Pretoria, 1994.

SATYANDRANATH RAGUNANAN 'MAC' MAHARAJ

Member of Parliament,
African National Congress, 1994.
Minister of Transport, 1994.

Mac Maharaj was born on 27 April 1935, the fourth of the eight children
of Mr and Mrs NR Maharaj of Newcastle, Natal. He matriculated at St
Oswald's School in 1952 and enrolled for a BA degree at the University
of Natal, Durban, as a part-time student.

While at university, Maharaj served on the Students' Representative
Council, campaigned against the segregation of students and supported
the boycott of the separate graduation ceremonies held at that time. In
addition he edited the student newspaper, *Student Call*, from 1955-56.
Maharaj completed his BA in 1955; in 1956 the 'Non-European' section
of the university opened a law faculty where he completed the first year
of an LLB. However, the faculty closed down in 1957.

Following the arrests of Congress leaders for the 1956 treason trial, Maharaj was asked to take over the running of the *New Age* newspaper. He decided to leave for the United Kingdom in August 1957 as he was unable to obtain a permit to study law in the Cape or the Transvaal. In 1959 he became a part-time student at the London School of Economics where he began his LLB again. In 1960, following the Sharpeville massacre, the Congress movement asked him to return to South Africa and devote himself more fully to political work. He returned to South Africa on 2 May 1962 with his first wife, Ompragash.

Maharaj worked for a firm of attorneys in Johannesburg while spending a great deal of his time on political matters. In July 1964, he was arrested in Johannesburg, charged and convicted with four others on charges of sabotage in what became known as the mini-Rivonia trial. Maharaj was sentenced to 12 years' imprisonment which he served on Robben Island. While in prison, he completed a BAdmin, an MBA and the second year of a BSc degree before his release on 8 December 1976.

On his release, Maharaj was served with a five-year banning order prohibiting him from leaving his Merebank, Durban, home at night. His wife had left the country in 1974 on an exit permit and was living in London.

Maharaj was refused permission to take up employment in central Durban and could therefore not earn a living. Following instructions from the ANC, he left South Africa in July 1977 and was deployed by the organisation in Lusaka. A senior official in the political department of the ANC, Maharaj was elected to its national executive committee at the 1985 Kabwe Conference.

From 1987 to 1990, Maharaj worked underground within South Africa, as part of Operation Vula. Following the unbanning of the ANC and the South African Communist Party in February 1990, he had to leave the country and re-enter legally under an indemnity from prosecution, agreed to between the ANC and the government. On his return, he assisted in the organisation and restructuring of the SACP. He appeared with the-then·SACP's general secretary Joe Slovo at a press conference when it was announced that the party would be calling its first legal conference in July 1990.

At this launch, held on 29 July 1990, it was announced that Maharaj was a member of the SACP's central committee, and he was also named as a member of the party's 22-person interim leadership group.

On 26 July 1990, just three days before the launch of the party, security police detained Maharaj in Johannesburg under section 29 of the Internal Security Act, following police allegations of an ANC/SACP/Umkhonto we Sizwe plan (code-named Operation Vula) to seize power in the event of the failure of ANC negotiations with the government. Initially charged under the Arms and Ammunition Act,

Maharaj had additional charges added later. In October 1990, Maharaj and eight others were charged with terrorism and, alternatively, illegal possession of arms, ammunition and explosives. It was alleged that they had conspired to create a national underground network to recruit, train, arm and lead a 'people's army' or 'revolutionary army' to seize power from the government by means of an armed insurrection. The accused were released in November 1990 on bail, and all charges dropped on 25 March 1991 after the accused had received partial immunity with respect to Operation Vula.

Following his release Maharaj resigned from his ANC and SACP posts and quit politics. However, he was re-elected to the ANC's national executive committee at the organisation's Durban conference in July 1991 and was re-elected in December 1994.

In 1991 Maharaj became a member of the secretariat of the Convention for a Democratic South Africa (Codesa) which brought together most South African political organisations to negotiate a new constitutional dispensation.

In 1994 he served as one of the joint executive secretaries of the Transitional Executive Council and in the April elections of that year stood as candidate number 16 on the ANC's national list to the national assembly.

In May 1994 Maharaj was appointed Minister of Transport in the government of national unity.

Maharaj is married to Zarina and they have two children.

SOURCES

1. Sean Moroney and Linda Ensor, *The Silenced*, South African Institute of Race Relations, Johannesburg, 1979.
2. *Daily News*, 8 December 1976.
3. *Daily News*, 18 March 1977.
4. *Post*, 9 April 1986.
5. Interviewed by Peter Gastrow, Goree Island, Senegal, July 1987.
6. *Daily Mail*, 30 July 1990.
7. *Sunday Tribune*, 24 March 1991.
8. *Daily News*, 6 July 1991.
9. *Profile 94*, South African Communication Services, Pretoria, 1994.

CLARENCE MLAMI MAKWETU

*President, Pan-Africanist
Congress, 1990.
Member of Parliament,
Pan-Africanist Congress,
1994.*

Born on 6 December 1928 in Hoyita, in the district of Cofimvaba, Transkei, Clarence Makwetu was the second of the five children of Minah and Gqongo Makwetu, a peasant from whom Makwetu learnt crop farming.

Makwetu grew up in Hoyita and after passing Standard Four at the local school moved to Keilands Mission in the Stutterheim district where he completed Standards Five and Six. Between 1943 and 1945 he attended school in Queenstown, studying for his Junior Certificate, after which he went to Lovedale, near Alice, where he matriculated.

Makwetu was drawn into the political struggle by the 1952 Defiance Campaign organised by the African National Congress (ANC). He joined the ANC Youth League in 1954.

By May 1959 he had become part of the Africanist faction within the ANC which broke away to form the Pan-Africanist Congress (PAC). Issues which led to the split included the ANC's linkages with non-African organisations and the role of whites in the Congress Alliance.

One of Makwetu's main reasons for supporting the PAC was its commitment to restoring the land to its rightful owners, the African people.

Following the break with the ANC, the PAC formed branches in the Cape Town townships of Nyanga and Langa as well as in the squatter areas at Windermere and Crawford. A visit to Cape Town by PAC leaders Robert Sobukwe and Potlako Leballo led to the growth of support for the organisation. On 18 March 1960 the PAC announced its anti-pass campaign and on the eve of the campaign, Sunday 20 March, large meetings were held in Langa and Nyanga.

The following day about 6 000 men who had gathered in Langa were urged to march to the Langa police station and surrender themselves for deliberately leaving their passes at home. Makwetu, by then a prominent PAC branch secretary at Langa New Flats, repeated an earlier insistence that there should be no violence. However, when police indicated they would view the march as an attack, the marchers dispersed.

The massacre at Sharpeville later that day did not halt the anti-pass campaign in Cape Town. On Friday 25 March, Makwetu, Philip Kgosana and other PAC leaders led a demonstration to Cape Town's Caledon Square police headquarters. The crowd was relaxed and PAC marshalls were in control but Kgosana was arrested. Later that morning the police chief, Colonel IBS Terblanche, agreed to negotiate and Makwetu told him that the marchers wished to surrender themselves for being without passes. Terblanche indicated that he had no intention of making any arrests and that for the next month people would not have to show their passes in Cape Town. Kgosana was released later that day and the crowd dispersed.

The government declared a state of emergency on 30 March 1960. Makwetu was detained from March to August 1960 and the PAC banned on 8 April. In August 1961 he was arrested in Cape Town and escorted to the Transkei where he was again detained from September 1961 to February 1962. Following his release he returned to Cape Town, but was arrested in May and sent back to Cofimvaba. There he was arrested in September and held in detention until he was charged for furthering the aims of the PAC in April 1963. He was tried at Engcobo, Transkei, and sentenced to five years imprisonment. On his way to Robben Island, Makwetu was taken to Stellenbosch where he faced further charges, but was acquitted.

After his release from Robben Island, Makwetu was taken back to the Transkei where he was restricted for two years until 1970. He then found employment near Qamata as a clerk with a firm of building contractors, earning R39 a month. Faced with this meagre salary, he obtained a plot of land linked to an irrigation scheme and began crop farming, a skill he had learned from his father.

In June 1976 Makwetu was detained without trial, being released in May 1977. In July 1977 security police arrested him in Queenstown and took him to Pietermaritzburg, Natal, where he was held until November 1977.

Makwetu was arrested in July 1979 by the Transkei police and detained until October of that year. After his release he was home for one month before being banished and restricted to Libode where he spent five years. When his term of banishment was over he returned to Qamata where he farmed green mealies and vegetables.

In 1989 Africanists decided that they could no longer work

underground only, and following a series of meetings, the Pan-Africanist Movement (PAM) was launched on 2 December 1989 in Johannesburg. PAM's founding congress elected Makwetu as leader. He stated that the PAM did not intend to replace the PAC, but to accommodate Africanists who could no longer operate underground.

The congress adopted a declaration which stated that the struggle by Africans was against oppression and dispossession of land. It was to be led by the African working class to ensure democracy and the redistribution of resources, particularly land. Guiding principles of the declaration included non-racialism, non-collaboration, the recognition of universal human rights, and a planned economy in which transport, electricity supply, mining and water supply should be in the hands of the state. The provision of housing was also seen as a duty of the state as were free health-care facilities, free education, and state-backed plans to reduce illiteracy. The declaration also argued for independent trade unions, religious freedom, equality of the sexes and the right of all people over the age of 21 to vote and stand in elections.

PAM's concept of non-racialism incorporated white, Indian and coloured people into the category of 'African' if they were committed to the guiding principles of Africanism.

In March 1990, following the unbanning of the PAC on 2 February, PAM members held a congress at which it was decided to rename the organisation 'PAC internal'. Makwetu was elected president in December 1990. In February 1991 Makwetu and Nelson Mandela of the ANC addressed the Harare meetings of the Frontline states, the Organisation of African Unity and the liberation movements. They were encouraged to start a unity process of anti-apartheid forces in South Africa.

During 1991 Makwetu held talks with the ANC and the Azanian People's Organisation (Azapo) in an attempt to forge a Patriotic Front to unite the major liberation organisations around a minimum set of demands, including the election of a constituent assembly. This led to the October Patriotic Front conference.

The PAC also participated in talks leading up to the Convention for a Democratic South Africa (Codesa), but the question of participation in Codesa nearly led to a split in the PAC when delegates from a large number of branches declared their autonomy from the leadership. At a conference called by the delegates in Katlehong, the PAC leadership was accused of selling out. A special congress of the PAC was then called on 16 December where the majority voted to boycott Codesa and a split in the organisation was averted.

The PAC declined to sign the Peace Accord in September 1991, which led to the creation of peace structures in an effort to contain the violence which had become endemic in certain areas in South Africa. The PAC continued with guerilla activity and attacks were made on policemen, some of whom were killed.

The PAC did not participate in Codesa which broke down in May 1992. However, when negotiations were resumed in March 1993, the PAC dropped its insistence that talks be held outside South Africa and were represented. Makwetu, however, remained suspicious of the process, stating in August that the talks would not lead to liberation, but would perpetuate white domination. The PAC did not play a role in the Transitional Executive Council which was established to level the playing fields in preparation for the elections.

In the first democratic general election in April 1994, Makwetu headed the PAC list for the national assembly. The organisation fared poorly, winning only 1,3% of the vote and thereby gaining five of the 400 seats in parliament. As MP, Makwetu serves on the parliamentary portfolio committees on agriculture, water affairs and forestry; defence; and land affairs.

At the PAC's national congress held at the end of 1994 Makwetu's leadership of the organisation was challenged by recently returned exile, Dr Motsoko Pheko. However, Makwetu managed to retain the presidency and Pheko was elected his deputy.

Makwetu is married to Mandisa and they have two sons. They live in Cofimvaba, near Queenstown.

SOURCES

1. Correspondence with Clarence Makwetu, February 1990.
2. Tom Lodge, *Black Politics in South Africa*, Ravan Press, Johannesburg, 1983.
3. *Sunday Tribune*, 17 December 1989.
4. *Weekly Mail*, 6 December 1991.
5. *Natal Witness*, 2 August 1993.
6. South African Institute of Race Relations, *Race Relations Survey 1993/94*, Johannesburg, 1994.

NELSON ROLIHLAHLA MANDELA

*Deputy President, African
National Congress, 1990-91.
President, African National
Congress, July 1991.
Member of Parliament, African
National Congress, 1994.
State President of South Africa,
1994.*

Nelson Mandela was born on 18 July 1918 at Qunu, near Umtata, the son of Nonqaphi Nosekeni and Henry Mgadla Mandela, chief councillor to the paramount chief of the Thembu. He spent his early childhood in the Transkei, being groomed to become a chief. In 1930, when his father died, Mandela was placed under the care of his guardian and cousin, David Dalindyebo, the acting paramount chief of the Thembu.

Mandela matriculated at Healdtown Methodist Boarding School and thereafter attended Fort Hare University College where he became involved in student politics. It was at Fort Hare that he met Oliver Tambo, and they were both expelled in 1940 as a result of their participation in a student strike.

Mandela left the Transkei, partly to avoid an arranged tribal marriage, and moved to Johannesburg where he was employed as a mine policeman. When he was traced by his relatives, he again went into hiding. Shortly after, he met Walter Sisulu who assisted him in obtaining articles with a legal firm. Completing a BA degree by correspondence in 1941, he then studied at the University of the Witwatersrand towards an LLB. In December 1952, Mandela and Oliver Tambo opened the first black legal partnership in the country.

Together with Sisulu and Tambo, Mandela participated in the foundation of the African National Congress Youth League in 1944 and in 1948 he served as its national secretary. In 1949 the ANC endorsed the 'Programme of Action' submitted to its annual conference by the Youth League, and the national executive of the ANC changed character when more radical members like Mandela and Sisulu were elected to it.

Both Mandela and Sisulu were distrustful of working with other racial groups, but Mandela modified his views during the 1952 Defiance Campaign, eventually becoming one of the leading proponents of united action against government policy.

In late 1950 Mandela became national president of the Youth League, and in 1952 was appointed national 'volunteer-in-chief' of the Defiance Campaign. In this capacity he travelled around South Africa enlisting disciplined volunteers prepared to break apartheid laws. The campaign officially opened on 26 June 1952 with Mandela and 51 others breaking curfew regulations as their first act of defiance.

In December 1952 Mandela and a number of others were arrested and charged under the Suppression of Communism Act. Mandela was sentenced to nine months' imprisonment with hard labour, suspended for two years. He was also served with a banning order prohibiting him from attending gatherings for six months, or from leaving the Johannesburg magisterial district. For the following nine years his banning orders were continually renewed.

Although Mandela, by now deputy national president of the ANC, was banned from gatherings, he continued to work with small groups of Congress members. He was instrumental in the formulation of the 'M Plan' (named after him) whereby ANC branches were to be broken down into cells to cope with the possibility of underground activity.

In September 1953 renewed bans required Mandela to resign officially from the ANC. From then on, except during the years of the treason trial, Mandela's leadership was exercised secretly.

In December 1956 Mandela was one of 156 political activists arrested and charged with high treason. Four-and-a-half years later, on 29 March 1961, Justice Rumpff found the accused not guilty. As well as being an accused, Mandela played a legal role in the trial as the original defence lawyers withdrew during the 1960 state of emergency.

In 1959, with the treason trial still continuing, the ANC planned an anti-pass laws campaign. It was, however, pre-empted by the Pan-Africanist Congress (PAC) which called for mass anti-pass protests on 21 March 1960. It was during one of these protests that the Sharpeville massacre took place. Shortly thereafter, both the ANC and the PAC were banned, and the government declared a state of emergency.

During the emergency approximately 1 800 political activists, including Mandela, were imprisoned without charge or trial.

An ad hoc committee of black leaders, including Duma Nokwe, Govan Mbeki and Alfred Nzo, called an All-In Africa Conference in Pietermaritzburg in March 1961 which was attended by leaders from various political groupings. Mandela's banning order was due to expire on the eve of the conference and, anticipating its renewal, he went into hiding and made a surprise appearance at the conference. As a result, he was appointed honorary secretary of the All-In National Action Council, constituted to organise demonstrations against the proclamation of South Africa as a republic on 31 May, to campaign for a national convention, and for a three day stay-at-home strike on 29, 30 and 31 May 1961 in support of these issues.

Evading arrest for incitement, Mandela went underground. He and Sisulu travelled secretly around the country organising the strike, and Mandela (nicknamed the Black Pimpernel at the time) remained a fugitive for the next 17 months.

Mandela called off the three-day stay-at-home protest on its second day after massive police repression of strikers. The failure of this action was important in changing his political thinking, and he became more committed to the formation of Umkhonto we Sizwe (the Spear of the Nation) as a military wing of the ANC.

At about this time, Mandela and some of his colleagues concluded that violence in South Africa was inevitable, and it would be unreasonable for African leaders to continue with their policy of non-violence when the government met its demands with force. The decision to form Umkhonto we Sizwe (MK), however, was not made by the ANC itself, but by individuals within the organisation, and Mandela became MK's first commander-in-chief.

Early in 1962 Mandela was smuggled across the border and on 11 January made a surprise appearance at the Pan-African Freedom Movement Conference in Addis Ababa. His address to the conference, a few weeks after the first sabotage attacks by Umkhonto, explained and justified the turn to violent action.

During this trip he received guerilla training in Algeria before travelling to London where he met leaders of British opposition parties.

He returned to South Africa in July, and on 5 August was captured near Howick, Natal. Mandela was tried in Pretoria's Old Synagogue and in November 1962 sentenced to five years' imprisonment for incitement and illegally leaving the country. He began this sentence in Pretoria Central Prison.

While Mandela was in prison, police raided the underground headquarters of the African National Congress at Lilliesleaf Farm, Rivonia, arresting, among others, Walter Sisulu, Govan Mbeki, Raymond Mhlaba, Ahmed Kathrada, Dennis Goldberg and Lionel Bernstein. Police found documents relating to the manufacture of explosives, Mandela's diary of his African tour and copies of a draft memorandum – 'Operation Mayibuye' – which outlined a possible strategy of guerilla struggle.

The Rivonia trial commenced in October 1963 and Mandela was brought from jail to join the other eight accused being tried for sabotage, conspiracy to overthrow the government by revolution, and assisting an armed invasion of South Africa by foreign troops.

Mandela's statement from the dock after conviction received world-wide publicity. On 12 June 1964, all eight of the accused, including Mandela, were sentenced to life imprisonment.

The following night Mandela was flown to Cape Town en route to Robben Island Prison where he was held until April 1982, when he was transferred to Pollsmoor Prison in Cape Town.

A massive 'Release Mandela Campaign' was launched in 1982 both within South Africa and abroad. This included worldwide celebrations of Mandela's 70th birthday in 1988, marked by a 12-hour music concert broadcast to over 50 countries. In addition, many foreign countries pressured the South African government to release Mandela, who had become the world's most famous political prisoner.

On 13 August 1988 Mandela was taken to Tygerberg hospital for treatment of fluid around the lung. It was subsequently revealed that he was suffering from tuberculosis. The following month he was transferred to the Constantiaberg Medi-Clinic where he was treated until December, when he was moved to a warder's home in the grounds of the Victor Verster Prison, near Paarl.

From July 1986 onwards Mandela had contact with government representatives, firstly with Minister of Justice Kobie Coetzee, and subsequently with the Minister of Constitutional Development, Gerrit Viljoen. This eventually led to his meeting with State President PW Botha in July 1989 at Tuynhuys. In December 1989 he met the new state president, FW de Klerk. In addition to meeting government representatives, Mandela was able to meet with senior members of the United Democratic Front, the Congress of South African Trade Unions and other political groups. On 2 February 1990, in his opening of parliament speech, State President De Klerk announced the unbanning of the ANC, the South African Communist Party and the PAC and indicated that Mandela would be released in the near future. After a further meeting with De Klerk on Friday, 9 February, Mandela was released on Sunday, 11 February. He immediately addressed a mass rally in the centre of Cape Town. Subsequent welcome rallies in Soweto and Durban drew hundreds of thousands of people.

In March 1990, when Mandela travelled to Lusaka to meet the ANC's national executive committee, he was appointed deputy president of the organisation. He then travelled to Sweden to meet the ANC president, Oliver Tambo, but cut short the rest of his proposed trip abroad as a result of the increased unrest within South Africa.

In May 1990, Mandela headed the ANC delegation which held talks with South African government representatives at Groote Schuur. In June, he began a six-week tour of Europe, the United Kingdom, North America and Africa. His reception by heads of state, and hundreds of thousands of citizens of the countries he visited, confirmed his stature as an internationally respected leader.

In July he attended the Organisation of African Unity (OAU) summit held in Addis Ababa, but had to leave for Kenya when he contracted pneumonia.

In August talks resumed with the South African government and in the same month Mandela visited Norway. This was followed by visits to Zambia, India and Australia.

In February 1991 Mandela met with Chief Mangosuthu Buthelezi, president of Inkatha, in an attempt to put an end to the violence sweeping Natal and the Transvaal. However, despite their pledges to work towards peace, the violence continued. Mandela then issued an ultimatum to the government, setting a deadline by which it had to end the violence, and fire the Ministers of Defence and Law and Order. He indicated that the ANC would quit the negotiation process if these demands were not met. However, the government failed to meet these demands.

In April 1991 Mandela attended a meeting between the ANC and the PAC in Harare where they resolved to work together to oppose apartheid. A joint sub-committee was established to approach the European Community to reverse its decision to lift bans on steel imports from South Africa. The meeting also resolved to convene a conference of anti-apartheid organisations to support the demand for a national constituent assembly.

In June 1991 Mandela attended the OAU summit in Abuja, Nigeria, following which he travelled to the United Kingdom and Belgium. In July, at the ANC conference held in Durban, he was elected ANC president, succeeding an ailing Oliver Tambo. The following month Mandela travelled to countries in South America.

In September 1991 he signed the National Peace Accord on behalf of the ANC. This agreement between a number of political organisations, including the ANC, Inkatha Freedom Party and the National Party, established structures and procedures to attempt to end the political violence which had become so widespread.

In October 1991 a meeting of the Patriotic Front was held in Durban in an attempt to bring together all anti-apartheid groupings in the country. All attended with the exception of the Azanian People's Organisation. Policy regarding future negotiations was formulated and the ANC and the PAC began preparatory meetings for the Convention for a Democratic South Africa (Codesa). However, the PAC could not see its way clear to participating in the convention.

In November Mandela travelled to West Africa and the following month met United States President, George Bush.

The first meeting of Codesa, set up to negotiate procedures for constitutional change, was held in December 1991. At the end of the plenary session, after De Klerk had raised the question of disbanding Umkhonto we Sizwe, Mandela delivered a scathing personal verbal attack on him. Mandela argued that even the head of an 'illegitimate, discredited minority regime should have certain moral standards'. During 1992, Mandela continued his programme of extensive international travel, visiting Tunisia, Libya and Morocco. He and State President de Klerk jointly accepted the Unesco Houphouet-Boigny Peace Prize in Paris on 3 February. At the same time the two men attended the World Economic Forum in Davos, Switzerland.

On 13 April 1992 Mandela called a press conference at which he stated that he and his wife, Winnie, had agreed to separate as a result of differences which had arisen between them in recent months. Later in' April Mandela, FW de Klerk and Mangosuthu Buthelezi addressed a gathering of more than a million members of the Zion Christian Church at Moria, near Pietersburg, and committed themselves to end the ongoing violence and move speedily towards a political settlement.

In May 1992 the second plenary meeting of Codesa was held, but the working group dealing with constitutional arrangements deadlocked when the ANC and government could not reach agreement on certain constitutional principles. Codesa's management committee was asked to find a way out of the logjam but by 16 June (Soweto Day) no progress had been made and the ANC called for a mass action campaign to put pressure on the South African government.

While visiting the Scandinavian countries and Czechoslovakia in May, Mandela suggested that FW de Klerk was personally responsible for political violence in South Africa. He likened the violence in South Africa to the killing of Jews in Nazi Germany. Mandela also criticised what he felt was the stranglehold imposed on the South African press by unrepresentative white-owned conglomerates. However, he expressed support for a critical, independent and investigative press.

Following the Boipatong massacre of June 1992, Mandela indicated that negotiations with the government would not be resumed until ANC demands for an election to a constituent assembly, a transitional government, and state steps to end political violence were met.

At the end of June 1992, Mandela addressed the heads-of-state summit of the Organisation of African Unity in Dakar, Senegal. As a result, the OAU agreed to raise the issue of South Africa's political violence at the United Nations. During July, Mandela and representatives of other South African parties addressed the UN security council. Mandela asked the UN to provide continous monitoring of the violence, and submitted documents which he claimed proved the 'criminal intent' of the government, both in the instigation of violence and in failing to halt it. He maintained that the government was conducting a 'cold-hearted strategy of state terror to impose its will on negotiations'.

During July 1992, Mandela visited the Olympic Games in Barcelona, where a South African team was participating for the first time in 30 years. On his return to South Africa, he involved himself in the ANC's mass action campaign calling for disciplined and peaceful protest.

Following violent incidents between ANC supporters in the Transvaal, Mandela admitted that the organisation had disciplinary problems with some of its followers, particularly in township self-defence units. He promised to take action against those who abused positions of power and authority.

During 1992, Mandela indicated that the ANC had shifted its economic thinking, particularly with regard to nationalisation. This was no longer viewed as an ideological imperative, but merely one policy option. He continued to stress the need to redress economic imbalances, but noted that the ANC was aware of both local and international business hostility towards nationalisation.

In September 1992 Mandela indicated that he was prepared to meet De Klerk on condition that he agreed to the fencing off of hostels, the banning of the public display of dangerous weapons and the release of political prisoners. They met at the end of the month and these bi-lateral talks resulted in the signing of a Record of Understanding by the two leaders which enabled negotiations to be resumed.

During 1992 and 1993 Mandela continually made calls for peace. Following the assassination of ANC/SACP leader, Chris Hani, in April 1993, he again called for restraint, discipline and peace, but at a a rally in Soweto's Jabulani Stadium he was booed by a militant crowd when he tried to convey a message of peace in the wake of the killing.

In May 1993, Mandela caused a political row when he suggested that South Africa's voting age should be lowered to enable 14-year-old children to vote. However, he was persuaded to accept that only people aged 18 or more could vote in the April 1994 elections.

In September 1993, while on a visit to the USA, he urged world business leaders to lift economic sanctions and to invest in South Africa.

During the latter half of 1993 and early 1994 Mandela campaigned on behalf of the ANC for the 1994 election and addressed a large number of rallies and people's forums. At the same time, he continued to attempt to draw the Freedom Alliance partners (white right wing groups, the IFP, the Bophuthatswana and Ciskei governments) into the election process. However, he ruled out the possibility of delaying the election date to accommodate them.

In March 1994, following a civil uprising in Bophuthatswana which led to the downfall of the Mangope government, Mandela guaranteed striking civil servants their jobs, but harshly criticised the looting that had occurred during the unrest. In April, last-minute talks were held in the Kruger Park between Mandela, De Klerk, Buthelezi and Zulu King

Goodwill Zwelithini to try to break the deadlock on IFP participation in the elections. The meeting was unsuccessful and was followed by an attempt at international mediation. This, too, failed, but a last-minute effort by Kenyan academic, Washington Okumu, brought the IFP back into the election process. Mandela and De Klerk then signed an agreement regarding the future status of the Zulu king.

Mandela contested the April 1994 election at the head of the ANC's list for the National Assembly. He personally voted in Inanda, near Durban, on 27 April 1994 and early in May the Independent Electoral Commission announced that the ANC had won 62% of the national vote. Mandela subsequently indicated that he had been relieved that the ANC had not achieved a two-thirds majority in the election as this would allay fears that it would unilaterally re-write the constitution. He stated that he stood for a government of national unity with each party sharing in the exercise of power.

On 9 May 1994 Mandela was elected unopposed as president of South Africa in the first session of the National Assembly. His presidential inauguration took place the next day at the Union Buildings in Pretoria and was attended by the largest gathering of international leaders ever held in South Africa, as well as about 100 000 celebrants on the lawns in front of the building. The ceremony was televised and broadcast internationally. In his inaugural speech Mandela called for a 'time of healing' and stated that his government would fight against discrimination of any kind. He pledged to enter into a covenant to build a society in which all South Africans, black and white, could walk tall without fear, assured of their rights to human dignity – 'a rainbow nation at peace with itself and the world'.

In Mandela's State-of-the-Nation speech to parliament in May he announced that R2,5 billion would be allocated in the 1994/95 budget for the government's reconstruction and development programme. His pragmatic economic policy was welcomed by business in general.

Mandela continued to draw the white right wing into the negotiation process and in May 1994 held a breakthrough meeting with the leader of the Conservative Party (CP), Ferdie Hartzenberg. Negotiations also involved a possible meeting with AWB leader Eugene Terre Blanche.

In June Mandela attended the OAU summit held in Tunis and was appointed second vice-president of the organisation. The following month he held talks with his Angolan, Mozambican and Zairean counterparts in an attempt to further peace-making efforts in Angola. His participation in the peace process was welcomed by Unita leader, Jonas Savimbi.

In September 1994 Mandela made a crucial speech at the annual conference of the Congress of South African Trade Unions (Cosatu) where he called on the labour movement to transform itself from a liberation movement to one which would assist in the building of a new South Africa. He warned that workers would lose their jobs if production costs rose because of unnecessary labour unrest and he called on workers to assist in making the ANC's reconstruction and development programme work.

In July 1994 Mandela underwent eye surgery for a cateract. The operation was complicated by the fact that his tear glands were damaged by the alkalinity of the stone at Robben Island where he had done hard labour breaking rocks.

In January 1995 the government of national unity nearly collapsed over an alleged secret attempt by two former cabinet ministers and 3 500 police to obtain indemnity on the eve of the April 1994 elections. At a cabinet meeting on 18 January, Mandela attacked Deputy President de Klerk stating that he did not believe that De Klerk was unaware of the indemnity applications. He went on to question De Klerk's commitment to the reconstruction and development programme. At a press conference on 20 January De Klerk maintained that this attack on his integrity and good faith could seriously jeopardise the future of the government of national unity.

In April 1995 Mandela fired his estranged wife, Winnie, from her post as Deputy Minister of Arts, Culture, Science and Technology, following a series of controversial issues in which she was involved. She challenged her dismissal in the Supreme Court, claiming that it was unconstitutional. She had obtained an affidavit from IFP leader Mangosuthu Buthelezi to the effect that he had not, as a leader of a party in the government of national unity, been consulted about this dismissal. This was a constitutional requirement. Winnie Mandela was then briefly reinstated before being dismissed again, Mandela having consulted with all party leaders involved in the government of national unity.

In May 1995, following the dispute between the IFP and the ANC regarding international mediation for the new constitution, Buthelezi called on Zulus to 'rise and resist' any imposed constitutional dispensation. Mandela accused Buthelezi of encouraging violence and attempting to foment an uprising against central government. In this context, he threatened to cut off central government funding to KwaZulu/Natal, indicating that he would not allow public funds to be used to finance an attempt to overthrow the constitution by violent means. Although a subsequent meeting between the two leaders seemed cordial in tone, the matter of mediation remained an unresolved point of conflict.

Mandela has travelled frequently since 1992, visiting the United Kingdom, Belgium, Portugal, Spain, the USA, Zambia and Taiwan. He has received a number of joint awards with FW de Klerk including the Prince of the Asturias Prize for International Co-operation (Spain, 1992);

the Philadelphia Liberty Medal (USA, 1993); the Nobel Peace Prize (Norway, 1993); and has received honorary degrees from over fifty universities around the world. He donated part of the Nobel Peace Prize award to charities for children and also announced that he would contribute R150 000 of his annual salary to a presidential trust fund created to aid street children and child detainees.

Mandela's autobiography, *Long Walk to Freedom*, was published in 1994, and soon became one of the year's best selling books in South Africa.

Mandela has a son and a daughter from his first marriage to Evelyn Ntoko, a nurse. Their third child was killed in a car accident. In 1958 he married Nomzamo Winnie Madikizela, from whom he is now separated, and they have two daughters. He has eighteen grandchildren.

SOURCES

1. Ruth First (ed), *No Easy Walk to Freedom: Articles and Trial Addresses of Nelson Mandela*, London, 1980.
2. Mary Benson, *The Struggle for a Birthright*, Harmsondsworth, 1966.
3. Gwendolen Carter, Thomas Karis and Gail Gerhart, *From Protest to Challenge. A Documentary History of African Politics in South Africa, 1882-1964, volume 4*, Stanford, 1977.
4. Ronald Segal, *Political Africa*, London, 1961.
5. *Weekly Mail*, 21 March 1986.
6. *Weekly Mail*, 18 April 1986.
7. *Daily News*, 9 February 1990.
8. Francis Meli, *South Africa Belongs to Us: A History of the ANC*, Harare, 1988.
9. *Natal Mercury*, 18 April 1991.
10. *Daily News*, 21 December 1991.
11. *Daily News*, 3 February 1992.
12. *Natal Mercury*, 4 February 1992.
13. *Natal Mercury*, 21 March 1992.
14. *Daily News*, 13 April 1992.
15. *Natal Mercury*, 20 April 1992.
16. *Natal Mercury*, 26 May 1992.
17. *Daily News*, 27 May 1992.
18. *Natal Mercury*, 15 June 1992.
19. *Natal Mercury*, 16 July 1992.
20. *Natal Mercury*, 29 July 1992.
21. *Natal Mercury*, 3 August 1992.
22. *Sunday Tribune*, 11 September 1992.
23. *Natal Mercury*, 24 May 1993.
24. *Natal Witness*, 24 May 1993.
25. *Natal Mercury*, 23 June 1993.

26. *Natal Mercury*, 24 June 1993.
27. *Guardian Weekly*, 23 July 1993.
28. *Washington Post*, 25 September 1993.
29. *Natal Witness*, 17 February 1994.
30. *Daily News*, 9 May 1994.
31. Nelson Mandela, *Long Work to Freeedom*, MacDonald Purnell, 1994.
32. *Argus*, 19 January 1995.
33. *Sunday Times*, 22 January 1995.
34. *Cape Times*, 17 February 1995.
35. *Weekly Mail & Guardian*, 13 April 1995.
36. *Cape Times*, 4 May 1995.

NOMZAMO ZANIEWE WINNIFRED MANDELA

President, Women's League,
African National Congress, 1993.
Member of Parliament,
African National Congress, 1994.
Deputy Minister, Arts, Culture,
Science and Technology, 1994-95.

Born on 26 September 1934 at Bizana, Pondoland, Winnie Mandela is the daughter of Nomathamsanqa and Columbus Madikizela, a teacher and later Minister of Agriculture and Forestry in the Transkeian government. Mandela attended school at Bizana and Shawbury, enrolling at the age of 16 at the Jan Hofmeyr School of Social Work. Thereafter, she took a post as the first African medical social worker at Baragwanath Hospital, Soweto.

In 1957 she met Nelson Mandela, a member of the African National Congress executive and an accused in the treason trial. They married in 1958 and three months later she was arrested for her role in an anti-pass campaign.

Mandela served on the national and provincial executives of the ANC Women's League and on the national executive of the Federation of South African Women. In addition, she chaired the Orlando branch of the ANC until the organisation was banned in 1960.

In 1962 Mandela was banned in terms of the Suppression of Communism Act and restricted to Orlando, in Soweto. As a result she had to relinquish her job as a social worker with the Child Welfare Society. More stringent banning orders were served on her in 1965 and in 1966 and she remained under banning orders continuously until 1975.

In 1967 Mandela was charged on two occasions for contravening her banning order and sentenced to one year's imprisonment, with all but four days suspended. In May 1969 she was detained under section 6 of the Terrorism Act and held in solitary confinement for 17 months. After two trials, both ending in acquittal, she was released from prison in September 1970, but served with a new banning order which included house arrest. She was charged on numerous occasions for alleged contraventions of these restrictions, and in 1971 she received a suspended sentence for communicating with another banned person. In 1974 she served a six-month jail sentence for another contravention of her banning order.

Mandela's banning order expired at the end of October 1975. In December of that year she helped found the Black Women's Federation and later, in response to the 1976 Soweto riots, helped establish the Black Parents' Association which arranged legal and medical help for those affected by police action. Both groups were banned in the October 1977 clampdown on black organisations. She was detained from August to December 1976 under the preventive detention clause of the Internal Security Act. On 28 December 1976, she was issued with a new banning order.

In May 1977 Mandela's banning orders were amended and she was banished from her Soweto home to Phatakahle in Brandfort, Orange Free State. She was subsequently again charged on several occasions for contravening this banning order. In 1982 she was served with her fifth banning order which was renewed in June 1983.

In August 1985, after Mandela's home in Brandfort was fire-bombed, she returned to her home in Orlando West in defiance of her restrictions.

Her banning order was subsequently amended to allow her to live anywhere in South Africa, except in the Johannesburg and Roodepoort magisterial districts. On 21 December 1985 security police forcibly removed her from her Soweto home but she returned immediately. The following day she was arrested and detained overnight at the Krugersdorp police station. Following her Christmas visit to Cape Town to see her imprisoned husband, she returned to Johannesburg, again defying her banning order, and was arrested after a dramatic car chase seen by the local and international media. In February 1986 charges of contravening her restrictions were provisionally withdrawn.

In April 1986, in a statement which provoked considerable controversy, Mandela was quoted as having said that blacks would be liberated by means of matches and tyres (necklace killings by means of a burning tyre placed around a victim's neck). She later denied that she had called for violence and maintained that she had been quoted out of context.

In June 1988 Mandela's home was burnt down after it was attacked by a group of schoolchildren. It was alleged that the attack was not aimed at her personally, but at the Mandela United Football Club who guarded her, and who had allegedly attacked a Soweto schoolgirl. The incident, however, was an indication of the growing controversy surrounding Mandela and her actions.

In January 1989 Mandela was involved in a controversy surrounding the abduction of four youths from a mission house by her 'football club'. One of the abducted youths, 14-year-old Stompie Moeketse Seipei, was subsequently found murdered. She was urged by both her husband and Oliver Tambo, ANC president, to disband the club, and on 16 February 1989 the United Democratic Front (UDF) and the Congress of South African Trade Unions (Cosatu) issued a statement placing the entire blame for the conduct of the team on her. The statement expressed outrage at the reign of terror carried out by the football club which she had created, and distanced Cosatu and the UDF from her and her actions.

UDF and Cosatu representatives met with the ANC to discuss the issue: a subsequent ANC statement argued that while Mandela had made mistakes, extra-parliamentary groups should not ostracise her, but rather draw her back as a disciplined member, accountable to the movement and subject to its restraint and counsel. The ANC also suggested that the club had been infiltrated by provocateurs to discredit Nelson Mandela and the ANC.

The 'coach' of the 'football team', Jerry Richardson, was subsequently charged and convicted for the murder of Seipei. One of the key witnesses against Richardson implicated Mandela in assaults on Seipei and other abducted youths. In April 1991 Mandela herself was charged with eight counts of kidnapping and assault. Her defence centred around the issue of whether the children concerned had been abducted or whether they were taken to Mandela's home for safety, following complaints that they had been involved in homosexual activities at the church manse where they were staying as refugees. Mandela's defence team was accused of using homophobia as part of its strategy. Two of the prosecution witnesses disappeared during the course of the trial. One resurfaced to give evidence, but the other, who claimed he had been kidnapped by Mandela's supporters, was later traced to Lusaka where he was being held by the Zambian authorities. Mandela was convicted on four counts of kidnapping and on four counts of being an accessory to assault, and sentenced to sixyears' imprisonment. She subsequently won an application for leave to appeal, and in 1993 the Appeal Court found her guilty of kidnapping, but not of assault and ordered her to pay a fine of R15 000 and R15 000 compensation to the three surviving victims of the kidnapping and assault which took place at her home.

On 11 February 1990, following the unbanning of the ANC, Nelson Mandela was released from jail and the couple reunited. As the ANC began reconstituting its organisational structures within South Africa, Mandela took on an increasingly prominent role, and was appointed head of its welfare department.

At the April 1991 national congress of the ANC Women's League, Mandela was defeated in the election for presidency by Gertrude Shope, who received 633 votes to Mandela's 196 after Albertina Sisulu withdrew from the contest and asked her supporters to back Shope. However, Mandela was elected chairperson of the Women's League in the PWV area.

In July 1991, at the ANC's national conference held in Durban, Mandela was elected to the organisation's national executive committee.

On 14 April 1992, Nelson Mandela announced that he and Winnie Mandela were separating because of personal differences. She subsequently resigned from her position as head of the ANC's social welfare department. Shortly after, two of the co-accused in her trial – John Morgan and Xoliswa Falati – withdrew their previous corroboration of Mandela's alibi, and Falati stated that she had perjured herself to protect Mandela. In addition, a potential state witness against Mandela then held in a Zambian jail alleged that she was implicated in the murder of Dr Abu-Baker Asvat, who had examined Stompie Seipei after he had been assaulted in Mandela's home.

Mandela continued to campaign on ANC platforms, seemingly with substantial support among the more militant youth. She indicated that she would pursue her political activities within the ANC despite allegtions against her.

On 3 May 1992 Mandela was re-elected unopposed as chair of the PWV region of the ANC Women's League, but on 25 May a PWV inter-branch meeting suspended the regional executive committee, effectively removing Mandela from her position.

This was a sequel to a demonstration at the ANC's head offices, where a group of women had demanded Mandela's reinstatement as head of the social welfare department. Although Mandela denied orchestrating the demonstration, certain members of the Women's League felt that she was responsible for it. This move took place amidst allegations that Mandela and her deputy in the social welfare department had spent R400 000 while on a fund-raising trip abroad. Both denied these allegations.

In early September, amidst growing discontent over Mandela's conduct, she resigned from all posts she held in the organisation, but indicated that she remained a loyal ANC member.

In June 1993, Mandela was appointed chairperson of the Southern Transvaal region of the South African National Civic Organisation (Sanco), but the following month she was suspended for a year from the ANC Women's League for displaying 'defiance, insubordination and total disloyalty to the ANC, the league and the entire leadership of the organisation'.

However, at the annual general meeting of the ANC Women's League in December 1993, Mandela was elected president, beating veteran, Albertina Sisulu. In the same month she was elected deputy president of Sanco.

In April 1994 it was revealed that a secret ANC internal commission of inquiry held in 1993 had implicated Mandela in the disappearance of foreign funding and misappropriation of ANC funds. Mandela had refused to appear before the chairman of the commission, Oliver Tambo. The commission found that Mandela and the former deputy head of the ANC's social welfare department, Dali Mpofu, had failed to declare the proceeds of donations from a 1991 visit to the USA, that there was no record of this money being deposited into the department's bank account, and that there was unequivocal evidence of ANC funds amounting to R74 000 being deposited into Mandela's personal banking accounts. Mandela acknowledged the debt and it was reported that arrangements had been made between the ANC treasurer and Mandela regarding its repayment. Mandela subsequently dismissed these reports as lies.

In the first democratic general elections held in April 1994, Mandela stood as candidate number 31 on the ANC's list for the national assembly and became a member of parliament. In May she was appointed Deputy Minister of Arts, Culture, Science and Technology.

Soon thereafter, she attempted to obtain a restraining order against her co-accused in the kidnapping trial, Xoliswa Falati, who had been released from prison and who had threatened to reveal damaging evidence against Mandela at a press conference. Mandela was unsuccessful in her attempt, but to date Falati has not revealed any further information.

In August 1994, while speaking in parliament, Mandela apologised for failing to save the life of Stompie Seipei and accused 'white courts' and 'apartheid justice' for criminalising her. This caused controversy, especially in legal circles, as her appeal was dealt with by the chief justice who confirmed the conviction, but amended the sentence of imprisonment to allow for the alternative of a fine. Because the chief justice retained his position under the new democratic government, it was alleged that Mandela had abused her parliamentary privilege in criticising the judiciary. However, the parliamentary speaker ruled that she was within her rights to do so.

At the end of 1994 Mandela's relationship with convicted illegal diamond buyer, Hazel Crane, made headlines when Ms Crane was reported to have purchased a house for Mandela in Cape Town. This was followed by a court case in which it was alleged that Mandela had chartered a jet aircraft, using the letterhead of a non-governmental organisation dealing with poverty relief, to fly business associates to Angola to buy diamonds. In May 1995, this civil claim was postponed indefinitely when a medical certificate was placed before the court indicating that Mandela was too ill to attend the hearing. She was ordered to pay all costs of the postponement.

In December 1994 new elections for the ANC national executive committee were held at the ANC congress and Mandela was placed fifth on the list. In the same month she was elected treasurer of the Congress of Traditional Leaders of South Africa (Contralesa).

Soon thereafter, Mandela was faced with the resignations of eleven senior members of the ANC's Women's League national executive committee on the grounds of undemocratic leadership, lack of transparency and accountability, an inability to unite women and a long history of tensions within the league. Attempts by Deputy President Thabo Mbeki and President Mandela to resolve the crisis in the league failed, and Mandela did not attend meetings called to resolve the matter.

At the same time, Mandela was ordered to apologise for criticising the government of national unity when she stated at a funeral that the government had failed South Africans because it had not addressed apartheid imbalances and racism in the work place and she termed the ANC's 'indulgence' in reconciliation a weakness. She subsequently submitted her apology to President Mandela a few days later.

In February 1995 Mandela travelled to countries in West Africa to attend an international film festival, despite a request by the president that she cancel the visit in favour of attending important meetings being held in South Africa at that time. At the same time, the Democratic Party gave notice that it would demand explanations in parliament on allegations that Mandela 'gratuitously and improperly' used her position as Deputy Minister to interfere in a legal dispute between the Pretoria Regional Services Council and an electrical contractor. Documentation was released which showed, in the view of the DP, that she had used the office, authority, stationery and staff of her deputy ministry to interfere in a matter which fell outside her realm of authority.

While Mandela was in West Africa, police raided her Soweto home and the offices of the Co-ordinated Anti-Poverty Programme (Capp), which she headed, in search of documents related to possible charges of corruption in regard to low-cost housing provision. She cut short her trip and challenged the validity of the search warrants in the Supreme Court. She won the case, and the documents were returned to her by police.

On the weekend of 25 March 1995, she attacked the government of national unity for spending R2,5-million to entertain a 'British queen' (Elizabeth II): this was viewed by many as a direct attack on State President Mandela.

On Monday 27 March, President Mandela announced that Winnie Mandela's appointment as Deputy Minister had been terminated with immediate effect. Mandela then brought an application to the Supreme Court, challenging her dismissal on the grounds that it had been unconstitutional. She had obtained an affidavit from IFP leader and cabinet minister Mangosuthu Buthelezi to the effect that, as a leader of a party in the government of national unity, he had not been consulted prior to her dismissal. This was a requirement in terms of section 88 of the constitution. Mandela was then briefly reinstated as Deputy Minister before being dismissed again, following consultation between the State President and all leaders of participating political parties in the government of national unity. Mandela publicly tendered her resignation the day before her dismissal was due to take effect. The next day, she entered a private clinic where she was treated for a severe electrolyte imbalance.

Mandela remains a Member of Parliament, president of the ANC Women's League, and a member of the ANC's national executive committee.

Winnie Mandela has two daughters, Zenani and Zindziwa, and several grandchildren.

SOURCES

1. Sean Moroney and Linda Ensor, *The Silenced*, South African Institute of Race Relations, Johannesburg, 1979.
2. Supplement to *Fair Lady*, 23 March 1983.
3. *The Star*, 'South Africa's Black History Makers', No.62.
4. *Natal Mercury*, 27 August 1964.
5. *Daily News*, 3 March 1971.
6. *Daily News*, 15 October 1974.
7. Pamphlet issued by Students' African Movement, University of the Witwatersrand.
8. Tom Lodge, *Black Politics in South Africa since 1945*, Ravan Press, Johannesburg, 1983.
9. *Argus*, 23 December 1985.
10. *Sunday Times*, 29 December 1985.

11. *Cape Times*, 31 December 1985, 19 February 1986 and 15 April 1986.
12. *Weekly Mail*, 2 May 1986.
13. South African Institute of Race Relations, *Race Relations Survey, 1988-89*, Johannesburg, 1989.
14. *Natal Mercury*, 17 February 1989.
15. Fatima Meer, *Higher Than Hope*, Skotaville, Johannesburg, 1988.
16. *The Star*, 28 July 1990.
17. *City Press*, 12 May 1991.
18. *Natal Witness*, 14 May 1991.
19. *Sunday Tribune*, 19 April 1992.
20. *Sunday Times*, 19 April 1992.
21. *Natal Witness*, 7 September 1992.
22. *Natal Witness*, 3 June 1993.
23. *Daily News*, 23 November 1993.
24. *Financial Mail*, 17 December 1993.
25. *Saturday News*, 9 April 1994.
26. *Natal Mercury*, 26 August 1994.
27. *Sunday Times*, 22 January 1995.
28. *Sunday Times*, 12 February 1995.
29. *The Citizen*, 13 February 1995.
30. *Sunday Tribune*, 26 February 1995.
31. *Weekly Mail & Guardian*, 13 April 1995.
32. *Cape Times*, 11 May 1995.

NOEL CHABANI MANGANYI

Director General of Education,
August 1994.

Born at Mavambe, near Louis Trichard in the Northern Transvaal, on 13 March 1940, Chabani Manganyi is the son of Sophie and Frans Manganyi, a migrant worker. He grew up in Mavambe attending various schools in the area before matriculating in 1959 from the Douglas Laing Smit Secondary School at Elim, near Louis Trichard.

In 1960 Manganyi enrolled at the University of the North (Turfloop) for a BA degree majoring in English and Psychology which he completed at the end of 1962. During this time he served on the Students' Representative Council (SRC) and was active in student politics. He was also involved in the debates which eventually led to a breakaway by black universities from the National Union of South African Students (Nusas) and the establishment of the Black Consciousness South African Students' Organisation (Saso).

Manganyi was awarded his Honours degree in Psychology in 1964. He started work as a personnel officer at ASEA Electric SA (Pty) Ltd while continuing his studies part-time. He completed his MA in 1968 at the University of South Africa (Unisa) and his DLitt et Phil in 1970 (Unisa) for his thesis on body image in paraplegia.

Manganyi then undertook his internship for Clinical Psychology at Baragwanath Hospital's Neurosurgery Unit, near Johannesburg, and registered with the South African Medical and Dental Council the following year as a clinical psychologist.

In 1970, Manganyi was sponsored by the United States-South Africa Leadership Exchange Programme (USSALEP) to visit the United States of America. In 1973 he received a two-year grant from the Ford

Foundation to study in the Department of Psychiatry at the Yale University School of Medicine where he completed a post-doctoral fellowship in Clinical Psychology in 1975.

Following his return to South Africa in 1976 Manganyi was appointed professor and chair of the Department of Psychology at Fort Hare University (now the University of the Transkei). From 1977-80 he served as the university's dean of the Faculty of Arts.

From 1981-90 Manganyi was visiting professor and senior research fellow at what was then known as the African Studies Institute of the University of the Witwatersrand. During this period he undertook several research trips to Paris, the United Kingdom and the United States of America. He published several books and research papers and was a visiting scholar at Yale University in 1985.

Following his return from Yale University, he combined his part-time private practice of psychology with the establishment of the first centre for the study and professional remediation of violence in South Africa (the Political Violence and Health Resources Project) which was supported by the Ford Foundation in New York. It was also during his term at the University of the Witwatersrand that Manganyi worked extensively in the Supreme Court as an expert witness for the defence in political trials, including those of Oscar Mpetha and Robert McBride.

In 1991 Manganyi was appointed vice-chancellor and principal designate of the University of the North. During his term as principal, Manganyi was a member of the joint working group on education established by the National Party government, various educational organisations and Nelson Mandela. He remained principal of the university until the end of 1992. In 1993 he accepted a position as executive director of the private sector's Joint Education Trust, a position he held until his appointment as director-general of education in August 1994.

Manganyi's immediate priorities include the enhancement of efficiency in the recently-established Department of National Education as well as the facilitation of the establishment of viable provincial departments of education.

Manganyi is married to Dr Peggy Sekele. He has two adult daughters from a previous marriage and three step-daughters.

SOURCES

1. *Curriculum vitae* supplied by Dr Chabani Manganyi.
2. *Educamus*, 40 (3), 1994.
3. Interviewed 15 February 1995, Cape Town.

MOSIBUDI MANGENA

*President, Azanian People's
Organisation, 1994.*

Born in Tzaneen on 7 August 1947, Mosibudi Mangena was the youngest of the seven children of Tlodipjane and Rephard Mangena.

He attended Mawasha Primary School (1955-56) in Tzaneen; Jaarskraal Primary School (1957-63) at Ga-Maja in the Pietersburg area; and Lethabong Primary School (1964) in Wallmansthal near Pretoria. Mangena attended Wallmansthal Secondary School (1965-67) where he obtained his Junior Certificate with distinction. He then proceeded to Hebron Training Institute (1968-69) where he matriculated.

He applied for admission to the University of the Witwatersrand to study mechanical engineering, but rules governing the entry of Africans into the engineering school required that they first obtain a BSc degree from a black university as they could not attend lectures in science faculty departments. This meant that for Mangena and other black applicants, the engineering degree would take seven years of study instead of the usual four. In order to comply with these regulations, Mangena enrolled at the University of Zululand (Ngoye) for a BSc degree.

During his first semester at university, students from the black section of the University of Natal came to the Ngoye campus on behalf of the South African Students' Organisation (Saso) to address the student body. Their message was that black people had been oppressed and brutalised by whites during three centuries of colonisation and racism which had led blacks to lose their dignity and inner sense of worth and self-esteem; that whites were a united power block while blacks were a fragmented and powerless mass; that there was an urgent need for blacks to organise themselves into a united force if they were to change their lot; and that liberation was an act of self-activity and not an act of charity by any other external being.

Many Ngoye students, including Mangena and Nicodemus Mthuli ka Shezi, identified with Saso and joined the organisation, becoming active in its local branch. In 1971 Mangena was elected to the Students' Representative Council (SRC), representing science faculty students, and by this time the entire Ngoye student body had affiliated to Saso through its SRC. However, his activities in Saso and the SRC resulted in friction between Mangena and the university authorities, especially following an article he had written arguing in favour of economic sanctions. When Mangena narrowly failed his second year examinations at the end of 1971 he strongly believed the university had deliberately penalised him because of his political activities and he decided to discontinue his studies.

Mangena moved back to Pretoria where he joined the Pretoria branch of Saso (Preso) in 1972, becoming its chairman the same year. While living in Mamelodi he participated in the Saso literacy campaign in the Winterveld area. During this time he worked as head of a quality control laboratory in a brick-making factory at Olifantsfontein, near Tembisa township. He resigned after three months when he discovered that a white junior employee earned more than double his salary despite his higher qualifications.

In mid-1972 Mangena was asked by Mthuli Shezi to convene the interim structure of the Black People's Convention (BPC) in the Pretoria area, a political organisation established for Black Consciousness adherents in the general community. Mangena led the delegation from the Pretoria branch to the inaugural conference of the organisation at Hammanskraal on 16-17 December 1972 where he was elected BPC national organiser. It was at this time that Mangena's close friend, Shezi, was pushed in front of a moving train by a white railway worker and subsequently died as a result of his injuries.

Mangena spent the first part of 1973 touring the country on behalf of the BPC, organising, establishing branches and raising funds.

In June 1973 he was arrested in the Johannesburg offices of the BPC, and transferred to Port Elizabeth where he was detained for over three months under section 6 of the Terrorism Act. He was brought to trial in the Eastern Cape Supreme Court, and charged with attempting to recruit two policemen for military training while on a train trip to Port Elizabeth. Convicted, he was sentenced to five years' imprisonment on 3 October 1973.

Mangena served his sentence on Robben Island and on his release was banned for five years and banished to Mahwelereng, near Potgietersrus, Northern Transvaal.

Following the post-June 1976 flight of thousands of black youths to neighbouring countries and further afield, a decision was taken to dissolve all Black Consciousness organisations in exile and form one united body. As a result the Black Consciousness Movement of Azania (BCMA) was launched in London on 12 April 1980 with the tasks of providing a political home for BCM activists in exile; establishing a military wing; working for unity among all the components of the Azanian liberation movements; and organising international solidarity for the Azanian liberation struggle.

On 3 August 1981, at the request of the BCMA, Mangena and his family left for Botswana, two years before his banning order was due to expire. He was elected chairperson of the Botswana region of the BCMA in December 1981, and in August 1982 was elected chairperson of the central committee of the BCMA.

Mangena studied intermittently through the University of South Africa before his arrest and while on Robben Island. However, he studied more consistently while under banning orders in Mahwelereng and during the first five years of his exile in Botswana. He completed a BSc degree in 1979, BSc Honours in 1981 and an MSc degree in Applied Mathematics in 1986.

In September 1989 his book, *On Your Own*, a narrative of the development of the Black Consciousness Movement, was published.

Following the unbanning of organisations in February 1990 and the start of the negotiation process the BCMA called for unity among the liberation movements and workers' organisations; for the democratisation of the negotiating process through the establishment of a constituent assembly; for the method of establishing the constituent assembly to be negotiated at a neutral venue outside South Africa under the chairmanship of an impartial mediator; and for the new constitution to contain mechanisms for the redistribution of land and wealth.

The BCMA did not return to take part in the elections because it believed that the Kempton Park agreements and the constitution upon which the elections were based entrenched white supremacy in South Africa. It believed no fundamental change would occur and that the existing racial inequalities in land ownership, in the ownership patterns in the economy and in the delivery of social services would continue. It did not suspend the armed struggle for the same reasons, but it did not engage in any armed activity after the April 1994 elections.

In October 1994 the Azanian People's Organisation (Azapo), a Black Consciousness grouping within South Africa, called a conference at which it was resolved to merge Azapo and BCMA, but to retain the name Azapo. Mangena, who had returned to South Africa from Zimbabwe on 27 July 1994, was elected president.

Mangena is married to Thabile Kubheka and they have two children.

SOURCES

1. Correspondence with Mosibudi Mangena, February 1990.
2. Mosibudi Mangena, *On Your Own*, Johannesburg, 1989.
3. *Sowetan*, 3 April 1991.
4. Correspondence with Mosibudi Mangena, February 1992.
5. Correspondence and discussion with Mosibudi Mangena, November 1994.

TREVOR ANDREW MANUEL

Member of Parliament,
African National Congress, 1994.
Minister of Trade, Industry
and Tourism, 1994.

Born in Kensington, Cape Town, on 31 January 1956, Trevor Manuel was one of the four children of Philma and Abraham Manuel, an employee of the Cape Town City Council.

After matriculating at Harold Cressy High School in 1973, Manuel was employed by a construction company where he remained for seven-and-a-half years, reaching the post of civil engineering technician. He resigned in 1981 to work voluntarily as a community organiser for the Cape Areas Housing Action Committee (Cahac). In March 1982 Manuel became a field worker for the Education Resources Information Centre (Eric), an agency supplying literature to community organisations.

As a young boy, Manuel became aware of the South African political situation when, in 1960, his black neighbours were forced to move in police vans from Kensington, a mixed area, to Guguletu, a black area. His first formal political involvement was his participation – with the encouragement of his father – in the Labour Party Youth in 1969.

However, he dropped out of its activities as a result of peer pressure at school and his belief that Labour Party participation in the Coloured Representative Council was a futile exercise.

During 1973 Manuel's views were further influenced by students at the University of the Western Cape, and he developed a world view largely defined by Black Consciousness. The following year he became involved with the Young Christian Workers, a mainly-Catholic group emphasising worker issues. At this stage he was employed by a construction company and made contact with migrant workers from the Ciskei. He visited their hostels frequently and learnt of their living conditions and families in the 'homeland'. This had a profound influence on Manuel as he compared his lifestyle with that of the workers. In 1975, as a result of his contact with migrants from the Ciskei, he spent ten days at Mgwali, a 'black spot' in the Eastern Cape.

This period was one of restlessness for Manuel and he was greatly influenced by his friendship with Toufie Bardien, a former member of the Coloured People's Congress, who had been banned for 15 years.

In 1975 Manuel volunteered to serve on an action committee in the Kensington/Factreton area to protest against busfare increases. The attempt to initiate a bus boycott failed, but a youth group developed out of the campaign in an early attempt at a political organisation aiming to tackle community projects. The group eventually collapsed due to differences in political outlook, but through its activities, Manuel came into contact with activists from other areas, including Johnny Issel and Peter Jones.

In 1976 Manuel participated in an adult literacy scheme for migrant workers and during the uprising of that year undertook support work for those arrested, raising bail and obtaining legal assistance.

In 1979 he became involved in the publishing of a community newspaper, *Kenfacts*. In addition, he joined the Kensington/Factreton Tenants and Ratepayers Association and convened its working committee. He made contact with the newly-established *Grassroots* community newspaper and served on its editorial committee.

The Tenants and Ratepayers Association played a supportive role in the 1980 school boycott. Manuel was elected to the bus action committee which spearheaded the bus boycott, and as one of the few activists not detained in that period, he faced the task of keeping the boycott alive.

In 1980 Manuel became a member of the steering committee of the Umbrella Rentals Committee which had been established to co-ordinate resistance to rent increases in nine communities. This committee was later transformed into the Cape Areas Housing Action Committee, of which Manuel became secretary. It was at this stage that Manuel resigned from his construction company job to work in a voluntary capacity for Cahac.

In 1983 he attended the Anti-South African Indian Council Committee conference in Johannesburg, where the concept of a united democratic front against the proposed new constitution and Koornhof Bills was put forward. His involvement in the founding of the UDF in the Western Cape led to his appointment as the region's secretary and at its national launch in August 1983, Manuel was elected to the UDF national executive.

In September 1985 Manuel went into hiding in the wake of arrests of top-ranking UDF activists, but on 22 October 1985 he was detained under section 29 of the Internal Security Act. On 15 November, while still in detention, he was banned from attending any meetings until 31 August 1990.

He was released on 21 November, but his banning order kept him under virtual house arrest. Following court cases in which banning orders were overturned, particularly those of Eastern Cape UDF officials Mkhuseli Jack and Henry Fazzie, Manuel's ban was lifted on 25 March 1986 when it was ruled that it did not comply with the provisions of the Internal Security Act. He immediately reaffirmed that he would be deeply involved in the fight to end apartheid and called for the release of all political prisoners and the return of exiles.

On 15 August 1986 Manuel was detained in terms of state of emergency regulations and held at the Sea Point police station, before his transfer to Victor Verster Prison, Paarl. He was released on 7 July 1988, but under severe restrictions. Ten weeks later, on 21 September 1988, he was again detained under emergency regulations and held at Pollsmoor Prison, Cape Town. He was released on 17 February 1989, again under restriction orders which included house arrest at night; reporting twice daily to the Athlone police station; and confinement to the Wynberg magisterial district.

During the Mass Democratic Movement defiance campaign organised in August and September 1989 to coincide with the general election, Manuel defied his restriction order to speak at a press conference in Athlone on 2 August. On 28 August he was detained and went on a hunger strike. He was transferred from the Mannenberg police station to Grootvlei Prison, near Bloemfontein, and released on 26 September, again under severe restrictions. During this time he worked as a projects and policy developer for the Mobil Foundation in Cape Town.

Following the unbanning of the ANC in February 1990, Manuel was appointed its deputy co-ordinator in the Western Cape with the responsibility of opening an office and helping with the establishment of structures in the area. He was elected publicity secretary of the ANC in the Western Cape at its first regional conference in 1990. In July 1991 Manuel was elected to the national executive of the ANC at its congress held in Durban, and thereafter elected to serve on its national working committee.

In 1992 Manuel became head of the ANC's Department of Economic Planning. Lacking any formal education in economics, he had to familiarise himself with key issues and helped to develop ANC policy, taking into account pressures from the unions, business and the ANC constituency. He also served on the ANC committee dealing with socio-economic reconstruction.

Manuel represented the ANC on the National Peace Committee established in terms of the National Peace Accord signed in September 1991. He also served on its sub-committee dealing with socio-economic reconstruction and development.

In the April 1994 general election Manuel stood as an ANC candidate for the national assembly and became a member of parliament. In May of that year, he was appointed Minister of Trade, Industry and Tourism. He is therefore responsible for improving South Africa's competitiveness in the global market and developing an export culture after years of economic policies orientated towards import replacement. He will also oversee South Africa's compliance with the new General Agreement on Tariffs and Trade (GATT) and the phasing out of the general export incentive scheme. In addition, he will have to deal with the survival of the country's motor, textile and clothing industries. In June 1994 he was appointed leader of the House and at the ANC's Bloemfontein conference held in December 1994 he was re-elected to the organisation's national executive committee.

Manuel is married to Lynne (born Matthews) and they have three children.

SOURCES

1. *Herald*, 28 September 1985.
2. *Argus*, 23 October 1985.
3. *Cape Times*, 16 November 1985.
4. *Argus*, 21 November 1985.
5. *Cape Times*, 23 November 1985.
6. *Argus*, 26 March 1986.
7. Interviewed 17 May 1984, Cape Town.
8. *South*, 11 June 1987.
9. *Herald*, 8 July 1988.
10. *Argus*, 21 September 1988.
11. *Argus*, 18 February 1989.
12. *Argus*, 2 August 1989.
13. *Argus*, 28 August 1989.
14. *Argus*, 5 September 1989.
15. *Cape Times*, 27 September 1989.
16. *Daily News*, 23 June 1994.

17. Anton Harber and Barbara Ludman (eds), *A-Z of South African Politics*, *Weekly Mail & Guardian*/Penguin Books, Johannesburg, 1994.

GILL MARCUS

Member of Parliament,
African National Congress, 1994.

Born on 10 August 1949 in Johannesburg, Gill Marcus was the second of the four children of Molly and Nathan Marcus, an accountant. Both her parents subsequently worked for the African National Congress (ANC) abroad for 15 years until they retired.

Marcus grew up in Johannesburg and attended Barnato Park High School, Berea, matriculating in 1966. She then enrolled at the University of the Witwatersrand for a BCom degree, but left after two years for the United Kingdom with her family in 1969. There she completed her degree through the University of South Africa in the mid-1970s.

In London her family opened a salad bar and Marcus worked there. She came from a politicised home and felt she could make a contribution towards solving the political problems in South Africa. She believed that the ANC was the only vehicle through which this could be done. In 1970 she began to work with the information department of the ANC and from 1976 became the editor of a weekly ANC news bulletin outlining events in South Africa. She remained editor until 1990 and also served as the ANC's deputy secretary for Information and Publicity from the mid-1980s. In the latter capacity she was responsible for compiling information on the ANC's activities for international distribution.

Following the unbanning of the ANC in February 1990 the movement asked Marcus to return to South Africa to help establish its information department. While setting up the department, Marcus served as ANC media spokesperson.

At the ANC's July 1991 conference Marcus was elected to the organisation's national executive committee and was re-elected in December 1994. In 1991 she was co-opted onto the ANC's national working committee and was elected to this committee in February 1995.

In the April 1994 elections Marcus stood as an ANC candidate for the National Assembly and became a member of parliament. She was then elected chairperson of the joint standing committee on finance. In this capacity she has been instrumental in changing the role and function of the 55-member committee which gives consideration to all budgetary bills presented to parliament. A number of working groups have been established to deal with, inter alia, taxation, macro-economic policy, finance, relations with the provinces and the budgetary process. In addition, twice-weekly meetings are held to discuss policy issues. Marcus has attempted to open up the process of the committee to facilitate the development of a broader understanding by the public regarding financial issues.

Marcus also serves on the Public Accounts portfolio committee and is deputy chairperson of the Audit Commission.

In terms of the ANC's policy of allocating constituency areas to its members of parliament, Marcus is responsible for the Tsitsikamma area of the Eastern Cape which includes the towns of Storms River, Humansdorp, Uitenhage and Jeffreys Bay. She therefore spends time in this area holding meetings and serving all constituents, regardless of political party affiliation.

Gill Marcus is single.

SOURCE

Interviewed 23 February 1995, Cape Town.

VINCENT JOSEPH MATTHEWS

Member of Parliament,
Inkatha Freedom Party.
Deputy Minister of Safety
and Security, 1994.

Born in Durban on 17 June 1929, Joe Matthews was one of the five children of Frieda and ZK Matthews, a professor, academic lawyer and anthroplogist at the University College of Fort Hare.

Matthews attended Lovedale School in Alice where he completed his primary education and then enrolled at St Peter's Secondary School in Rosettenville, Johannesburg, where he first became politically active. He joined the African National Congress (ANC) Youth League at St Peter's which was formed in 1944 and served as its branch chairman. He subsequently became chairman of the ANC Youth League in Rosettenville.

Following his matriculation in 1947, Matthews attended the University College of Fort Hare and graduated in 1950 with a BA in English and History. During this time, he came into contact with Nelson Mandela and Mangosuthu Buthelezi. He became a close friend of the latter at whose wedding he served as best man. In 1948 he chaired the ANC Youth League until 1950 when he became its national secretary under the presidency of Mandela. He became president of the Youth League in 1952.

After graduating Matthews taught for a period at Newall School and in 1952 became active in the ANC's Defiance Campaign and later the Congress of the People Campaign of 1955 which culminated in the drafting of the Freedom Charter. However, he was unable to attend the meeting in Kliptown as he was under banning orders issued in September 1953. The order included a ban on his teaching and he could not be quoted. In addition he not attend a gathering of more than two people. During this period, he undertook political work underground.

While banned during 1954-56 Matthews completed his LLB degree through London University as an external student. He then completed legal articles with JH Spilkin, attorneys, in Port Elizabeth from 1957-58.

On 5 December 1956 Matthews and his father were among 156 political activists arrested and charged with high treason. Most of those charged were released on bail and the trial began in 1958. Matthews and his father were among those acquitted in what was to be a marathon four-and-a-half year trial for key leaders such as Mandela.

In 1959 Matthews drafted a discussion paper for the ANC leadership in which he argued that the Bantu Self-Government Act of that year could be used to establish structures to promote political unity among Zulus in Natal.

Matthews joined the South African Communist Party (SACP) in 1957 and served on its central committee from 1962-70. However he subsequently developed doubts as to whether the ideology could work in practice and became estranged from the party.

In 1960, following the anti-pass campaign which led to the Sharpeville massacre and the banning of the ANC, a state of emergency was declared. During the emergency, Matthews was among some 1 800 political activists imprisoned without charge or trial. He was subsequently released. He then escaped to Lesotho, and his wife and family followed shortly afterwards. Other than flights via Jan Smuts Airport, Johannesburg, Matthews did not set foot in the country again until his return in 1991.

In 1965 he was awarded his MA in History at the School of Oriental and African Studies at the University of London, while serving at the same time as the ANC representative in its London office. He was also the first editor of the ANC journal *Sechaba* in 1966.

In 1970 Matthews moved to Botswana where he became assistant secretary in the office of Prime Minister Sir Seretse Khama. In 1972 he was appointed assistant attorney general for Botswana, a post he held until 1976. At that time he played a low-key political role and helped the ANC to operate in Botswana.

In 1976 Matthews opened a private law practice and remained in Gabarone until 1984 when he returned to the United Kingdom. In the late 1980s he lived in Canada and the Netherlands where he wrote articles for papers and journals and undertook academic work. In March 1991 he privately applied to return to South Africa. He attended the ANC congress held in Durban in 1991 as a representative of the veterans.

Matthews returned to South Africa in March 1991. He settled in Durban where he wished to establish a legal practice. He resumed his contacts with Buthelezi and ANC colleagues and in December 1992 was appointed chief executive officer of the Inkatha Freedom Party (IFP). In this capacity, he has served as spokesperson for the party and attended the multi-party negotiations in April 1993.

In the April 1994 general election, Matthews was second on the IFP's list for the national assembly and was elected to parliament. In May he was appointed Deputy Minister of Safety and Security in the government of national unity.

During March 1995, Botswana authorities announced that they were reviewing charges of trust fund embezzlement against Matthews, which allegedly took place while he practised as a lawyer in that country. They indicated that a request to South Africa for the extradition of Matthews was possible.

In 1951 Matthews married Regina Thelma Phillips from Durban. They have seven children.

SOURCES

1. *People in Politics*, Second Quarter 1993, Institute for a Democratic South Africa (Idasa), Durban, 1993.
2. *Profile 94*, South African Communication Services, Pretoria, 1994.
3. *Weekly Mail and Guardian*, 17 March 1995.

THABO MVUYELWA MBEKI

*National Chairperson, African
National Congress, 1993-94.
Deputy President, African
National Congress, 1994.
Member of Parliament,
African National Congress, 1994.
First Executive Deputy
President of South Africa, 1994.*

Born in Idutywa, Transkei, on 18 June 1942, Thabo Mbeki was one of the four children of Epainette and Govan Mbeki.

Mbeki attended primary schools in Idutywa, Queenstown and Butterworth and high school at Lovedale, Alice. He joined the ANC Youth League in 1956 while at Lovedale and undertook organisational work within the school. Following a student strike in 1959 the school closed down and its students were expelled. Mbeki remained at home to study and sat his matriculation examinations at St John's High School, Umtata, in 1959. During 1960 and 1961, Mbeki completed his A-Level examinations through the South African Committee for Higher Education in Johannesburg, and in 1961-62 undertook the first year of an economics degree as an external student with the University of London.

During this period the ANC was declared unlawful, and Mbeki became involved with its underground, mainly in the Witwatersrand and Pretoria areas. During 1961, Mbeki was active in mobilising students and youth in the May stay-at-home in protest against the creation of a Republic. In addition, after the ANC decided that it was necessary to form an organisation for black students, the African Students' Association was formed in December 1961 in Durban. Mbeki was elected secretary, but the organisation subsequently collapsed when many of its members were arrested during the 1962-64 period.

When in Johannesburg, Mbeki stayed with Duma Nokwe, secretary general of the ANC while it was still legal, and the underground work Mbeki and his colleagues did among the youth was supervised by Nokwe and Walter Sisulu.

Mbeki left South Africa in 1962 on the instructions of the ANC. He went through Bechuanaland (now Botswana) into Southern Rhodesia (now Zimbabwe) where he was arrested and kept in a Bulawayo prison for six weeks. The Southern Rhodesian authorities intended to deport him to South Africa, but after his case was raised in the British House of Commons by a Labour member of parliament, Mbeki and his colleagues were granted political asylum in Tanganyika (now Tanzania) by Julius Nyerere. He subsequently left for the United Kingdom to study at the University of Sussex. In 1966 he was awarded an MA in Economics.

While at university, Mbeki was active in the student leadership of the ANC and became involved in the mobilisation of the international student community to take a stand against apartheid. Between 1967 and 1970, Mbeki worked for the ANC office in London and, following military training in the Soviet Union in 1970, he moved to Lusaka. He served as assistant secretary of the revolutionary council of the ANC before spending a year in Botswana from 1973-74, where he held discussions with the Botswana government about opening an ANC office in that country. After returning to Lusaka for six months he served as acting ANC representative in Swaziland from 1975 to April 1976. From December 1976 to February 1978 he was ANC representative in Nigeria, again returning to Lusaka at the end of that appointment.

Mbeki was appointed to the ANC national executive committee in 1975 and in 1978 was made political secretary in the office of the president. He was subsequently appointed ANC director for information.

In 1985, following the ANC's Kabwe conference, Mbeki added secretary for presidential affairs to his activities, also sitting on the ANC's political and military council. After the death of Johnny Makatini, Mbeki took over as head of the ANC's department of international affairs in 1989.

From 1985 onwards, Mbeki led many of the ANC delegations which met groups of South Africans representing different constituencies within the country.

Following the unbanning of the ANC and the release of Nelson Mandela in February 1990, Mbeki formed part of the ANC team which met South African government representatives at Groote Schuur in Cape Town in May.

At the ANC conference held in Durban in July 1991 Mbeki was elected to the organisation's national executive committee, receiving the second highest number of votes polled. He was subsequently elected to the ANC's national working committee.

Mbeki attended the plenary sessions of the Convention for a Democratic South Africa (Codesa) in December 1991 and May 1992. He served on the Codesa working group dealing with transitional arrangements and also served as an ANC representative on the National Peace Committee.

In June 1993 the ANC Youth League formally requested that Mbeki be made deputy president of the organisation and heir apparent to Nelson Mandela. On 30 August he was elected national chairman of the ANC, replacing the late Oliver Tambo.

In the general election of April 1994, Mbeki stood as candidate number three on the ANC's list to the national assembly and became a member of parliament. In May, following a struggle between himself and Cyril Ramaphosa, he was appointed first executive deputy president of South Africa. In this he had the support of most of the ANC formations and alliance partners.

Mbeki is married to Zanele, a social worker by profession, who is active in social development programmes including education administration and assisting refugees.

SOURCES

1. Interviewed 7 October 1986, Lusaka.
2. *Daily News*, 3 March 1990.
3. *Daily News*, 24 June 1993.
4. *Natal Mercury*, 31 August 1993.
5. *Financial Mail*, 10 September 1993.
6. *Natal Mercury*, 4 May 1994.
7. *Curriculum vitae* submitted by the office of the Deputy President, August 1994.

TITO TITUS MBOWENI

Member of Parliament,
African National Congress, 1994.
Minister of Labour, 1994.

Born on 16 March 1959 in Bordeaux, Tzaneen, Northern Transvaal, Tito Mboweni was the youngest of the three children of Peggy and the late Nelson Mboweni, a hotel chef.

Mboweni attended Bordeaux Primary School from 1966-73 and Dumela Secondary School from 1974-76. He then attended Bankuna High School where he matriculated in 1978. Mboweni's father worked in Johannesburg and Mboweni spent part of his time there, especially during school holidays. It was there that he first became aware of the influx control regulations as the municipal police occasionally came to check on his father's pass, often late at night. He also found it upsetting and undignified when his parents were stopped for pass checks.

While at secondary school Mboweni learnt from his teachers about past political struggles, particularly regarding Nelson Mandela, the African National Congress prior to its banning and the Black Consciousness South African Students' Organisation. During this period, debate concerning the creation of bantustans alerted him to other political issues.

While at high school, he met students from other parts of South Africa, including some from Soweto schools who had served on the Soweto Students' Representative Council, and who had had to leave their schools to be educated elsewhere. This created a very intense political environment at the school which was combined with input from Radio Zimbabwe, broadcast from Maputo by the Zimbabwe liberation movement. In addition, students at Bankuna held school boycotts in an attempt to engage its authoritarian management.

In 1979 Mboweni registered at the University of the North (Turfloop) for a BCom degree and became involved in student politics. After a Sharpeville memorial service on 21 March a student leader, Ngoako Ramathlodi (now premier of the Northern Transvaal), was expelled, resulting in a student boycott demanding his reinstatement. This led to police intervention to break the boycott. Mboweni's contact with Ramathlodi was to develop into a close friendship.

Strikes and police contact were frequent occurrences at Turfloop and the Students' Representative Council was banned by university authorities. However, activist students formed the University of the North Drama Society which became an important organising body for them and to which they were able to recruit potential leadership. Mboweni became active in the society which also included members of the ANC underground. Besides its underground political work, members of the society produced protest drama which included plays written by Ramathlodi.

This was the first time that Mboweni came into contact with the Freedom Charter and he also read speeches made by Nelson Mandela before his imprisonment. It was also the beginning of his real contact with the ANC.

During this period attempts were being made to form new organisations within South Africa including the Congress of South African Students and the Azanian Students Organisation (Azaso) and to strengthen the trade unions. Early in 1980, Mboweni helped to establish the Turfloop branch of Azaso and was elected to its executive, serving as correspondence secretary. A major student strike took place at Turfloop that year and student leaders were harrassed. The boycott ended in July 1980 and, by August, Mboweni felt discouraged and decided to leave the country to fight the struggle by other means.

On 9 August 1980, Mboweni and a fellow student crossed the Caledon River near Ladybrand into Lesotho. Ramathlodi had left South Africa earlier in 1980 for Lesotho and Mboweni joined him there.

During the following year Mboweni participated in the ANC's political education programme. This involved intensive political study, including the history of colonisation; wars of resistance; post-colonial states and experiences; the history of the ANC; the development of the South African economy; and the rise of the trade unions. At that time, the head of the ANC in Lesotho was Chris Hani.

From August 1981-85 Mboweni attended the National University of Lesotho, completing a BA Honours in Economics, with political science as a minor course. While there he was active in an ANC structure known as the Roma Unit. About 200 students from within South Africa were studying at the university and, when they returned home during holidays, formed a link between the ANC cadres and home. In addition, they organised the Committee for Action and Solidarity with Southern African Students which included progressive students from Southern Africa as well as those in the ANC. This organisation also published a journal, *Vanguard*.

In 1985 Mboweni was chairperson of the Federation of Academic Societies, a powerful organisation which was disliked by the Lesotho government. Mboweni led a major strike and Lesotho soldiers warned him that he would be detained. The ANC President, Oliver Tambo, called Mboweni and Ramathlodi to ANC headquarters in Lusaka, Zambia, to account for their activities and to point out that they were damaging the relationship between the ANC and the Lesotho government. However, after Mboweni and Ramathlodi had put forward their case, some of the more progressive ministers of the Lesotho government became closer to the ANC students.

While in Lesotho Mboweni became part of the ANC's underground effort and made contact with people from South Africa, helping to smuggle literature into the country.

At the end of November 1985 Mboweni left Lesotho for the United Kingdom and from then until June 1986 attended Sheffield University studying towards a MPhil degree. He subsequently studied at the University of East Anglia, Norwich, and in 1987 completed his MA in development economics.

While in Britain Mboweni participated in the sanctions campaign against South Africa. On completing his studies he remained in Britain to work with Aziz Pahad on the ANC's Regional Political-Military Council, responsible for political education and organising political classes for people coming from South Africa, including trade unionists and youth activists. During this time he also undertook consultancy work for Unesco.

Towards the end of 1988 Mboweni was asked to return to Africa and went to Lusaka to work for the Internal Political Committee, a sub-committee of the Political-Military Council. There he worked under the leadership of Ruth Mompati and Steve Tshwete and his colleagues included Joel Netshitenze, Jeremy Cronin, Ronnie Kasrils, Sue Rabkin and the late Joe Slovo. As an economist Mboweni also became involved with the ANC's economics department, headed by Max Sisulu. During this time Mboweni was asked to make contact with the business and professional sector within South Africa, including lawyers, teachers and social workers. He also increasingly worked with unionists.

Following the unbanning of the ANC in February 1990 the

organisation held a Conference on Economic Policy in May in Harare together with the South-African based Economic Trends Group and the Congress of South African Trade Unions.

Mboweni returned to South Africa in May 1990 to attend a conference organised by the Consultative Business Movement and then travelled back to Lusaka. The ANC decided to establish its economics department inside South Africa as it was felt that economic policy was one of the crucial issues outside of the negotiations. Mboweni, having received indemnity, returned in June 1990 to establish the department.

In 1991 Mboweni spent a four-month sabbatical at the Institute for Social Development at the University of the Western Cape.

In the April 1994 general election Mboweni stood as an ANC candidate for the national assembly and became a member of parliament. In May he was appointed Minister of Labour. At the ANC's conference in Bloemfontein held in December 1994, Mboweni was elected to the organisation's national executive committee.

In January 1995 Mboweni was made one of the Global Leaders for Tomorrow by the World Economic Forum based in Geneva.

Mboweni is separated from his wife and has two sons.

SOURCE

Interviewed 24 February 1995.

FRANK THEMBA MDLALOSE

Premier, KwaZulu/Natal
Province, 1994.
Minister of Labour, 1994.

Frank Mdlalose was born on 29 November 1931 at Nqutu, the son of Tabitha Mthembu, a teacher, and Jaconiah Zwelabo Mdlalose, a general dealer. He attended local primary schools in Nqutu from 1937 to 1942, entering the Polela Institution before attending St Francis High School, Mariannhill, where he matriculated in 1949. Between 1950 and 1952, he studied for a BSc degree at the University of Fort Hare, Alice, and completed his University Education Diploma in 1953.

Mdlalose came from a conservative Catholic school where politics had not been discussed, but once at Fort Hare his interest was aroused through the influence of Mangosuthu Buthelezi, who was completing his BA there at the time. Buthelezi suggested that he should attend an African National Congress (ANC) Youth League meeting to be held at Ntselamanzi township, near Fort Hare, but Mdlalose's elder brother, Edward, who was also a student, felt Mdlalose was too young and naive to participate.

However, Mdlalose attended the meeting and was surprised to discover that one of the speakers was his brother, Edward. From that time onwards, Mdlalose became increasingly involved in political activity, eventually serving as chairman of the Victoria East branch of the ANC Youth League, which consisted almost entirely of Fort Hare students, as the League had been banned from the campus. In addition, he was elected to the university's Students' Representative Council in 1952 and 1953.

Mdlalose's ideas were influenced by Professor ZK Matthews, president of the ANC in the Cape and vice-principal of the university. In addition, he consulted frequently with Dr J Njongwe, who replaced Matthews when he left for the United States, and who became acting ANC president in the Cape and volunteer-in-chief for the Defiance Campaign in that province.

Mdlalose played an active role in the Defiance Campaign which was launched on 26 June 1952. He and other students led people into the town of Alice after curfew hours and sat on 'whites only' benches at the station. In August, after a particularly large group of volunteers had been arrested and charged, a number of supporters sang outside the court and accompanied the accused to their cells. This led to a police charge and students, including Mdlalose, were severely beaten.

Following the completion of his University Education Diploma in 1953, Mdlalose became a medical student at the University of Natal and qualified as a doctor in 1958.

His experience at this university was different from that at Fort Hare. In Natal, the medical students were isolated from the main campus, living in a residence in Wentworth. Students participated occasionally in ANC meetings held in town and Mdlalose sometimes visited his friend, ANC Natal secretary, MB Yengwa, at whose office he met ANC President Albert Luthuli.

In 1955, the Congress of the People was called at Kliptown, Johannesburg, and the Freedom Charter was adopted there. Mdlalose had reservations about the Charter as he felt it was more socialist than nationalist in content. He also believed that members of the South African Communist Party (SACP) had too great an influence on the ANC. By 1959 a clear split had developed within the organisation and many, including Mdlalose, thought of forming the breakaway Pan-Africanist Congress (PAC), spearheaded by Robert Sobukwe. However, Mdlalose made the decision to remain with the ANC in an attempt to counter its left wing.

In 1959 Mdlalose participated in the potato boycott as a protest against the use of pass laws offenders as prison labourers on the farms of the Eastern Transvaal.

Mdlalose completed his internship at King Edward VIII Hospital, Durban, and then, in 1960, established a private practice in Atteridgeville, outside Pretoria. Following a period (1962-70) in Steadville Township, Ladysmith, he moved to Madadeni. During this time he had continued contact with Buthelezi and visited him occasionally. In 1974, Buthelezi asked Mdlalose for his ideas on forming a new political organisation, and in March 1975 he was invited to a meeting in Melmoth, Natal, where the new organisation's constitution was discussed.

Arising from this meeting, Inkatha yeNkululeko yeSizwe was launched. Dr AH Zulu served as its first national chairman, but in 1976 Mdlalose was elected to this position at Inkatha's second national conference. Since moving to Madadeni, Mdlalose has acquired widespread business interests. He was chairman of the Madadeni town council from 1971 to 1977, and in addition has served on the following bodies: Bantu anti-tuberculosis association, Madadeni (1970-78); Mangosuthu Madadeni scholarship fund committee (1974-78); Ladysmith Bantu child welfare society (chairman, 1966-70); council, Medical University of Southern Africa (1976 to date).

In 1978 Mdlalose was elected to the KwaZulu legislative assembly and was appointed Minister of Interior. In 1983 he became Minister of Health and Welfare, a portfolio he shared with ESC Sithebe in 1986.

Mdlalose participated in the Natal Indaba which commenced in April 1986 and served as leader of the Inkatha delegation to this gathering.

In July 1990 Mdlalose succeeded Oscar Dhlomo as Minister of Education and Culture in KwaZulu.

Following the 2 February 1990 unbanning of the ANC and the release of political prisoners, violence in Natal and the Transvaal between supporters of the ANC and Inkatha began to escalate. Mdlalose worked with John Nkadimeng of the ANC, especially in the Mpumalanga area, in an effort to stop the fighting. He also served on a national 12-a-side committee and on a four-a-side Peace Implementation Committee which included representatives of Inkatha and the ANC. Mdlalose was present at the peace meeting between Mandela and Buthelezi on 29 January 1991, and subsequent to that meeting he and Jacob Zuma, then chair of the Southern Natal region of the ANC, moved into trouble spots jointly in an effort to stop the violence.

In March 1991 Mdlalose was relieved of his portfolio as Minister of Health and became Minister without Portfolio attached to the office of the Chief Minister. Buthelezi indicated that Mdlalose's huge responsibilities linked to the position of Inkatha national chairman as well as his work implementing programmes aimed at ending the violence demanded that he be relieved of other portfolios.

Mdlalose also served as chairman of the KwaZulu/Natal Joint Executive Authority and was a key figure in the IFP's negotiation team on the constitutional future of South Africa.

Mdlalose headed the IFP delegation at the Convention for a Democratic South Africa (Codesa) in December 1991. Inkatha refused to sign Codesa's declaration of intent but agreed to continue to work within the Convention. Mdlalose represented the IFP on the Codesa working group dealing with the future of the TBVC states. Following the breakdown of the Codesa talks, the IFP agreed in January 1993, as part of the Concerned South Africans' Group (consisting of the IFP, KwaZulu government, the Conservative Party, the Bophuthatswana government and the Ciskei government), to a multi-party planning conference to prepare for multi-party negotiations. Mdlalose served on the ten-person planning committee which prepared the ground for new negotiations at the World Trade Centre, Kempton Park. He also became co-leader of the IFP's delegation at the talks. However, in July 1993 the IFP and the KwaZulu government walked out of the negotiation forum and suspended their participation after the chairman of the council decided that sufficient consensus existed for the adoption by the forum of an election date in April 1994 despite the objections of all Cosag members. The decision was subsequently challenged in the Supreme Court, but the court dismissed the application.

Mdlalose was a member of the executive of the National Peace Committee, formed after the National Peace Accord was agreed to in September 1991.

In the general election held in April 1994, Mdlalose stood as the leader of the IFP's list for the KwaZulu Natal Legislative Assembly. The IFP won 51% of the vote in the province. On 11 May he was elected unopposed as the region's premier at the KwaZulu/Natal Assembly's inaugural sitting. He called for peace and extended a hand of friendship to the ANC. However, problems arose over the allocation of portfolios in the KwaZulu/Natal cabinet and a reshuffle took place within days. In addition, the issue of the capital of the province led to a boycott by ANC representatives who refused to attend meetings in Ulundi.

Mdlalose, whose interests include child welfare, tennis and boxing, married Eunice Nokuthula Sikhosana in 1956 and they have three sons and two daughters.

SOURCES

1. Dee Shirley Dean, *Black South Africans. A Who's Who. 57 Profiles of Natal's Leading Blacks*, Cape Town, 1978.
2. *KwaZulu Legislative Assembly, 1972-82*, Bureau of Communication, Department of the Chief Minister, KwaZulu Government Service, Ulundi.
3. Interviewed 11 July 1986, Durban.
4. *Sunday Tribune*, 31 March 1991.
5. *Saturday News*, 9 March 1991.
6. *Natal Mercury*, 12 May 1994.
7. *Weekly Mail*, 13 May 1994.

GEORG MEIRING

*Chief, South African Defence
Force, 1990.*

Georg Meiring was born in Ladybrand, Orange Free State, in 1939. He matriculated at the local high school and then attended the University of the Orange Free State where he graduated with a BSc degree in physics in 1959. He went on to obtain an MSc at the same university where he lectured in Applied Physics for a period.

In 1963 Meiring joined the Permanent Force as a captain and specialised in signals. In 1974 he was appointed director of signals at army headquarters and in 1975, director of telecommunications in the SADF. In 1977 he was appointed director of logistical staff at army headquarters and in 1978 officer commanding, Witwatersrand Command. In 1981 he was promoted to major-general and transferred back to headquarters as chief of army staff (logistics). The following year he was made deputy chief of the army and from 1983-86 Meiring served as general officer commanding the South West Africa Territory Force (about 19 000 men) in Namibia. During this time he was involved in pre-Namibian independence negotiations in Lusaka, Zambia, and the Joint Monitoring Commission period of co-operation with Angola.

Meiring then became general officer commanding the Far North Command and in April 1989 was re-appointed deputy chief of the army. In 1990 he became chief of the army with the rank of lieutenant-general.

Meiring and his wife, Annchen, have five children. He is a keen hunter and cook, reads extensively and enjoys spending time on his smallholding.

SOURCE

1. *People in Politics*, Fourth Quarter 1993, Institute for Democracy in South Arica (Idasa), Durban, 1993.

KENNETH RASELABE MESHOE

Leader, African Christian
Democratic Party, 1994.
Member of Parliament, African
Christian Democratic Party, 1994.

Born in Pretoria on 18 January 1954, Kenneth Meshoe was the fourth of the seven children of Bertha and Edward Meshoe, a police captain. He was raised in a Christian home where the children were taught obedience and discipline.

Meshoe grew up in Pretoria, attending Hofmeyr High School until Standard Nine. In 1972 he matriculated at Maripi High School, Acornhoek, Eastern Transvaal, and then studied at the University of the North for a Secondary Teachers Diploma. During his matriculation year, Meshoe came into contact with the Rev Shadrack Maloka who became his role model in terms of his lifestyle and commitment to Christianity.

Meshoe began teaching in January 1976 at GH Franz High School in Bochum in the Pietersburg area, specialising in General Science, Agriculture and Bibilical Studies. After three months, he realised that he was not suited to the teaching profession and chose to go into the full-time ministry of evangelism. He joined an organisation called Christ for All Nations which preached the gospel throughout Africa.

In 1983-84 Meshoe underwent theological training at the Shekinah Bible Institute in Tennessee, USA, and in 1986 he lived in Zimbabwe for a year. In 1987 he returned to Tennessee to further his studies and returned to South Africa in January 1988. In March he started an independent charismatic church in Vosloorus and also served as a marriage counsellor, holding seminars in the township. He also held seminars on marriage in Zimbabwe, Malawi and Zambia which were organised through the church. Meshoe remained with the church until his involvement with the African Christian Democratic Party (ACDP) in 1993.

Meshoe had no background in political activism and had never been involved in politics because his Christian leaders discouraged this. However, following the September 1990 violence in Vosloorus, Christian leaders began to ask themselves what they could do to stop the violence. Meshoe's church prayed and Meshoe believed that as a result of these prayers, the violence stopped. He therefore concluded that Christians could help to influence events in society. Following biblical research, he concluded that Christians, as citizens, should be politically involved. He began talks with colleagues about this issue and over a two-year period met many like-minded Christians.

In 1992 the Christian Democratic Movement was formed and in September 1993 came into contact with Dr Johan van der Westhuizen. Discussions then began regarding the creation of a new centrist federal party based on Christian principles.

The African Christian Democratic Party was launched on 9 December 1993 in Johannesburg with 250-300 delegates present. Meshoe was elected interim leader, becoming president of the party at its annual general conference at the World Trade Centre in January 1994.

In the general election of April 1994, the ACDP won two seats in the National Assembly and three in provincial parliaments. Meshoe became a member of parliament. In this capacity he serves on the parliamentary portfolio committees of health, home affairs, constitutional affairs and welfare.

It is Meshoe's view that Africans are conservative and religious and that the changing norms in society which affect their families could lead them to support the ACDP which emphasises family values.

Meshoe is married to Lydia and they have three children.

SOURCE

Interviewed 11 August 1994, Cape Town.

ANTHON TOBIAS MEYER

Member of Parliament,
National Party, 1994.
Deputy Minister of Land Affairs,
1994.

Tobie Meyer was born on 14 March 1939 in Kareedouw in the Langkloof, Eastern Cape, the eldest of the two sons of Hannah and Hudson Meyer, a farmer. Although his parents did not actively participate in politics or community affairs, the Meyers took a keen interest in political events, especially the National Party victory in 1948 which they celebrated. His brother is Roelof Meyer, Minister of Constitutional Affairs.

He attended Kareedouw Primary and High School in Uniondale, matriculating at Hoërskool Brandwag in Uitenhage. When his father died in 1956, Meyer had to take over the family farm, Hudsonville, at a very young age. His election as secretary of the Kareedouw Farmers' Association was the first step in a long career of community and organised agricultural service, which eventually led to politics.

After a few years Meyer sold the farm and moved to Ficksburg, Orange Free State, where he was again approached to serve as secretary of the farmers' association in 1968. Eight years later he decided to return to dairy and beef farming in the Eastern Cape and sold the farm in Ficksburg.

When Meyer moved back to the Tsitsikamma in 1976, agriculture in the region was very depressed and underdeveloped. He had not intended to play a role in organised agriculture but was persuaded to become chairman of the Humansdorp Farmers' Association. Despite a lack of funds, the association was voted the best in the Eastern Cape within four years. In 1983 Meyer was selected as South African Farmer of the Year.

As chairman of the farmers' association, Meyer served on the Eastern

Cape Agricultural Union and was elected president in 1983. In the latter capacity he served on its general board and on various other committees of the South African Agricultural Union.

By serving the farming community, Meyer became involved in development projects in the region. He served on the Regional Development Advisory Committee of Region D and the National Regional Development Advisory Council, through which he helped to establish sound relationships between all the agricultural role players in the Eastern Cape, as well as Ciskei and Transkei.

On his own farm Meyer introduced the concept of a partnership relationship between labour and management. Despite initial criticism and ridicule from neighbours, the success of this management style motivated many farmers to follow his example.

Meyer also served on the control board of the South African Broadcasting Corporation and as a director of Volkskas Bank.

His brother's involvement in student and national politics sharpened Meyer's own political interest. When the 1987 general election was announced, he decided to stand as a National Party (NP) candidate in order to help promote the political development of the region. After being elected member of parliament for Cradock, Meyer resigned from his positions in agricultural organisations.

In parliament he played a role in matters relating to agriculture. He served as secretary of the NP study group on agriculture; member of the Select Committee for Public Accounts; and vice-chairman of the Commission for Co-operation and Development.

Meyer was appointed Deputy Minister of Agriculture on 8 April 1991 and became Deputy Minister of Land Affairs on 1 July 1993. He served on the sub-council for regional and local government and traditional authorities of the Transitional Executive Council (TEC) from December 1993-May 1994.

In the first democratic elections in April 1994, Meyer was elected a member of the National Assembly on the NP list. On 10 May he was appointed Deputy Minister of Land Affairs in the government of national unity.

Meyer is married and farms in the Humansdorp district.

SOURCES

1. *People in Politics*, Third Quarter 1994, Institute for Democracy in South Africa, Durban, 1994.
2. *Profile 94*, South African Communication Services, Pretoria, 1994.

ROELOF PETRUS MEYER

Member of Parliament,
National Party, 1994.
Minister of Constitutional Affairs
and of Communication, 1992-94.
Minister of Provincial Affairs and
Constitutional Development,
1994.

Roelof Meyer was born in Port Elizabeth on 16 July 1947, the youngest of the two sons of Hannah and Hudson Meyer, a farmer in the Humansdorp district of the Eastern Cape. His brother is Tobie Meyer, Deputy Minister of Land Affairs. He attended primary school in Kareedouw, and after the family moved to the Orange Free State he went to high school in Ficksburg where he matriculated in 1964.

Following a year's military service at the airforce gymnasium, Pretoria, Meyer enrolled at the University of the Orange Free State, Bloemfontein, and completed his BCom and LLB degrees. While at university he was active in student politics, serving as chairman of the Students' Representatives Council from 1969-70 and as national president of the Afrikaanse Studentebond (ASB) in 1970-71.

On completion of his degree he began work as a legal adviser with Federale Volksbeleggings in Cape Town. In 1973 he began his legal articles with a firm of attorneys in Pretoria, eventually becoming a professional assistant and later a partner in the firm. In 1978 his firm moved him to Johannesburg. During this time, Meyer remained active in Afrikaner and political organisations and was national chairman of the Junior Rapportryers from 1976-78. While in Pretoria, he served on the National Party (NP) divisional council of the Rissik constituency.

In August 1979 Meyer fought and won a by-election in the Johannesburg West constituency when the sitting MP, Dawie de Villiers, left to become South African ambassador in London. As an MP, Meyer served on the NP study groups on national education, constitutional development and defence, and was senior whip of the Transvaal National Party.

On 1 December 1986 Meyer was appointed Deputy Minister of Law and Order. He held this portfolio at a time the country was under a state of emergency. He argued that detentions of activists had played a necessary role in achieving stability. He also claimed that youths in detention were not innocent children, but that many were perpetrators of stone throwing, murder and other acts of violence.

In 1988 Meyer became Deputy Minister of Constitutional Development and Planning and in the cabinet reshuffle after the September 1989 general election was appointed Deputy Minister of Constitutional Development and of National Education.

Until his appointment to the cabinet, Meyer served on the board of the Stellenbosch Farmers' Winery.

Following the unbanning of the African National Congress and the release of Nelson Mandela in February 1990, Meyer formed part of the government delegation to the May talks with the African National Congress at Groote Schuur, Cape Town, and continued to play a key role in the negotiation process. During this period he, together with his Minister Gerrit Viljoen, was relieved of the national education portfolio in order to concentrate on constitutional development.

Following the August 1991 cabinet reshuffle, Meyer was appointed Minister of Defence and Communication and on 1 June 1992 replaced Gerrit Viljoen as Minister of Constitutional Affairs and Communication.

Meyer presently serves as deputy leader of the Transvaal National Party. He was also a NP representative on the National Peace Committee and served on the Convention for a Democratic South Africa's (Codesa) working group on transitional arrangements.

In 1993 he took over as the government's chief negotiator and was instrumental in steering the negotiations at the World Trade Centre to their successful conclusion. He served on the planning committee of the multi-party negotiating process and was one of two government delegates. From December 1993-April 1994 Meyer served on the management committee of the Transitional Executive Council.

In the April 1994 general election, Meyer stood on the NP's list for the national assembly and once again became a member of parliament. In May he was appointed Minister of Provincial Affairs and Constitutional Development in the government of national unity. The portfolio includes the development of a new constitution and the introduction of administrative and operating procedures in the new provinces. Later that month he was given the additional portfolio of local government and is therefore responsible for overseeing the holding of local government elections.

In June 1993 Meyer and Cyril Ramaphosa, the chief ANC negotiator, were awarded honorary law degrees by the University of Massachusetts. They were also named Men of the Year by the *New National* newspaper.

He is married to Carene (born Lubbe) and they have four children.

SOURCES

1. South African Institute of Race Relations, *Race Relations Survey, 1987-88*, Johannesburg, 1988.
2. *Negotiation News*, 2, 25 May 1992.
3. Interviewed 13 November 1986, Johannesburg.
4. *Daily News*, 12 June 1993.
5. *Natal Mercury*, 27 May 1994.
6. *Profile 94*, South African Communication Services, Pretoria, 1994.

RAYMOND MHLABA

Premier, Eastern Cape
Province, 1994.
National Chair, South African
Communist Party, 1995.

Raymond Mhlaba, the son of a policeman, was born in the Fort Beaufort district of the Eastern Cape on 12 February 1920. He completed ten years of schooling, the last two at Healdtown, before being forced to leave school for financial reasons.

Mhlaba was employed as a laundry worker by a Port Elizabeth dry cleaning factory and remained there until he was fired after a laundry workers' strike in April 1948 when 200 workers walked out of city laundries after being refused a two-shillings-and-sixpence weekly raise.

During this time he became active in the trade union movement and in 1943 joined the South African Communist Party. The following year he joined the African National Congress (ANC) and remained active in both organisations, serving as Port Elizabeth Communist Party branch secretary until the party was banned, as well as Port Elizabeth ANC branch chairman from 1947-53. He was also active in the Council for Non-European Trade Unions.

In 1949 Mhlaba chaired the Eastern Cape bus boycott action committee which led a boycott lasting nearly four months. In 1952 he was chosen as the Port Elizabeth Defiance Campaign's volunteer-in-chief and, on 26 June of that year, led a group of defiant protesters through the 'Europeans Only' entrance to the New Brighton railway station, thus becoming the first ANC leader arrested in the campaign.

He was subsequently arrested and detained on several occasions in the 1950s and early 1960s and charged with treason in the 1956 treason trial. Although banned under the Suppression of Communism Act, Mhlaba was elected to the ANC Cape executive committee in 1954 and continued his political activities.

After the ANC was banned, Mhlaba went underground and joined one of the first groups that left the country to do military training during August/September 1961, prior to the formation of Umkhonto we Sizwe (MK). He completed his training and returned to South Africa in February/March 1962, serving as MK's commander-in-chief for a period.

Mhlaba was arrested at Lilliesleaf Farm, Rivonia, in July 1963 and charged with 193 acts of sabotage. The trial was held in the Pretoria Supreme Court and on 12 June 1964 Mhlaba, together with Nelson Mandela, Walter Sisulu, Govan Mbeki, Denis Goldberg, Elias Motsoaledi and Andrew Mlangeni, was sentenced to life imprisonment.

A colleague of Mhlaba has claimed that the evidence given against Mhlaba in the Rivonia trial – that he personally supervised and participated in the Port Elizabeth blasts of 16 December 1961 – was false, as Mhlaba was undergoing military training at the time and was therefore not in the country. During his trial, Mhlaba refused to provide details of his movements at the time.

Mhlaba served his sentence on Robben Island until his transfer to Pollsmoor Prison in 1982.

On 15 October 1989 he and other Rivonia trialists were released from prison and Mhlaba returned to Port Elizabeth. After his release, and the subsequent unbanning of the ANC, he became a member of the ANC's interim internal leadership group. At the relaunch of the SACP as a legal political party, Mhlaba was named as chairman of its interim leadership group.

At the July 1991 ANC congress held in Durban, Mhlaba was elected to the organisation's national executive committee. He was re-elected in December 1994.

In the general election of April 1994 Mhlaba stood as head of the ANC's list for the provincial legislature in the Eastern Cape and was returned as premier. In this position he is responsible for the amalgamation of the bureaucracies of the Cape Provincial Administration, the Ciskei and the Transkei.

As premier Mhlaba has had to deal with numerous crises, particularly in the previous Transkei region. In February 1995 a mutiny by Transkei police was put down by force and at the same time Mhlaba was involved in attempting to negotiate the release of a hostage being held by awaiting-bail prisoners. In the latter case, it became necessary to call in a special task force to storm the prison cell.

At the SACP's ninth national congress, held in April 1995, Mhlaba was elected unopposed as national chair of the party.

Mhlaba, a widower until March 1986, has eight children. While in Pollsmoor Prison, he married Dideka Heliso, mother of three of his children.

SOURCES

1. *Daily News*, 11 October 1989.
2. Thomas Karis, Gwendolen Carter and Gail Gerhart, *From Protest to Challenge. A Documentary History of African Politics in South Africa, 1882-1964*, Vol 4, Standford, 1977.
3. *Cape Times*, 28 March 1986.
4. *Daily News*, 3 October 1989.
5. Francis Meli, *South Africa Belongs to Us*, Harare, 1988.
6. *Daily Mail*, 30 July 1990.
7. *Cape Times*, 27 February 1994.

JOHANNES MODISE

Member of Parliament,
African National Congress, 1994.
Minister of Defence, 1994.

Joe Modise, the only child of Miriam and Ezekiel Modise, was born in Doornfontein, Johannesburg, on 23 May 1929. He attended primary school in Kliptown and completed Standard Eight at the Fred Clark Memorial School, Nancefield. He continued studying privately up to his matriculation.

Modise worked as a driver for various employers including a clothing factory, a leather goods manufacturer and a grocery wholesaler.

After joining the African National Congress (ANC) Youth League in Newclare in about 1947, Modise played an active role in resisting the Sophiatown removals and in 1954 was arrested after trying to defend people against police assaults. Modise served as a part-time organiser for the ANC in the early 1950s and was particularly active during the period when the government was introducing Bantu education. Most of his organising work was among the youth.

In 1956 he was one of the 156 Congress activists accused of treason, although charges were dropped against him in the late 1950s.

Following the banning of the ANC after the 1960 Sharpeville shootings, Umkhonto we Sizwe (MK), the military wing of the ANC, was formed with Modise serving as a member of its high command. He participated in the MK's initial sabotage operations. Modise was responsible for the departure of the first MK recruits to leave South Africa for military training. In 1962 he was asked to resign his job as a lorry driver to work as a national full-time MK organiser.

Towards the end of 1962 some of the Umkhonto cadres were arrested in Northern Rhodesia and deported to South Africa. Early in 1963 it became clear that the South African authorities were looking for him after some of those captured had, under interrogation, implicated him in their departure from South Africa for military training.

The Umkhonto high command decided that Modise should leave the country to do military training and take charge of its military personnel abroad. In addition, he was entrusted with the procurement of armaments and was asked to organise the shipment of weapons into South Africa. Modise underwent military training in Czechoslovakia (1963) and the Soviet Union (1964). At the end of 1964 he returned to Tanzania.

In the meantime the first commander of Umkhonto we Sizwe, Nelson Mandela, was arrested as was his successor, Raymond Mhlaba. Wilton Mkwayi acted briefly as commander, but when he too was arrested in 1965, the ANC national executive requested Modise to take over MK's leadership. At the same time (1965) he was appointed a member of the ANC's national executive committee.

Modise remained in Tanzania in 1965 and was involved in efforts to re-organise MK and arrange for new cadres to go into training. He tried to set up a route back to South Africa via Botswana and in 1966 lived in Lusaka for longer periods while carrying out reconnaissance from Botswana.

In the second half of 1966, Modise remained in Zambia to plan joint operations between MK and the Zimbabwe People's Revolutionary Army (Zipra), the armed wing of the Zimbabwe African People's Union (Zapu), under the leadership of Joshua Nkomo. Joint operations took place in the south-western part of Rhodesia, near Wankie.

In 1968 an attempt was made to push through the eastern part of Rhodesia and Modise spent ten days in that country carrying out extensive reconnaissance. The aim was to entrench both Umkhonto and Zapu cadres among the local population in order to open up a route through the eastern highlands and the game reserve into the North-eastern Transvaal. However, the 1968 group collapsed.

From 1970-76, Modise directed the building up of underground structures in South Africa and from 1976 military action again commenced with a strong emphasis on 'armed propaganda' for the ANC.

Modise's position on the national executive of the ANC was confirmed at the Kabwe conference in 1985 and he also served on the military committee of the ANC and on its political-military council.

Following the unbanning of the ANC and the release of Nelson Mandela in February 1990, Modise formed part of the ANC team which participated in talks with the South African government at Groote Schuur in Cape Town in May.

In July 1991 Modise was re-elected a member of the ANC's national executive committee at its congress in Durban. He also served on its national working committee. At MK's national conference, held in Venda in 1991, Modise was reconfirmed as commander of the ANC's army.

During 1993 Modise was involved in negotiations with top officials of the South African Defence Force (SADF) regarding the integration of MK cadres into the force. He also served on the defence sub-council of the transitional executive council from December 1993 to April 1994.

In the general election of April 1994 Modise stood as candidate number 23 on the ANC's election list to the national assembly and became a member of parliament. In May he was appointed Minister of Defence. His immediate priorities in this capacity were the establishment of a civilian department of defence and scrutiny of defence accounts.

Attempts to appoint his senior MK colleagues as generals in the defence force were met with resistance due to lack of available positions and the high qualifications of defence officers from the TBVC states.

The May 1994, Modise served papers on the *Weekly Mail & Guardian* newspaper advising it of his intention to seek an interdict to restrain the publication of further material on the SADF's former Directorate of Covert Collection (DCC). Modise was criticised from within the ANC on the grounds that it was the organisation's policy to encourage full disclosure of former covert action and he was urged to withdraw the interdict.

Modise was re-elected to the ANC's national executive committee at its December 1994 conference in Bloemfontein.

In 1992 Modise suffered a mild stroke. He is married to Jackie Molefe and has two children. His son, Thabo, a former MK cadre and major in the SADF, died in February 1995 of a heart ailment.

SOURCES

1. Interviewed 7 October 1986, Lusaka.
2. *Sunday Tribune*, 14 June 1992.
3. *Sunday Tribune*, 22 May 1994.
4. *Sunday Times*, 22 May 1994.
5. *Daily News*, 1 June 1994.
6. *Natal Witness*, 11 June 1994.
7. *Cape Times*, 22 February 1995.

PETER RAMOSHOANE MOKABA

Member of Parliament,
African National Congress, 1994.

Peter Mokaba, the second of the four children of Priscilla and Albert Mokaba, was born on 7 January 1958 in New Look Location, Pietersburg, Northern Transvaal.

He attended the Roman Catholic Pre-school at New Look until the family was forced to move to Mankweng, about 28 kilometres east of Pietersburg. As there was no school in Mankweng at the time, he first attended lower primary school in Motolo, a nearby rural village. However he later moved to Pula-Madibogo Lower Primary in Mankweng, and continued at Dikolobe Senior Primary and Hwiti High School.

During the 1976 revolt, Mokaba became one of the leaders of the student movement in the north that organised school boycotts in Mankweng and the surrounding areas. Because of vigilante and police action at the time, he and others slept in the mountains until captured in November 1977. Mokaba was arrested on a charge of public violence and detained for a month in terms of the Terrorism Act. He was finally acquitted of the charges when all 28 state witnesses refused to give evidence against him.

As a result of his political activities, both the South African and Lebowa governments prohibited Mokaba from attending school. He studied at home and completed his matriculation in 1978. Thereafter, he worked as a labourer at the silicon mines in the area, and at a construction company. At the same time he became involved in drama activities and journalism, reporting for the *Voice of the North* and becoming a member of the Writers Association of South Africa (Wasa).

In 1979 Mokaba became a teacher at Makgoka High School in Moria, near Boyne, where he taught mathematics and science. He also taught karate in a number of villages in the Northern Transvaal, and has a black belt in karate. In addition he served as president of the Mankweng softball club and was on the executive committee of the Dynamic Bullets football club.

In 1980 he enrolled at the University of the North (Turfloop) for a BSc. While at university Mokaba helped to establish a local branch of the Azanian Students Organisation (Azaso). He also became a member of the university's cultural committee and continued to teach karate. Mokaba attempted to maintain a a low political profile at university as his admission as a student was conditional on his keeping out of political activity.

However, 1980 was a year of riots and protests at educational institutions including Turfloop. Mokaba was raided by the security police and eventually, as a result of pressure, was forced to leave the campus. At the end of June 1982 Mokaba was detained under section 6 of the Terrorism Act. He was subsequently charged with membership of the African National Congress (ANC); possession of arms of war; membership of Umkhonto we Sizwe (the ANC's military wing); attempting to recruit members for the ANC; and having undergone military training in Angola, Mozambique and Swaziland. Mokaba was found guilty and sentenced to six years imprisonment which he began serving on Robben Island.

In September 1984 Mokaba won an appeal against his conviction on the grounds of irregular behaviour by the trial magistrate and the investigating officer. As he was about to be released, he was arrested on the same charges. On 1 March 1985 Mokaba was retried, found guilty of being in possession of a Makarov pistol and sentenced to three years imprisonment suspended for five years.

On 3 March Mokaba attended a United Democratic Front (UDF) conference at the University of the North where it was decided to form a regional branch of the organisation. Mokaba served on the area committee for Mankweng as well as the interim regional structure.

While Mokaba had been on Robben Island, the Mankweng Youth Congress was formed. He was elected patron of this and other youth congresses which were established in the Northern Transvaal. As a member of the Mankweng Youth Congress, Mokaba was asked to form a civic association, and the Mankweng Civic Association was launched on 12 April 1985 with Mokaba as its publicity secretary. In addition he became an executive member of the newly-formed Detainees Support Committee (Descom).

On 18 April 1985 Mokaba helped organise a Northern Transvaal youth conference where a co-ordinating structure was established with a view to the formation of a national youth organisation. Mokaba was elected to the executive as education officer.

During 1985, Mokaba served as UDF publicity secretary in the Northern Transvaal and was briefly detained on two occasions. On 14 July 1985 he was detained under section 28 of the Internal Security Act (preventive detention) and spent nine months in jail.

In July 1986 a consultative youth conference was organised in Cape Town where Mokaba was elected education officer of the interim committee of the National Youth Organisation (NYO). He organised a workshop on 25-26 October 1986 in Pretoria at which all regions were represented. Despite the state of emergency those attending managed to evade the police and were able to organise a national consultative conference in Cape Town which decided on a constitution for the South African Youth Congress (Sayco).

The Northern Transvaal Youth Congress was launched in November 1986 with Mokaba as regional education officer.

The Sayco launch in Cape Town on 28 March 1987 took place under difficult conditions with many of the conference representatives being wanted by the police. Mokaba was unanimously elected president.

As Sayco president and a UDF member, Mokaba motivated and helped to establish the Congress of Traditional Leaders of South Africa (Contralesa) as well as the Northern Transvaal People's Congress which aimed to organise migrant workers in the hostels. Mokaba motivated and drew up the constitutions for both organisations and held workshops with the chiefs during 1987 in preparation for the Contralesa launch.

On 21 March 1988 Mokaba was arrested in Johannesburg under section 29 of the Internal Security Act and held at John Vorster Square before being transferred to the Pietersburg Prison. On 12 April his mother was detained by security police under emergency regulations after she had seen Mokaba in chains at police headquarters in Pietersburg. This led to an attempt by his sister to obtain a court order to restrain police from torturing Mokaba, but the application was unsuccessful. On 23 May 1989 he was charged with being a commander of Umkhonto we Sizwe structures in the Northern Transvaal and of being in control and possession of an arms cache. His trial took place in the Pietersburg Regional Court and once again state witnesses refused to testify against him, and he was acquitted.

Although Sayco was one of the 17 organisations severely restricted in the February 1988 government crackdown, a decision to continue to operate had been made in December 1987. Mokaba had remained in touch with the organisation during his detention and on his release he took up his Sayco presidential duties, participating in the Defiance Campaign during the general election.

During December 1989, Mokaba participated in the Congress for a

Democratic Future. He also served on the National Reception Committee which co-ordinated the schedule of released political prisoners.

In April 1990, at Sayco's first open national congress at Kanyamazane, near Nelspruit, Mokaba was re-elected president. The congress mandated the organisation's central executive committee to consult with the ANC youth section about relaunching the defunct ANC Youth League inside South Africa. On 27 October 1990 he became provisional chairman of the ANC Youth League.

In May 1991 Mokaba was arrested with 14 others when he led a demonstration at the Union Buildings, Pretoria, demanding that government take firm action to stop political violence. During May 1991 the press reported that the ANC had investigated Mokaba as an alleged security police agent. The ANC responded that he was regarded as a fully-fledged member of the organisation, in good standing, and that the ANC did not doubt his bona fides. At the 1991 ANC Conference held in Durban, Mokaba was elected to the organisation's national executive committee. In December 1991 he was elected president of the ANC Youth League, a post he held until January 1994.

In June 1993 Mokaba became the centre of a controversy when, despite a directive by the ANC to cease using the inflammatory slogan 'Kill the Boer, Kill the Farmer', he repeated it at a Soweto Day rally at Orlando stadium at which ANC President Nelson Mandela was present. Despite calls from other political parties for the ANC to take action, he was not disciplined.

In the April 1994 general elections Mokaba stood as an ANC candidate for the national assembly and became a member of parliament. In parliament he chairs the select committee on environmental affairs and tourism.

Mokaba became chairman of the National Tourism Forum in 1993 and in 1995 an investigation was launched into the forum's affairs after allegations were made of irregular payments. Mokaba maintained that he was innocent of any wrong-doing, having initiated the investigation himself in February 1994. However, it was alleged that he received a substantial salary from the forum which was paid in addition to his salary as a member of parliament.

In December 1994 Mokaba was re-elected to the ANC's national executive committee at its congress in Bloemfontein.

Mokaba is divorced. He has one daughter.

SOURCES

1. *South*, 21 April 1988.

2. *Weekly Mail*, 3 April 1987.
3. *Weekly Mail*, 20 April 1990.
4. *Weekly Mail*, 30 May 1991.
5. *Weekly Mail*, 13 December 1991.
5. Interviewed 23 January 1990, Johannesburg.
6. Interviewed 9 October 1991, Durban.
7. *Natal Mercury*, 18 June 1993.
8. *Sunday Times*, 12 February 1995.
9. *Cape Times*, 1 March 1995.

POPO SIMON MOLEFE

Premier, North West Province, 1994.

Born in Sophiatown, Johannesburg, on 26 April 1952, Popo Molefe was adopted by his aunt, Sanah Tsatsimpe. In 1960 the family moved to Soweto and he attended the Atamelang Lower Primary School in Naledi, and the Tau-Pedi Higher Primary School. His studies were interrupted for financial reasons, but he later attended Naledi High School where he was head prefect in 1976.

While at high school he joined the Black Consciousness-oriented South African Students' Movement (Sasm) and participated in the school's debating society. As head prefect Molefe became involved in the campaign against the government's policy of equalisation of Afrikaans and English as media of instruction in the schools, and on 13 June 1976 Sasm called a meeting which decided to organise protest marches in Soweto.

After police opened fire on a group of marchers, the 1976 revolt broke out, and the Soweto Students' Representative Council was formed in which Molefe played a leading role.

On 18 August 1976 police detained Molefe, holding him for seven months. On his release in 1977 he continued with political work in the Black People's Convention (BPC) and did not return to school.

After the banning of the BPC in October 1977, Molefe and others called a conference to create a new political organisation, the Azanian People's Organisation (Azapo), in April 1978. Molefe became the first chairman of the Soweto branch.

Initially, Molefe viewed South African politics as a conflict between black and white, believing the solution involved replacement of the white government by a black one. However, his views gradually changed, particularly during the 1976 rebellion when he saw black police confronting black students. He realised that opponents could hide behind the same skin colour, and that there were whites who were prepared to sacrifice everything for the same ideals as his own.

Joe Qabi, an ANC activist subsequently assassinated in Zimbabwe, was a major influence in Molefe's change of view. He encouraged Molefe to commit himself to the concepts enshrined in the Freedom Charter and the principles of non-racialism.

From 1980 onwards, ideological differences developed within Azapo over the Freedom Charter, and Molefe lost confidence in the ability of the Black Consciousness Movement to bring about change in South Africa. He resigned from Azapo in 1981.

Molefe became co-ordinator for the Anti-Republic Day Celebration Committee and in December 1982 he was elected to the Soweto-based Committee of Ten. In this capacity he worked as co-ordinator of its education and training committee.

When the idea of the United Democratic Front (UDF) emerged in January 1983, Molefe participated in the discussion and planning of its formation. He was appointed secretary of the Transvaal region and became a member of the advance planning committee dealing with the national launch of the UDF in Cape Town. In August 1983 Molefe was appointed UDF national general secretary and subsequently played a prominent role in the UDF's campaigns to oppose the tricameral constitutional dispensation, and boycott elections to the Houses of Representatives and Delegates in the tricameral parliament.

After leaving school Molefe worked as a shop assistant, a microfilm machine operator, a records clerk and a photographic printing machine operator. When he became the UDF's national general secretary, he worked full-time for the organisation. His UDF work continued when he was re-elected to the position at the UDF's first annual conference held in April 1985 in Azaadville, Krugersdorp.

Molefe was subsequently detained and in June 1985 was one of 22 people accused of treason relating to the 1984 civil disturbances in the Vaal Triangle. He and other accused were repeatedly denied bail on the grounds that they posed a threat to state security. The accused were alleged to have conspired with each other, the ANC and the South African Communist Party to promote unrest at a national level in order to overthrow the government by revolutionary means. In November 1988 Molefe and four others were convicted of treason. After the judge ruled that the dominant part of the UDF leadership had acted as the internal wing of the ANC, Molefe received a ten-year sentence. However, on 15 December 1989 the Appeal Court quashed all the convictions, and Molefe was released.

Following the unbanning of the ANC and the release of Nelson Mandela in February 1990, Molefe was appointed to its interim leadership committee which was charged with the task of establishing internal structures for the organisation.

At the ANC's July 1991 conference held in Durban, Molefe was elected to the organisation's national executive committee and also served on its national working committee.

In September 1992, Molefe was appointed head of the ANC's elections department, formed to prepare the organisation for participation in future national elections.

In the April 1994 general elections Molefe stood as head of the ANC's list for the North West provincial legislature and became premier of the region when the ANC won 83% of the vote. Molefe indicated that he planned to develop a new civil service from former members of the Bophuthatswana and Transvaal administrations and would try to counter right-wing presence in the province by creating an atmosphere of security regarding property, culture and language.

However, political in-fighting developed between Molefe and Rocky Malebane-Metsing, a member of the executive council with the portfolio of Agriculture in the provincial legislature, who had led an abortive coup against the previous administration in 1988. In November 1994 Molefe and Malebane-Metsing both stood for the position of chairperson of the ANC in the region at its regional conference, with Molefe being elected. Despite attempts at reconciliation, Molefe eventually fired Malebane-Metsing from his post on the executive council, on the grounds of his 'undemocratic tendencies'. A group of Malebane-Metsing's supporters then launched a 'Re-instate Rocky' campaign with threats to bring the regional government to its knees. Following ANC intervention, Molefe was told to find a way of accommodating Malebeane-Metsing and he was then appointed Molefe's special adviser.

However, a government inquiry into a R15 million loan granted by the parastatal Agribank to a Jamaican national for the purchase of a farm revealed that the loan was approved by Malebane-Metsing while he was agriculture MEC and that this was in contravention of the law. The matter was then handed over to the police.

In February 1995 Malebane-Metsing claimed at a press conference that Molefe had hired three assassins to kill him and his colleague, Dr John Lamola, and he would therefore not take up his post as special adviser. He laid a charge of attempted murder at the Potchefstroom police station. Molefe, who denied these allegations, indicated that he was prepared to assist the police in their investigations.

Molefe is married to Boitumelo Elizabeth Plaatje, a nursing sister, and they have three children.

SOURCES

1. Interviewed 16 April 1984, Johannesburg.
2. *Frontline*, June 1987.
3. *Natal Mercury*, 16 December 1989.
4. *Argus*, 18 December 1989.
5. *Sunday Times*, 8 May 1994.
6. *Sunday Tribune*, 11 September 1994.
7. *Sunday Times*, 26 February 1995.

MOHAMMED VALLI MOOSA

Member of Parliament,
African National Congress, 1994.
Deputy Minister of Provincial
Affairs, 1994.

Born in Johannesburg on 9 February 1957, Mohammed Valli Moosa was the fifth of the nine children of Ayesha and Wally Moosa, a shop assistant.

Valli spent his early years in Johannesburg where he attended the Gold Street Primary School. After the government moved the Indian community to Lenasia in the early 1960s, Valli attended the Lenasia State Indian High School, where he matriculated in 1974. When he was refused ministerial permission to attend the University of the Witwatersrand in 1976 he enrolled at the University of Durban-Westville for a BSc degree in mathematics and physics.

There he joined the Black Consciousness-oriented South African Students' Organisation (Saso), serving on its university branch executive until the organisation's banning in 1977. Although he was involved in campaigns around conditions at the university itself, most Saso activities were geared to conscientising black people, and cultural programmes took priority. Valli maintains that for many in Saso, Black Consciousness was not seen as a long-term ideological perspective, but as a means to activate and conscientise people. When the Black Consciousness organisations were banned, Valli was not among those who supported the launch of a new Black Consciousness political organisation.

Recognising the need for the development of a grassroots approach to politics, Valli participated in the formation of civic associations, residents' associations, township youth groups and trade unions from 1977 onwards.

During 1979, he taught in Chatsworth, Durban, and participated in the

Natal Indian Congress (NIC) campaign against elections for local affairs committees. He also became involved in Phoenix, a community made up of people resettled from other parts of Durban. Valli helped set up the Phoenix working committee and various local residents' associations.

Between 1980 and 1982 Valli taught in Johannesburg. He was dismissed from his post, probably as a result of his political involvement. When he returned to Johannesburg in 1980, Valli hoped to help revive Congress politics in the Indian community, particularly Lenasia, where he lived. He participated in the formation of a number of residents' associations and began to work with high school students, establishing the 'Time To Learn' tuition programme. He was also involved in Pulse Films, a film society which aimed to bring more politicised members of the community together.

In April 1980, during the school boycotts, Valli was detained for two weeks at John Vorster Square, Johannesburg.

The Anti-South African Indian Council Committee (Anti-Saic) was launched in 1982 to campaign against elections to the Indian Council. Valli believes that this firmly re-established Congress politics in the Indian community. At the Anti-Saic conference which rounded off the campaign in January 1983, a call was made to form a united front in opposition to the proposed tricameral parliament and the Koornhof Bills. A national interim committee was established to do the groundwork for the formation of the United Democratic Front (UDF). In June 1983, when the Transvaal region of the UDF was formed, Valli was elected to its executive committee as general secretary. He also participated in the national launch of the UDF in Cape Town in August 1983 where he was elected to the national executive committee of the organisation.

Valli helped revive the Transvaal Indian Congress in 1983 and was elected to its executive committee in May that year.

In 1984 the UDF sent Valli abroad to mobilise support for the organisation among governments, the international community and anti-apartheid organisations.

As a result of the arrest of UDF general secretary Popo Molefe in 1985, Valli became acting national general secretary at the 1986 UDF conference. He had gone into hiding during the 1985 state of emergency until March 1986, and although he had not yet been appointed acting general secretary, became responsible for maintaining the UDF head office. During this time he and others worked under extremely difficult conditions and severe repression to ensure the continued existence of the UDF.

During the 1986 state of emergency Valli went into hiding, but was detained from January to April 1987 at the Randburg police station. He was re-arrested together with Murphy Morobe, UDF acting publicity secretary, in Port Elizabeth in July 1987. He was held at St Albans Prison for about ten days before being transferred to Johannesburg where he remained until September 1988 when he and two others escaped and sought refuge in the Johannesburg consulate of the United States where they spent five weeks.

In mid-December 1988 Valli and Morobe travelled abroad, visiting a number of countries including the United Kingdom, the US and the USSR. They spent time with ANC representatives in Lusaka and Harare before returning to South Africa in February 1989.

When Valli emerged from the consulate, the UDF was a restricted organisation, but he continued to operate as a leader of the Mass Democratic Movement (MDM). He was centrally involved in the planning of the Defiance Campaign which led to his detention on 18 August 1989 under emergency regulations. After being held for six weeks, he was released under severe restrictions.

Prior to his detention he had been involved in reviving the anti-apartheid conference initiative which had been banned in 1988 and on his release became involved in organising the Conference for a Democratic Future, held in Johannesburg on 9 December 1989. This brought together a range of anti-apartheid groupings which adopted guidelines for a transitional and constitutional process.

At the time imprisoned ANC leaders were released in 1989 and 1990, Valli served on the National Reception Committee established to organise their post-release programmes.

When the ANC was unbanned in February 1990, Valli was seconded by the UDF to work for the ANC and appointed secretary of the movement's internal leadership core, chaired at the time by Walter Sisulu. When the ANC's national executive committee relocated from Lusaka, Zambia, to Johannesburg, Valli was appointed secretary of the ANC's political committee. He played a role in the preparatory committee organising the ANC conference held in Durban in July 1991, and at that conference was elected to the ANC's national executive committee.

In August 1991 the UDF was disbanded. The following month Valli was elected to the ANC's national working committee and took over the negotiations portfolio in August 1991. He served as the co-ordinator/secretary of the ANC's negotiations commission.

Valli attended the Patriotic Front Conference held in October 1991 where an attempt was made to unify all anti-apartheid organisations.

He served as an ANC representative at the first preparatory meeting for the Convention for a Democratic South Africa (Codesa) held in November 1991 and subsequently became part of the ANC's negotiating team at the Codesa plenary sessions in December 1991 and May 1992. He represented the ANC on Codesa working group two which dealt with constitutional principles and a constitution-making process. This working group failed to reach consensus before the meeting of Codesa 2 and as a result the management committee of Codesa had to take over the issues in an attempt to break the deadlock. However, negotiations eventually broke down and the ANC embarked on a campaign of rolling mass action. Following bi-lateral meetings between the ANC and the South African government, a Record of Understanding was signed between the two parties. This eventually led to a resumption of talks between all parties at the World Trade Centre and Valli continued to play a strategic role during the negotiation process.

In the April 1994 general elections, Valli stood as candidate number 25 on the ANC list and became a member of parliament. In May he was appointed Deputy Minister of Provincial Affairs in the government of national unity.

He was re-elected to the ANC's national executive committee at its Bloemfontein congress in December 1994.

In February 1995 Valli was given the responsibility of taking political control of the Masakhane ('Let us build each other') campaign which attempted to deal with the non-payment of rents and services by township dwellers. Non-payment began in the 1980s as a protest against illegitimate local government structures, and became entrenched. Payments continued to be withheld even after the new government was elected. As a result, local authorities faced massive debts and services broke down in many areas.

Valli is married to Elsabe Wessels, a journalist.

SOURCES

1. Interviewed 21 November 1989, Johannesburg.
2. Telephonic interview, 4 June 1992.
3. *Profile 94*, South African Communication Services, Pretoria, 1994.
4. *Cape Times*, 1 March 1995.

ANGELA THOKO MSANE

Member of Parliament,
African National Congress, 1994.
Deputy Minister of Agriculture,
1994.

Born in Mankayane, Swaziland, on 2 June 1965, Thoko Msane was the youngest of the three children of Assiena (born Motha) and Vusumusi Msane, both of whom were teachers. As her parents lived at the school at which they worked, Msane spent her early years in the extended family of her maternal grandparents who were farmers.

In 1974 Msane's father returned to South Africa where he was born and the family settled at Mpumulanga Township near Hammarsdale, Natal. Msane completed Standards 3-5 at Okhozini School in Mpumulanga and then attended Ohlange High School at Inanda where she matriculated.

Msane first became aware of political issues during the 1976 student revolt which had a profound impact on her. When visiting the city, she became aware of the existence of apartheid and of separate facilities for whites and blacks. This was foreign to her as she had previously lived in Swaziland where relationships between the races had been different.

It was at Ohlange High School that she began to deal concretely with political issues. Political discussions, debates and the reading of newspapers were encouraged to increase student awareness of both the issues of the day and the history of the liberation movement. In 1980 Msane and a nucleus of students at Ohlange High School joined the Congress of South African Students (Cosas).

After she matriculated in 1981, Msane trained as a secretary at Turret College. She then worked as a legal secretary/receptionist at Mafika Mbuli and Company, a firm of attorneys, before taking up a position in Durban as receptionist/secretary with Diakonia, an ecumenical church agency, in March 1985. In 1987 she became a programme officer for Diakonia's social action network unit which attempted to motivate the church to play a more active role in society. The unit assisted churches to deal with the day-to-day issues of their congregants. Diakonia played an important role in relief and advocacy work and also provided a platform for raising issues concerning repression.

At the same time, Msane served as joint treasurer of the Natal Organisation of Women (NOW), an affiliate of the United Democratic Front (UDF) which had been formed in 1983 to oppose the tricameral parliament and other apartheid institutions and legislation. Her work with NOW made her aware of gender inequalities and the struggles of women, particularly young women, in times of violence. In 1987 Msane served on the Women's Advisory Committee of the South African Council of Churches (SACC) and in the same year attended the International Children's Conference in Harare, Zimbabwe.

Msane also became a member of the Young Women's Christian Association (YWCA) and began to deal with issues such as youth empowerment and development, assisting in the planning of programmes to help young people. In 1989 Msane was asked by the YWCA to take up the position of national youth programme co-ordinator of the South African Council of World-Affiliated YWCAs. She began to consider the strategic position of the YWCA as a vehicle to mobilise young women around issues which affected them. As a result a larger percentage (25%) of young women were brought onto the decision-making level of the organisation, despite resistance from older women. Msane served as National Deputy Secretary General of the SA Council of the World-Affiliated YWCA from 1993 to April 1994.

The YWCA is an affiliate of the SACC and in 1989-90 she served on its Youth Executive which began to grapple with the crisis of margina-lised youth in South Africa. The SACC and the South African Catholic Bishops Conference had created the Joint Enrichment Project (JEP) to analyse these issues and to bring the issue of marginalised youth onto the agenda. A conference was held in 1991 and JEP was mandated to meet with youth organisations to develop proposals to deal with the problem. Msane served on the planning co-ordinating committee to prepare for a youth summit which was held in 1992. A National Youth Development Committee was formed and Msane served on this body. She subsequent-ly participated in the process which led to the establishment in September 1993 of the National Youth Development Forum which deals with issues impacting on young people, and brings together youth structures and people with expertise to contribute towards youth development.

In 1991 Msane served as a member of the Women's Development Bank and in 1993 became an alternative member of the executive of the SACC.

From 1992-94 Msane served as national general secretary of the National Women's Coalition, a broad, inclusive organisation of women from across the political spectrum and civil society with the aim of focusing on issues faced by South African women and recommending changes. Msane played a key role in the process of bringing women together and learned that regardless of political differences, social background and income levels, women were able to come together to deal with issues which affected them. Out of this process a Charter of Women's Rights was produced and this contributed towards South African society beginning to deal with the reality of the oppression of women.

While a member of NOW in the 1980s, Msane was involved in consultations with the then banned liberation movement, especially the ANC Women's Section, on the possible revival of the Federation of South African Women which had been active in the 1950s. During 1987-88 consultations also took place regarding the move towards a negotiated settlement and Msane was involved in discussions on the implications for a post-apartheid South Africa.

Following the unbanning of the ANC in 1990, Msane was active in establishing its structures in Umlazi. Arising out of her work with the youth, Msane was approached by the ANC Youth League to stand for election to the National Assembly in the April 1994 general election. She was placed number 108 on the ANC list and became a member of parliament.

In May 1994 Msane was appointed Deputy Minister of Agriculture. She plans to deal with the issue of women in agriculture, taking into account the key role they play in small-scale or subsistence farming in the rural areas. She believes that the Department will need to formulate policies to meet the needs of that sector by improving resources and servicing the needs of women farmers through re-organising extension work.

Msane has undertaken various post-matric courses and completed her Diploma in Personnel and Training Practice (1989) and her Certificate in Public Relations (1990). In 1991 she completed her Diploma in Journalism, and in 1993 was awarded a Diploma in Business and Financial Management. She has also presented papers at various conferences in Zimbabwe, Zambia, Norway, South Africa and Germany.

Thoko Msane is married, and has a daughter and twin sons.

SOURCE

Interviewed 6 June 1994, Durban.

CELANI JEFFREY MTETWA

Minister of Police Services,
KwaZulu/Natal, 1994.

Born in Msinga, Natal, on 10 October 1926, Celani Mtetwa was the son of Juana and Luke Mtetwa. He attended Mzweni Primary School in Msinga from 1935-42 and then St Cyprian's High School in Sophiatown, Johannesburg, where he completed his Junior Certificate in 1945. He then found work as a despatch clerk in Johannesburg from 1946-49 and subsequently became a clerk with the Johannesburg City Health Department from 1950-59.

In 1959 he returned to Msinga to take up the unpaid position of deputy chief of the Majozi tribe. He became the official facilitator and mediator in factional disputes which were common in the area, as well as mediator on issues involving government authorities.

Mtetwa worked as a travelling salesman in the Msinga area from 1961-72 and then became the owner of a Msinga trading store. In 1958 he became a member of the Inyanda Chamber of Commerce (Natal and Zululand African Chamber of Commerce) and served as the chairman of its Northern Natal region from 1970-74.

Mtetwa served on the Msinga local council from 1961-69 and the Msinga Regional Authority from 1969 onwards. He became a member of the KwaZulu Territorial Authority (1970-72); the KwaZulu Legislative Assembly (1974-94); and the central committee of Inkatha yeNkululeko yeSizwe after its founding in 1975. He also served as chairman of its security and defence committee until 1994.

He became Minister of Justice in the KwaZulu government in 1976. His portfolio included the administration of justice in KwaZulu; the provision of auxiliary services for an adequate system of law and procedure; and legal advice to the KwaZulu government departments. At a later stage, Correctional Services (prisons) was added to his portfolio.

During the 1980s, when King Goodwill Zwelithini, the Zulu monarch, was prevented from speaking to the press, Mtetwa was appointed his spokesman and journalists had to obtain permission for interviews with the king through his department. It was a condition of interviews with the king that he be present during them.

Since 1993 Mtetwa has headed the security division of the Inkatha Freedom Party. He also served as a member of the executive committee of the Msinga Regional Authority with the portfolios of Justice and Education.

Mtetwa, who is deputy chief of the Majozi tribe, stood as an Inkatha Freedom Party provincial candidate in the April 1994 elections in which the IFP won a slim majority in KwaZulu/Natal. In May he became KwaZulu/Natal Minister of Police Services, a crucial portfolio considering the violence in the province and the negative image of the KwaZulu police in many areas.

Mtetwa is married to Gladys Jabulile Nene and they have four children.

SOURCES

1. *KwaZulu Government Diary 1986*, Izwi Lama Afrika Abumbene on behalf of the KwaZulu Government, 1986.
2. Dee Shirley Dean, *Black South Africans. A Who's Who. 57 Profiles of Natal's Leading Blacks*, Oxford University Press, Cape Town, 1978.

SANKIE DOLLY MTHEMBU-NKONDO

Member of Parliament,
African National Congress, 1994.
Deputy Minister of Welfare,
1994-95.
Minister of Housing, 1995.

Born on 23 March 1951 in Sophiatown, Sankie Mthembu was the youngest of five children from a working class family. At the age of two her family was forcibly removed to Meadowlands under Group Areas legislation. Her father, who died in 1977, was a chef for the Chamber of Mines, and her mother, Emma Mthembi now on pension, was a domestic worker.

After matriculating from Sekano-Ntoane High School in 1970, Mthembu enrolled at the University of the North (Turfloop). During the early 1970s, Turfloop was one of the most politically active universities in the anti-apartheid struggle, and political debates concerning Black Consciousness empowered the students to fight for better campus conditions and to challenge broader political issues. In the five years that Mthembu was a student, the university was closed three times due to strikes – once in protest over the detention of students following a pro-Frelimo rally in 1974.

Mthembu obtained a BA degree and a teaching diploma in June 1976. However, the repression following the school protests against the use of Afrikaans as a medium of instruction, and the arrest of Black Consciousness activists, stopped her from becoming a teacher in the Bantu education education system, and she joined the underground structures of the African National Congress (ANC).

By the middle of June 1977 the wave of repression prompted her and Zinjiva Nkondo, whom she married when he was released from prison, to leave the country. She was trained as a journalist and worked for the ANC media section as a journalist and announcer for Radio Freedom in

Lusaka, Zambia, and in Tanzania. She was also involved in literacy projects. Nkondo's work as print and radio journalist brought her into contact with most sections of the ANC and enabled her to travel widely.

As editor of the ANC's women's journal, *Voice of Women,* she became a strong proponent of gender issues and served on the national executive and council of the ANC's Women's Section.

Because her work involved substantial travelling and attendance at international conferences and forums, the ANC's department of international affairs offered to train her as a diplomat.

Nkondo then worked at the ANC office in Nigeria and during 1983 was sent to Sweden as administrative secretary for 18 months. In December 1989 she was posted to Bonn, as chief ANC representative to Germany and Austria. Following the unbanning of the ANC in February 1990, she returned to South Africa on numerous occasions for conferences and consultations. In October 1993 she was recalled from Bonn to the ANC head office in Johannesburg to take up the post of deputy head of the ANC's Department of International Affairs.

In the general election of April 1994 Nkondo stood as an ANC candidate and in May she was appointed Deputy Minister of Welfare in the government of national unity. In January 1995, following the death of Joe Slovo, Nkondo was appointed Minister of Housing.

At the December 1994 ANC conference, Nkondo stood as one of the candidates for the post of ANC deputy secretary-general, but was defeated by Cheryl Carolus.

Apart from contributing poetry to a variety of publications, Nkondo's anthology, *Flames of Fury,* was published by the Congress of South African Writers in 1990.

Nkondo, who is divorced, has one daughter.

SOURCES

1. *People in Politics,* Third Quarter 1994, Institute for Democracy in South Africa (Idasa), Durban, 1994.
2. *Sunday Times,* 8 January 1995.

THENJIWE MTINTSO

Member of Parliament,
African National Congress, 1994.

Thenjiwe Mtintso was born in Orlando East on 7 November 1949, the daughter of Hannah Plaatje, a cleaner at the Baragwanath Hospital. Her father, whom she never met, was the veteran communist, Ghana Makabeni.

Mtintso spent her school years at Bury High School in Transkei, but was forced to leave school for financial reasons. She returned to abject poverty in Soweto where she continued her studies. She started working in a factory at the age of 16 after her sister, who paid for her education, died. She worked for an insurance company as a filing clerk. She also studied part-time and obtained her matric through Damelin.

Having obtained a bursary, she enrolled for a BSc degree at the University of Fort Hare during 1972. Shortly thereafter, Mtintso became a member of the South African Students' Organisation (Saso), a Black Consciousness grouping based at the universities. She joined striking students, resulting in her first banning from the campus. The following year she was banned again for the same offence.

Mtintso became involved in the Black People's Convention, an off-campus Black Consciousness organisation, and settled in King William's Town where she worked for the Dependents Conference of the Border Council of Churches which supported ex-political prisoners and detainees. She was also a founder member of the Zimele Trust Fund which was a self-employment programme for ex-political prisoners and detainees.

In King William's Town she met activists close to Black Consciousness leader Steve Biko, who was retricted to the town. Biko, who became a major influence in her political growth, also had a direct hand in her joining the *Daily Dispatch* newspaper as a reporter under the editorship of Donald Woods in 1975. Biko suggested to Woods that Mtintso should be employed so that the *Daily Dispatch* would have a black journalist in contact with the community. As a reporter she became involved in the founding of the first union for black journalists.

In the clampdown on Biko and fellow political activists during 1976, Mtintso was also arrested. Following her release, she was banned and restricted to Orlando East. The entire grouping around Biko was removed and restricted across the country. During the next two years, Mtintso spent a total of 18 months in detention during which period she was tortured both physically and psychologically. Recognising that her mother and toddler son were contiually being harrassed by the police, Mtintso decided to leave the country, and in December 1978 she and her son left South Africa, crossing through Transkei into Lesotho. In Lesotho she joined the World University Services for eight months while considering her political future.

While closely aligned to Black Consciousness politics inside South Africa, Mtintso joined the African National Congress (ANC) in Lesotho the following year. She became active in the Lesotho Front under the leadership of the late Communist Party secretary general, Chris Hani. Mtintso edited several political publications including *Umkhonto Lerumo* (The Spear). She was also responsible for recruitment inside the country and the handling of underground political structures in the Orange Free State and the Cape.

In 1980 Mtintso received military training in Angola and East Germany where she was trained in intelligence and counter-intelligence work. She returned to Lesotho the following year where she worked in the political-military structures until 1982. She then left for Cuba for political training at the FMC Political School in Havana where she studied for a year.

She once again returned to Lesotho where she worked in the ANC military command until 1985. The same year she was seconded to the Botswana Front as the head of the Regional Political Military Council responsible for the deployment of cadres into the country, supplying logistics and reporting to the political-military structures in Lusaka the first woman to head a front.

In January 1989 Mtintso was transferred to Uganda where she was responsible for the opening of the first ANC mission in Uganda and the setting up of ANC camps in the country, which had to be built from scratch. The move followed an agreement with the Angolan government that ANC training camps would be relocated in anticipation of the Namibian settlement.

In 1990 Mtintso returned to South Africa to attend an ANC Women's

League conference. Compelled to remain and assist her mother, she enrolled at the University of the Witwatersrand for a BA in Social Work.

At the internal launch of the South African Communist Party (SACP) in 1991, Mtintso was elected to its central committee and its politburo. She had joined the party in Lesotho in 1990. She also heads the Gender Department of the SACP on a volunteer basis. The ninth national congress of the SACP, held in April 1995, re-elected Mthinso to its central committee. In this election, she received the highest number of votes from delegates.

Mtintso was part of the negotiating team of the SACP at the Convention for a Democratic South Africa (Codesa) where she served in working group four which deliberated the future of the TBVC homelands.

Mtintso served as a member of the Sub-Council on Intelligence in the Transitional Executive Council from December 1993 until May 1994.

In the April 1994 general elections Mtintso stood as an ANC candidate and became a member of parliament. She serves as a member of the parliamentary joint standing committee on defence and the rules committee.

SOURCES

1. *People in Politics*, First Quarter 1994, Institute for Democracy in South Africa (Idasa), Durban, 1994.
2. 'The Women's Directory 1994-95, Political Addendum', *Femina* in association with Old Mutual.

SYDNEY PHOLISANI MUFAMADI

Member of Parliament,
African National Congress, 1994.
Minister of Safety and Security,
1994.

Sydney Mufamadi was born on 28 February 1959 in Alexandra Township, Johannesburg, the son of Masindi and Reuben Mufamadi, a driver. His father had two wives, and there were eight children in the family.

Mufamadi grew up in Venda, where his mother sold liquor illegally to supplement the family income. Mufamadi attended school in Venda. Following the 1976 Soweto uprising, when student discontent spread into other areas, Mufamadi became a member of the Zoutpansberg Students' Organisation which led the school boycotts in Venda during October 1977. Many students were arrested and others, including Mufamadi, went underground. When schools re-opened, Mufamadi was refused re-admission and was unable to complete Standard Nine. After the unbanning of the African National Congress (ANC), he indicated that he had been active in its underground while at high school.

Mufamadi moved to Johannesburg, where his father was living, and enrolled with an international correspondence college to write his GCE examinations. His involvement in the Azanian People's Organisation led to a two-month spell of detention-without-trial at John Vorster Square, Johannesburg, under section 6 of the Terrorism Act.

During 1980 Mufamadi worked as a private teacher at Lamula Secondary School, Soweto, where he assisted members of the Congress of South African Students (Cosas). When he left the job in 1981 to work as a messenger for a firm of attorneys, he joined the General and Allied Workers' Union (Gawu) and participated in the 16 June stayaway of that year. His employer saw a newspaper photograph of Mufamadi addressing a commemoration service, and he was fired. He then worked in a voluntary capacity for Gawu, and at its national conference in April 1982 was elected its general secretary. He was re-elected to this post in 1984.

In 1983 Mufamadi attended the launch of the United Democratic Front (UDF) in Cape Town, and was later elected Transvaal publicity secretary of the organisation, a position he held until 1990. He was involved in all UDF campaigns in this capacity.

In 1984 Mufamadi was detained twice in the Ciskei, during April and again in September. Following the successful Transvaal Regional stayaway in November 1984, Mufamadi was subpoenaed to appear as a state witness at the trial of some of its organisers. However, charges were withdrawn when some of the accused left the country, and Mufamadi was not called to testify.

From June to November 1985, when the government had declared a partial state of emergency, Mufamadi operated underground to avoid detention, resurfacing to help organise and attend the launch of the Congress of South African Trade Unions (Cosatu) in December 1985. At the inaugural rally in Durban, Mufamadi was elected assistant general secretary. He again operated underground from June to October 1986, but openly resumed his work despite the continuing state of emergency. Police again detained him on 8 June 1987.

In 1988 Mufamadi headed a planning committee to organise an anti-apartheid conference in Cape Town which aimed to include delegates from a broad spectrum of anti-apartheid organisations. On 21 September 1988 the government prohibited the holding of the conference and restricted its organisers, including Mufamadi, for a ten-day period.

During January 1990, Mufamadi was one of the internal leaders of the Mass Democratic Movement who travelled to Lusaka, Zambia, with the recently released Rivonia trialists to meet with the African National Congress executive committee.

When the South African Communist Party (SACP) relaunched as a legal organisation on 29 July 1990, Mufamadi – who had joined the party in the early 1980s while it was still banned – was named as one of its 22-person interim leadership group. In December 1991 he was elected to the party's central committee. He was re-elected at the party's ninth national congress, held in April 1995.

At the ANC congress held in Durban in July 1991, Mufamadi was elected to the movement's national executive committee. He was subsequently elected by the NEC to serve on its working committee. He did not stand for re-election as Cosatu's assistant general secretary in 1991.

Mufamadi served as the SACP's delegate on the Convention for a Democratic South Africa (Codesa) working group dealing with the future of the TBVC states. He also served as an ANC representative on the National Peace Committee and was a member of its executive committee.

In the run-up to the first democratic elections in April 1994, Mufamadi served on the sub-council on law and order of the Transitional Executive Council.

In the general election, Mufamadi stood as candidate number nine on the ANC's list for the national assembly and became a member of parliament. In May 1994 he was appointed Minister of Safety and Security in the government of national unity.

He indicated that his priorities included the integration of the South African Police and the former homeland police forces; the formulation of a national crime prevention strategy; the restructuring of the South African Police Service (SAPS) on national and regional levels; the demilitarisation and professionalisation of the SAPS (possibly including a civilian rank structure); the reallocation of resources to reach regional and local levels; making the SAPS more representative in terms of race and gender; and the elimination of salary disparities between the various agencies which comprise the SAPS.

On 22 August 1994 Mufamadi announced certain measures to deal with the increasing numbers of attacks on the police and a soaring crime rate. In October 1994 Mufamadi published a green paper setting out significant and fundamental shifts in approach to the function of the police from law enforcement to community service with certain democratic checks and controls.

Mufamadi is married to Nomsa and they have three children.

SOURCES

1. *Cape Times*, 9 June 1989.
2. South African Institute of Race Relations, *Race Relations Survey 1988/89*, Johannesburg, 1989.
3. Interviewed 12 November 1986, Johannesburg.
4. Jeremy Baskin, *Striking Back. A History of Cosatu*, Johannesburg, 1991.
5. *Natal Witness*, 26 May 1994.
6. *Natal Witness*, 23 August 1994.
7. *Natal Mercury*, 23 August 1994.
8. *Natal Witness*, 3 November 1994.

PIETER WILLEM ADRIAAN MULDER

Member of Parliament,
Freedom Front, 1994.

Born on 26 July 1951 in Krugersdorp, Pieter Mulder was the eldest of the four children of Suzanne (born De Wet) and Cornelius Petrus (Connie) Mulder, a member of parliament and National Party cabinet minister.

Mulder attended the Acacia Park school in Cape Town and the Randfontein Afrikaans Medium school. During his high school years he lived with his grandmother and attended the Hoërskool Riebeeck and matriculated in 1968. He was head boy of his school and won its Victor Ludorum award.

In 1969 Mulder underwent military training in the navy at Saldhana Bay. After completing an officer's course, he served on a minesweeper in Simonstown, winning an award as best officer of the intake.

In 1970 Mulder enrolled at Potchefstroom University where he completed his BA (Communication) in 1973, an MA in 1976 and a DPhil in 1978. As a student, he served as chairman of the Students' Representative Council and as deputy president of the Afrikaanse Studentebond. In 1974 he became a lecturer in communication at the university, and won an Abe Bailey Scholarship to visit the United Kingdom for three months. In 1981 Mulder visited the United States, and undertook post-doctoral studies in international communication at the University of Wisconsin, Madison.

In 1984 Mulder was appointed professor and head of the Department of Communication at Potchefstroom University. He became vice-president of the lecturers' union and a member of the Public Relations Institute of South Africa.

In 1985 Mulder was elected to the Potchefstroom Town Council and in the 1987 general election was an unsuccessful candidate for the Conservative Party (CP) in Potchefstroom. In March 1988 he stood in a by-election in Schweizer-Reneke, a marginal seat in a rural area, winning the seat then, and again in the 1989 general election.

Mulder came from an intensely political family. His grandfather was a commissar in the Transvaal Republic in 1899 and fought in the Anglo-Boer war. When rebellion broke out in 1914 he sided with the rebels and was jailed. Mulder's father was a National Party member of parliament from 1958 and became a cabinet minister. Widely tipped to succeed John Vorster as prime minister, he resigned after exposure of his involvement in the notorious 'information scandal' of 1978.

Self-determination of the Afrikaner is paramount in Mulder's political thinking, and he maintains that the Afrikaners fought against the British to rid the country of colonialism, not because they were anti-black. He argues that racism and the self-determination of the Afrikaner people are two different issues. Mulder had been a member of the NP until the CP was formed in 1982. He was a founder member of the CP and was elected to its head committee. He headed its Transvaal information committee and was its spokesman on broadcasting, media, information and films. In 1992 he became vice-chairman of the CP in the Transvaal.

During the negotiations towards a settlement in South Africa in 1992 and 1993, Mulder and his brother, Corne, together with General Constand Viljoen formed part of the *Volksfront* delegation. The *Volksfront* served as an umbrella body for various conservative organisations including the CP. When they succeeded in having Principle 34 on self-determination included in the Bill of Rights and the *Volkstaat* Council added to the interim constitution, Mulder felt that the way was now open for future negotiations on the self-determination of the Afrikaner. He therefore felt that it was essential for the CP to contest the coming general elections. However, the CP leadership refused to accept the changes which were imminent in the country and declined to participate in the elections. Mulder and six other CP members of parliament indicated that they would take part and he was therefore expelled from the party in March 1994.

Mulder then joined the Freedom Front (FF) under the leadership of General Viljoen, and was candidate number two on the FF's candidate's list for the national assembly. The FF won nine seats in the national assembly and Mulder was returned as a member of parliament. He is currently chairman of the Freedom Front. In parliament Mulder is the FF spokesperson on the media and foreign affairs and serves on the portfolio committees dealing with foreign affairs and communications.

Mulder is married to Triena (born Roestorf) and they have five children. They live in Potchefstroom.

SOURCES

1. Interviewed 9 April 1991, Cape Town.
2. *Curriculum vitae* supplied by Pieter Mulder.
3. Telephonic interview, 27 February 1995.

YVETTE LILLIAN 'MAVIVI' MYAKAYAKA-MANZINI

Member of Parliament,
African National Congress, 1994.

Mavivi Myakayaka was born on 19 January 1956 in Alexandra township, Johannesburg, the fourth of the eight children of teachers Gius Gottfried and Ella (born Mavanyisi) Myakayaka.

At the age of two Myakayaka contracted polio and spent the next two years at a hospital for the disabled in Roodepoort. During this period, the Manzini family moved to Soweto where she later attended primary school. During her high school years, her father was recruited to teach in the newly established Gazankulu homeland and the family moved to Tzaneen in the Northern Transvaal where she obtained a Junior Certificate at Bankuna High School in Letaba, near Tzaneen. In 1974 she matriculated from the Lemana High School at Elim near Louis Trichardt.

In 1975 Myakayaka enrolled at Turfloop University to study Social Work and found herself on a politically volatile campus where student detentions were rife. Several students including the current African National Congress (ANC) secretary general, Cyril Ramaphosa, were detained following a pro-Frelimo rally organised by the students. Conscientised by the apartheid system and the poverty of the townships,

Myakayaka did not become involved in active politics until she attended Turfloop University. There, she participated in the local branch of the South African Students Organisation (Saso), a Black Consciousness grouping based at the universities, and also made contact with the ANC in Swaziland during the latter part of her first year. She subsequently conducted underground political work for the organisation. Her task was to help Umkhonto se Sizwe cadres locate police stations and military installations in the area and also to work within the student movement.

By mid-1976, following a two-month detention by security police, Myakayaka was advised by her ANC handlers to leave the country. She crossed the border into Botswana and, having gained refugee status, she obtained a United Nations Development Programme scholarship. In 1979 she completed her BA at the University of Zambia, with majors in Political Science, Sociology and Development Studies.

During 1980 she took up her first full-time position with the ANC in the media department of the Women's Section where she edited the magazine, *Voice of Women*, and produced a weekly radio programme. She was elected to the executive committee and the secretariat of the Women's Section which aimed to promote the demand for women's rights in parallel with the demand for national liberation.

During 1988 Myakayaka-Manzini enrolled for a Masters degree at the Institute for Social Studies in the Hague, Netherlands, focusing on women in development. Her thesis was entitled 'Women's Liberation and the Struggle for National Liberation – Present Challenges – a Case Study of South Africa.' She returned briefly to Lusaka and then travelled back to South Africa when she was chosen as one of the ANC women in exile to return to the country to rebuild the ANC Women's League in anticipation of its relaunch in August 1990.

During 1991 Myakayaka-Manzini served on the Gender Advisory Committee, a sub-committee of the Convention for a Democratic South Africa (Codesa) which was established to identify and advise negotiators on gender discrimination. During extended negotiations in the multi-party negotiating process, she served as adviser to the ANC team.

From December 1993 to May 1994 Myakayaka-Manzini served on the Transitional Executive Council's sub-council on the status of women.

She was also employed by the Gender Research Project of the Centre for Applied Legal Studies which focused on customary law, the constitution and law reform, and was active in the National Women's Coalition.

In the April 1994 general election she stood as an ANC candidate and became a member of parliament. There, she serves on the select committees on Rules and Constitutional Affairs (including provincial affairs and local government). She also serves on the select committee on abortion and sterilisation.

Myakayaka-Manzini is married to Manala Manzini. They have a nine-year-old son and live in Berea, Johannesburg.

SOURCES

1. *People in Politics, First Quarter 1994*, Institute for Democracy in South Africa, (Idasa), Durban, 1994.
2. 'The Women's Directory, 1994-95, Political Addendum', *Femina* in association with Old Mutual, 1995.

SIPO ELIJAH MZIMELA

Member of Parliament,
Inkatha Freedom Party, 1994.
Minister of Correctional
Services, 1994.

Sipo Mzimela was born in Durban on 19 June 1935, the second of the four children of Maria and Allison Mzimela, a carpenter. He grew up in Clare Estate and later Mayville in Durban, attending the Ket Maria Roman Catholic School in Mayville.

In 1951 Mzimela attended boarding school at St Chads in Ladysmith and the following year moved to the Ohlange Institute. From 1953-54 he studied at Adams College, Amanzimtoti, where he trained as a teacher, and he taught in Cato Manor (Mkhumbame) from 1955-60. Mzimela's parents were supporters of the African National Congress (ANC) and he grew up in a politicised home.

While a student at Ohlange Institute which was founded by John Dube, a former ANC president, Mzimela attended a rally to launch the ANC's Defiance Campaign in 1952. Following the rally which was addressed by ANC President, Albert Luthuli, Mzimela joined the organisation. From then on he became politically active and was arrested in the Defiance Campaign. He participated in efforts to subvert the imposition of Bantu education through joint action with other teachers. By 1958 ANC teachers were aware that they were under surveillance and that there were informers in the schools.

Following the banning of the ANC in 1960, Mzimela and two colleagues left South Africa together in December 1961. They travelled to Swaziland where Mzimela remained until May 1962. Mzimela then travelled to Rhodesia where he had relatives who were members of the Zimbabwe African Peoples' Union (Zapu) and he took cover under their umbrella. However, the Rhodesian Special Branch became aware of his presence and he was arrested. Mzimela had, by then, a Rhodesian identity document and as a result, he was released. However, the Rhodesian authorities made contact with the South African special branch and he was under threat of rearrest when he left Rhodesia for Zambia in October 1962. Thereafter, he travelled to Tanzania where the ANC had offices with headquarters in Dar es Salaam. Thousands of cadres of the liberation movements of Mozambique, Angola, Namibia, Rhodesia and South Africa were gathered there.

At the end of 1962, Mzimela was sent to Czechoslovakia for further education. He first studied the language in Dobruska before attending university in Prague where he studied Marxist theory and philosophy. However, he came to believe there was a glaring contradiction between the theory and practice of communism, with the Czech population generally worse off than people in South Africa under the apartheid regime. Mzimela concluded that communism was not a viable system, and in October 1964 left Czechoslovakia for West Germany, where he studied German in Munich before enrolling at the University of Bochum to study business and economics.

Mzimela was then employed by the *Contenantaleversicherungen* where he remained until 1974. He was responsible for the company's foreign insurance department, based in Dortmund.

From a very young age Mzimela had wanted to be a priest, but left the church after the Sharpeville massacre in 1960 on the grounds that the Dutch Reform Church's view that apartheid was consistent with the will of God was unacceptable. While at the University of Bochum in 1973 he joined the Students' Christian Movement and returned to the church. His desire to become a priest resurfaced and in 1974 Mzimela moved to the United States of America to study for the priesthood in the Anglican church at the General Theological Seminary in New York. He was ordained in December 1976 and then went on to University in New York where he completed his PhD in Ethics.

As soon as he arrived in the USA, Mzimela joined the ANC delegation at the United Nations and served on its team which aimed to have South African foreign minister, Pik Botha, expelled from the General Assembly.

From 1977 Mzimela became deputy ANC representative to the United Nations and the USA, with Johnny Makathini as chief representative. At the end of 1980 he took leave in New Jersey to write his dissertation. He also served parishes in Atlantic City.

In 1984 Mzimela left the USA to teach at St Paul's United Theological College in Kenya where he remained for two years. While he was in Kenya, the ANC held its Kabwe consultative conference and it was Mzimela's view that it was at that point that the ANC and the South African Communist Party (SACP) merged. Mzimela therefore resigned from the ANC.

During this time Mzimela met with hundreds of young South Africans in Kenya who had left ANC and Pan-Africanist Congress camps. These refugees were stranded as they were not recognised by either the Kenyan government or the UN High Commission for Refugees. When he returned to the USA in 1986, Mzimela initiated the South African Education Fund with the aim of moving such refugees out of Kenya. A number of them were able to travel to the USA to study.

Mzimela then joined the St Bartholemews's Episcopal Church in Atlanta, Georgia. During this time he concentrated on educational issues, wrote some articles on South Africa and addressed meetings in the USA.

Following the unbanning of organisations in February 1990 Mzimela returned to South Africa and met with Chief Mangosuthu Buthelezi, leader of the Inkatha Freedom Party (IFP), whom he had known since 1953. Mzimela decided to join the IFP and, as there was no-one representing the organisation in the USA, took on this role from 1991. He returned to South Africa for the negotiations at the Convention for a Democratic South Africa (Codesa) as an IFP delegate and participated in the final stages of the delicate negotiations which led to IFP participation in the April 1994 elections.

Mzimela fought the election as the IFP's third nominee on its Natal provincial list for the national parliament, and in May 1994 was appointed Minister of Correctional Services in the government of national unity.

Soon after taking office, Mzimela was faced with large-scale prison riots over the issue of amnesty. He met a delegation of prisoners at Modderbee Prison who believed that, once there was majority rule, they would be released. The riots were dealt with mainly through negotiation and matters were brought under control with Mzimela announcing a six-month blanket sentence reduction.

Mzimela is married to Gail (born De Costa) and has one step-daughter. He has two daughters from a previous marriage.

SOURCES

1. Interviewed 20 June 1994, Cape Town.
2. *Weekly Mail*, 17 June 1994.

JAYASEELAN 'JAY' NAIDOO

Member of Parliament,
African National Congress, 1994.
General Secretary, Congress of
South African Trade Unions,
1985-93.
Minister without Portfolio in the
President's Office responsible for
the Reconstruction and
Development Programme,
1994.

Born in Durban on 22 December 1954, Jay Naidoo was one of the seven children of a court interpreter. He matriculated from Sastri College, Durban, in 1972 and, following a few years of travelling and working in South Africa, enrolled at the University of Durban-Westville for a BSc degree in 1975.

While at school, Naidoo became a follower of the Black Consciousness philosophy, and these ideas were reinforced by the influence of his older brother, a South African Students Organisation (Saso) office bearer in the 1970s.

After the June 1976 unrest, Naidoo left the university, returning in 1977. That year he was instrumental in reviving Saso on the campus and in the Durban area. However, following the October 1977 clampdown on Black Consciousness organisations and the banning of Saso, Naidoo once again left the university and did not complete his degree.

From 1976 until his entry into the trade union field in 1979, Naidoo worked in the communities of Phoenix and Chatsworth, taking up issues such as transport, rent and child care. He began working in the trade union movement, initially as a volunteer, and became an organiser for Federation of South Africa Trade Unions (Fosatu) unions in Pietermaritzburg. Naidoo moved through the ranks and in 1983 was elected general secretary of the Sweet, Food and Allied Workers' Union (SFAWU) which he and Chris Dlamini, president of the union, helped to forge into one of Fosatu's strongest affiliates.

On 30 November 1985, following four years of negotiation between various unions and federations, the Congress of South African Trade Unions (Cosatu) was formed in Durban, and Fosatu dissolved. Cosatu claimed 500 000 members from 33 affiliates at the time of its launch.

Naidoo was elected general secretary of Cosatu at its launch, a position he held until 1993.

In December 1985 Naidoo went to Harare, Zimbabwe, to speak at the conference of the World Council of Churches. At the same time he met representatives of the African National Congress (ANC) and South African Congress of Trade Unions (Sactu). This was followed up in March 1986 when a seven-person Cosatu delegation, including Naidoo, met a joint ANC/Sactu delegation for two days of talks in Lusaka, Zambia.

During 1987-88, Naidoo was involved in the 'Living Wage' and 'Hands off Cosatu' campaigns. The latter was launched after numerous attacks on union officials and property, including the bombing of Cosatu House in Johannesburg.

In September 1988 Naidoo's passport was confiscated as he was about to board a flight to Australia. He was subsequently refused a passport to attend an October conference at White Plains, USA, leading seven black South Africans to walk out of the conference in protest.

In 1989 Naidoo participated in talks between the United Democratic Front, Cosatu and Inkatha in an effort to find a peaceful solution to political violence in Natal, but the talks eventually broke down.

On behalf of Cosatu, Naidoo addressed the relaunch of the South African Communist Party as a legal organisation, held on 29 July 1990. He reaffirmed Cosatu's commitment to its revolutionary alliance with the ANC and SACP in this speech.

In August 1990 Naido and other Cosatu officials were charged with kidnapping and assaulting a security policeman allegedly spying on the federation's head office. In October 1991, Naidoo was found guilty and fined R2 000 (or one year's imprisonment) with a further one year suspended for three years. However, on appeal, the conviction for assault was overturned in March 1992, although the verdict on kidnapping was upheld. In 1994 the hearing on appeal was postponed *sine die.*

In November 1991 Naidoo called for a macro-economic negotiating forum comprising employers, major political parties and the state. He spearheaded the two-day anti-VAT (value-added tax) strike of that month, called after negotiations between the Co-ordinating Committee on VAT and the government had deadlocked over taxation on basic foodstuffs, medicines, electricity and water.

Following the breakdown of negotiations in the Convention for a Democratic South Africa (Codesa) in May 1992, the ANC/SACP/Cosatu alliance launched a mass action campaign in an attempt to pressurise the government to accept a constituent assembly and transitional government, and take firm steps to end political violence. Naidoo filled a high profile role in this campaign which included marches in major cities and a two-day general strike. Naidoo was also involved in negotiations between Cosatu and the South African Co-ordinatiog Committee on Labour Affairs (Saccola), an employers' federation, in unsuccessful attempts to avert the strike.

In September 1993 Naidoo and other trade unionists resigned from their positions in the unions in order to play a role in the ANC/SACP/Cosatu alliance's election campaign and to stand as candidates for the ANC. Naidoo stood in the April 1994 election as number six on the ANC's list to the National Assembly and became a member of parliament. In May he was appointed Minister without Portfolio in the government of national unity. The position concentrates on co-ordinating ⸺and implementing the reconstruction and development programme which involves working closely with all government departments.

Naidoo is married to Lucie Page, a French Canadian journalist, and they have two children. Naidoo also has a stepson from his wife's previous marriage.

SOURCES

1. South African Institute of Race Relations, *Survey of Race Relations 1985, 1987/88 and 1988/89,* Johannesburg, 1986, 1988, 1989.
2. *Herald,* 8 December 1985.
3. *Sunday Tribune,* 15 December 1985.
4. *New Nation,* 16 January 1986.
5. *Daily News,* 7 March 1986.
6. *Sunday Tribune,* 1 June 1986.
7. Telephonic discussion, 28 February 1987.

  8. *Daily News,* 29 August 1990.
  9. *Daily News,* 17 October 1991.
 10. *Daily News,* 7 November 1991
 11. *New Nation,* 8 November 1991.
 12. *Sunday Tribune,* 22 October 1991.
 13. *Daily News,* 24 March 1992.
 14. *Natal on Saturday,* 6 November 1993.
 15. *Post,* 23 February 1994.

JAYENDRA NAIDOO

---

*Executive Director, National
Economic Development and
Labour Council (Nedlac), 1995.*

Born in Durban on 5 September 1960, Jayendra Naidoo was the son of Sakunthula and MJ Naidoo, an attorney and president of the Natal Indian Congress (NIC) from 1973-79.

He grew up in Durban, attending Sastri College and the Gandhi Desai High School where he matriculated in 1976. The following year he began a law degree at the University of Durban-Westville and became involved in the activities of the South African Students' Organisation (Saso), a Black Consciousness grouping. Subsequent to the banning of Saso, Naidoo became involved in community-based struggles which led to his leaving the university in 1979 to become a full-time community activist in areas around Durban, including Phoenix, Tongaat and Cato Manor. He returned to campus in 1980, the year of ongoing student boycotts, but left university in 1981 without completing his degree.

In 1982 Naidoo joined the trade union movement as an organiser and worked for the National Union of Distributive and Allied Workers. Through a process of mergers the union eventually became part of the South African Commercial, Catering and Allied Workers' Union (Saccawu), and in 1987 Naidoo was elected national education co-ordinator of the union.

Naidoo's union activities at this time were largely undertaken in Natal, involving recruitment, education, negotiations and media. He served as national co-ordinator of a number of major strikes at this time, including those at the Spar Group (1985), Pick 'n Pay (1986) and OK Bazaars (1986-87).

From 1987-89 Naidoo served as a Ccawusa delegate on Cosatu's central executive committee and worked on Cosatu's commission on organisational development and training, as well as a range of other union committees. From 1988 onwards, he was actively involved in the peace process in Natal and served on the joint working committee formed in 1989.

Following the unbanning of the African National Congress (ANC) in February 1990, Naidoo was elected chair of its Durban Western Areas branch. In March 1991 he stood down from that position, as well as the joint working committee on peace, to popularise debates on political economy and make them more accessible to Cosatu's leadership and membership.

Naidoo served on the ANC and Cosatu's co-ordinating committee for the National Peace Accord. He was a member of the ANC/SACP/Cosatu alliance team which negotiated the terms of the Peace Accord, and chaired its management committee. Following publication of the draft Peace Accord, Naidoo chaired its editing committee which produced the final document.

From 1991-94 Naidoo served on the national peace secretariat, which was charged with the establishment of dispute resolution committees throughout the country, and on its sub-committee dealing with a code of conduct for the South African Defence Force. He was also the full-time Cosatu negotiations co-ordinator which included responsibility for negotiating the establishment of a national economic forum with the state and employers.

During July 1992, Naidoo was involved in talks with the South African Co-ordinating Committee on Labour Affairs (Saccola), an employers' federation, concerning the breakdown of negotiations in the Convention for a Democratic South Africa (Codesa). A draft Charter for Peace, Democracy and Reconstruction emerged from these talks, to help curb political violence, combat poverty, mediate in industrial disputes, and assist in bringing parties back to the negotiating table.

Naidoo continued working on the process committee of the National Economic Forum, and in January 1995 Minister of Labour, Tito

Mboweni, announced Naidoo's appointment as executive director of the National Economic Development and Labour Council (Nedlac), a statu- tory body established to bring together business, labour and state inter- ests with effect from 1 February. Nedlac replaced the National Economic Forum and the National Manpower Commission and deals with changes to economic and social policies and legislation prior to implementation. The council has four chambers, namely labour, trade and industry, monetary policy and public finance and development.

It is Naidoo's view that Nedlac is a forum where key constituencies can negotiate legislation and policy that will impact on them. Matters envisaged on Nedlac's agenda include new labour legislation and the implementation of the Gatt agreements.

Naidoo and his fiance have one daughter. He has two children from a previous marriage.

SOURCES

1. Interviewed May 1991, Durban.
2. *Sunday Tribune,* 19 July 1992.
3. *Sunday Times,* 15 January 1995.
4. *Sunday Times,* 12 February 1995.

BALDWIN SIPHO NGUBANE

Member of Parliament,
Inkatha Freedom Party, 1994.
Minister of Arts, Culture, Science
and Technology, 1994.

Born on 22 October 1941 at a mission station at Inchanga, in the Camperdown district of Natal, Ben Ngubane was the youngest of the six children of Anastasia and Alfred Ngubane. Ngubane's father was involved in church work and also did some farming. He was a councillor to the local chief and was skilled in the use of herbs.

Most of Ngubane's schooling took place at the Mariannhill Mission, near Pinetown, and he matriculated in 1960. He then taught Latin at Mariannhill for two years and during this time undertook special courses in mathematics and physical science to enable him to study medicine. He then enrolled at the Medical School of the University of Natal, Durban, and graduated MB ChB in 1971.

Ngubane worked as a doctor at the King Edward VIII hospital in Durban and also at the Ngwelezana Hospital until 1975 when he became district surgeon in the Empangeni area, a post he held until 1991 when he became Minister of Health in the KwaZulu government.

Ngubane came from a family involved in traditional politics and his first brush with broader political issues was during his time at medical school. He became a member of the Students' Representative Council, the House Committee of the Alan Taylor Residence and the Medical Students' Council. He also became active in national student politics, serving as vice-president of the National Union of South African Students (Nusas). He worked with Steve Biko during the time Biko was active in Nusas and attended the union's congress at Rhodes University where black students were accommodated in an old church building as they were not permitted to stay in the university residences. Black students led by Biko decided to form a black students' organisation in order to address issues related to blacks and the Black Consciousness-oriented South African Students' Organisation was established.

Ngubane differed with Biko in that he believed that it was possible to continue to work through Nusas and force the universities to take a united position against the government. He felt that the formation of a student organisation which excluded a section of the student community played into the hands of the government. Ngubane supported the Black Consciousness call towards self-reliance, self-help and a heightening of self-esteem and saw the contact between Black Consciousness activists and democratic whites in a positive light.

In 1975 Inkatha yeNkululeko yeSizwe (Freedom of the Nation) was formed with the mission to oppose the de-nationalisation of black people and the refusal of independent status for KwaZulu. Ngubane joined Inkatha in 1976 and in 1978 was elected to represent the Enseleni district in the KwaZulu legislative assembly.

During this time, Ngubane served as a member of the Red Cross Natal Region from 1977; as a delegate of the South African Red Cross Society at international congresses of the Red Cross in 1978, 1981, 1983 and 1985; as a member of the Council of the University of Zululand, a position he held until 1994; and as a member of the Natal Boxing Board of Control from 1991.

He undertook post-graduate academic work and studied at the University of the Witwatersrand for a Diploma in Tropical Medicine (1983) and completed his MPraxMed (Master in Family Medicine and Primary Health) (1986) at the University of Natal.

Ngubane also travelled to the USA, Germany, Switzerland, England, Benin and Senegal.

In 1991 Ngubane was appointed Minister of Health in the KwaZulu government, a post he held until 1994.

In 1992 Ngubane served on the Convention for a Democratic South Africa (Codesa) working group which dealt with constitutional principles and constitution making, but the negotiations collapsed over the issue of percentages necessary to amend entrenched clauses and fundamental rights in the constitution.

The African National Congress (ANC) then undertook a campaign of rolling mass action. This led to government concessions on various issues and the signing of a bilateral Record of Understanding between itself and the ANC. When negotiations resumed in April 1993 Ngubane was again involved on behalf of the Inkatha Freedom Party (IFP). The IFP eventually withdrew from the negotiations along with its partners in the Concerned South African Group (Cosag) which included the Conservative Party and the governments of the Ciskei and Bophuthatswana.

The IFP initially refused to participate in the April 1994 elections, but following intensive negotiations at a meeting with the Zulu king, ANC and government representatives at the Kruger Park and later through several mediation attempts, the IFP agreed to fight the elections, two weeks before the election date.

Ngubane headed the KwaZulu Natal regional list to the National Assembly and following the elections was appointed Minister of Arts, Culture, Science and Technology in the government of national unity. The main function of this new ministry is to bring about technical advancement and development which can underpin the government's reconstruction and development programme and the revitalisation of the South African economy. Regarding the arts, the government is committed to achieving national untiy and promoting a national culture in South Africa's multi-cultural population. In addition, the Ministry is committed to provide access to training and information for those people who have been denied such access in the past.

Ngubane is married to Sheila (born Buthelezi) and they have four children.

SOURCES

1. Interviewed 24 June 1994, Cape Town
2. *Curriculum vitae* supplied by the Ministry of Arts, Culture, Science and Technology, June 1994.

JOSEPH MBUKU NHLANHLA

Member of Parliament,
African National Congress, 1994.
Deputy Minister of Intelligence,
1994.

Born on 4 December 1936 in Sophiatown, Joe Nhlanhla was one of the five children of Christina Toli (born Buhali) and Samuel Nhlanhla, a shoemaker and a priest in the informal African churches.

By the time Nhlanhla began school at the age of seven, his family had bought property in Alexandra, where he grew up. He attended a local primary school and then enrolled at Kilnerton High School, where he matriculated in 1956.

Nhlanhla joined the African National Congress (ANC) and was active in the Alexandra Youth League. During this time he was involved in the anti-pass campaign, as well as the 1957 bus and potato boycotts. He served as secretary of the Alexandra Youth League and was a member of the Transvaal executive committee of the ANC Youth League. Nhlanhla was one of the first to be arrested during the 1960 state of emergency, when he was detained on 28 March. On his release a few days before the lifting of the emergency, he was confined to the magisterial area of Johannesburg.

After the ANC was banned, Nhlanhla joined its underground structures. In April 1964 he left South Africa to join the ANC's military wing, Umkhonto we Sizwe (MK), in Tanzania. He was selected to go to Moscow where he studied economics at the Plekhanov Institute from October 1964 until 1969. He headed the ANC youth and student structure in the USSR and organised conferences for ANC students studying there.

In 1970 Nhlanhla returned to Tanzania, serving as head of the ANC youth and students structure until 1973, when he became the ANC's chief representative in Egypt and the Middle East. During this time he represented the ANC on the Afro-Asian People's Solidarity Organisation, the forerunner of the Non-Aligned Movement.

In 1978 Nhlanhla was recalled to ANC headquarters in Lusaka to become the organisation's national administrative secretary. In 1981 he became a member of the ANC's national executive committee.

In 1983, Nhlanhla was appointed secretary of the ANC's Political-Military Council, established to deal with internal mobilisation within South Africa. In 1987, when the intelligence and security section of the ANC was reorganised, Nhlanhla was appointed to head the Department of Intelligence and Security.

Following the unbanning of the ANC in February 1990, Nhlanhla returned to South Africa in April. He had previously had clandestine contact with representatives of the South African government in the late 1980s, after the ANC had received indications that a negotiated settlement with the apartheid government might be possible.

Nhlanhla served on the steering committee preparing for the Groote Schuur conference between the ANC and the South African government which took place in May 1990, and was present at the conference as a member of the ANC delegation.

Nhlanhla attended the Convention for a Democratic South Africa (Codesa) held in December 1992, and served on its working group dealing with interim government. He subsequently became involved in negotiations on the future of the intelligence services in South Africa.

Nhlanhla stood as an ANC candidate in the general election of April 1994 and became a member of parliament. In July it was announced that he was to be appointed Deputy Minister, Intelligence, reporting directly to President Mandela with effect from February 1995. In this post, Nhlanhla chairs the National Intelligence Co-ordinating Committee which oversees the country's four intelligence agencies – the National Intelligence Agency (domestic); the South African Secret Services (international); the police; and the military.

Nhlanhla is married to Mmabatho and they have one son.

SOURCES

1. Interviewed 12 March 1992, Johannesburg.
2. *Sunday Times,* 17 July 1994.
3. *Sowetan,* 27 February 1995.

CHARLES NQAKULA

Deputy General Secretary,
South African Communist Party,
1991-93.
General Secretary, South African
Communist Party, 1993.

Born in Cradock on 13 September 1942, Charles Nqakula was one of the nine children of Ida and Billy Nqakula. His mother was a washerwoman while his father was employed by Karoo farmers to destroy weeds.

Nqakula grew up in Cradock, attending the local primary school. He was a member of the Anglican Church where the local priest was former African National Congress (ANC) general secretary, James Calata. Nqakula was politicised at an early age, becoming part of a group selling Communist Party media, such as the *New Age* newspaper.

Nqakula's high school years were spent at Lovedale (1959-63), where he matriculated. He then worked as a waiter and wine steward in a hotel and later as a clerk in the local Department of Bantu Education. In 1966 he began working as a journalist for the *Midland News,* a regional weekly newspaper in Cradock. In 1973 he joined *Imvo Zabantsundu,* based in King Williams Town, and served as its political reporter. In 1976 he joined the staff of the *Daily Dispatch* in East London where he remained until 1981, when the government placed him under a banning order.

When Ciskei became legally independent later that year, his banning order became non-operative, as he was living in a village which, although just outside King Williams Town, fell into the Ciskei. As a result South African authorities revoked the banning order in 1982, but declared Nqakula a prohibited immigrant unable to enter South African territory.

While working for *Imvo,* Nqakula became a member of the Union of Black Journalists (UBJ) and was elected its vice-president in 1976. In October 1977 the union was banned in a government crackdown on organisations generally supportive of Black Consciousness. When Nqakula was invited on a study visit to Germany, the government withdrew his passport and he was unable to take up the opportunity.

In 1978 the Writers' Association of South Africa (Wasa) was formed to succeed the banned UBJ and the following year Nqakula was elected its vice-president. In 1980 the union was broadened to include others in the media industry who were not journalists, and renamed the Media Workers Association of South Africa (Mwasa). Nqakula was elected its vice-president.

During 1980, Nqakula was detained and held at Fort Glamorgan, East London, for a week. Subsequently, he was frequently detained either by the South African or the Ciskeian authorities, including a six-week period in August-September 1983. During this time he was elected publicity secretary of the Border region of the United Democratic Front (UDF).

At the end of 1982 Nqakula started the *Veritas* news agency in Zwelitsha, but towards the end of 1983 was arrested in East London for being in South Africa without a visa.

By this time, Nqakula had become an underground operative for the African National Congress (ANC), specialising in propaganda. He also undertook work for the South African Communist Party (SACP), but was only officially drawn into SACP ranks in 1985, after leaving South Africa.

In October 1984 Nqakula left South Africa, travelling to Lesotho, Tanzania and Zambia. He then moved to Angola where he underwent military training in the ANC and joined Umkhonto we Sizwe (MK). He travelled to the Soviet Union and East Germany for further military training and in 1988 infiltrated back into South Africa as one of the commanders of Operation Vulindlela, with a mission to build viable underground political and military structures. Nqakula served as Vula's commander in the Western Cape region and remained in the country following the unbanning of the ANC and the SACP, emerging from the underground just before the July 1991 ANC conference when he was granted amnesty by the government.

Nqakula served on the interim leadership group of the SACP and as convenor of its national organising committee. He was also a member of its political committee and served on the party's secretariat. At the December 1991 conference of the SACP, these structures were dissolved and a new central committee elected. Nqakula was elected deputy general secretary of the party and therefore also served on its central committee and politburo, which is charged with the day-to-day administration of the party programme of action.

Following the assassination of Chris Hani in April 1993, Nqakula was appointed as general secretary of the party. He was re-elected to this post at the SACP's ninth national congress, held in April 1995.

In 1994 he declined to stand for a parliamentary seat on the grounds that the SACP needed to be built up at the grassroots, and that this was where his energies were required. At the ANC's Bloemfontein congress held in December 1994, Nqakula was elected to the organisation's national executive committee.

Nqakula is a composer of choral music and a poet. He has published a book of Xhosa poetry entitled *Ukhanyo* (Light) which has been prescribed in schools teaching Xhosa since 1974. He has also contributed to other publications.

Nqakula is married to Gertrude (born Sixaba), a teacher, and they have three children.

SOURCES

1. Interviewed 30 October 1991, Johannesburg.
2. Information provided by South African Communist Party, May 1995.

EMMANUEL BONGINKOSE 'BLADE' NZIMANDE

Member of Parliament,
African National Congress, 1994.
Deputy National Chairperson,
South African Communist Party,
1995.

Born in Edendale, Pietermaritzburg, on 14 April 1958, 'Blade' Nzimande was one of the three children of Nozipho Alice and Phillip Sphambano, a Shangaan herbalist from Mozambique.

Nzimande attended the Roman Catholic School, Henryville, and then

Plessiers Lower Primary School before going on to Mthethomusha School in Edendale, the first school in the area established under the new Bantu education system. He matriculated in 1975 at Georgetown High, Edendale.

While at school he participated in youth clubs which were gatherings for cultural and sporting events, and were not particularly political in nature. He first became politically aware when Harry Gwala was released from Robben Island prison in 1973 and this was widely discussed in the community.

In 1976 Nzimande enrolled at the University of Zululand to study towards a BA degree, majoring in Public Adminstration and Psychology. He became involved in student activity, including a food boycott and demonstrations against the award of an honorary doctorate to Mangosuthu Buthelezi in May 1976. During that time the Black Consciousness-oriented South African Students' Organisation (Saso) was prominent on campus, but Nzimande's political views later shifted towards the Congress Alliance.

Following the shooting of demonstrating students in Soweto on 16 June 1976, the administration building of the university was burnt down and the university subsequently closed down for a period.

Nzimande returned to university in 1977 and completed his degree in 1979. After graduating, he returned to Edendale and joined the Azanian Students' Organisation (Azaso) which eventually broke away from the Black Consciousness Movement, alligning itself with the Congress or Charterist tendency.

For Nzimande the shift from Black Consciousness to the Charterist position was facilitated by weekly Zulu broadcasts from Radio Freedom and Radio Moscow. In this way he and his colleagues became acquainted with the policy of the African National Congress (ANC) and they started to receive underground ANC documents. While active in Azaso Nzimande completed his Psychology Honours degree at the University of Natal, Pietermaritzburg, in 1980, and obtained his Masters degree in Industrial Psychology in 1981. More recently, he has been awarded a PhD for a thesis in the field of personnel management.

In January 1982 Nzimande moved to Durban, and at that stage was active in the Dambuza Youth Organisation which affiliated to the United Democratic Front (UDF) after its launch in 1983.

In 1982 Nzimande undertook his internship in Industrial Psychology in the personnel department of Tongaat Hulett Sugar Ltd. There he met Jay Naidoo and began working informally with unions, addressing union seminars on job grading and other issues. He resigned his job in 1984.

Nzimande was then offered a post as a lecturer at the Umlazi branch of the University of Zululand where he founded the Department of Industrial Psychology on that campus. At the same time, he became increasingly involved with the trade unions and served on the editorial board of the *South African Labour Bulletin* in 1986. He also continued to assist with trade union seminars teaching the history of trade unionism.

In Umlazi he began to work on educational issues in mid-1986 and also held clandestine Marxist study classes with the youth. Nzimande lectured until June 1987 and then joined the University of Natal, Durban, to lecture in the Psychology Department. There he became involved in the Culture and Working Life Project, and initiated the cultural activities of the Dambuzo Cultural Organisation which produced a play on violence, *Koze Kube Nini* (Until When?), performed in the townships. He also wrote various articles on violence, and assisted in the presentation of seminars.

In the late 1980s Nzimande served on the local National Education Co-ordinating Committee (NECC) and in 1989 became a member of the National Reception Committee formed in anticipation of the release of political prisoners.

In the late 1980s Nzimande became part of the underground structures of the ANC and the SACP. Following the February 1990 unbanning of the these organisations he returned home to Umlazi and helped to form eight branches of the ANC in Umlazi, serving as secretary of the Bhekithemba Branch. Harry Gwala then asked him to serve on the regional interim committee of the ANC in the Natal Midlands Region as political education officer. In 1991 he was elected to the regional executive committee. He also served as assistant secretary to the interim leadership group of the SACP in the same region.

In August 1989 Nzimande was appointed director of the Education Policy Unit (EPU) which was formed as a joint venture between the University of Natal and the NECC, with the intention of establishing the effect of violence on education in Natal. He first held the post of director on the Durban campus, but in January 1991 the EPU opened on the Pietermaritzburg campus and moved there.

At the national congress of the SACP held in December 1991, Nzimande was elected to the party's central committee. He also served on its politburo, responsible for the day-to-day implementation of policy. In 1992 he was elected deputy chairperson of the Natal Midlands ANC regional executive committee. At the ninth national congress of the SACP, held in April 1995, Nzimande was elected deputy national chairperson of the party.

In the general election of 1994, Nzimande stood for the ANC and became a member of parliament. In this capacity, he was elected to serve as chairperson of the select committee on education.

Nzimande is married to Phumelele Ntombela and they have four children.

SOURCE

1. *People in Politics,* Second Quarter 1993, Institute for Democracy in South
   Africa (Idasa), Durban, 1993.
2. Information provided by South African Communist Party, May 1995.

ALFRED BAPHETHUXOLO NZO

Member of Parliament,
African National Congress, 1994.
Minister of Foreign Affairs, 1994.

Alfred Nzo was born on 19 June 1925 in Benoni, one of the five
children of Christina and Nkululeko Nzo, a clerical worker at
Modderbee mine, Benoni.

He attended the Roman Catholic Missionary School at Mariazell near
Matatiele where he completed his Junior Certificate in 1942. He matriculated at Healdtown Missionary Institute, Fort Beaufort, and then registered at the Fort Hare University College for a BSc degree. However, he
dropped out at the end of his second year in 1946. At university, Nzo
joined the African National Congress (ANC) Youth League.

He continued with his studies part-time at a Johannesburg technical
college and completed a health inspector's course under the Royal Sani-
tary Institute of London in June 1951. He then worked as a health inspector in Alexandra, but was fired in 1958 because of his political activities.

The 12 years he spent working in the field of public health made Nzo
aware of the poverty and frustration of the black community and this,
combined with his involvement in the ANC Youth League, led him to

take an active political role. Nzo participated in the May Day strike of 1950 and later the nationwide strike of 26 June. He assisted in the mobilisation of people during the 1952 Defiance Campaign and was also active in the campaign leading up to the Congress of the People and the adoption of the Freedom Charter in Kliptown on 26 June 1955.

In 1957 Nzo became secretary of the bus boycott co-ordinating committee which organised the Alexandra bus boycott from January to March of that year.

In 1958 Nzo was elected to both the Transvaal and national executive committees of the ANC. He lost his job at the end of 1958 because of his political involvement and on 2 January 1959 began full-time work as an office administrator at the ANC headquarters in Johannesburg.

After Nzo lost his job, his permanent residence permit in Alexandra was cancelled, making it illegal for him to live there. From 1959 onwards he was served with a series of banning orders and was frequently arrested under section 10 of the Urban Areas Act for not being in possession of a resident's permit. In 1961 he was imprisoned for five months.

In 1961 Nzo was restricted to Mofolo, and in November 1962 placed under 24-hour house arrest. During that year he was charged in the trial following the All-In Africa Conference held in March in Pietermaritzburg. On 24 June 1963, security police detained Nzo, holding him for 238 days. During this period he was released on two occasions but immediately re-detained. He was finally released in February 1964 with no charges being brought against him.

Following his release, the underground leadership of the ANC asked Nzo to leave the country and join the external mission which had been operating under the leadership of Oliver Tambo since 1960. Nzo left South Africa on 22 March 1964.

He served as the ANC's deputy representative in Cairo from September 1964 to August 1967, when he became chief representative in New Delhi, India. In April 1969 he was elected secretary-general of the ANC and transferred to the movement's headquarters at Morogoro, Tanzania. He subsquently moved to Lusaka, Zambia. As a member of the South African Communist Party (SACP), Nzo was awarded the Order of Friendship by the Soviet Union in 1985.

In 1989 ANC President, Oliver Tambo, suffered a stroke and Nzo took over many of his duties including intensive consultations with internal groupings from South Africa prior to the unbanning of the ANC in February 1990.

Following the unbanning of the ANC and the release of Nelson Mandela, Nzo formed part of the ANC delegation involved in talks with the government.

At the July 1991 ANC conference held in Durban, Nzo was defeated by Cyril Ramaphosa for the position of secretary-general. However, he was elected a member of the organisation's national executive committee and appointed deputy head of the ANC's security department. He later headed its Directorate of Intelligence. From December 1993-April 1994 Nzo served on the intelligence sub-council of the Transitional Executive Council.

In the April 1994 general election, Nzo was number 44 on the ANC's national list for the National Assembly, and he became a member of parliament. In May 1994 he was appointed Minister of Foreign Affairs. As Minister he participated in the integration of South Africa into various international institutions such as the Organisation for African Unity, the Non-Aligned Movement, and the Commonwealth.

At the ANC's Bloemfontein congress held in December 1994 Nzo was re-elected to the organisation's national executive committee.

He is married to Regina Vuyelwa and they have one son.

SOURCES

1. Thomas Karis, Gwendolen Carter and Gail Gerhart, *From Protest to Challenge. A Documentary History of African Politics in South Africa, 1882-1964,* Vol 4, Stanford, 1971.
2. *Sechaba,* May 1981.
3. Interviewed, 7 October 1986, Lusaka.
4. *Profile '94,* South African Communication Services, Pretoria, 1994.

ABDULAH MOHAMED OMAR

Member of Parliament,
African National Congress, 1994.
Minister of Justice, 1994.

Dulah Omar, one of the 12 children of Aysha and Mohamed Omar, a greengrocer/hawker, was born in Cape Town on 26 May 1934. He attended a small Moslem primary school in Salt River and the Wesley Training School after which he matriculated at Trafalgar High School in 1952. In his matric year Omar participated in a campaign to boycott national celebrations commemorating Jan van Riebeeck's arrival at the Cape.

Between 1953 and 1957 Omar attended the University of Cape Town where he completed BA and LLB degrees. While at university, he joined the New Era Fellowship, an educational, cultural and political forum linked to the Anti-CAD (Coloured Affairs Department) movement. He subsequently served as secretary of the Cape region of Anti-CAD. In addition, he became involved in the activities of the Non-European Unity Movement (NEUM) and participated in the campaign against separate education for blacks and whites. Omar was also active in opposing government moves to have coloureds removed from the common voters' roll.

Following graduation, Omar completed his legal articles in Cape Town. He then opened a legal practice in partnership with Cadoc M Kobus, the only African lawyer practising in Cape Town at the time.

When he opened his practice in 1960, Omar was approached by Pan-Africanist Congress (PAC) leaders to act for them in a legal capacity. The leadership was subsequently detained or arrested and Omar met and acted for many of them, including Robert Sobukwe. He also acted for members of the Coloured People's Congress (CPC), part of the Congress

Alliance which had adopted the Freedom Charter in 1955. Omar was asked to defend Robben Island prisoners who had fallen foul of prison regulations and met leaders of the African National Congress (ANC), including Nelson Mandela, Ahmed Kathrada, Govan Mbeki and others for whom he later acted.

During the early 1960s, Omar defended accused in the Poqo trials. In the 1970s he acted for the Black People's Convention (BPC) and the South African Students' Organisations (Saso), both part of the Black Consciousness Movement. He advised BPC members who set up the Black Community Programmes' self-help projects such as the establishment of co-operatives and appeared for PAC members in the 1978 Bethal trial.

On 23 August 1985 Omar was detained under section 29 of the Internal Security Act and held in solitary confinement at Pollsmoor Prison for eight weeks. Despite his poor health – he had suffered a heart attack in 1979 – he was made to sleep on the floor. In October of the same year Omar was again detained, this time under emergency regulations, and held at Victor Verster Prison, Paarl, until his release in December.

In 1985 Omar was elected first president of the Democratic Lawyers' Organisation, a body representing lawyers from across the political spectrum, and in 1987 helped found the National Association of Democratic Lawyers (Nadel), serving as its vice-president.

Following Omar's decision to play a political role in the UDF, he was elected chairperson of its Western Cape region in 1987. While attending a Defiance Campaign meeting in Durban in 1989, he suffered a further heart attack and stepped down from the chair of the UDF. In December 1989 he was elected vice-chairperson of its Western Cape region.

During 1990, evidence presented to the Harms Commission of Enquiry revealed that Omar had been the subject of an assassination attempt organised by the Civil Co-operation Bureau, a clandestine section of the South African Defence Force. Attempts were also made to kidnap his daughter.

Omar served as director of the Community Law Centre at the University of the Western Cape until his appointment as Minister of Justice. In this capacity, he participated in research and policy formulation regarding human rights and constitutional matters as well as issues dealing with the democratisation of the legal system, the judiciary and the legal profession. He also took a special interest in projects concerning children's rights; women's and gender rights; and policing in a democratic South Africa.

Omar stood as an ANC candidate in the first democratic elections in April 1994 and became a member of parliament. In May he was appointed Minister of Justice. He indicated that he intended to use his portfolio to transform the judicial system by inculcating a culture of human rights so that it would be seen to be legitimate in the eyes of society. His duties included the establishment of the Judicial Service Commission, the Constitutional Court, the Human Rights Commission, the Commission on Gender Equality and the public protector's office.

At the ANC's conference held in Bloemfontein in December 1994 Omar was elected to the organisation's national executive committee.

Omar is married to Farida (born Ally) with whom he has two sons and a daughter.

SOURCES

1. *South,* 11 June 1987.
2. Interviewed, 7 May 1988, Cape Town.
3. *Post,* 11 May 1994.
4. *Sunday Times,* 22 May 1994.
5. *Profile 94,* South African Communication Services, Pretoria, 1994.

AZIZ GOOLAM HOOSEIN PAHAD

Member of Parliament,
African National Congress, 1994.
Deputy Minister of Foreign Affairs,
1994.

Aziz Pahad was born in Schweizer-Reneke in the Western Transvaal on 25 December 1940, one of the five sons of Amina and Goolam Hoosein Ismail Pahad, a businessman. His parents were active in the Transvaal and South African Indian Congresses and his mother was arrested on three occasions while participating in the Passive Resistance Campaign and Defiance Campaign of 1952.

The family moved to Johannesburg when he was five years old and he attended the Ferreirastown Indian Primary School and the Central Indian High School, Johannesburg, established by the Congress Movement to oppose the residential racial segregation demanded by the Group Areas Act. Pahad matriculated in 1959.

Pahad's childhood was highly politicised and was characterised by participation in marches, distributing Congress literature and constant raids and harrassment by the police. He also met national leaders such as Nelson Mandela, Walter Sisulu, Albert Luthuli and Yusuf Dadoo, who were associates of his parents.

Pahad enrolled at the University of the Witwatersrand for a degree in Sociology and Afrikaans. There he became involved in the formation of the first Human Rights Society and was also a member of the Transvaal Indian Youth Congress.

Pahad and his brother, Essop, were banned in 1963 and forbidden to attend gatherings and participate in political activities. During this period Pahad was detained for short periods, often for violating his banning order.

In 1964, following the Rivonia trial, Pahad and his brother left South Africa for London. He enrolled at the University College of London and completed his Diploma in International Relations in 1966. In 1968 he was awarded an MA degree in International Relations from the University of Sussex.

During this time Pahad worked in the London office of the Anti-Apartheid Movement, co-ordinating its campaigns. He later became a member of the Revolutionary Council of the ANC which created underground structures for a political mass movement and consolidated and co-ordinated protests.

Because of the surveillance of ANC members in African countries, the council was based mainly in Europe from where it was safer to interact with internal members of the movement. Pahad, however, spent about a year in Angola and 18 months in Zambia as a member of the Revolutionary Council until it was dissolved in 1983 to make way for new structures in the ANC. He was elected to the ANC national executive committee (NEC) at the consultative conference held in Kabwe, Zambia, in 1985.

In 1987 Pahad was involved in preparations for the Dakar (Senegal) conference held in July. This conference publicly brought together for the first time a broad-based group of mainly white, Afrikaans South Africans with members of the ANC leadership. This highly publicised meeting placed the process of dialogue and negotiation high on the

ANC's agenda. Subsequent meetings were held in France and Germany.

After the ban was lifted on the ANC and other organisations in February 1990, Pahad was part of the ANC leadership group which returned to prepare for negotiations. At the July 1991 ANC conference held in Durban, Pahad was re-elected to the organisation's national executive committee. In the same year he became deputy head of the ANC's department of international affairs and a member of the national peace executive committee. When the Transitional Executive Council was established in December 1993, he served as a member of its sub-council on foreign affairs.

In the first democratic elections in April 1994, Pahad stood as candidate number 37 on the ANC's list for the National Assembly and became a member of parliament. In May he was appointed Deputy Minister of Foreign Affairs in the government of national unity.

At the ANC's Bloemfontein congress held in December 1994 Pahad was re-elected to the organisation's national executive committee.

Aziz and Sandra Pahad married in July 1994 and they have a daughter. He has a son from a previous marriage.

SOURCES

1. *People in Politics,* Second Quarter 1992, Institute for Democracy in South Africa (Idasa), Durban, 1992.
2. *People in Politics,* Third Quarter 1994, Idasa, Durban, 1994.
3. *Sunday Times,* 24 July 1994.
4. Anton Harber and Barbara Ludman (eds), *A-Z of Politics,* Weekly Mail & Guardian/Penguin Books, 1995.

NAKEDI MATHEWS PHOSA

Premier, Eastern Transvaal
Province, 1994.

Born on 1 September 1952 in Mbombela township, Nelspruit, Mathews Phosa was the second of the four children of Reshoketjoe and Paul Phosa, a school teacher. His mother was a nurse who served in Europe as a volunteer during the Second World War.

Politics was often discussed in Phosa's home, with his mother keeping the history of black resistance alive with stories about Nelson Mandela, then imprisoned on Robben Island.

Phosa spent his primary school years with his grandparents in Potgietersrus. In 1967 he became a boarder at the Maripi High School at Acornhoek in the Eastern Transvaal where he matriculated in 1971. Phosa was a keen student and participated in debating and drama. He also enjoyed boxing, karate and athletics.

Phosa had his first brush with security police while still at school. Pupils who had protested against and disrupted a whites-only event to be held at the school were interrogated by security police and were severely beaten by the headmaster.

In 1972 Phosa enrolled for a BProc LLB at the University of the North and joined the South African Students' Organisation (Saso), becoming publicity secretary for the Turfloop branch. As a student Phosa had to work part-time during holidays in order to assist his mother financially. His father had died in 1970 and, throughout his years at Turfloop, Phosa worked as a printing clerk at a construction company during his vacations.

After graduating in 1977, he served his articles with a Johannesburg legal firm. He returned to the Eastern Transvaal in 1980 and opened his own legal firm. He was actively involved in legal work until he went into exile in 1985.

Phosa had joined the African National Congress (ANC) and its military wing, Umkhonto we Sizwe (MK), in 1979. He initially operated as a political organiser in underground structures, conducting a number of campaigns. During this time he made several contacts with ANC structures in neighbouring countries and in Europe.

From 1981-83, while based in Nelspruit, Phosa led the campaign against the incorporation of KaNgwane into Swaziland together with former and KaNgwane chief ministers Enos Mabuza and Caiphus Zitha. In 1984 Phosa led the anti-tricameral parliament campaign in the Eastern Transvaal. In 1985 he led the rent boycotts which started in Piet Retief and spread throughout the region.

In April 1985 Phosa left the country after ANC intelligence sources uncovered a plot to assassinate him. While in exile he spent most of his time in Maputo, Mozambique. He was appointed regional commander of the Political-Military Committee of the region. Based in Maputo, he directed the ANC's political and military work in the Eastern Transvaal region. During this period, he also received political and military training in the German Democratic Republic (GDR).

In 1990 Phosa was among the first ANC members to return from exile to begin pre-negotiation talks with the government. He was closely involved in the setting up of joint meetings and the writing of the Groote Schuur and Pretoria Minutes. He was also involved in the planning of the National Peace Accord signed in September 1991.

Based at ANC headquarters in Johannesburg, Phosa headed the legal section of the ANC's Department of Constitutional and Legal Affairs. He served on the ANC's National Negotiations Commission which developed strategies for all negotiations activities of the organisation.

At the Convention for a Democratic South Africa (Codesa) he was a member of the working group dealing with the future of the homelands. Phosa was involved in behind-the-scenes negotiations on a number of security issues, including the release of political prisoners. He was a key negotiator in the process leading up to the signing of the Record of Understanding on 26 September 1992 between the ANC and the National Party and served as a member of the Police Board established in terms of the National Peace Accord to monitor the actions of the police force.

Phosa was chairperson of the ANC Eastern Transvaal Region and in that capacity was responsible for the overall organisational and political work of the movement in the region. As chairperson he also served as an *ex officio* member of the ANC's national executive committee.

Phosa has also served as a member of the national executive of the Black Lawyers' Assocation (1982-85) and was a member of the Board of Directors of Mapulaneng Enterprises from 1983-85. In addition, he was a founder member of the Lusito Lwesive Welfare Association in 1983.

In the general election of April 1994 Phosa headed the ANC list for the Eastern Transvaal province where the organisation won 81% of the vote, and he became premier.

Phosa has published Afrikaans and English poetry in the literary magazines *Standpunte, New Classic* and *Staffrider* under the name of Nakedi Phosa. He is currently compiling an anthology of poems.

Phosa, who speaks Northern Sotho, Swazi, Southern Sotho, Tswana, English, Zulu, Afrikaans and Portuguese, is married to Yvonne Nkwenkwezi, a social worker, and they have two children.

SOURCES

1. *People in Politics,* First Quarter 1993, Institute for Democracy in South Africa (Idasa), Durban, 1993.
2. Author's research undertaken for Idasa, 1994.
3. Anton Harber and Barbara Ludman (eds), *A-Z of Politics,* Weekly Mail & Guardian/Penguin Books, 1995.

SIPHO MILA PITYANA

Director General.
Department of Labour, 1995.

Born in Port Elizabeth on 21 August 1959, Sipho Pityana was the youngest of the three children of Ruth Pityana, a nurse and later a principal of a nursing college. His father was Mandla Ginya.

Pityana grew up in Port Elizabeth and then lived with relatives for two years in Uitenhage while his mother studied for a nursing education diploma at the University of Natal. It was there that he began school, attending a community school operating in a church. He later attended various Catholic boarding schools in the Transkei.

He returned to Port Elizabeth at the time his brother, Barney, an activist in the Black Consciousness Movement, was banned in 1973. Pityana then attended Newell High School until 1976 when the student upheavals sparked off in Soweto began to break out in Port Elizabeth.

Following the detention of two brothers and a sister-in-law, Pityana was detained by police under section 6 of the Terrorism Act iin September 1976. While in detention, he was severely tortured, and subsequently convicted of public violence and looting – activities which he denies involvement in – and sentenced to nine lashes.

Despite pressure from the security police to prohibit him from attending school, Pityana was readmitted to Newell High School where he completed Standard 8 in 1977. He became involved in the formation of the Port Elizabeth Students' Representative Council which brought together leaders from Port Elizabeth schools to co-ordinate student action.

In September 1977, Black Consciousness leader Steve Biko died while in police custody. This had a major impact on Pityana who had known him as a close associate of his brother. Pityana became involved in organising a school boycott against Bantu education and in response to Biko's death. The boycott began on 3 October, following Biko's funeral. On 10 October Pityana and nine members of the executive committee were detained by police under section 29 of the Internal Security Act, and held until mid-December.

In January 1978 Pityana was elected president of the SRC. Although the school boycott ended that year, Pityana was unable to return to school as security police detained him on two further occasions. Following his release in December 1978, he attended Osborne High School, Transkei, where he matriculated in 1980.

Pityana was then invited by the executive of the Motor Assembly and Component Workers Union of South Africa (Macwusa) to assist as a trade union organiser. During 1981, strikes at Firestone, Ford and General Motors were followed by strikes at other companies in the Port Elizabeth area. This coincided with a major clampdown by security police on the labour movement and its leadership, and in May 1981, Pityana was again detained under section 29 of the Internal Security Act. While in detention he was interrogated and tortured. On his release in February 1982, he was immediately served with a two-year banning order which involved severe restrictions.

He left the country on 15 August and travelled to Lesotho. On 2 December he travelled to Mozambique where he met with Chris Hani, then ANC head in Lesotho, and thereafter proceeded to the United Kingdom. There he completed his English 'O' and 'A' levels in Economics, History and Sociology at the Milton Keynes College for Further Education in 1984.

During this time he became connected with various ANC structures and pursued his trade union involvement through the South African Congress of Trade Unions (Sactu). On behalf of Sactu, he travelled to Canada, the USA and various European countries. In 1983, he made a submission to a United Nations Ad Hoc Working Group on repression of trade unions and trade unionism in South Africa.

In 1984, Pityana enrolled at the University of Essex where he completed his BA Hons degree in Government and Sociology. He was then employed by the International Defence and Aid Fund as a researcher investigating detentions in South Africa, developments in the labour movement and summary executions of opponents of apartheid. During this period, he made several submissions to UN bodies and other bodies and published a number of articles and papers.

In September 1988 Pityana registered with the Birbeck College of the University of London to study part-time for a masters degree in Politics and Sociology which he was awarded in 1990.

At the end of 1989 he was asked by the ANC to co-ordinate the Nelson

Mandela International Reception Committee which culminated in the international concert held in London in May 1990. He was also commissioned by the Commonwealth to participate in a study on South African human resource development strategy and contributed to the section dealing with small business and the informal sector.

Following the unbanning of the ANC in February 1990, Pityana returned to South Africa in June 1991. He joined the Community Agency for Social Enquiry (CASE), a research organisation, to take up a project initiated by the Congress of South African Trade Unions (Cosatu) involving a nationwide survey of Cosatu shop stewards. The report was published in January 1992 and Pityana was subsequently appointed deputy director of CASE. He was also active in various ANC structures and was a member of its research team at the time of the Convention for a Democratic South Africac (Codesa).

In February 1992, Pityana was appointed special assistant to Professor Sibusiso Bengu, then vice-chancellor of the University of Fort Hare, and in March 1994 became registrar (academic) at the university. At the end of February 1995, he resigned to take up the post of director general of the Department of Labour.

Pityana is married to Nonkululeku (born Moss) and they have two children. They live in Cape Town.

SOURCE

Interviewed 13 March 1995, Cape Town.

JEFFREY THAMASANQA RADEBE

Chairman, Southern Natal Region,
African National Congress, 1991.
Secretary, Natal Interim
Leadership Group, South African
Communist Party, 1990-91.
Minister of Public Works, 1994.

Born in Durban on 18 February 1953, Jeff Radebe was the youngest of the three children of Eleanor and Isaac Radebe, a driver for the Durban corporation. He attended the Dukemini Lower Primary School (1959-62), the Isilimela Higher Primary School (1963-66) and the Isibonelo High School, KwaMashu, where he matriculated in 1971.

From 1972-75 Radebe attended the University of Zululand where he completed his BJuris degree. He began serving legal articles in Durban in 1976.

In 1972 Radebe and others formed the KwaMashu Youth Organisation to discuss politics and focus on culture. About a year later some of Radebe's colleagues in KwaMashu left South Africa to join the African National Congress (ANC) and he eventually became involved in its underground activities. He left South Africa in 1997 and went to Tanzania where he worked for Radio Freedom, which fell under the ANC's Department of Information and Publicity.

In 1978 Radebe began a Masters degree in International Law at Leipzig, East Germany, and graduated in 1981. From 1981-82 he worked as the ANC's deputy representative in Dar es Salaam, Tanzania, and then moved to Lusaka in 1982 to work in the ANC's Department of International Affairs.

In 1983 Radebe moved to Lesotho where he liaised with the internal underground of the organisation. During this time, he worked with Moses Mabhida, then secretary general of the South African Communist Party (SACP) and Mabhida became an important influence in his life. In 1986, while on a mission within South Africa, Radebe was arrested in

Johannesburg and detained under section 29 of the Internal Security Act from April to June. He was charged with terrorism, undergoing military training and membership of the ANC. Found guilty, he was sentenced to ten years imprisonment which was reduced to six years on appeal.

In August 1986 Radebe was transferred to Robben Island. He became active in the ANC's political department and by the time he left was head of the department. He also served as hunger strike co-ordinator when prisoners embarked on an 11-day strike in 1990. On 9 June, following the unbanning of the ANC, Radebe was released from prison.

He returned to Durban and became regional co-ordinator of the National Association of Democratic Lawyers (Nadel). In November 1990 he was elected vice-chair of the Southern Natal region of the ANC and also served as secretary of the Interim Leadership Group of the SACP in Natal. Radebe became involved in the peace initiative in Natal and served on the joint peace committee between the ANC and the Inkatha Freedom Party and on the peace implementation committee.

In 1991 Radebe was elected chairman of the Southern Natal Region of the ANC.

In the April 1994 election, he stood as candidate number 14 on the ANC's list for the national assembly and became a member of parliament. In May he was appointed Minister of Public Works and is responsible for planning and controlling the construction of large projects such as dams, hospitals, schools, recreational facilities and housing projects. His department is one of the largest in the civil service with about 70 000 employees.

At the ANC congress in Bloemfontein in December 1994 Radebe stood for the post of ANC chairperson, but was defeated by Jacob Zuma.

The ninth national congress of the South African Communist Party, held in April 1995, elected Radebe to the central committee of the party.

Radebe is separated from his wife and has two children.

SOURCES

1. Interviewed 13 March 1991, Durban
2. *New African*, 3 December 1990.
3. *Post*, 11 May 1994.
4. *Profile '94*, South African Communication Services, Pretoria, 1994.

MATAMELA CYRIL RAMAPHOSA

General Secretary, National
Union of Mineworkers, 1982-91.
Secretary General, African
National Congress, 1991.
Chairperson, Constituent
Assembly, 1994.

Born in Johannesburg on 17 November 1952, Cyril Ramaphosa was the second of the three children of Erdmuth and Samuel Ramaphosa, a retired policeman. He grew up in Western Native Township and Soweto, attending a local primary school and Sekano-Ntoane High School in Soweto, before attending the Mphaphuli High School in Sibasa, Northern Transvaal, where he matriculated in 1971.

In 1972 Ramaphosa registered at the University of the North (Turfloop) for a BProc degree. He became involved in student politics and joined the South African Students Organisation (Saso) in 1972, serving as chairman of its university branch in 1974. In the same year, he was elected chairman of the Student Christian Movement.

In 1974, after a pro-Frelimo rally at the university, Ramaphosa was detained for 11 months under section 6 of the Terrorism Act. On his release, he became active in the Black People's Convention (BPC), holding posts on various committees. He obtained articles with a Johannesburg firm of attorneys at the same time.

In June 1976, following the outbreak of unrest in Soweto, Ramaphosa was again detained under the Terrorism Act, this time being held for six months at John Vorster Square. On his release, he continued his legal articles and studies, obtaining a BProc through the University of South Africa in 1981. He completed his articles in the same year, and joined the Council of Unions of South Africa (Cusa) as an advisor in its legal department.

In August 1982, the Cusa national conference resolved to form the National Union of Mineworkers (NUM), and in December Ramaphosa became NUM's first general secretary. The union, which initially represented 6 000 workers on eight mines, had by 1986 a membership of about 340 000. It became the first unregistered trade union recognised by the Chamber of Mines as representative of black mineworkers.

Ramaphosa was conference organiser in preparations leading to the launch of the Congress of South African Trade Unions (Cosatu), and delivered the keynote address at Cosatu's launch rally, held in Durban in December 1985.

In March 1986 he formed part of a seven-person Cosatu delegation which met with the African National Congress and the South African Congress of Trade Unions in Lusaka, Zambia.

In July 1986, after the declaration of a state of emergency, Ramaphosa went into hiding after security police swoops on the homes and offices of political activists. He travelled to the United Kingdom and appeared with NUM president, James Motlatsi, at a conference of the British National Union of Mineworkers.

In August 1987 a deadlock in NUM wage negotiations with the Chamber of Mines led to one of the largest strikes in the country's history, involving 40 gold and coal mines. The number of strikers was estimated at between 222 000 and 340 000, but workers were eventually called back to work without winning the increase they had demanded.

Ramaphosa was refused a passport to travel to Britain in September 1987, but a month later, when he became the first recipient of the Olaf Palme prize, was permitted to travel to Stockholm to receive it.

In December 1988, Ramaphosa and other prominent members of the Soweto community met Soweto's mayor to discuss the rent boycott crisis. He also played a prominent role in many of the campaigns of the Mass Democratic Movement, including resistance to the Labour Relations Amendment Bill.

In January 1990, Ramaphosa accompanied released ANC political prisoners to Lusaka, Zambia, where a three-day summit was held to discuss strategies for the ANC in the light of the new approach by State President de Klerk. Ramaphosa served as chairman of the National Reception Committee, which co-ordinated arrangements for the release of Nelson Mandela and subsequent welcome rallies within South Africa, and also became a member of the International Mandela Reception Committee together with others such as Fr Trevor Huddleston, Jimmy Carter and Mikhail Gorbachev.

At the ANC's national conference held in Durban in July 1991, Ramaphosa was elected general secretary of the organisation, ousting Alfred Nzo who had served in this capacity in exile for many years. In this capacity he became the head of the negotiations commission of the ANC and participated in the Conference for a Democratic South Africa (Codesa). He also served on its working group dealing with constitutional principles and the constitution-making process.

However, the working group was unable to agree on certain constitutional clauses and the initiative collapsed after the Boipatong massacre of June 1992. This was followed by an ANC campaign of rolling mass action to place the South African government under pressure to take action to halt the political violence, and accept a transitional government and constituent assembly. Ramaphosa was a key figure in behind-the-scenes negotiations with the government which eventually led to the signing of a Record of Understanding between Mandela and De Klerk in September of that year. When formal talks were resumed in 1993 Ramaphosa served on the ten-person planning committee of the multi-party negotiating process held at the World Trade Centre, Kempton Park, and represented the ANC as a delegate. From December 1993 to April 1994 he was a member of the management committee of the Transitional Executive Council charged with levelling the playing fields in the run-up to the elections.

In June 1993 Ramaphosa and Roelf Meyer, who headed the National Party negotiating team, received honorary law degrees from the University of Massachusetts for their contribution to democratisation in South Africa.

In the general election of April 1994 Ramaphosa stood as an ANC candidate and became a member of parliament. Tipped as a potential deputy president, he failed to be appointed to the post and was subsequently elected chairman of the constituent assembly.

He was re-elected secretary general of the ANC at its December 1994 conference in Bloemfontein. In this position he is responsible for party organisation.

Ramaphosa is divorced. He has three children.

SOURCES

1. Telephonic interview 21 September 1984.
2. South African Institute of Race Relations, *Race Relations Survey, 1983,* Johannesburg, 1984.
3. *Cape Times,* 27 October 1983.
4. *Sowetan,* 2 December 1985.
5. *Argus,* 19 September 1987.
6. *Argus,* 20 October 1987.
7. *Tribute,* May 1988.
8. *Work in Progress,* 59, June/July 1989.
9. *Natal Mercury,* 16 January 1990.
10. *Post* 25 September 1991.
11. *Daily News,* 16 June 1993.
12. *Natal Witness,* 5 March 1994.

NGOAKO RAMATLHODI

*Premier, Northern Transvaal
Province, 1994.*

Born in the village of Tauetswala, near Potgietersrus, on 21 August 1955, Ngoako Ramatlhodi grew up in a traditional household. His father was a mineworker.

He attended school in Tembisa on the East Rand before enrolling at the University of the North in 1977 to study law. There he joined the South African Students Organisation (Saso) which was banned by the government in October 1977. He also served as chairman of the Central Cultural Committee, which acted as the only voice of the students following the banning of the university's Students' Representative Council. He became a founder member of the Azanian Students Congress, which later became known as the South African Students Congress (Sasco).

In 1978 he joined the African National Congress (ANC) and worked underground at the university. In March 1979 he was expelled for attempting to organise a Sharpeville memorial service which led to student boycotts. He fought his case through the courts and was reinstated later that year. During his years as a student activist, Ramatlhodi was expelled three times and detained on several occasions.

In 1980 Ramatlhodi joined the ANC's military wing, Umkhonto we Sizwe (MK). On 17 July 1980 he left South Africa for Lesotho where he continued his studies at the National University of Lesotho (NUL). While a student at NUL, Ramatlhodi continued his MK activities, attending military camps in Angola during the university vacations. He also subsequently underwent six months' training in the Soviet Union. In the mid-1980s he was appointed head of MK's Political-Military Council in the Northern Front, which included the Northern Transvaal.

His student activities included serving as second secretary (1981-83) on the Committee for Action and Solidarity for Southern Africa (Cassas), an organisation which sought to unite Southern African students against apartheid. From 1982-83 Ramatlhodi was secretary for public and foreign affairs on the NUL SRC. In 1983-84 he was elected president of the SRC and became an *ex-officio* member of the university council. He completed his BA Law in 1984 and his LLB in 1986.

From 1986-88 Ramatlhodi lived in Zimbabwe where he served as head of the ANC's Political-Military Council at the movement's Zimbabwe mission. During this time he completed his MSc in International Relations at the University of Zimbabwe.

From 1988-92 Ramatlhodi served as political secretary and assistant to the ANC president, based in Lusaka and London, before returning to South Africa in July 1990. In this portfolio, he served as secretary to the political committee in the president's office and as secretary to the ANC Control Commission which was composed of the top five members of the national executive committee including the president and the secretary general. The function of this committee was to identify bottlenecks in the organisation and to ensure organisational effectiveness. In addition, he personally assisted the ANC president (then Oliver Tambo), consulting closely with him on a daily basis, travelling and attending meetings with him and at times serving as his special envoy. He also helped to draft the president's speeches and supervised the staff in his office.

On his return to South Africa following the unbanning of the ANC, Ramatlhodi was appointed deputy registrar/executive assistant to the principal of the University of the North (Turfloop) and also lectured in Public International Law. At the end of 1991 he became chairman of the ANC's Northern Transvaal region and a member of the organisation's national executive committee.

In the April 1994 elections, Ramatlhodi led the ANC's provincial list for the Northern Transvaal and won with a 96% majority, thereby becoming premier of the region.

Known as a poet and dramatist, Ramatlhodi is married to Ouma and they have one son.

SOURCES

1. *Sunday Tribune,* 20 March 1994.
2. *Weekly Mail & Guardian,* 13 May 1994.
3. *Weekly Mail & Guardian,* 1 July 1994.
4. *Curriculum vitae* submitted by Office of the Premier, Northern Transvaal Province, 4 July 1994.

RENIER STEPHANUS SCHOEMAN

Member of Parliament,
National Party, 1994.
Deputy Minister of Foreign
Affairs, 1991-94.
Deputy Minister of Education,
1994.

Renier Schoeman, the third of the four children of Helena and Marthinus Johannes Schoeman, a policeman and later a member of the administrative staff of the South African Broadcasting Corporation, was born in Durban on 10 October 1944.

He grew up in Durban and matriculated from Northlands Boys High in 1962. Joining the Department of Manpower in an administrative position, he also began part-time studies at the University of Natal, Durban, towards a BA degree, majoring in Political Science and Afrikaans/Nederlands.

When Schoeman left school he joined the *Nasionale Jeugbond,* the youth wing of the National Party, where he played a leading role. Schoeman was active in student politics at university and represented part-time students on the Students Representative Council from 1964 to 1966. He chaired the Natal University Conservative Students Club between 1966 and 1968, and in 1967 was national president of the Federation of Conservative Students Associations, which functioned on English-speaking campuses. He played an active role in the anti-National Union of South African Students (Nusas) campaign from 1963 to 1967. He attended the 1968 Afrikaner Studentebond (ASB) congress, where he was elected national director of student relations, becoming responsible for links with all universities. In 1969 he was elected vice-president of the ASB.

After Schoeman graduated in 1967 he enrolled for a Social Science degree, which he did not complete. In September 1967 he was transferred to the Department of Tourism and in January 1971 became assistant private secretary to Frank Waring, Minister of Tourism, Indian Affairs, Sport and Recreation. Owen Horwood, who had been principal of Natal University during Schoeman's time there, took over from Waring in 1972, and this marked the start of a long association with Schoeman, who became his private secretary in 1974. He continued in this position when Horwood became Minister of Finance in 1975 and in this capacity he travelled abroad on numerous occasions, attending five meetings of the International Monetary Fund and World Bank as a member of the official South African delegation. He also visited major cities in Europe, North America, Israel and the Far East.

In February 1981 Schoeman left the civil service and became provincial secretary and chief executive officer of the National Party in Natal. He saw the party through the 1981 elections, the 1982 breakaway by the Conservative Party and the 1983 referendum over the tricameral parliament. In November 1985, Schoeman became the nominated MP for Natal. In January 1987 he relinquished his post as provincial secretary and was appointed director of information for the National Party in Natal.

Schoeman won the Umhlanga seat from the Progressive Federal Party in the 1987 general election. As an MP, he participated in National Party caucus study groups on constitutional development, environmental affairs, trade and industry, finance, information, and the SABC.

In the 1989 election Schoeman lost his seat to Kobus Jordaan of the Democratic Party. He was then indirectly elected to parliament by the electoral college of Natal National Party MPs. At the end of 1989 it was announced that he would take over from Con Botha as the National Party's chief director of federal information services and as editor of the *Nationalist* from February 1990. This entailed leadership of the party's overall information, marketing and public relations efforts countrywide.

On 1 July 1991 Schoeman was appointed Deputy Minister of Foreign Affairs and in that position he occasionally travelled abroad as part of the state president's entourage.

In October 1991 Schoeman mooted the idea that South Africa should form an Indian Ocean Rim economic bloc in order to compete with powerful regional associations of states.

In the April 1994 general election Schoeman stood as a NP candidate and was returned as a member of parliament. In May he was appointed Deputy Minister of Education in the government of national unity.

Schoeman is married to Vida and they have two children.

SOURCES

1. Interviewed 1 December 1989, Durban.

2. *Daily News,* 16 October 1991.
3. Author's research 1995.

MOSIMA GABRIEL TOKYO SEXWALE

Chairperson, PWV Region,
African National Congress, 1991.
Premier, PWV Region, 1994.

Born in Johannesburg on 5 March 1953, Tokyo Sexwale was the third of the six children of Godlieve and Frank Sexwale, a senior clerk in the Johannesburg general hospital.

Sexwale attended St Martin's Primary School in Johannesburg and Orlando West High School where he matriculated in 1972. He then attended the University of Botswana, Lesotho and Swaziland, initially at its Lesotho campus and thereafter in Swaziland.

Sexwale became politically aware at an early age and remembers hearing the first Umkhonto we Sizwe (MK) actions and the sound of a bomb which exploded at the Dube Post Office near his home on 16 December 1961. During the 1970s he was a staunch Black Consciousness supporter and a member and leader of the South African Students' Movement (Sasm). As head prefect of his school, he opened classrooms over weekends and political meetings were held in the school.

Sexwale became involved with the African National Congress (ANC) inside South Africa through his contact with other students at high school. He made contact with the ANC during his student days and became involved in underground structures in 1971, helping to distribute pamphlets and ANC insignia. His underground cell was inspired by the ANC, but at that time was not controlled by it.

At university, Sexwale completed a diploma in business studies and registered for a BCom. During this time he worked with Thabo Mbeki, Jacob Zuma and Stanley Mabizela in Swaziland, and became part of the machinery which facilitated contact with structures inside South Africa. However, his ANC activities were detected by the Swazi authorities, and attempts were made to arrest him in 1975. He left Swaziland for the Soviet Union, via Mozambique and Tanzania, where he underwent political and military training in Moscow. During this time he also stayed in Simfiropol, near the Black Sea, where he completed studies in conventional warfare and an officer's course.

The ANC then instructed Sexwale to return to South Africa and join a group already inside the country. While crossing into the country carrying weaponry and pamphlets, Sexwale and a group of colleagues were stopped by the police on suspicion of having crossed the border illegally. Their suitcases were searched and they were transported in a landrover for further questioning. However, Sexwale threw a hand grenade through the driver's window and by the time it exploded they had all jumped off the moving vehicle.

The group retreated to Swaziland and later returned to South Africa. Underground work within the country involved political instruction of cell members, and offering military training throughout the Transvaal. Sexwale and others were arrested in 1977, and charged in what became known as the Pretoria Twelve trial. He was convicted in 1978 and – after the state called for the death penalty – sentenced to 18 years imprisonment.

Sexwale was jailed on Robben Island and during this time he served on the prisoners' recreation committee, a key structure as it was recognised by the prison authorities. As a result most issues raised by prisoners were routed through it. He also studied towards his BCom, although his study privileges were withdrawn on four occasions, and by the time he left prison he still had four courses left to complete his degree.

Sexwale was released on 9 June 1990 under political amnesty following the unbanning of the ANC and the Groote Schuur agreement between the South African government and the ANC. In September 1990 he was elected to the ANC's executive committee in the PWV area. He was also appointed head of the special projects department of the ANC, dealing, inter alia, with matters pertaining to Umkhonto we Sizwe (MK).

In September 1991 he was elected chair of the ANC's PWV region and as a result became an *ex-officio* member of the organisation's national executive committee.

Sexwale served on the Witwatersrand regional dispute resolution committee, set up in terms of the National Peace Accord agreed to in September 1991.

Sexwale rose to national prominence following the assassination of his friend and neighbour, SACP secretary general Chris Hani, when he appeared on television shortly after the murder and again at the funeral where he showed his ability to control excited and militant crowds.

In the April 1994 general election, Sexwale headed the ANC's PWV list, becoming provincial premier after the organisation won 58% of the vote in the region. Soon after his installation, Sexwale visited three Inkatha Freedom Party-dominated hostels on the East Rand in an attempt at reconciliation and to defuse potential violence. He gave instructions that the two railway lines to Katlehong be re-opened and announced that 150 000 houses would be built in the PWV in 1994.

Sexwale is married to Judy van Vuuren and they have two children. He has two children from his first marriage. Sexwale lives in Houghton.

SOURCES

1. Interviewed 12 March 1992, Johannesburg.
2. *Sunday Times,* 20 October 1991.
3. *Natal Mercury,* 30 May 1994.

SAM SHILOWA

*Member, Central Committee,
South African Communist Party,
1991.
General Secretary, Congress of
South African Trade Unions,
1993.*

Born on 30 April 1958 in the village of Olifantshoek, Gazankulu, Sam Shilowa was the youngest of the seven children of Anna and Johannes Shilowa, a peasant farmer.

Shilowa attended Khamanyani primary school in Olifantshoek and the Akani High School until his dismissal in his matriculation year, 1979, for political activities. He then left the rural area for Johannesburg.

In Johannesburg Shilowa found work with the Anglo-Alpha Cement company. He also registered for his matriculation examination and passed that year. During 1982, after leading a strike, he became involved in the trade union movement. He remained with the company until February 1986 when he was fired for his political activities.

Shilowa then joined the Pritchard Services Group, a security company. By this time he was organising for the trade unions, and also working underground for the South African Communist Party (SACP) and the African National Congress (ANC). He felt that a position in security services would provide a good cover for his activities. Shilowa began to organise workers in the Transport and General Workers Union (TGWU) and was elected a shop steward in 1987. He was subsequently elected vice-chairperson of his branch and a member of the TGWU's national executive committee in 1987. In the late 1980s Shilowa also worked within structures of the United Democratic Front (UDF) and was elected regional vice-chairperson for the Witwatersrand region in 1990.

In 1990 Shilowa was elected second vice-president of the TGWU, and the following year became president, a position he held until his election as assistant general secretary of the Congress of South African Trade

Unions (Cosatu). Shilowa had been promoted to the post of security officer in Pritchard Services and continued to work for the company until
July 1991 when he began to work full-time in his new Cosatu post.

Following the unbanning of the ANC and the SACP, Shilowa served
briefly as publicity officer of the ANC's Dobsonville branch. He remains
a branch member. In addition he served as a member of the interim working group of the SACP's Transvaal region.

During 1991 Shilowa participated in peace process meetings on behalf
of the SACP, called with representatives of business and the churches in
an effort to stop the violence affecting the townships. He attended the
signing of the National Peace Accord in September 1991 and served as
Cosatu's representative on the National Peace Committee.

He was a member of the ANC's delegation to the December 1991
Convention for a Democratic South Africa (Codesa). In the same month,
he was elected as a member of the SACP's central committee.

In 1993 Shilowa was part of the SACP's negotiating team at the multi-
party talks at the World Trade Centre. Following the September 1993
resignation of Cosatu general secretary, Jay Naidoo, Shilowa was elected
to succeed him.

At the ANC's Bloemfontein congress held in December 1994,
Shilowa was elected to the organisation's national executive committee.
The appointment was controversial within the union movement and he
was asked to resign from the committee as it was felt that he would not
have the time to do justice to both positions. He therefore tendered his
resignation.

Shilowa was elected to the central committee of the SACP at its ninth
national congress, held in April 1995.

Shilowa is married to Wendy Luhabe.

SOURCES

1. Interviewed 13 March 1992, Johannesburg.
2. *Financial Mail,* 24 September 1993.
3. *City Press,* 21 August 1994.
4. Information supplied by the South African Communist Party, May 1995.

STELLA MARGARET NOMZAMO SIGCAU

Member of Parliament,
African National Congress, 1994.
Minister of Public Enterprises,
1994.

Born on 4 January 1937, Stella Sigcau was the eldest of the three children of Paramount Chief Botha Sigcau of East Pondoland who became the first state president of the Transkei when it assumed independence in 1976.

As the daughter of a paramount chief, Sigcau was politically conscientised from childhood and this was reinforced at Lovedale College in Alice where she attended school in the early 1950s. While a student at the University of Fort Hare, Sigcau joined the African National Congress (ANC) Youth League. She graduated with a BA degree majoring in Anthropology and Psychology and became a teacher. She subsequently worked in Natal and KwaZulu.

Sigcau's husband, Ronald Tshabalala, died in 1964 and in 1968 she became politically active at the request of her father, then leader of the Transkei National Independence Party.

That year Sigcau won the Lusikisiki seat from the opposition Democratic Party, and became a member of the Transkei Legislative Assembly. She was appointed Minister of Roads and Works and over the next 20 years handled several ministerial portfolios, including energy, education, interior and posts and telecommunications. During this time she was the only woman in the cabinet.

Aware of issues around women's rights, Sigcau undertook to challenge discriminatory traditions and laws in an active campaign to empower rural Transkeian women. She was instrumental in having single mothers granted land ownership rights in the region, but was herself forced by Transkei prime minister, Chief Kaizer Matanzima, to resign from the cabinet in 1977 because she was unmarried and pregnant.

Soon after the opening of the parliamentary session in 1978, Sigcau led most of the Pondoland MPs across the floor to sit in the opposition and formed the Democratic Progressive Party. However, she rejoined the ruling Transkei National Independence Party in August 1980. In 1981 she was appointed to the cabinet of George Matanzima as Minister of Telecommunications, replacing ousted Minister of the Interior, Saul Ndzumo.

Following the resignation of Chief George Matanzima as a result of corruption charges in October 1987, Sigcau became prime minister of the Transkei. She defeated two male rivals, Kholisile Nota and Ngangomhlaba Matanzima, in the struggle for the premiership. On 30 December of the same year she was removed from power in the military coup led by her defence force chief, Major General Bantu Holomisa, who accused her government of corruption and Sigcau personally receiving a bribe in return for the granting of gambling rights. She denied receiving the bribe, but admitted that she had received R50 000 from a senior official in the form of a bursary for her daughter's education.

Sigcau dropped out of the political scene for a few years and disbanded the Transkei National Independence Party in 1990. When the Transkei government was invited to participate in the Convention for a Democratic South Africa (Codesa), Holomisa consulted with a number of existing organisations to nominate delegates to join the government delegation. In the process Sigcau, who is a member of the national executive committee of the Congress of Traditional Leaders of South Africa (Contralesa), was nominated.

She also became active in ANC structures and at one stage headed the ANC Women's League in the Transkei.

In December 1993 the Transitional Executive Council (TEC) was established to level the playing fields in the run-up to the election. Sigcau served on the TEC sub-council on foreign affairs.

In the April 1994 general election Sigcau stood as an ANC candidate and became a member of parliament. In May she was appointed Minister of Public Enterprises. At the ANC's December 1994 congress in Bloemfontein Sigcau was elected to the organisation's national executive committee.

Sigcau's home is on a farm in the Lusikisiki district and she has two children.

SOURCES

1. *Daily News,* 1 December 1977.

2. *Daily News*, 25 April 1978.
3. *Daily News*, 19 August 1980.
4. *Die Burger*, 10 October 1987.
5. *Rapport*, 11 October 1987.
6. *Financial Mail*, 16 October 1987.
7. *Sunday Times*, 10 January 1988.
8. *Negotiation News*, 25 May 1992.
9: *Profile '94*, South African Communication Services, Pretoria, 1994.

SIZAKELE WHITMORE SIGXASHE

Director General, National
Intelligence Agency, 1995.

Born in Viedgesville, Umtata, on 21 June 1937, Sizakele Sigxashe was one of the three children of Alice and William Sigxashe, both self-employed agricultural workers. Sigxashe grew up in Viedgesville and attended Xugwala Primary School and St John's College, Umtata, where he matriculated. He enrolled at Fort Hare University in 1958 and obtained a BA degree in English and Xhosa in 1961.

Sigxashe joined the African National Congress (ANC) in 1959 while at university and served as a member of the executive committee of the organisation's Youth League. He also joined the South African Communist Party (SACP).

On completion of his degree he was sent by the underground leadership of the liberation movement to the Soviet Union for further studies in finance and banking. In 1970 he completed his PhD in Political

Economy at the Kiev Institute of National Economy. In the same year he joined the ANC's military wing, Umkhonto We Sizwe (MK).

In 1972 Sigxashe was appointed lecturer in Development Studies at the University of Dar es Salaam (Tanzania) and was promoted to senior lecturer in 1974.

In 1976 he was assigned to the ANC's Military Intelligence Section as a researcher and was seconded to the Angolan Defence Ministry. During 1981 he served as secretary for the ANC's Department of Information and Publicity, based in Lusaka, Zambia. In 1983 he became a member of the National Directorate of the Department of Intelligence and Security (DIS) and headed the Information Processing and Research Section. In addition, he served on the ANC's Political-Military Council.

In 1983 Sigxashe became a member of the central committee of the SACP and in 1985, at the ANC's Kabwe conference, was elected to the movement's national executive committee on which he served until 1991. Sigxashe headed the DIS during a period of restructuring.

Following the unbanning of the ANC and SACP in February 1990, Sigxashe returned to South Africa in March 1991. He continued with his work in the DIS and during 1994 frequently acted for the director general of the National Intelligence Agency in his absence.

In February 1995 Sigxashe was appointed director general of the National Intelligence Agency.

SOURCE

1. *Curriculum vitae* provided by the National Intelligence Agency, February 1995.

ZWELAKHE SISULU

*Group Chief Executive, South
African Broadcasting Corporation,
1994.*

Born in Soweto on 17 December 1950, Zwelakhe Sisulu is the third of the five children of Albertina and Walter Sisulu.

Sisulu attended Salesian and St Christopher's School, Swaziland, where he completed his 'A' levels. In 1975 he enrolled in a journalism course run by South African Associated Newspapers and was subsequently employed as a journalist on the *Rand Daily Mail*. He later joined the staff of the *Sunday Post* as news editor, a position he held until he was banned by the government in December 1980.

Following the banning of the Union of Black Journalists in October 1977, the Writers' Association of South Africa was established with Sisulu as president. The association was expanded to include all black media workers and in October 1980 the Media Workers' Association of South (Mwasa) replaced it, again with Sisulu as president.

In August 1979 Sisulu was sentenced to nine months imprisonment for refusing to answer questions in connection with the trial of Thami Mkhwanazi, a *Post* reporter who subsequently received a seven-year prison sentence for offences under the Terrorism Act. However, in November 1980, Sisulu's sentence was set aside.

Sisulu played a crucial role in a two-month union recognition strike by Mwasa members during 1980. This was achieved in December of that year. On 29 December 1980 he was served with a three-year banning order.

In July 1981 Sisulu was detained under section 6 of the Terrorism Act and subsequently under section 12 (b) of the Internal Security Act which allowed for detention of potential state witnesses. He was released in

February 1982 without being charged or called as a witness, after 251 days in detention.

In 1982 Sisulu was sentenced to 18 months imprisonment for refusing to testify against members of the exiled South African Revolutionary Youth Council, but both his conviction and sentence were set aside on appeal. The same year his banning order was lifted and he was awarded a medal by the Rothco Chapel, based in Texas, for his 'commitment to freedom and truth'.

In 1984 Sisulu was awarded a Niemann Fellowship for a year's study at Harvard University, Boston. In early 1986 he was appointed as the first editor of *New Nation*, a newspaper published by the South African Catholic Bishops' Conference.

During 1986, Sisulu was detained twice under the state of emergency regulations. While in detention, he was held for some time in solitary confinement and was also hospitalised for depression. He was released in December 1988 with stringent restriction orders preventing him from returning to his post as editor of *New Nation*.

In 1989 Sisulu returned to *New Nation* as editor and chief executive, a post he held until the end of 1993 when he was appointed executive assistant to the group chief executive of the South African Broadcasting Corporation, Wynand Harmse. He became chief executive of the SABC in 1994.

Other awards received by Sisulu include the Pringle Award from the South African Society of Journalists (1986); the Union of Swedish Journalists Award (1987); the International Human Rights Law Group Award, USA (1988); and the CASA Award, Netherlands, (1988).

In December 1978 Sisulu married Zodwa Mdladlamba, a radiographer, and they have three children.

SOURCES

1. South African Institute of Race Relations, *Survey of Race Relations in South Africa, 1979,* Johannesburg, 1980.
2. *Post,* 7 August 1979.
3. *Rand Daily Mail,* 30 December 1980.
4. *Sowetan,* 26 February 1982.
5. *Weekly Mail,* 17 January 1986.
6. *Weekly Mail,* 4 July 1986.
7. *Daily News,* 19 July 1986.
8. *Daily News,* 3 December 1988.
9. *Sunday Tribune,* 15 October 1989.
10. *Learn & Teach,* June 1991.
11. *Financial Mail,* 17 December 1993.
12. Author's research, 1995.

ZOLA SIDNEY THEMBA SKWEYIYA

Member of Parliament,
African National Congress, 1994.
Minister of Public Service and
Administration, 1994.

Zola Skweyiya was born in Cape Town on 14 April 1943, the only child of Simon and Winnie Skweyiya, workers in the Simonstown dockyard. He spent his early childhood moving from place to place while attending the Retreat Presbytarian School.

Skweyiya was politicised at a young age, as both his father and uncle were involved in civic association activities. Lack of access to land and educational facilities for Africans in the Cape Peninsula left an indelible impression on the young Skweyiya. In the interests of a better education, he was sent to Lovedale High School in the Eastern Cape, where his contemporaries included Chris Hani and Thabo Mbeki. Politics at Lovedale was divided between supporters of the African National Congress (ANC) and the Non-European Unity Movement, and Skweyiya found himself identifying with the former. As he could not afford to travel home during school holidays, he began spending the holidays with his aunt in Port Elizabeth. Here the ANC group from Lovedale received political instruction from ANC/South African Communist Party stalwart Govan Mbeki.

After matriculating, Skweyiya enrolled for a BA in English and History at the University of Fort Hare in 1961. This was a period of intense political activity on the campus in reaction to the banning of the ANC and Pan-Africanist Congress and the subsequent crackdown on black political leaders. Punitive action against political activists on the campus followed and Skweyiya's study loan was withdrawn for his second year. He returned to Cape Town and a few months later travelled to Johannesburg with Chris Hani, who was arrested along the way. He then travelled to Botswana where he joined Thabo Mbeki and others who had earlier left South Africa illegally. From there different groups made their way to Tanzania, where Oliver Tambo was setting up headquarters for the ANC in exile.

Following Zambian independence in 1964 Skweyiya moved to the ANC's new headquarters in Lusaka, and was attached to the Department of Information and Publicity where he edited *Spotlight* magazine, the forerunner of *Sechaba*.

In 1968 Skweyiya won a scholarship to Leipzig University in the German Democratic Republic where he graduated in international and constitutional law. He returned to Lusaka in 1973 and was posted to the ANC's International Department. A year later he returned to Leipzig to write his doctoral thesis on racial discrimination in international law with special reference to South Africa and Rhodesia.

Returning to Lusaka in 1978 Skweyiya worked in the ANC's president's office and the international department, dealing mainly with research on the land question and human rights issues. In 1981 he became the ANC representative to the Organisation of African Unity (OAU) in Addis Ababa with the tasks of establishing an office in order to create closer co-operation between the two organisations; achieving ANC recognition as the sole representative of the South African people; and strengthening relations with African countries.

One of the successful projects Skweyiya embarked on for the ANC in Ethiopia was securing one hour of ANC broadcast time each day on the radio station, 'Voice of the Gospel'. This broadcast could be heard all over Africa, including South Africa.

In late 1984 Skweyiya was called back to Lusaka to set up the ANC's legal department and constitutional committee together with SACP veteran, Jack Simons, who chaired the committee. Their task was to draw up guidelines for a future constitution for South Africa and these were published in 1987.

Planning for a post-apartheid South Africa became a major focus for the department and as a result the Swedish funded Post-Apartheid South Africa (PASA) project was set up to focus on the economic and legal issues. A number of conferences involving experts from inside the country followed. Another major area of focus for the legal department was securing legal assistance and defence for the Umkhonto we Sizwe (MK) soldiers arrested inside the country which required close networking with the legal profession.

Following the unbanning of the ANC in February 1990 Skweyiya returned to South Africa in June that year to set up the ANC's legal department at its headquarters in Johannesburg. He became involved in networking between the ANC, the legal profession and academic institutions in the process of policy formulation. He helped to establish the

Centre for Development Studies and the South African Legal Defence Fund at the University of the Western Cape.

Apart from constitutional work, the legal department investigated the judiciary and its role in a post-apartheid South Africa and established programmes to prepare disenfranchised South Africans and the ANC for democratic elections. He also served as co-ordinator of the ANC's civil service unit.

Skweyiya represented the ANC on the UN Commission for Human Rights from 1984. He was elected to the ANC's national executive committee at its July 1991 conference in Durban and became a member of its working committee. He was re-elected to the national executive at the ANC's December 1994 conference.

In the April 1994 general election, Skewyiya stood as an ANC candidate and became a member of parliament. In May he was appointed Minister of Public Service and Administration.

Skweyiya is divorced. He has a son, Voyo Pamilele.

SOURCES

1. *People in Politics,* Second Quarter 1992, Institute for Democracy in South Africa (Idasa), Durban, 1992.
2. *Weekly Mail & Guardian,* Special Supplement, May 1994.
3. Author's research, 1994.

PIERRE DERKSEN STEYN

Secretary for Defence, 1994.

Born on 25 November 1942 in Swellendam, Cape Province, Pierre Steyn was the eldest of the two children of Stella Helena and Jan Frederik Steyn, both teachers. He spent his early years in Swellendam before moving to Bellville at the age of five. He attended Bellville Primary School and later Bellville High School where he matriculated in 1959.

He then underwent a pilot's training course as a volunteer with the South African Air Force. After completing the academic training programme at Stellenbosch University, he began studying towards a BMil degree at the Military Academy in Saldanha, graduating in 1963.

In 1964 Steyn completed a flying instructor's course and served as an instructor at the flying training school at Dunnottar during that year. From 1965-67 he taught aeronautics at the Military Academy.

Steyn was then transferred to Number 1 Squadron based in Pietersburg, Northern Transvaal, where he flew Sabre jets. In 1969 he moved to Number 2 Squadron in Waterkloof, Pretoria, where he remained until 1975, filling various positions in the squadron. During this time he served as a tactical reconaissance pilot.

From 1975-78 Steyn served as a military attache/representative abroad and on his return to South Africa spent three years as senior staff officer, projects, in the air force and played an active role in acquiring and developing weapon systems for the air force. From 1982 to 1984 he was commanding officer of the Hoedspruit air force base and in 1985, when he was promoted to brigadier, served as director of force preparation of the air force. In 1986 Steyn was promoted to major-general and became inspector-general of the air force before serving as chief of air staff, operations, from 1987-88 when he directed and planned joint operations.

The following year he became deputy chief of staff, operations, of the South African Defence Force (SADF) and in the same year completed his MBL degree through the University of South Africa. In 1991 he was promoted to lieutenant-general with the post of chief of staff, personnel, and in 1993 was transferred to the post of chief of defence force staff.

In 1992, arising out of the Goldstone Commission investigations, the existence of the Directorate of Covert Intelligence, associated with military intelligence, was revealed with allegations regarding its involvement in illegal activities. State President De Klerk then appointed Steyn to investigate the allegations of unlawful conduct of members of the SADF. At the end of 1992, as a result of initial investigations, De Klerk acted against 23 members of the SADF, putting some on early retirement and others on leave pending further investigations. Steyn's investigations were concluded in July 1993 and he submitted a number of reports to the state president. These resulted mainly in the restructuring of the organisation responsible for gathering military intelligence.

In November 1993 Steyn retired from the SADF. He then became a defence management consultant for companies in both the private and public sectors. In 1993 he took up a directorship with the Institute for Defence Policy and part of the research which he directed concerned the creation of a defence secretariat within the Ministry of Defence. In August 1994, he was appointed to the position of secretary for defence. This involves heading a secretariat staffed by civilians who deal with defence policy, secure the necessary resources and effect the necessary control over the expenditure of financial resources and the application of other resources of the state. The defence secretary serves as the civilian adviser to the Minister of Defence, functioning at the same level as the chief of the National Defence Force, who serves as military adviser to the minister.

Steyn married Fiona (born Stopforth) in 1967 and they have three daughters.

SOURCE

Interviewed 21 February 1995, Cape Town.

MAKHINKETI ARNOLD STOFILE

Member of Parliament,
African National Congress, 1994.
Treasurer General, African
National Congress, 1994.

Born on 27 December 1944, Makhinketi Arnold Stofile, a Presbyterian minister, matriculated from Newill High School in Port Elizabeth in 1964. From 1965-68 he worked as a machine operator in a textile factory in Port Elizabeth after which he enrolled at the University of Fort Hare for a BA degree which he completed in 1971. He then studied towards his Theology degree, graduating in 1974 and completed his BTh Honours in 1975 and his BA Honours in 1977. In 1979 he was awarded a Masters degree in Theology.

In 1972 Stofile worked as a part-time tutor, and from 1973-86 was employed by the University of Fort Hare as a senior lecturer in Theology and Philosophy of Religion. From 1975 to date, Stofile has served as a minister of the Presbyterian Church of Southern Africa.

In 1981 Stofile completed his post-graduate Diploma in Theology at Tubingen University in Germany. This was followed by an MA degree at Princeton University, USA, in 1983.

Stofile was active in provincial and national sports administration from 1969 and he rose to prominence when, as general secretary of the Border region of the United Democratic Front (UDF), he was sent to New Zealand to campaign against the proposed 1985 Kiwi rugby tour. As a rugby administrator in the South African Council on Sport (Sacos), he gave evidence in the New Zealand high court case which led to the cancellation of the tour.

While employed as a lecturer at the University of Fort Hare in 1986, Stofile was detained by Ciskei police under section 26 of the Ciskei National Security Act at the height of a controversy between workers and university authorities regarding the recognition of a trade union.

Stofile was again detained by the Ciskei security police in October 1986. In March 1987 he and others were charged in the Ciskei Supreme Court, Bisho, with terrorism, possession of arms and harbouring terrorists. Stofile was the first UDF executive member to be connected with the armed struggle. After a controversial trial, he received an 11-year sentence on the main count of promoting the activities of the African National Congress (ANC) and another one year to run concurrently for two counts of possessing a Soviet-made pistol and ammunition.

Prior to his appearing in court, Stofile's wife, Nambitha, was detained in January under section 26 of Ciskei's National Security Act. An application was brought on Stofile's behalf for an urgent interdict to prevent the police from assaulting her. She was released after a week in detention.

In December 1989 Stofile was released by Ciskei on humanitarian grounds. A month after his release from jail, Stofile again became involved in sports politics and joined the campaign against the English rebel cricket tour of South Africa.

Following the unbanning of the ANC in February 1990, Stofile became a member of its interim leadership core with the task of assisting to set up ANC structures within South Africa. Later in 1990 he was elected chairperson of the Border region of the ANC, a post he held until 1991 when he accepted the post of senior lecturer in the Religious Studies Department of the University of the Transkei, teaching Systematic Theology. From 1992-94 Stofile was director of the Department of Public Relations and Development at the University of Fort Hare.

In the general election of April 1994 Stofile stood as an ANC candidate and became a member of parliament. He was appointed chief whip of the ANC.

At the ANC's conference held in Bloemfontein in December 1994, Stofile was elected the organisation's treasurer-general. He also serves on the boards of various non-governmental organisations.

Stofile is married and has three children.

SOURCES

1. *People in Politics*, Third Quarter 1991, Institute for Democracy in South Africa (Idasa), Durban, 1991.
2. *Curriculum vitae* submitted by the Office of the Chief Whip, 6 March 1995.

EUGENE NEY TERRE BLANCHE

*Leader, Afrikaner
Weerstandsbeweging, 1973.*

Eugene Terre Blanche was born in Ventersdorp, Transvaal, on 31 January 1944, the son of Anna Francina (born Lourens) and Villebois-Mareuil Terre Blanche. He attended the Ventersdorp Primary School and the Hoërvolkskool, Potchefstroom, where he matriculated in 1963.

The following year he joined the police force and served as a volunteer in Namibia. He was also a member of the special police unit guarding the residences of the state president and prime minister.

After four-and-a-half years he left the police force, having reached the rank of warrant officer, and began farming. He became active in the Herstigte Nasionale Party and stood (unsuccessfully) in Heidelberg as a parliamentary and provincial candidate.

In 1973 he and six others launched the Afrikaner Weerstandsbeweging (Afrikaner Resistance Movement – AWB) at a meeting in a Heidelberg garage. Initially the organisation operated secretly, but following the tarring and feathering of historian Professor Floors van Jaarsveld while delivering an address on the desanctification of the Day of the Covenant in 1979, it came into the public eye. As a result of this incident, Terre Blanche and 13 supporters were prosecuted on charges of assault, trespass, crimen injuria and malicious damage to property.

The AWB aims to achieve white security and reunification of the Afrikaner *volk* through a resistance and freedom movement and the creation of a *volkstaat*. It proposes a separate area for coloureds in the Western Cape where they can 'achieve their full potential'. The Indian community, according to AWB policy, is a foreign entity in South Africa with no claim to its own parliament; a limited form of self-government under strict conditions within a specific area could be considered, however.

Terre Blanche believes that foreign investors and exploiters should not be permitted access to South African mineral assets. He recommends decentralisation of industries to keep blacks away from white areas.

In December 1982 police uncovered a number of arms caches in a swoop on AWB members. Nine men, including Terre Blanche, were detained in terms of security legislation. In July 1983, he and three associates were charged with terrorism and accused of possessing arms, ammunition and explosives. In October 1983, Terre Blanche was found guilty and sentenced to two years' imprisonment, suspended for five years.

Earlier in the year, Terre Blanche had received a suspended sentence and a fine of R300 for illegal possession of arms and ammunition.

Early in 1986 Terre Blanche announced the establishment of Brandwag (Sentry), an armed commando-type organisation under the aegis of the AWB. He claimed that Brandwag did not promote violence, but would meet violence with violence to protect whites and their property. The organisation is based on a pyramid structure of councils operating at local, regional, and national levels.

At the end of December 1988 West Rand police announced that they were investigating a charge of malicious damage to property against Terre Blanche after a gate was damaged at the Paardekraal monument. Sensational newspaper reports about the monument incident, and his relationship with journalist, Jani Allen, who was with him at the time, followed. There were calls for his resignation amidst accusations that he was a drinker and a womaniser who had embarrassed the AWB. He responded by expelling four senior members for disloyalty, and then summoned a meeting of the 300-strong AWB executive. At the meeting held in Pretoria on 22 January, a full vote of confidence in Terre Blanche's leadership was passed. In May 1989 he was acquitted on charges arising from the Paardekraal incident. During the 1989 election campaign Terre Blanche tried to unify the far-right, and urged the CP and HNP to fight the election together.

The Jani Allen affair was again raised in mid-1989 with the release of telephone answering machine recordings of Terre Blanche asking to meet her. Allen also claimed that he had fallen asleep in the passage outside her apartment after she had ignored his pleas to be admitted late one night. Terre Blanche denied the claims and threatened to sue Allen if she continued her allegations. He denied any intimate relationship with her and claimed the whole matter was part of a smear campaign.

In July 1992, Jani Allen sued Channel Four, a British television station, for libel, accusing it of suggesting she had had an affair with Terre Blanche. This arose from a Channel Four documentary, *The Leader, the*

Driver and the Driver's Wife. Following a highly publicised court case, in which a witness testified that Allen and Terre Blanche had been intimate, Allen lost the case. Terre Blanche denied all allegations of an affair with Allen.

In May 1990 the AWB's para-military wing, the *Wenkommando,* was launched, with Terre Blanche maintaining that its function was solely a protective one. In 1991 he announced the formation of the *Ystergarde,* a special unit composed of highly training cadres, the members of which would wear a black uniform. In addition the AWB has a special force to deal with the safety of its leaders and property (Aquilla), and a youth corps known as the *Stormvalke.* In many towns the AWB has established units known as *Brandwagte* which function as vigilante committees.

In March 1991 Terre Blanche indicated that in order to oppose the reform process AWB supporters in industry and state employ would initiate strike action, while farmers would withhold production. He reiterated that they would fight against any imposed agreement with the African National Congress (ANC). He also confirmed that paramilitary training of AWB supporters was taking place.

In August 1991 Terre Blanche led a protest against then-State President FW de Klerk, when he addressed a meeting of National Party supporters in Ventersdorp. Right-wingers were armed with handguns, whips, hunting rifles, batons and knives and appeared to be determined to storm the NP meeting. Some 2 000 AWB supporters, led by Terre Blanche, marched towards the hall, but were blocked by police. Teargas was used to disperse the marchers and a street battle ensued which left three right-wingers dead and many injured. Following the incident Terre Blanche stated that the organisation was preparing its commando units for revolution.

In February 1992 a referendum was called for the white community to indicate its support or opposition to the process of political reform associated with FW de Klerk. Terre Blanche originally indicated that the AWB would boycott the referendum, but eventually entered an alliance with the Conservative Party and the Herstigte Nasionale Party against the reform process. The 'no' vote gained only 30 per cent of the poll.

In March 1993 Terre Blanche continued to call on whites to arm and defend themselves. In June 1993, after storming through a heavy police cordon, a group of AWB supporters drove an armoured vehicle through the front doors of the World Trade Centre in Kempton Park where national negotiations for a new constitution were taking place. The group smashed windows as members of the negotiating teams fled. In July of that year, Judge Goldstone asked police to open a docket against Terre Blanche for failing to respond to a summons to appear before his committee of inquiry into the incident. Terre Blanche responded by saying that he would not be intimidated nor threatened and would not appear before the committee.

In September 1993 Terre Blanche stated that the AWB was demanding an Afrikaner homeland of up to 25 per cent of South Africa's territory and he was not prepared to negotiate with the ANC for a smaller area.

The Afrikaner *Volksfront* was formed in 1993 to bring together all right-wing white groupings and Terre Blanche became a member of its executive council. In March 1994 the *Volksfront* was asked by the Bophuthatswana national security council to help prop up the Mangope government which was under threat from striking civil servants and mutinying members of the Bophuthatswana Defence Force. About 500 AWB cadres joined the *Volksfront* men at the local air force base, but were asked to withdraw following a confrontation between Terre Blanche and chief of the BDF, Major-General Jack Turner. Terre Blanche allegedly refused to take orders, and reneged on his agreement to withdraw his men. On 11 March AWB members opened fire on BDF troops at the Molopo military base and their chief of staff was ordered to withdraw by Colonel Jan Breytenbach, head of the AVF force. As they left they began firing at random and shortly thereafter three AWB members were shot in the street.

The failed attempt to intervene in Bophuthatswana was a major blow to the organisation and to Terre Blanche personally. He subsequently focused mainly on attempts to assist fellow right-wingers brought to court on charges concerning pre-election bombings, attempting to obtain indemnity for them.

In February 1995 he appeared before the parliamentary select committee on justice which was considering draft legislation concerning the Truth and Reconciliation Commission. There he indicated that the 'war was over' and pleaded that right-wingers facing charges relating to pre-election violence be treated in the same way as others who had received indemnity.

Terre Blanche has written drama and poetry, and one of his dramas, *Sybrand die Watermaker,* was prescribed in Cape secondary schools during 1982 and 1983. He is married to Martha Maria Elizabeth Jansen van Vuuren, and they have one daughter. They live on a farm in Ventersdorp, Western Transvaal.

SOURCES

1. *Curriculum vitae* supplied by office of the AWB.
2. AWB pamphlet, *Ontwaak Blanke Suid-Afrika. Die Weerstand Groei.*
3. South African Institute of Race Relations, *Survey of Race Relations in South Africa 1979, 1983,* Johannesburg, 1980, 1984.

4. *Sunday Times,* 12 December 1982.
5. *Cape Times,* 25 June 1983.
6. *Cape Argus,* 14 July 1983.
7. *Cape Times,* 12 October 1983.
8. *The Star,* 9 May 1984.
9. *Vaderland,* 17 May 1984.
10. *Weekly Mail,* 28 February 1986.
11. *Weekly Mail,* 2 May 1986.
12. *Natal Witness,* 20 October 1988.
13. *Natal Witness,* 31 December 1988.
14. *Sunday Tribune,* 1 January 1989.
15. *Daily News,* 4 January 1989.
16. *Daily News,* 22 January 1989.
17. *Daily News,* 10 May 1989.
18. *Natal Witness,* 15 July 1989.
19. *Sunday Times,* 30 July 1989.
20. *Daily News,* 31 July 1989.
21. *Natal Witness,* 8 November 1989.
22. *Sunday Times,* 11 August 1991.
23. *Natal Mercury,* 29 January 1992.
24. H Kotze, and A Greyling, *Political Organisations in South Africa A-Z,* Tafelberg, Cape Town, 1991.
25. SA Institute of Race Relations, *Race Relations Survey 1991/92 and 1993/94,* Johannesburg, 1992 and 1994.
26. *Daily News,* 5 May 1993.
27. *Daily News,* 7 July 1993.
28. *Sunday Times,* 13 March 1994.
29. Author's research, 1995.

STEVE VUKILE TSHWETE

Member of Parliament,
African National Congress, 1994.
Minister of Sport and Recreation,
1994.

The eldest of five children, Steve Tshwete was born in Springs on 12 November 1938 but, while he was still an infant, his family moved to Peelton, Eastern Cape. He attended various school in Cape Town, East London and Ginsberg, King Williams Town, where he played first team rugby and was head prefect.

Tshwete became involved in politics while at school, joining the African National Congress (ANC) as a teenager. After the banning of the ANC in 1960 he became national secretary of the African Students' Association, an ANC front chaired by Thabo Mbeki. He attended the All-In-Africa conference in Pietermaritzburg in 1961 where it was decided to oppose the creation of a Republic and call for a national convention. However, after the demands were not met and the peaceful strike which was called failed, ANC activists began to consider alternative strategies and a decision was taken to turn to armed struggle. Tshwete became active in Umkhonto we Sizwe in the Border area, and was involved in planning sabotage actions.

In June 1963 he was captured and detained. In February 1964 he and five other members of MK's Border regional command were charged with sabotage and furthering the aims of a banned organisation. He was not convicted on the counts of sabotage, but received five years on each of the remaining three charges, totalling 15 years imprisonment which he served on Robben Island.

While in prison, he was president of the prisoners' athletics association and served as political commissar of the general section of the prison, playing a key role with the arrival of young political prisoners following the 1976 protests. During this period he completed a BA degree.

Following his release on 22 March 1979, he was banned and banished to Peelton, Ciskei. After the banishment order expired in 1982, he played a major role in preparing for the launch of the United Democratic Front (UDF) in August 1983. He was detained, but elected president of the UDF's Border region in his absence. He continued to play a role in sport and was elected to the Border Rugby Union, a non-racial sporting body.

Tshwete was frequently detained and harassed by South African authorities, and in October 1984 was declared a prohibited immigrant in 'white' South Africa. This forced him to apply for a visa each time he left the nominally independent Ciskei to enter South Africa. During this time he was employed as a teacher, but lost his job because of his political activities. Confined to the Ciskei, Tshwete went underground and left South Africa in 1985. In 1987, the 1984 order declaring him an illegal immigrant in South Africa was overturned on appeal, although he was by then in exile.

In Lusaka, Zambia, Tshwete joined the ANC's administration department and was appointed to head the movement's committee charged with organising its 75th anniversary celebrations held on 8 January 1987. In 1988 he was co-opted to the national executive committee of the ANC and appointed political commissar of Umkhonto we Sizwe, in charge of the political education of ANC cadres. However, in August 1988 he was removed from this position, officially because his appointment to the national executive gave him other duties. However, he had previously been involved in a controversial stand regarding the legitimacy of civilian targets in Umkhonto we Sizwe attacks.

Still maintaining a keen interest in sporting matters, Tshwete helped organise a meeting of the Federation Professional League and the National Soccer League in Lusaka during 1988, assisting these organisations to bring about sports unity in soccer.

Following the unbanning of the ANC in February 1990, Tshwete returned to South Africa, and played a role in defining the Groote Schuur Minute of May, when the ANC met with a government delegation in Cape Town. He was appointed national organiser of the ANC charged with building up the internal structures of the organisation, and was later appointed the movement's sports liaison officer.

Tshwete has played a major mediating role in moves to bring about unity in South African sport, paving the way for its re-entry into international sport. He was involved in talks between the South African Cricket Board and the South African Cricket Union, leading to the launch of the United Cricket Board of South Africa. In May 1991 he travelled abroad with Ali Bacher of the SA Cricket Union where they undertook the groundwork necessary for South African cricket's re-entry into international competition. During 1991 he played a key role in the unification of South African rugby, chairing the steering committee to oversee the transition period until unity was complete. He was also involved in unity talks in athletics and other sports, the results of which enabled South African participation in the 1992 Barcelona Olympics.

Tshwete accompanied the South African cricket team to Australia in February and March 1992, where it participated in the World Cup. In that year he won the Jack Cheetham award in recognition of his devotion to South African sport.

At the 1991 ANC Congress in Durban, Tshwete was elected to its national executive committee and also served on its national working committee. He was re-elected at the organisation's December 1994 Congress.

On 7 September 1992, Tshwete participated in an ANC march from King William's Town to Bisho in the Ciskei. The crowd was fired upon by Ciskei security forces and Tshwete was injured. Later that day, he participated in a short sit-in at the South African embassy in Bisho to protest against the South African government's refusal to remove Ciskei's military leadership from office.

In the first democratic general election of April 1994, Tshwete stood as an ANC candidate and became a member of parliament. In May he was appointed Minister of Sport and Recreation.

Tshwete is married to Pamela, a paramedic, and they have two children.

SOURCES

1. *Die Suid-Afrikaan,* September 1987.
2. *Weekly Mail,* 30 October 1987.
3. *Weekly Mail,* 4 December 1987.
4. *New Nation,* 4 April 1990.
5. *Weekly Mail,* 8 March 1991.
6. *Daily News,* 19 June 1991.
7. *Weekly Mail,* 13 December 1991.
8. *Natal Mercury,* 8 September 1992.
9. *Profile '94,* South African Communication Services, Pretoria, 1994.

DESMOND MPILO TUTU

*Anglican Archbishop of
Cape Town, 1986.*

Born in Klerksdorp on 7 October 1931, Desmond Tutu attended mission schools before becoming a pupil at the Johannesburg Bantu High School (now Madibane High) in Western Native Township from 1945-50. He obtained his teaching diploma from the Pretoria Bantu Normal College in 1953, at the same time completing a BA degree, awarded in 1954.

Between 1955 and 1958 Tutu taught at Krugersdorp's Munsieville High School, leaving to enter St Peter's Theological College for training as a priest. He was ordained as a deacon in 1960 and then as a priest in 1961, serving title in Benoni location. In 1962 Tutu moved to the United Kingdom where he lived in Golders Green, London. During this period he obtained his BA (Hons) in 1965 and his MA in theology in 1966. The same year he returned to South Africa, visiting Israel *en route.*

Tutu then taught at the Federal Theological Seminary at Alice in the Eastern Cape. When the seminary was taken over by the state, he moved to the National University of Lesotho as a theology lecturer.

In 1972 Tutu was appointed associate director of the Theological Education Fund of the World Council of Churches, based in Bromley, Kent. His family moved to London and Tutu remained in this post until 1975 when he was appointed Anglican Dean of Johannesburg.

In 1976 Tutu became Bishop of Lesotho and served in that capacity until 1978 when he returned to Johannesburg to take up the post of general secretary of the South African Council of Churches (SACC).

In the same year, while attending an Anglican Bishops' conference in England, he was instrumental in altering a resolution condemning South Africa's apartheid policy to include other countries violating human rights.

In September 1979, while in Denmark, Tutu condemned Denmark's ongoing purchase of South African coal on the grounds that this led to increasing dependence on South Africa. On his return, he was summoned to meet the Ministers of Co-operation and Development and Justice and reportedly asked to retract his statement or face possible action against himself and the SACC. Following a meeting of its executive council in October, the SACC announced that an apology or retraction would constitute a denial of Tutu's prophetic calling, but expressed its willingness to begin discussions with the government on fundamental reform.

Tutu was one of 54 marchers, mainly priests, arrested under the Riotous Assemblies Act in May 1980 for protesting against the detention of Rev John Thorne of the Congregational Church, who had been held in connection with the coloured school boycott. In July all were convicted and sentenced to a fine of R50 or 50 days imprisonment.

Tutu's passport had been confiscated in March 1980, a few days before he was due to travel to Switzerland, but it was returned to him in January 1981 and in March he visited the United States of America. While there he met Kurt Waldheim, secretary general of the United Nations and Jean Kirkpatrick, US ambassador to the UN. He also addressed the UN Special Committee Against Apartheid. He then travelled to Britain and Europe, meeting the Pope and holding discussions with other church leaders. On his return to South Africa, his passport was again confiscated.

In 1982 Tutu was granted a temporary travel document to attend a convention in the US, but was refused a full passport. In December 1983 he again visited the US, attending the 50th anniversary of the birth of US civil rights leader, Martin Luther King.

In 1984 Tutu was awarded the Nobel Peace Prize. In February 1985 he relinquished his position as SACC general secretary and was appointed Anglican Bishop of Johannesburg. He travelled widely throughout the world after becoming a Nobel laureate, calling for punitive and economic sanctions against South Africa as a non-violent form of pressure to force the government to change its apartheid policies.

During July 1985, Tutu spoke out against the violence then erupting in black townships, and threatened to leave South Africa if killings by burning, including 'necklace' killings continued. He consistently called for a cessation of 'black-on-black' violence and also condemned bomb attacks in South African cities, while appealing for talks to resolve conflict.

At the same time, Tutu offered his services as an intermediaary between the government and black leaders, but then-State President PW Botha refused to grant him an interview. However, in February 1986 Tutu, Beyers Naude and Allan Boesak met Botha at his official residence in Cape Town in an effort to mediate in the crisis developing in

Alexandra, Johannesburg. Tutu subsequently met with Botha on two occasions in June and July 1986. In January 1986 Tutu announced that he had met officials of the then-banned African National Congress (ANC) and Pan-Africanist Congress (PAC) while on a visit abroad.

On 14 April 1986 Tutu was elected Anglican Archbishop of Cape Town and enthroned in St George's Cathedral, Cape Town, in September 1986.

He travelled extensively during 1987, visiting Australia, Britain, the US and Mozambique. In March he met members of the national executive committee of the ANC in Lusaka, Zambia, indicating after the meeting that while he agreed with the aims of the organisation to achieve a non-racial, democratic South Africa, he could not associate himself with its strategy of armed struggle.

At an August 1987 meeting in Togo, Tutu was unanimously elected head of the All-Africa Conference of Churches and in this capacity he visited Nairobi in December where he repeated his appeal for comprehensive mandatory sanctions against South Africa.

On 24 February 1988, following the restriction of 18 anti-apartheid organisations, Tutu and Boesak led a march of 25 church leaders and 70 others from St George's Cathedral in Cape Town. The marchers intended handing a petition to the state president at the Houses of Parliament but, after ignoring a police instruction to disperse, the group was arrested, but subsequently released without charge.

Tutu, Boesak and Jakes Gerwel, then rector of the University of the Western Cape, were instrumental in the formation of the Committee for the Defence of Democracy, which planned to continue with the activities of the restricted organisations. However, before the end of the month, the committee itself was outlawed.

In April 1988 Tutu called for a break in diplomatic relations with South Africa, as well as economic and financial sanctions. During the municipal elections of October 1988, Tutu urged black people not to vote. The following month he formed part of an SACC delegation which met with ANC leaders.

In July 1989 the Mass Democratic Movement (MDM) launched a defiance campaign and peaceful mass action directed against apartheid laws. Tutu and other church leaders stated in August that they would embark on a peaceful and non-violent defiance campaign in solidarity with the MDM. Following a march to the Manenberg Police Station demanding the release of detained students and teachers, Tutu and other church and community leaders were teargassed by riot police outside a Guguletu church.

Following the unbanning of the ANC in February 1990, Tutu called on the organisation to end the armed struggle against the South African government. However, an ANC spokesperson indicated that the ANC would continue to fight until the grievances which had led people to take up arms had been dealt with. Later in the year, however, the ANC suspended its armed struggle.

In 1991 Tutu argued that, following policy changes by the government, sanctions should be reviewed.

During 1993 Tutu facilitated and chaired a meeting between ANC President, Nelson Mandela, and the Chief Minister of KwaZulu, Mangosuthu Buthelezi, in an attempt to defuse the violence between supporters of the two organisations.

Since 1978 Tutu has been awarded over fifty honorary degrees by universities in various countries including South Africa, the United States of America, Australia, the United Kingdom, Germany, Norway, Brazil, Trinidad, Canada and France. His collections of sermons and speeches include *Crying in the Wilderness* (1982); *Hope and Suffering* (1983) and *The Rainbow People of God: South Africa's Victory over Apartheid* (1994).

Tutu married Leah Nomalizo Shinxani on 2 July 1955 and the couple have four children.

SOURCES

1. South African Institute of Race Relations, *Survey of Race Relations in South Africa, 1978, 1979, 1980, 1981, 1986, 1987/8, 1988/9, 1989/90, 1991/92 and 1993/94,* Johannesburg, various years.
2. *Daily Dispatch,* 22 September 1976.
3. Desmond Mpilo Tutu, *Hope and Suffering,* compiled by Mothobi Mutloatse, Johannesburg, 1983.
4. *Daily News,* 7 January 1984.
5. *Daily News,* 24 July 1984.
6. *SA Foundation News,* September 1985.
7. *Cape Times,* 21 January 1986.
8. *The Argus,* 23 January 1986.
9. *Daily News,* 13 June 1986.
10. *Daily News,* 3 July 1986.
11. *Daily News,* 21 July 1986.
12. *Daily News,* 3 September 1986.
13. *Curriculum vitae* supplied by the office of Archbishop Tutu, February 1995.

ANDRE ISAK VAN NIEKERK

Member of Parliament,
National Party, 1994.
Minister of Agriculture, 1994.

Born in Eshowe, Zululand, on 7 October 1938, Kraai van Niekerk was the son of Evadne (born Van Rooyen) and Louis Jacobus Nel van Niekerk, a farmer. Van Niekerk grew up in Eshowe where he attended local schools until moving to Grey College, Bloemfontein, where he matriculated in 1956.

Van Niekerk enrolled at the University of Stellenbosch and completed his BSc in agriculture in 1961. He then taught science at the Eshowe Bantu Training College for one year, before returning to Stellenbosch to complete his honours (1963) and MSc (1965).

From 1964-67 van Niekerk was employed as a research worker at the Department of Agriculture Technical Services at the university. In 1968 he was awarded a British Council Bursary, and studied for a year in Scotland at the Rowett Institute of Animal Nutrition. The following year he undertook research at the Wageningen Agriculture University in the Netherlands, having received a scholarship granted by the Agrarish Institute of the Netherlands. On his return he studied full-time at the University of Stellenbosch until the end of 1970, and in 1971 went sheep farming. He completed a doctorate in 1977.

During his farming career, Van Niekerk became active in organised agriculture and served on the executive of the Cape Agricultural Union.

Van Niekerk joined the National Party (NP) while at university, but his interests remained in the agricultural field rather than in politics. However, in 1981 he was invited to stand for the Prieska constituency in the general election and he won the seat.

As a member of parliament, Van Niekerk served on the select committee that investigated the Mixed Marriages Act and section 16 of the Immorality Act. He also served as a member of the standing committee on agricultural economics and water affairs, and the agricultural study group of the NP caucus.

On 1 December 1986 Van Niekerk was appointed Deputy Minister of Agriculture, and on 21 September 1989 he became Minister of Agriculture and Water Supply in the ministers' council, House of Assembly (later known as Agricultural Development). He was appointed Minister of Agriculture in April 1991.

Van Niekerk served on the committee dealing with land reform, and had to deal with resistance by white farmers to changes in the Land Act. He was also instrumental in the establishment of the agricultural research council.

In the April 1994 general election Van Niekerk stood as an NP candidate and was returned as a member of parliament. In May he was appointed Minister of Agriculture in the government of national unity.

Van Niekerk is married to Theresa (born Claassens), a music teacher at the Conservatoire in Stellenbosch. They have three sons and live in Stellenbosch.

SOURCES

1. Interviewed 14 May 1991, Cape Town.
2. *Profile '94,* South African Communication Services, Pretoria, 1994.

MARTHINUS CHRISTOFFEL JOHANNES VAN SCHALKWYK

Member of Parliament,
National Party Randburg,
1990-94.
Member of Parliament,
National Party, 1994.

Born in Pietersburg on 10 November 1959, Marthinus van Schalkwyk was the eldest of the three children of Hesther Helena and Johannes Machiel van Schalkway, a farmer and station master.

Van Schalkwyk attended Groenvlei Laerskool, near Tabazimbi, and later Northam Laerskool, between Tabazimbi and Rustenburg. He then moved to Pietersburg Hoër Afrikaans Skool where he matriculated in 1977. While at high school he devoted a great deal of time to sport, particularly rugby, and was appointed a prefect.

From 1978-79 Van Schalkwyk underwent two years national service in the Armour Corps and the Special Service Battalion. During this time he served on the Namibia/Angola border.

In 1980 he enrolled at the Rand Afrikaans University (RAU) for a BProc degree which he completed in 1983. He then obtained his BA Hons in Political Science (1984) and his MA (1989). While at university he received the Award for Academic Achievement of the Transvaal Lawyers Association and an Abe Bailey Travel Scholarship to England and Europe.

Van Schalkwyk played an active role in student politics and served as president of the Students' Representative Council (SRC); national president of the *Afrikaanse Studentebond* (ASB); chairman of Youth for South Africa and federal youth leader of the National Party (NP).

Van Schalkwyk had grown up in a home of staunch NP supporters. He had two grandfathers who had been involved in the *Ossewabrandwag* (OB) in the late 1930s and early 1940s, but who resigned to join the NP when the OB became too militant. At university, he participated in the first talks between the ASB and the Inkatha Youth Brigade and later between the ASB and the South African Youth Congress (Sayco).

From 1985-90 Van Schalkwyk lectured in Political Science at RAU and the University of Stellenbosch. During this time he withdrew from active NP politics. His interest was revived following President de Klerk's speech of 2 February 1990 when he announced the unbanning of the African National Congress (ANC) and outlined his vision of the future. In addition, in the late 1980s he was involved in talks held in Botswana between youth from Afrikaans campuses and the ANC Youth League. He also made contact with the ANC in Zambia in order to lay the groundwork for subsequent visits.

When Wynand Malan resigned from parliament in 1990, Van Schalkwyk stood for the NP in the Randburg constituency and won the seat. As MP he served on NP study groups on finance, trade and industry, law and order, constitutional development and justice. He also served on the law and order and justice standing committees of parliament until 1994.

In the April 1994 elections, Van Schalkwyk stood for the NP and was returned to parliament. During the elections he served as a member of the NP's campaign management team. He currently serves on the NP study groups on finance and economic affairs; constitutional affairs and public enterprises (broadcasting). He is also a member of the parliamentary joint committee on the reconstruction and development programme.

Van Schalkwyk is the director of media, information, publications and international relations of the NP and chairs its Witwatersrand North Region. He is also a member of the PWV executive committee of the NP.

Van Schalkwyk is married to Suzette and they have one son.

SOURCES

1. Interviewed 10 August 1994, Cape Town.
2. *Curriculum vitae* submitted by MCJ Van Schalkwyk, August 1994.

CONSTAND LAUBSCHER VILJOEN

Leader, Freedom Front, 1994.

One of twin boys born on 28 October 1933 on a farm in the Standerton district in the Eastern Transvaal, Constand Viljoen was the son of Geesie and Andries Viljoen, a farmer.

His parents were supporters of General Jan Smuts and his South African Party, which later became the United Party, but when Smuts joined with the Afrikaner nationalist, General Hertzog, his father lost interest in politics. However, his mother continued to be a life-long Smuts supporter. His father died when Viljoen was 14 years old.

In 1952 he joined the South African Defence Force (SADF) and entered the South African Gymnasium. Viljoen completed his BSc (Mil) (Pretoria) and became a permanent force cadet from 1953-54. Thereafter he rapidly rose through the ranks becoming chief of the army from 1976-80, and then taking over from General Magnus Malan as commander of the SADF.

While chief of the army, Viljoen took part in several military incursions into Angola and gained a reputation as a general who led from the front. During this time, about 200 km into Angola, the Ratel in which he was travelling was blown up by a double landmine, but he was uninjured. In addition he was known to have parachuted into Angola, accompanying supplies to his troops.

In 1985 he retired from the SADF and settled on his farm in the Ohrigstad area to breed cattle and produce paprika for export.

Viljoen remained out of the public eye until 1993 when he became active in Afrikaner right-wing politics. In April 1993, following the assassination of South African Communist Party secretary general, Chris

Hani, by right-wing elements, a Committee of Generals (which later became the directorate of the Afrikaner *Volksfront)* was formed. Viljoen was a member of this committee which linked up with the Conservative Party's mobilisation programme established as a response to the party's defeat in the March 1992 referendum. The aim of the Committee of Generals was to unify the right and harness it to the idea of creating an Afrikaner *volkstaat.*

On 6 May 1993 Viljoen attended a mass meeting of farmers from the Transvaal and the Orange Free State held at the Olen Park Stadium in Potchefstroom. There, Viljoen was called upon to speak on security matters affecting the farmers and received a standing ovation.

On 7 May 1993 the Afrikaner *Volksfront,* under the chairmanship of Viljoen, and headed by a committee of former SADF and SAP generals, was launched in Pretoria. With Viljoen at the helm, the AVF became the new driving force of the right wing. It succeeded in bringing together all the major parties of the right wing into a coalition aiming at 'self-determination of the Afrikaner'. A nine-person executive council was elected under the chairmanship of hardline CP leader, Ferdi Hartzenberg.

However, this duality of leadership was the cause of continuous internal friction among *volkstaaters,* white supremacists, CP hardliners, those willing to negotiate and those advocating a military option. An added cause of internal tension was the membership of Eugene Terre Blanche and his *Afrikaner Weerstandsbeweging* (AWB). This tension was exacerbated in June 1993 when heavily armed right-wingers, led by Terre Blanche and the AWB, stormed the multi-party negotiating council at the World Trade Centre, Johannesburg.

Viljoen continued to support a negotiated resolution for a *volkstaat* and held secret meetings with representatives of the African National Congress (ANC) in an effort to guarantee Afrikaner rights to self-determination.

At a mass right-wing rally in Pretoria on 29 January 1994 held to establish a *Volksfront* transitional authority, Viljoen faced a hostile crowd when he attempted to gain support for a non-violent alternative to securing a *volkstaat.* He indicated that such an Afrikaner homeland could be brought about with the co-operation of the ANC and the National Party (NP). He read out a resolution that supported a Boer homeland, but also urged Afrikaners to vote for the *Volksfront* in the coming April elections to prove that they had a mandate for self-determination. This clashed with the position taken by Hartzenberg who had publicly denounced negotiations as part of a broader communist plot and participation in the elections as unpalatable.

Debate within the AVF regarding participation in the election continued and on 4 March 1994 the party met a midnight deadline for registration in the upcoming non-racial general election.

At the same time, a political crisis in the Bophuthatswana homeland had developed when its president, Lucas Mangope, a member of the Freedom Alliance with the AVF, was overthrown. Viljoen displayed his military muscle when some 4 000 of his 'troops' entered Bophuthatswana on his orders. However, he withdrew his men when AWB intervention made co-operation with the defence force impossible.

That evening, 4 March, Viljoen learned that the AVF's chief ally in the Freedom Alliance, the Inkatha Freedom Party (IFP) had submitted papers to register provisionally for the elections. Later that night, Viljoen and other leadership figures requested provisional registration of the *Vryheidsfront* (Freedom Front), with himself as leader.

However, on the following day, 5 March, the *Volksraad* (the AVF's transitional parliament) dismissed Viljoen's attempt to register a *volkstaat*-supporting party. Following a nine-hour crisis meeting in Pretoria, Hartzenberg announced that they would not take part in the elections. This was a major defeat for Viljoen and for those in the right wing who maintained that the only way of demonstrating support for an Afrikaner *volkstaat* was through the ballot.

On 12 March Viljoen resigned from the AVF, precipitating a split in the organisation. When announcing his resignation in order to take up the leadership of the registered Freedom Front (FF), Viljoen indicated that conflict between himself and the leadership of the AVF had reached an *impasse.* He maintained that he was no longer politically acceptable in the organisation and he criticised the undisciplined and uninvited role of the extremist AWB in the Bophuthatswana crisis. The AWB responded by calling him 'a political Judas goat sent by the Broederbond/ANC/ NP/Communist Party alliance to lead us to the slaughter.'

Viljoen was supported by a number of CP members of parliament as well as the Committee of Generals and subsequently received endorsement from a large number of right-wing structures such as town councils.

Following his decision to participate in the election, negotiations between Viljoen, the government and the ANC continued and it was agreed that proposals for a *volkstaat* would be considered if sufficient support for it was demonstrated in the April 1994 elections. Viljoen suggested that such a *volkstaat* would be economically linked to South Africa, but Afrikaners would be able to control their own political destiny. Viljoen, as leader of the FF, signed such an accord with the ANC and government in Cape Town on 23 April 1994.

In the April 1994 general election the FF contested all nine provinces. The key theme of the campaign was that minorities should be better protected and that self-determination would bring peace. The FF won 2,2 per cent of the vote and was able to take nine seats in the National Assembly.

Viljoen is married to Christina (Risti) Susanna (born Heckroodt) and they have five children.

SOURCES

1. *Sunday Star,* 9 May 1993.
2. *Sunday Tribune,* 9 May 1993.
3. *Weekly Mail,* 7 May 1993.
4. *Weekly Mail,* 14 May 1993.
5. *Financial Mail,* 21 May 1993.
6. *Natal Witness,* 26 June 1993.
7. *Financial Mail,* 1 October 1993.
8. *Financial Mail,* 3 December 1993.
9. *Sunday Times,* 6 March 1994.
10. *Sunday Tribune,* 6 March 1994.
11. *Natal Witness,* 8 March 1994.
12. *Sunday Times,* 13 March 1994.
13. *Negotiation News,* 14, 15 March 1994.
14. *Sunday Times,* 20 March 1994.
15. *Sunday Tribune,* 20 March 1994.
16. *Leadership,* 13(1), 1994.

LEON WESSELS

Member of Parliament,
National Party, 1994.
Deputy Chairman, Constituent
Assembly, 1994.

Leon Wessels, the son of Susanna Elizabeth Gertruida (born Reyneke) and Willem Adriaan Wessels, a policeman, was born in Kroonstad, Orange Free State, on 19 April 1946. The family moved to Johannesburg where he started school, but shortly thereafter settled in Vryburg where he attended the Stellaland Laërskool. He completed his primary education at Port Natal School, Durban, and in 1963 matriculated from the Monument Hoërskool, Krugersdorp.

Wessels attended the South African Police College from 1964 to 1966, serving as an instructor and member of the mounted police. In 1967 he enrolled at Potchefstroom University where he completed a BJur et Comm degree in 1970 and LLB in 1972. While at university he was awarded a medallion for leadership, academic achievement and service to the student community. In 1971 Wessels won an Abe Bailey scholarship to the United Kingdom.

Wessels served as chairman of the Students' Representative Council in 1971 and as president of the *Afrikaner Studentebond* between 1971 and 1973.

A key white student issue at the time involved contact with black students organised into the Black Consciousness-oriented South African Students Organisation (Saso), which was dominant on black campuses. Wessels was part of a Potchefstroom student delegation which held an official contact visit with the Students Representative Council of the University of the North. There he met Abraham Ongeposte Tiro and Aubrey Mokoena, both leading Black Consciousness exponents, and the meeting had a great influence on his views of the South African situation. Tiro was subsequently assassinated in a bomb blast widely believed to be the work of South African agents.

Having worked as a prosecutor during university holidays, Wessels joined the Johannesburg bar as an advocate in 1973. In 1974 he was elected member of the Transvaal Provincial Council for Krugersdorp, and in same year served on the council of the Federation of Junior *Rapportryers*. From 1974 until 1977 he was leader of the *Nasionale Jeugbond* in the Transvaal and served as an *ex-officio* member of the Transvaal executive and head committees of the NP.

Wessels was elected member of parliament for Krugersdorp on 30 November 1977. As an MP, he chaired the NP's caucus group on law and order and was secretary of the foreign affairs group. In addition, he was a member of the NP's Transvaal organisation committee and its youth committee.

In April 1988 Wessels was appointed Deputy Minister of Law and Order, and in the cabinet reshuffle after the September 1989 elections he became Deputy Minister of Foreign Affairs.

He was appointed Minister of Planning, Provincial Affairs and National Housing on 1 October 1991, and his portfolio was changed the following month to Minister of Local Government, National Housing and of Public Works. On 1 June 1992 he became Minister of Local Government and National Housing and of Manpower.

Wessels participated in the Convention for a Democratic South Africa (Codesa) held in December 1991 and May 1992. He served as the South African government representative on the Codesa working group which dealt with time-frames and implementation of decisions.

In the run-up to the first democratic election held in April 1994, Wessels served on the Transitional Executive Council sub-council on foreign affairs. In the election he stood as a NP candidate and was returned to parliament. He serves on the parliamentary portfolio committee on labour and as alternate on the mineral and energy affairs committee. In May he was elected deputy chairman of the constituent assembly.

Wessels was a director of the Oude Meester group and VEKA Beperk. He was a member of the Transvaal junior horse jumping team in 1960, and has run the Comrades Marathon twice (1983 and 1985). During 1985 he completed the Argus cycle tour and plays squash and golf.

Wessels is married to Tersia Susara (born Van Loggerenberg) and they have two children.

SOURCES

1. Interviewed 1 April 1986, Acacia Park.

2. *Curriculum vitae* submitted by the Department of Local Government and National Housing and of Public Works, June 1992.
3. *Profile '94,* South African Communication Services, Pretoria, 1994.

ABRAHAM WILLIAMS

Member of Parliament,
National Party, 1994.
Minister of Welfare and
Population Development, 1994.

Born in Saldhana, Cape Province, on 12 December 1940, Abe Williams was the second of the ten children of Jeanetta and Adam John Williams, a fisherman.

He grew up in Saldhana, attending St Andrews Primary School and Schoonspruit High School, Malmesbury, until Standard 8. He then attended the Athlone Training College in Paarl and completed a Lower Primary Teachers Certificate in 1959. In 1960 he undertook a Higher Primary Woodwork course and became a specialist woodwork teacher.

Williams then taught for two years at Windermere Primary School in Cape Town before returning to Saldhana where he taught at the St Andrews Primary School for 13 years. This was followed by a year-and-a-half at Winsley Primary School in Bellville before he became principal of Belhar Primary School in the mid-1970s. He moved to Cape Town with the aim of improving his education and completed his matriculation privately in 1973.

Williams studied part-time at the University of the Western Cape for a BA degree, majoring in History and Biblical Studies and graduated in 1981. The following year he enrolled at the University of Stellenbosch to study full-time for a BEd degree.

In 1983 Williams was seconded to the Department of National Education to assist the South African Rugby Board's sport education programmes and worked very closely with the late Danie Craven, then president of the Rugby Board.

Williams had become involved in local politics in Saldhana and served as secretary of the area's advisory committee to the local council. He also gave evidence to the Commission of Inquiry into Beach Apartheid and the Erica Theron Commission which investigated coloured affairs. He coached the Tigers Rugby Club in Saldhana and in 1970 was involved in the organisation of the tour by the Proteas (a South African coloured rugby team) to England.

In 1972 Williams was appointed organising secretary of the South African Rugby Federation and that year attended an international rugby conference in the United Kingdom. He became secretary of the Federation in 1976.

Williams's involvement in rugby administration continued and he managed the first Craven Week coloured side. He fought for the integration of Craven Week rugby and the opening of sports facilities to all races. He also became involved in devising development programmes for rugby.

In 1981 Williams was the assistant manager of the Springbok rugby team tour to New Zealand and the United States of America which was highly controversial and which involved demonstrations against the tour in New Zealand. During the 1983/84 rugby season, he acted as assistant manager of the Craven Week team during their visit to Wales.

In 1984 Williams entered into politics on a full-time basis and stood for the Labour Party in the Mamre constituency, which included Atlantis and other areas on the Cape west coast. He became a member of the House of Representatives and won his seat again in the 1989 elections. In 1986 he served as national organiser of the Labour Party and in 1989 he became its national secretary.

In 1989 Williams was appointed Deputy Minister of Education and Culture in the House of Representatives, but resigned in 1991 both from the Labour Party (LP) and as Deputy Minister in order to join the National Party (NP). This move was precipitated by his belief that the LP was no longer making political inroads while the National Party had made major changes in moving away from apartheid policies. On 30 August 1991 he was appointed Deputy Minister of National Education and of Local Government and National Housing.

When the NP took over control of the House of Representatives in January 1992, Williams became the Minister of Education and Culture in its new Ministers' Council. He also served on the government's delegation to the Convention for a Democratic South Africa (Codesa).

On 1 April 1993 Williams was appointed Minister of Sport in the cabinet, and was also responsible for the portfolio of welfare in the Ministers' Council, House of Representatives.

Williams stood as a NP candidate in the April 1994 general election and became a member of the National Assembly. In May he was appointed Minister of Welfare and Population Development in the government of national unity.

Williams is married to Esme and they have two children.

SOURCES

1. Interviewed 24 June 1994, Cape Town.
2. *Curriculum vitae* supplied by Abraham Williams, June 1994.

SIFISO THOKOZANI ZULU

Official Spokesperson for
King Goodwill Zwelethini, 1994.

Born on 26 October 1952 at Pholela Mission in the district of Nkandla in Northern Natal, Sifiso Thokozani Zulu was the youngest of four children. His father, Prince Aaron Zulu, was a school principal and his mother, Christina Zulu, a teacher.

Sifiso Zulu claims his royal heritage through his father, Prince Aaron, who was a son of Prince Sifile, himself a son of Prince Mthonga, brother of King Cetshwayo and son of King Mpande.

Zulu grew up at the Pholela Mission where he attended Macela

Primary School. As a member of the royal family he frequented the palace of King Cyprian. He then attended Melmoth Entembeni Secondary School and Vryheid State High School in 1970. There he was appointed a prefect and won numerous trophies for his debating skills. It was also there that he first became involved in royal functions, organising a talk by Prince Mcwayizeni Zulu in the local Mondlo township.

When he matriculated in 1971, Zulu joined the KwaZulu government's Department of the Interior as a township superintendent. His first posting was in Umlazi H Section, and thereafter he served in various other sections. The Department then sponsored his studies at the University of Zululand and he completed a diploma in public administration in 1978.

On returning to work in the Department, Zulu was promoted to township manager, serving in Gamalake Township on the South Coast where he had to deal with a rent boycott and huge township debt. At the same time, he came into conflict with Chief Minister of KwaZulu, Mangosuthu Buthelezi, as he felt that Buthelezi had taken control of Inkatha, originally established by King Solomon to consolidate links between the Zulu nation and the Royal House, and had disbanded the Royal Council for his own personal gain.

Zulu first clashed directly with Buthelezi when he invited Prince Clement Zulu to address a Shaka Day rally in Gamalake. He was summoned to appear before the KwaZulu Legislative Assembly to explain his actions.

According to Zulu, his opposition to Buthelezi resulted in his being subject to harassment and assassination attempts; summonses to appear before the KwaZulu Legislative Assembly; twice-weekly audits of his office; being forced to fire staff for minor offences; and being frequently transferred from post to post.

He resigned in January 1983 and secured a position as liaison officer in the South African Department of Foreign Affairs. As head of the guest section, Zulu's job involved promoting the image of the South African government and its homeland policies. He organised liaison meetings with public opinion formers, business people and citizens of high standing within KwaZulu. He also introduced foreign visitors to members of the communities. During this period he travelled extensively throughout Southern Africa. However, in 1985 Zulu's father became ill and he was forced to resign to take over the family businesses – a supermarket and a refuse removal concern.

In 1989 Zulu enrolled for a Bachelors degree in Public Administration at the University of Bophuthatswana. He supported himself by working for the Bophuthatswana government as head of administration in the Department of State Affairs and Civil Aviation and completed his degree in 1991.

In 1993 he was summoned by King Goodwill Zwelethini, the Zulu king, to return to Natal to assist him in breaking away from the control of Inkatha and Buthelezi.

The animosity between Zulu and Buthelezi finally came to a head during an October 1994 public clash at the South African Broadcasting Corporation (SABC) studios in Durban when Buthelezi stormed into the studio where Zulu was participating in a live programme on current affairs. After this incident, Buthelezi claimed not to know Zulu.

Shortly after this incident, Zulu was appointed official spokesperson for the king who by that time had severed all relations with Buthelezi and Inkatha. This position, however, is unpaid and Zulu continues to support himself by undertaking part-time research work for the Department of Social Anthropology at the University of Natal.

Zulu sees the role of the royal house as being four-fold: to curb instability in the province; to achieve unity, peace and reconciliation within the Zulu nation; to democratise traditional institutions and authorities; and to promote the Reconstruction and Development Programme. He maintains that his role as spokesperson is to prepare the ground for this agenda and to handle disinformation about the king and the royal house.

During the April 1994 elections, Zulu was appointed by the Independent Election Commission as a sub-regional analyst. He is also the founder and executive chairperson of the Polele Community Development Organisation, a community-initiated organisation aimed at promoting community development for disadvantaged remote rural communities within the district of Nkandla.

Zulu is also an executive member of the KwaZulu Natal CBO Network, an executive member of the Zulu Royal House Peace and Development Programme and represents the Royal House on a number of other development forums. He is not aligned to any political party.

Zulu is married to Bongi Agrineth, a nurse, and they have two daughters and one son.

SOURCES

1. *Weekly Mail & Guardian,* 30 September 1994.
2. Interviewed by Sara Blecher Collins, 21 October 1994.

JACOB ZUMA

*Chairperson, African National
Congress, 1994.
Minister of Economic Affairs
and Tourism, KwaZulu/Natal,
1994.*

Born on 12 April 1942 at Nkandla, Zululand, Jacob Zuma was the eldest
child of Nobhekisisa and Gcinamazwi Zuma. When his father, a police
sergeant, died at the end of World War II, his mother became a domestic
worker and Zuma spent his early years moving between Zululand and
the suburbs of Durban, where his mother worked. He did not attend
school, having the responsibility of looking after the family's stock. One
of his cousins taught him to read and write Zulu and he borrowed
friends' school books in an attempt to teach himself.

By the age of 15 he was taking on odd jobs to supplement his mother's
income. He came into contact with the African National Congress
(ANC), and was also influenced by his elder brother, Mntukabongwa, a
trade unionist. By 1959 he had joined the ANC.

Following the banning of the ANC in 1960, Umkhonto we Sizwe was
formed and Zuma joined the organisation in 1962. He participated in
sabotage actions in Natal and then planned to leave South Africa for
military training abroad. However, in 1963, whilst on his way out with a
group of 45 recruits, he was arrested near Zeerust in the Western Transvaal. He and others, including Andrew Mlangeni, were charged with
conspiring to overthrow the state, but the charges against Mlangeni were
dropped when he became an accused in the Rivonia trial. In December
1963 Zuma was convicted of conspiring to overthrow the government by
means of violence, and sentenced to ten years imprisonment which he
served on Robben Island. Conditions on the Island were difficult, but
during this time Zuma managed to study formally for the first time.

After his release Zuma helped mobilise internal resistance and was instrumental in the establishment of ANC underground structures in Natal between 1973 and 1975. When a close colleague, Harry Gwala, was arrested in 1975, Zuma left South Africa. For the next 12 years, based first in Swaziland and then in Mozambique, he dealt with thousands of young exiles who poured out of the country in the wake of the Soweto uprising, clandestinely slipping back into South Africa on a number of occasions.

Zuma rose rapidly through ANC ranks. In 1978 he became a member of its national executive committee and was re-elected to the executive at the 1985 Kabwe Conference. He served on the ANC's political and military council when it was formed in the mid-1980s and also served as ANC chief of intelligence. In addition, Zuma was the ANC chief representative in Maputo, Mozambique, until forced to leave in 1984 after the signing of the Nkomati Accord, when he moved to Lusaka.

Following the unbanning of the ANC in February 1990, Zuma was one of the first ANC exiles to return to South Africa to make arrangements for the return of other senior ANC leaders.

After the May 1990 talks between the ANC and the South African government at Groote Schuur, a working group was established to advise on 'norms and mechanisms' for dealing with the release of political prisoners; the granting of immunity to political offender; the definition of political offences; and the time-scale for implementing recommendations. The ANC appointed Zuma to lead its team on this working group.

In November 1990 Zuma was elected chairperson of the ANC's southern Natal region. He had previously been a key figure in arranging talks with Inkatha regarding the violence in Natal, holding discussions with Mangosuthu Buthelezi, KwaZulu Chief Minister.

As head of the ANC's intelligence network, Zuma served on the joint government-ANC working group which investigated the practicalities of the ANC suspending the armed struggle in terms of the Pretoria Minute.

At the July 1991 ANC congress held in Durban, Zuma was elected deputy general-secretary of the organisation.

In December 1991 he attended the Convention for a Democratic South Africa (Codesa) and served as the ANC representative on its working group dealing with creating a climate for free political participation and the role of the international community.

During 1993 Zuma played a key role in attempts to bring the Inkatha Freedom Party and the white right wing into the electoral process. In addition, he built up a working relationship with the Zulu king, Goodwill Zwelithini. In the same year he was reprimanded by the Motsuenyane commission of inquiry into torture in ANC detention camps in Angola in that he was found to have inadequately supervised an investigation into the wrongful arrest of David Mbatha in 1988 on suspicion of being an enemy agent.

In January 1994 Zuma was elected the ANC's candidate for the premiership of the KwaZulu/Natal province and to lead it in the April election. During the campaign leading up to the April 1994 elections, Zuma's home in Nkandla was attacked twice.

In the general election of April 1994, Zuma was elected a member of the KwaZulu/Natal legislative assembly. In May he was appointed KwaZulu/Natal Minister of Economic Affairs and Tourism in the provincial government of national unity. At the ANC's Bloemfontein congress in December 1994 Zuma was elected chairperson of the organisation.

Zuma is married to Nkosazana (born Dlamini), who was appointed Minister of Health in May 1994. They have five children and he has five further children from other marriages.

SOURCES

1. *Weekly Mail,* 23 March 1990.
2. *Leadership,* 9, March 1990.
3. *New Nation,* 12 April 1990.
4. *Weekly Mail,* 18 May 1990.
5. *Vrye Weekblad,* 12 July 1991.
6. *Post,* 12 January 1994.
7. *Weekly Mail,* 22 April 1994.
8. *Daily News,* 27 April 1994.
9. *Weekly Mail,* 18 February 1994.
10. ANC Press Centre release, 29 April 1994.

NKOSAZANA CLARICE ZUMA

Member of Parliament,t
African National Congress, 1994.
Minister of Health, 1994.

Nkosazana Clarice Dlamini, the eldest of eight children, was born on 27 January 1949 in Pietermaritzburg at what is now Greys Hospital to Rose Ndlela and Williebrod Dlamini. Zuma's father was a primary school teacher in the Polela district of KwaZulu near the Drakensberg and her early years were spent in this rural area at vrious schools as she followed her father from post to post.

Zuma enjoyed a close relationship with her parents who brought up their sons and daughters with no division of labour between the sexes. Her mother believed that bringing up her children in this way would lead to greater independence. In addition, the children were always included in discussions on family matters and were often asked to contribute their opinions where there were family problems. Her parents also believed strongly in the value of education for girls, something which was not widely supported in their community at that time.

Zuma's father was very involved in the Catholic Church, while her mother participated in the Young Women's Christian Association, school committees and the Polela Health Centre where she taught nutrition and worked on the health committee.

Whilst in Standard Three and Four, Zuma lived with an aunt in Umlazi, outside Durban. She then returned to the rural area where, despite a lack of electricity or equipment, dedicated teachers made the best of the poor conditions. Her father discouraged her from her chosen career as a lawyer, and she was sent to Adams Mission to complete a three-year matriculation in chemistry, mathematics, physics and biology in order to qualify her to enter medical school.

The ethos of Adams Mission School was one that was to have a great influence on Zuma. It was a school with strong discriminatory practices and one incident in particular moulded her political conciousness. Black and white teachers had different staff rooms with separate cups from which to drink their tea. One day the cups in the black staffroom ran out and an elderly African teacher, for whom the students had a great deal of respect, asked that a cup be fetched from the other staffroom. After he had drunk from it, one of the white teachers entered the room, picked up the cup and smashed it to the ground 'to make sure that it never ended up back in the white staff room'.

Zuma matriculated in 1967 and decided against enrolling immediately for medicine, choosing to do a BSc degree at the University of Zululand with majors in Zoology and Botany. Whilst at university she joined the Catholic Society. When the Black Consciousness-oriented South African Students' Organisation (SASO) was formed she became an active member, involving herself in campus politics, and demonstrating against the installation of Chief Mangosuthu Buthelezi as university chancellor.

During 1972 Zuma worked as a research technician at the University of Natal Medical School and in 1973 registered for her medical degree on the same campus.

Although she was very active in SASO, becoming its vice-president in 1976, Zuma came to realise that the Black Consciousness philosophy was only a step towards liberation and that it in itself could not achieve freedom for her people. On a university visit to Swaziland in 1975 she met exiled members of the then-banned African National Congress (ANC), including Thabo Mbeki and Albert Dhlomo, and she was recruited for underground ANC work. She served as secretary of the Medical Students' Representative Council during 1975/76 and while vice-president of SASO was put under police surveillance.

By 1976 the Bureau for State Security (BOSS) had become aware that she was part of an ANC cell operating in Durban and whilst living in the Alan Taylor university residence in Wentworth, a Durban suburb, she managed to escape arrest during a raid by the security branch. She left the country for Botswana soon afterwards and was transferred to Tanzania to work in the ANC office and for Radio Freedom.

During this time Zuma addressed an Organisation of African Unity conference in Addis Ababa, Ethiopia, and represented the ANC at the International Students Union Conference in Ghana. She toured Europe with the ANC, visiting Czechoslovakia, Holland, Germany, Sweden, Britain and Ireland. In 1977 she was sent to England to help ANC representative, Reg September, with solidarity work. She was elected chairperson of the ANC Youth Section in the United Kingdom.

Later that year Zuma enrolled at the University of Bristol to complete her MBChB. There Professor Bill Hoffenberg, a South African exile, helped to have British university entrance rules waived to allow her to continue with her degree which she had abandoned in her fifth year.

Zuma completed her medical degree in 1978 and in the same year led an ANC delegation to the World Youth Conference in Moscow and travelled to Nigeria on behalf of the liberation movement. During 1978/79 she worked at Frenchay Hospital in Bristol as a house officer in surgery and during 1979/80 as a house officer in the Canadian Red Cross Memorial Hospital in Berkshire near London. In 1981 Zuma applied for work at the the Mbabane Government Hospital in Swaziland where she remained until 1985 in the Department of Paediatrics.

In 1982 she married Jacob Zuma, whom she had originally met in Tanzania and their first two children, Msholozi and Gugulethu, were soon born. At the end of 1985 Zuma returned to England where she completed a Diploma in Tropical Child Health at the School of Tropical Medicine in Liverpool on a scholarship from the African Education Trust. From 1987-89 she worked at the Paediatric Attachment of Wittington Hospital in London. From 1986-89 she was a member of the Regional Health Committee of the ANC in Great Britain and in 1987/88 was the vice-chair of the Regional-Political Committee of the ANC (GB).

From 1988-90 Zuma served as Director of the Health and Refugee Trust and Development Organisation (HEART) in England. Thereafter, she moved to Zambia where she had two more children, Nukuthula and Thuthukile.

In 1990 Zuma was one of the first exiles to return to South Africa, following the unbanning of the ANC in February of that year. She served on the task force established to re-organise the Women's League of the ANC in Natal. In the same year she was elected as an additional member to the regional executive committee of the ANC in Southern Natal and was a member of the organising committee for the national conference of the ANC held in July 1991.

From 1990-92 Zuma chaired the Southern Natal Regional Health Committee of the ANC and in 1992 was a member of the Gender Advisory Committee of the Convention for a Democratic South Africa. She served on the executive committee of the ANC for Southern Natal and chaired the ANC Women's League of Southern Natal from 1991.

In 1990 she was appointed a research scientist at the Medical Research Council in Durban and her research interests included illegal abortion, women and Aids, Aids and opinion leaders and primary health care models in South Africa. In 1992 Zuma became a member of the steering committee of the National Aids Co-ordinating Committee of South Africa, a trustee of the Health Systems Trust and a member of the board of the Centre for Social and Development Studies at the University of Natal.

Following the ANC win in the general election of April 1994, Zuma became a member of the National Assembly. In May she was appointed Minister of Health.

At the ANC's December 1994 congress in Bloemfontein Zuma was elected a member of the national executive committe.

Following her return to South Africa, Zuma moved to Durban with her four children. Zuma is married to Jacob Zuma, chairperson of the ANC and a member of the executive council of the KwaZulu/Natal provincial assembly. They have five children.

SOURCES

1. *People in Politics,* Second Quarter 1994, Institute for Democracy in South Africa (Idasa), Durban, 1994.
2. *Profile '94,* South African Communication Services, Pretoria, 1994.

GOODWILL ZWELITHINI

Zulu Monarch, 1971.

Born on 14 July 1948 at Nongoma, Goodwill Zwelithini was the eldest son of King Cyprian and his second wife, Queen Thomo.

He was educated at the Bekezulu College of Chiefs and a private school, during which time he lived at his father's official residence at

Khethomthandayo with his mother. In addition, he received formal instruction in Zulu customs and traditions.

When Prince Goodwill's father died in 1968, a regent acted as king until Goodwill completed his education. This led to a dispute between the royal family and the South African government, whose candidate for the regency was different to the royal family's choice.

Goodwill was installed as the eighth paramount chief of the Zulus at a traditional ceremony at Nongoma on 3 December 1971, attended by some 20 000 people.

The legal status of KwaZulu was changing at the time, and a new constitution for the territory was being drawn up in which the king's role was to be mainly ceremonial, and politically subservient to the chief minister. This led to serious tensions between Goodwill and Chief Minister Mangosuthu Buthelezi, and the first decade of his reign was characterised by a simmering feud between the two.

In 1975, the year in which Inkatha was formed, Goodwill was publicly accused by Buthelezi of involvement in party politics. As a result, the KwaZulu government insisted that the king obtain cabinet approval to travel outside the Nongoma tribal authority area.

In 1979 Buthelezi accused the king of seeking support from the Mozambican government, and of claiming that the KwaZulu government was the 'lackey of the whites'. Goodwill was also accused of conspiring to form a political party (Inala) which aimed to give the king the power to appoint KwaZulu's chief minister.

The KwaZulu administration then distributed a 'protocol guide' which limited the King's constitutional role. As a result, Goodwill refused to address the KwaZulu Legislative Assembly and there were rumours that he would be ousted.

Buthelezi objected to the king's conduct, maintaining that he had failed to carry out his constitutional duties. Goodwill's salary was cut and an inquiry launched into allegations of misconduct. Buthelezi indicated that these allegations included his involvement in political activities and support for an armed revolution.

In August 1979, the king was present during a lengthy debate in the KwaZulu Legislative Assembly in which he denied a host of serious allegations made against him, including the claim that he had advocated the use of violence to overthrow the Zulu state. Following the debate, Goodwill dramatically rushed out of the assembly, leaping from the royal box and running out of the building. There were rumours at the time that he was bewitched. He returned to his palace at Nkuzane. Later the assembly voted to end the enquiry and restore his full salary.

In 1980, Buthelezi announced that the king would not be permitted to give interviews with the press unless arranged through the office of the KwaZulu Minister of Justice, who would be present at such interviews.

However, from 1982 the rift between Goodwill and the KwaZulu government began to heal. During 1985, violence between supporters of the United Democratic Front (UDF) and Inkatha broke out in Natal. After the African National Congress (ANC) criticised the leadership of KwaZulu, the king demanded an apology from ANC President Oliver Tambo for allegedly insulting the 'Zulu nation' and 'Zulu royalty'. At much the same time, Goodwill also publicly opposed the implementation of economic sanctions against South Africa.

While opposing the strategies of the ANC and the UDF, the king committed the Zulu nation to bringing about radical change and adopted an anti-apartheid stance. He called on all Zulus to support what he referred to as Inkatha's non-violent political strategies and warned of a backlash against those who took up arms.

In 1989 he attacked ANC leaders recently released from prison for spurning the 'Zulu nation' by not inviting him and Mangosuthu Buthelezi to their welcome-back rally.

In the same year, he called for unity among the black population and a halt to violence and this theme continued into 1991 when he called for peace at a May Day rally. At the same time, he called on the ANC to stop attacking him and KwaZulu. He maintained that when KwaZulu was attacked, he was attacked, and argued that the ANC was fostering anti-Zulu feelings.

During 1992 Goodwill's status at the Convention for a Democratic South Africa (Codesa) became a major area of dispute. It was agreed in principle that traditional leaders would be represented at Codesa, but the question of whether this should be as observers or delegates was not resolved. As a result, Buthelezi refused to attend the plenary session of Codesa 2 in May. The Inkatha Freedom Party (IFP) demanded that the king, who it claimed represented the Zulu nation as opposed to a political party, should be given full delegate status with 12 representatives and four advisors.

In July 1992 Jacob Zuma, then deputy secretary-general of the ANC, and other senior ANC officials, held talks with Goodwill in an attempt to pave the way for a meeting between the king and ANC President Nelson Mandela. However, no meeting took place and the issue of the status of the king continued to simmer.

In May 1993 at a rally in Wema, near Durban, Goodwill called on supporters to stop the violence but in July he addressed 60 000 of his subjects at an historic *iMbizo* (meeting of the people) in Durban and demanded guarantees from President de Klerk and Nelson Mandela regarding the region's sovereignty. He stated his view that any Zulu who believed KwaZulu should become part of a unitary state was a traitor to the nation. He also indicated his support for the stand taken by the KwaZulu government at the negotiation forum when it had walked out in protest at the setting of an election date before a constitution had been finalised.

In February 1994 the ANC announced far-reaching concessions to the Freedom Alliance, of which the IFP formed part, but the king's office opposed them on the grounds that they did not go far enough.

In February 1994, King Goodwill met with State President FW de Klerk in Durban and indicated that he was preparing to promulgate the 'Constitution of KwaZulu/Natal' which would establish a monarchy in the region based on its 1834 boundaries. He had earlier indicated to his supporters that he had come to the end of the road following failed negotiations to accommodate Zulu aspirations and stated that he was not prepared to negotiate the sovereignty of the Zulu kingdom. It was the king's view that the new interim constitution negotiated at the World Trade Centre did not offer any space in which Zulus could survive as a nation and had no legitimacy to impose itself on them. He therefore rejected the constitution. He subsequently warned that the final test could come down to 'competition between the ballot box and the ability of the Zulu people to resist'.

In March 1994 Goodwill called on all Zulus to defend their freedom and sovereignty against anyone in South Africa who dared to challenge this. This statement caused alarm in KwaZulu/Natal and resulted in threats of war from the ANC. A statement from the Organisation of African Unity said that attempts by the king to declare a sovereign Zulu state posed a serious threat to peace and stability.

In April 1994 the king and Chief Minister Buthelezi met with De Klerk and Mandela in the Kruger National Park in an effort to break the deadlock before the April elections, but the meeting was unsuccessful. However, following the intervention of Kenyan mediator, Washington Okumu, a memorandum of agreement between the IFP, the ANC and the National Party agreed 'to recognise and protect the institution, status and role of the constitutional position of the King of the Zulus and the Kingdom of KwaZulu, which institutions shall be provided for in the Provincial Constitution of KwaZulu Natal immediately after the holding of the said elections.' In terms of the agreement Goodwill and his successors would probably be granted extensive ceremonial and advisory functions, the right to install all chiefs in the kingdom and the creation of a royal constabulary.

Following the general election in April 1994 and the return of an IFP majority in KwaZulu/Natal, there were rumours of a rift between the king and Buthelezi, who was now a member of the cabinet in the government of national unity. Buthelezi accused the ANC leadership in the province of trying to drive a wedge between them. However, it was noted that Goodwill had not attended post-election functions of the IFP and had also failed to attend a ceremony where he was to be introduced to the KwaZulu/Natal cabinet.

Divisions between Goodwill and Buthelezi continued to grow through 1994 with incidents of stoning at the king's palace by IFP supporters. The king established a Royal Council of advisors and marginalised Buthelezi from his court; his spokesperson, Prince Sifiso Zulu, stated that Buthelezi was not regarded as the king's traditional prime minister. In turn, Buthelezi mobilised large numbers of *amakhosi* (chiefs) in an attempt to prove that a substantial section of traditional leaders were loyal to him.

In January 1995 Buthelezi was unanimously elected chairman of the executive committee of KwaZulu/Natal's House of Traditional Leaders. This House had been established in 1994 but had been rejected by King Goodwill on the grounds that there had been no consultation with him as to its functions and that it undermined his status as king. In February 1995 the tension between the king and Buthelezi again came to the fore when, in the wake of the IFP walk-out from parliament in protest against lack of progress regarding international mediation, the king stated that such mediation, as agreed to prior to the elections, was no longer required.

In June 1994 Goodwill was awarded an honorary doctorate in Philosophy by the University of Zululand. Both Mandela and Buthelezi attended the ceremony.

Goodwill has five wives, and lives in Nongoma.

SOURCES

1. *Southern Africa Today,* November 1986.
2. *The Citizen,* 8 May 1992.
3. *Sunday Tribune,* 26 July 1992.
4. C Ballard, *The House of Shaka,* Emoyeni Books, 1988.
5. *Natal Mercury,* 12 July 1993.
6. *Natal Witness,* 15 February 1994.
7. *Natal Mercury,* 18 February 1994.
8. *Sunday Tribune,* 20 February 1994.
9. *Daily News,* 21 February 1994.
10. *Sunday Times,* 20 March 1994.
11. *Sunday Tribune,* 15 May 1994.
12. *Natal Witness,* 4 June 1994.
13. *Daily News,* 21 June 1994.
14. *Daily News,* 27 June 1994.
15. Author's research, 1995.

JUN 1 9 1996

3 2183 01247 3175

61 302EWC **8071**
07/96 FM
02-014-01 GBC